FIGHTING SON

FIGHTING SON

A Biography of
Philip F. La Follette

JONATHAN KASPAREK

Wisconsin Historical Society Press

Published by the
Wisconsin Historical Society Press

Publication of this book was made possible in part by a gift from
La Follette Godfrey & Kahn, Attorneys at Law. Additional funding was provided
by a grant from the Amy Louise Hunter fellowship fund.

www.wisconsinhistory.org/whspress

Photographs identified with PH, WHi, or WHS are from the Society's collections; address inquiries about such photos to the Visual Materials Archivist at the above address.

Publications of the Wisconsin Historical Society Press are available at quantity discounts for promotions, fund-raising, and educational use. Write to the above address for more information.

Printed in the United States of America
Designed by 2econdShift Production Services

10 09 08 07 06   1 2 3 4 5

Library of Congress Cataloging-in-Publication Data

Kasparek, Jonathan.
  Fighting son : a biography of Philip La Follette / Jonathan Kasparek.
    p. cm.
  Includes bibliographical references and index.
  ISBN-13: 978-0-87020-353-4 (pbk. : alk. paper)
  ISBN-10: 0-87020-353-3 (pbk. : alk. paper)
  1. La Follette, Philip Fox, 1897–1965. 2. Governors—Wisconsin—Biography. 3.
Wisconsin—Politics and government—1848–1950. 4. Progressivism (United States
politics) I. Title.
  F586.L3K37 2006
  977.5'03092—dc22

2006007567

∞ The paper used in this publication meets the minimum requirements of the American National Standard for Information Sciences—Permanence of Paper for Printed Library Materials, ANSI Z39.48-1992.

On the front cover: WHi Image ID 35021

For Abby, James, and William

Contents

Acknowledgments ix

Introduction xi

CHAPTER ONE
A Very Political Beginning 1

CHAPTER TWO
Apprenticeship 25

CHAPTER THREE
The Ghost at the Banquet 63

CHAPTER FOUR
Republican Victory 89

CHAPTER FIVE
The Progressive Party 125

CHAPTER SIX
A Stolen Utopia 173

CHAPTER SEVEN
Third Term Controversies 197

CHAPTER EIGHT
Strange Bedfellows and Failed Crusades 223

EPILOGUE
The Legacy of the Great Experiment 251

Notes 263

Bibliography 307

Index 319

Acknowledgments

No writer writes alone. For every hour spent in solitude hunched over a keyboard, many more are spent discussing the project with colleagues, conferring with archivists and librarians, or complaining to friends. Over the past eight years, I have accumulated debts to many people who have assisted in many ways, formally and informally, knowingly and unknowingly.

This book began as a dissertation at the University of Wisconsin–Madison. My advisor, Professor John Milton Cooper Jr., supported this project from the beginning, encouraging my interest in the La Follette family and Wisconsin politics and pointing me in the right direction at critical points. He and the other members of my committee, Stanley Schultz, James Leary, Paul Boyer, Diane Lindstrom, and John Coleman, oversaw the process from inception to completion. Their guidance made the end result a vastly better product, although the responsibility for errors or omissions lies solely with the author.

Fred Risser, Bronson La Follette, Gaylord Nelson, and Frank Zeidler generously shared their recollections of the political events of the 1940s. I am particularly grateful to Judith Sorem and Robert La Follette III for discussing their father as a politician and as a parent. Their memories added depth to a person I knew only through decades-old correspondence. The staffs of the Wisconsin Historical Society and the Library of Congress unfailingly assisted with the vast accumulation of La Follette papers, always cheerfully deposited at my table and always meticulously organized. Grants from the WHS Amy Louise Hunter fellowship fund and from La Follette Godfrey & Kahn, Attourneys at Law, made this book possible. My friends and colleagues both in and outside of the University of Wisconsin department of history frequently offered suggestions and criticism that were always helpful, if not always welcome. Ronald Mershart listened patiently to my complaints throughout the process and urged me to soldier on, and Jack Holzhueter provided moral support as well as insight on Wisconsin history. To the Teaching Assistants' Association (AFT local 3220) I owe a special debt: without its organizers and volunteers, the tuition waiver and TA salary I relied on for most of my time in graduate school would not have been.

Shepherding the manuscript from dissertation to published form turned out to be a much greater task than I imagined, and I owe thanks to many at the Wisconsin Historical Society for their efforts. Kate Thompson read the work critically and guided the editorial effort with skill and patience, providing suggestions for revision that invariably improved the text. Sara Phillips provided insightful editorial advice and suggestions. John Nondorf conducted illustration research, exploring the depths of the WHS's Visual Materials Archive and unearthing many striking photographs. Joe Heiman created the election maps to illustrate brilliantly the fortunes of candidate La Follette. The Wisconsin Historical Society is fortunate to have such talented people on its staff.

My parents-in-law, Daniel and Jo Markwyn, read early drafts critically and provided many helpful comments. They even seemed to appreciate the crash course in Wisconsin history. My parents, James and Carol Kasparek, provided emotional and financial support throughout my apparently endless college and graduate school career. They perhaps at times regretted the frequent admonition to stay in school, but their own interest in history and example of hard work set me on this path long ago.

My wife, Abby Markwyn, has lived with Phil almost as long as I have. As our life evolved to include two academic careers, two children, and another dissertation, she unfailingly supported this project. At the most discouraging points in the preparation of this biography, she has been my inspiration. Our children, James and William, reminded me again and again that as important as it is to read letters and microfilm, it is just as important to read *Goodnight Moon*. That balance made the completion of this book possible.

Introduction

On April 25, 1929, Philip Fox La Follette spoke to a large crowd gathered in the United States Capitol to witness the unveiling of the newest addition to Statuary Hall: a marble statue of his father, the late Senator Robert M. La Follette Sr. Almost four years had passed since the senator's death, long enough for him to be enshrined in the building where he had served for six years in the House of Representatives and for twenty years in the Senate, where he was often controversial, sometimes isolated, and always fiercely dedicated to the principles of open democracy, free speech, and business regulation. During his years in office, La Follette had inspired both devoted loyalty and passionate hatred, and no one was quite sure how to characterize his legacy. In his home state of Wisconsin, he remained an enormously popular figure even after his death. He had won reelection to the United States Senate in 1922 by the largest majority (nearly 81 percent) ever afforded a statewide candidate, and more than fifty thousand people shuffled past his casket as he lay in state in the capitol rotunda in Madison—even the banks and stores were closed, as if to celebrate some newly declared civic holiday. For years afterward, admirers held observances at his grave on the anniversary of his birth.[1]

On a national scale, La Follette's reputation was decidedly more mixed. Many newspapers noted his stubbornness and his fiery—if sometimes abrasive—oratory and dismissed him as an egoist, a dangerous radical, or an astute political boss. The *New York Times* printed a sentimental narrative of his last illness but could not help noting the ramifications of his death, which "removed from American life by far the strongest opponent of what are termed by political radicals 'the predatory interests.'" Other newspapers were more blunt. The *St. Paul Pioneer Press*, though it conceded to his early reforms, called him a negative force with few constructive ideas to offer. Likewise, the *Portland Oregonian* declared that at the end of his career he·was a danger to the nation. The *Outlook*, Theodore Roosevelt's old mouthpiece, declared at La Follette's death that he was above all else a rebel, one "whose only ground for rebellion was a lack of understanding of [his] own country." The *Saturday Evening Post* also took great delight in depicting him as the agitator of the discontented, especially during his presidential campaign in 1924. At times the denunciation La Follette suffered became subject to farce: Sinclair Lewis's fictional character George F. Babbitt declared his distrust of La Follette, "a man that's always talking about public ownership, and from that to communism and chaos there's only one step." La Follette had in fact moved from his initially modest reform proposals in the 1890s, such as the direct primary and railroad regulation, to more far-reaching policies, such as the nationalization of transportation and communications, but his personality remained consistently combative. As an insurgent he was not afraid to battle with politicians of any party, from the local bosses in Madison to national figures such as Roosevelt and Woodrow Wilson. He truly earned the sobriquet "Fighting Bob."[2]

La Follette, however, also generated a great deal of admiration from national left-wing circles, although *The Nation* and *The New Republic* were the only major national publications to depict him in a consistently favorable light. In September 1922, just after he won renomination to the United States Senate, *The Nation* ran a cartoon of him standing tall on a pile of lies and slanders as a benevolent Abraham Lincoln beamed down on him, saying, "I told you they couldn't fool all of the people all of the time." The editors of *The New Republic*, like those of *The Nation*, enthusiastically endorsed his independent presidential campaign. He also won support from the American Federation of Labor, the Socialist Party, the National Association for the Advancement of Colored People, and from prominent individuals such as Jane Addams, Felix Frankfurter, and Herbert Croly, all of whom wrote magazine articles supporting his candidacy. Progressives of many parties depicted La Follette, the standard-bearer of the variegated American left, less as an insurgent and more as an aged prophet promising to return the people to a mythical utopia envisioned by Jefferson and Lincoln.[3]

Such a return, however, was beyond Old Bob's powers. The saddest— and perhaps truest—accusation against La Follette was not that he was a radical or a political boss, but rather that the man had become quaint. He had been immersed in politics since the 1880s, and although his famous profile held true, his swept-back hair had grown white and he often looked tired. Not even his fiery speech could keep him from looking like a little old man giving the homily on Sunday morning. Later John Dos Passos looked back on La Follette's 1924 campaign and called him "an orator haranguing from the capitol of a lost republic," worn out by "incessant work and the breathed out air of committee rooms and legislative chambers." "Monopoly" and "money power" did not invoke the same fear and rage in the New Era that they had thirty years earlier, and the progressive platform itself was self-consciously dated. La Follette had outlived both Wilson and Roosevelt, but in his final years he was seldom in good health, increasingly absent from the Senate, and already fast becoming an icon rather than a productive statesman. After his death, people often seemed a bit lost when trying to sum up the career of a politician whose long life in office had seen him alternately worshipped and despised. "It's hard to know what to say about Bob La Follette," quipped Senator William E. Borah, "you know he lived a hundred fifty years." La Follette's death in many ways marked the end of the progressive era and sent a massive shock throughout Wisconsin as politicians and voters alike tried to understand his long and controversial career.[4]

Among those doing so in the Capitol that April day in 1929 was La Follette's younger son, Philip.* Although La Follette's accomplishments certainly merited such recognition, the memorial had an ironic twist: only a few years before, the Senate had been on the brink of expelling him for disloyalty, and he was for a time the most hated man in America. This irony did not escape Phil. Selected to express the family's appreciation to the people of Wisconsin for sending the statue to Washington, Phil chose not to discuss his father's reforms or even his popularity among Wisconsin voters. Rather, he recalled a day in April 1917 when La Follette sat in his Capitol basement office with a few close friends. "The World War was on us," Phil told his audience. "The rage and hatred of a vitriolic press and selfish profiteers were stirring to fever heat the passions of men. Friends were urging him to silence." La Follette became

---

*Although it is customary to refer to the subject of a biography by his or her last name, for the sake of clarity I will use first names throughout this work to distinguish between the many members of the family, except for Senator Robert M. La Follette Sr., whom I will refer to as "La Follette" to distinguish him from his son, Senator Robert M. La Follette Jr. Phil himself once remarked that everyone called him either "Phil" or "that so-and-so La Follette," and La Follette once said that half the state called him "Bob" and the other half "that-son-of-a-bitch."

one of only six senators to vote against war with Germany and brought down on himself a storm of verbal abuse. Despite this abuse, La Follette stood by his decision, and, in Phil's opinion, history proved him right. His statue, now literally enshrined with other American leaders, Phil said, was "lasting confirmation of his faith in the ultimate judgment of mankind."[5] For Phil, the Capitol memorial provided final proof that his father's stand, no matter how vilified at the time, was ultimately correct— that his insurgency would be recognized and embraced by history. Phil did more that day than provide a few appropriate remarks as one of several speakers; he alone clearly articulated the twin themes of La Follette's last years of public life: insurgency and vindication. As an insurgent, his father was an outsider, often lonely and misunderstood, but again and again Phil witnessed his father's vindication. Phil's life was entwined with politics from his childhood, and he absorbed his father's progressive ideals and inherited his father's abilities. More important, during the years before and after the First World War, he learned firsthand the difficulties of being an insurgent and the ultimate vindication it would bring.[6]

That Phil himself would enter politics was almost inevitable. From 1925 to 1927 he served one term as district attorney of Dane County, the office in which his father had begun *his* public career in 1880. During his term as district attorney, Phil gained a reputation for hard work and effective administration by virtually ending the liquor trade and organized crime in Madison. Perhaps more important, he became one of the principal leaders of the progressive faction of the Republican party during the 1920s, both before and after his father's death in 1925. As a lawyer in private practice, Phil held no public office between 1927 and 1931 but was instrumental in cultivating and campaigning for progressive candidates in the Republican primaries. Republicans dominated Wisconsin politics during the early decades of the twentieth century, but the party was divided into two main factions: Progressives who followed La Follette, and conservative Stalwarts who opposed progressive reforms, including such landmarks as the direct primary, income tax, workman's compensation, and regulation of industry.* Finding candidates who could defeat Stalwart candidates presented a major dilemma to Phil and other progressive leaders: how to promote one candidate all progressives could support without that candidate acting as a party boss. Progressives

---

*Capitalization bedevils historians of the Progressive Era. For the sake of clarity, *Progressive* will be capitalized when it refers to the La Follette faction of the Republican Party of Wisconsin or—between 1934 and 1946—the Progressive Party of Wisconsin. When referring to national *progressives*, those who supported the same general reforms as La Follette or the general ideas of reform, the term will be lowercased.

found an answer to that problem with Phil himself, who had the magic name and political ability to unite the progressive faction behind him. In 1930, Phil easily won the Republican nomination for governor just as the severity of the Great Depression had become apparent. It was an ideal opportunity for him to demonstrate that progressive ideals were still relevant, and his administration squarely addressed the principal problem of the day by establishing the nation's first unemployment compensation program.[7]

The economic dislocation of the Great Depression, however, vastly reshaped national and state politics. In 1932, the Wisconsin Democratic Party was swept into the state capitol on the coattails of Franklin Roosevelt. Most Democrats remained as conservative as they had been in the late nineteenth century, but the Roosevelt revolution buoyed conservatives on both sides, driving the Progressive faction to finally abandon the Republican Party and form its own independent party. An independent party allowed the Progressives to settle differences in a primary election, and it kept them from being swamped by conservatives because of voter defections to the Democrats. Phil was instrumental—although not solely responsible—for the formation of the party, and he was the only candidate who was ever able to hold together the coalition of old-time La Follette supporters, farm groups, labor unions, Socialists, and young liberals. He served two more terms as governor, from 1935 to 1939, although legislative gridlock and lack of funds from Washington frustrated his major goals.[8]

It has become commonplace to observe that Phil enjoyed politics. To a large extent this is true: as a child, he relished encounters with government figures, and later in life he liked the give-and-take of campaigning. He proved to be a good administrator and astonishing public speaker, one who viewed it as his task to persuade and convince his audience. He was usually successful. Yet there was much about politics that Phil hated. Requests for patronage irritated him, and he had little patience for politicians who seemed to put the demands of narrow interest groups or local constituencies ahead of the welfare of society as a whole. During his last two terms as governor, this frustration became intense as he struggled to hold the Progressive Party together while advancing an ambitious program of work relief and economic reform, all the time recognizing that the enormity of the problems made state-level relief inadequate and required federal help.

This frustration explains why Phil took the enormous step in 1938 to attempt to launch a national Progressive Party. When he was interviewed by the Norwegian newspaper *Morgenbladet* in 1936, he had to explain to the baffled reporter what *progressive* meant: "We investigate problems very thoroughly, whether it be a depression among the farmers, or unemployment. Out of this, shall we say scientific investigation of causes[,] we seek after remedies."[9] For Phil, progressivism was not so much a collection of political tenets as it was an approach. He believed that there was no social problem that could not be remedied if it was investigated thoroughly enough and if intelligent public servants crafted an appropriate response. Furthermore, he believed that there was no person who, presented with concrete facts and a workable proposal, would not support progressive measures, unless that person decided to put self-interest ahead of societal well-being.

These twin ideas—research and presentation—suggest the other path Phil's life might have taken. For a time in the late 1920s, he lectured at the University of Wisconsin law school and considered becoming an academic. It would have suited him better, perhaps, than politics. Throughout his life, Phil responded best to those whom he saw as intellectuals, and he relied on academics for advice. University faculty Harold Groves, Max Otto, Paul Raushenbush, Elizabeth Brandeis, Edwin Witte, John R. Commons, and others played important roles in preparing progressive legislation or providing political advice. Of the nonacademics he knew, those he most respected also were unusually intelligent. His fascination with General Douglas MacArthur stemmed from the fact that, as Phil noted in a 1951 book review, "MacArthur Has B-R-A-I-N-S."[10] Phil was a perceptive observer and an intellectual; he thought deeply about social issues and how he could best serve the progressive movement. Eventually, he decided that he could best serve the cause by entering politics and not by embarking on a university career, but throughout the twists and turns of his public life, the habits of careful observation and reflection provided the basis for his actions.

Phil La Follette's judgment occasionally failed him, of course, most spectacularly when he tried to launch the National Progressives of America in 1938 under a symbol that looked vaguely like a swastika. *He* knew what it meant, but he underestimated people's willingness to go along with his party in an age when few of the voting public remembered his father and more knew Huey Long, Charles Coughlin, Benito Mussolini, and Adolf Hitler. Phil all but abandoned the Progressive Party after 1939, when he became a major figure in the isolationist movement. Here, too, he thought he was following his father's example, but his opposition to the Roosevelt administration puzzled many. Some thought he had taken a sharp turn to the right, but in fact he was one of the few in

American public life still trying to use old progressive interpretations in a very different world.

Phil's criticism of the New Deal is not surprising. Much has been written on the continuity or lack thereof between old progressive-era reformers and New Dealers. Otis L. Graham demonstrated that in the 1930s most of the surviving key players in the progressive elements of both parties opposed New Deal legislation, and of these only a few were critics from the left. Despite his youthfulness, Phil fit this last category: he consistently argued for greater economic planning and government supervision of industries (à la Theodore Roosevelt's New Nationalism), although he himself had little use for the moral and social reforms that were major parts of turn-of-the-century reform. Yet he infused his public statements and personal correspondence with a profound sense of moral weight to rally supporters behind progressive proposals. Roosevelt, too, could sound almost jingoistically moral ("malefactors of great wealth"), but it is hard to believe he quite meant it when he thought, along with most of the New Dealers, that the Depression was new, uncharted territory. For progressives in general, and Phil in particular, the Depression was neither new nor unexpected; it was the latest in a long series of confrontations between organized and selfish wealth on one hand and the common folk on the other. Rather than bold, persistent experimentation, the Wisconsin Progressives sought to carefully research versions of traditional progressive proposals.[11]

This reapplication of progressivism to the world of the 1930s and 1940s met with limited success. The Progressive Party achieved electoral victories between 1934 and 1938 but went into steep decline once Phil was no longer actively cultivating the support of local leaders and shaping a platform of specific proposals. Without these elements, the party was easily overshadowed, at first by Roosevelt and the New Deal and later by the crisis in Europe. To govern, a party must articulate a program and give voters something to embrace; without Phil's intellectual reshaping of his father's beliefs, the Progressive Party became merely a poor vehicle for obtaining office. When he left the state to pursue his own course, first as an isolationist and then as an army officer, the party simply had nothing to hold itself together, and the most significant expression of liberal thought outside of the New Deal faded from the scene.

This book explores Phil's life from both a political perspective and a personal perspective. The successes and failures of Wisconsin progressives during the Great Depression were largely determined by Phil's ideas and his leadership. Without his efforts, the state would not have enacted the pioneering Unemployment Compensation program. Yet without his ambition, the Progressive Party would not have collapsed so completely after 1938. Phil's complex career seems puzzling, a contradictory collection of ideas and goals. As a young man he freely admitted to being a radical; later he seemed to have joined with reactionaries such as Charles Lindbergh and Douglas MacArthur. He wrote of the horrors of Nazi Germany, yet demanded the United States not intervene. Underpinning all of his political career was Phil's haunting desire to "do great things" and to apply progressive ideals born in the waning years of the nineteenth century to the postwar era—a desire that met with increasing perplexity in the eyes of his followers. Understanding this is key to understanding the person and the time.

CHAPTER ONE

A Very Political Beginning

Philip F. La Follette was born on May 8, 1897, the second son and third child of Robert M. and Belle Case La Follette. An older sister, Flora (known as Fola), had been born in 1882 and an older brother, Robert Jr., in 1895; a fourth child, Mary, was born in 1899. In many ways, Phil La Follette's childhood was like that of other middle-class children living in small towns in the Midwest. Winter brought sledding and skating; summer brought swimming and the circus, which Phil particularly enjoyed. But in other ways, Phil's childhood was unusual. Because of his father's prominence as a politician, it was steeped in politics, and even at an early age his father's importance strongly influenced his life; one of his earliest recollections was his grandmother telling him that he could no longer suck his thumb now that his father was governor. Belle often took Phil and Robert to hear their father address the legislature—and later the United States Senate—or to watch debates, and they freely read their father's mail at home and at his office. Sometimes they traveled along on campaign trips, and Belle even took them to the 1908 Republican Convention in Chicago.

Belle Case and Robert M. La Follette had met while undergraduate students at the University of Wisconsin in the 1870s. Belle was the star pupil; her husband-to-be was not and nearly failed to graduate. Both were well liked but had dramatically different personalities: he was the popular, glad-handing editor of the campus newspaper while she was considerably more reserved. Their contrasting personalities formed a good match, and despite Belle's initial reluctance, the two were engaged before they finished college.

Marriage was postponed, however, until La Follette could support a family. In 1879, Belle moved to Spring Green, Wisconsin, to teach school, and La Follette enrolled in the university's law school. Within seven months he had passed the state bar exam, and in just over a year was elected Dane County district attorney. By the end of 1881 they were married.

Belle's intellect and energy made it impossible for her to remain a conventional wife and mother while working to develop her own talents. In 1883, she enrolled in the University of Wisconsin law school, and in 1885 she was the first woman to graduate from that program. Although she never practiced, she viewed the law as a logical venue to develop one's ability to think and to speak. Her training also allowed her to support her husband, helping him prepare for legal cases.

She accompanied her husband to Washington in 1885 when he was sworn in as a congressman. Initially she found the social obligations tedious, but she enjoyed the cultural opportunities, including opera, concerts, and theater. At home, she assisted La Follette on his campaigns, helping him prepare speeches and traveling with him around the district. In politics and law, her aid was indispensable.[1]

Like Belle, the children learned more than just the public side of politics. At home the La Follettes included their children in the most intimate political discussions. Surprised visitors found the children listening solemnly to such national figures as United States Senators George Norris and William Borah, muckraking journalist Lincoln Steffens, and Supreme Court Justice Louis Brandeis and his wife, Alice. Old Bob had no secrets from his children and assured his sometimes skeptical visitors that they could trust the youngsters with confidential information—he saw his career as a family enterprise and often referred to the time "when we were governor." Naturally the children did not understand everything that was said, but they absorbed the information in increasing amounts, began to contribute their own ideas, and developed lasting friendships with some of the most influential leaders of the time. Phil would later turn to these familiar figures as his own political career advanced.[2]

But political life also took its toll on the La Follette family. Long separations, the stress of being in the public eye, and a high level of responsibility compromised family bonding. Like any child, Phil wanted his parents' affection and support, but this was not always evident in the bustle of political life. Phil was also a very energetic child, curious and always needing attention. His desire for affection translated into a lifelong pursuit to win his parents' approval; from a young age he felt the need to demonstrate his fitness as a progressive citizen and as a La Follette.

One of the most prominent features of Phil's childhood were the frequent, often long separations from his parents necessitated by his father's career. In 1899, Phil lived with his Grandmother Case on her Baraboo farm for nearly a year while Belle cared for her sick husband as he recovered from strain and overwork. Belle simply did not have the time to both nurse her husband and raise her children. The time Phil spent with his grandmother established a deep appreciation for the rhythms of rural life and the simple pleasures of a snug and safe home. His days included not only typical farm chores like gathering eggs but also time for play, including riding his grandmother's horse Charlie. Although the separation from his parents must have been painful for the two-year-old, Phil's early experience was positive, and he returned to Baraboo to spend summers at the farm until his grandmother's death in 1904.[3]

When his father was elected governor of Wisconsin in 1900, Phil's home became the governor's mansion, located on East Gilman Street between Lake Mendota and the state capitol. The neighborhood provided friends to play with and excellent hills for sledding. Even though the neighbors were generally conservative Republicans who opposed La Follette's reform program, it didn't bias their children against the young La Follettes. But politics were not entirely exempt from playtime. When he was about seven years old, Phil climbed on the porch railing of Chief Justice John Cassoday and to the delight of his playmates orated on the need for primary elections and railroad regulation. Such acting was made possible by the time Phil spent at the capitol and at home listening to his father and other political leaders discuss politics.[4]

Even as a young boy, Phil was impressed by the hard work of political leadership, particularly his father's role as an insurgent, fighting with authority and bucking convention. Some of his sharpest childhood memories reflected this elementary political education. In 1904, a year after La Follette had persuaded the Board of Regents of the University of Wisconsin to appoint his former classmate Charles Van Hise as president, former U.S. senator and university regent William F. Vilas appeared at the Executive Mansion to speak to the governor. Vilas, as the state Democratic leader, not only had opposed most of La Follette's reforms, he had also fought against the appointment of Van Hise, a fight he saw as a political battle and a chance to put the young governor in his place. After Phil ushered him into his father's study, Vilas stiffly admitted to his old rival that he had been wrong and La Follette had been right, turned around, and left.[5]

In January 1906, the happy days at the governor's mansion came to an end when La Follette resigned the governorship to become a United States senator. La Follette proudly carried his reform fight to Washington, but his election meant a painful separation for the family. Though the decision was difficult, the stress of congressional life and the search for another house forced the La Follettes to conclude their children would be better off in Wisconsin. La Follette and Belle traveled to Washington without them.[6]

The children stayed at Hillside Home School in Spring Green, about forty miles west of Madison. Hillside was a progressive boarding school run by Ellen and Jane Lloyd Jones, aunts of Frank Lloyd Wright. The combination home-school-farm blended fairly strict discipline emphasizing personal responsibility—for instance, students were fined one cent for any article of clothing or toy left lying around—with close affection. Each teacher was assigned a group of students to act *in loco parentis*. Academic work was balanced with farm and household chores. Although the schooling fit very well with the La Follettes' style of parenting, the experience was not a happy one for the children. Robert was desperately homesick, as was Mary.[7]

Phil seemed to cope better with the separation, although he, too, struggled with homesickness and longed to see his mother and father. Letters to his parents, often written with Belle in mind, voiced his loneliness and asked repeatedly for more attention from them. One letter, for instance, mentioned not once but three times that he had "just a little attack" of sore throat. Another suggested that Mary (and presumably he, too) could stay with one of his aunts because she was so homesick. When his parents failed to respond to his letters or his requests for candy he grew reproachful. On March 28, 1906, he wrote a short note: "Dear Mama, I want to know whether you got my letter or not." On April 25 he wrote: "Dear Papa and Mama, I hope you are feeling good. Write soon. I have not got any letter yet." Absorbed in a senator's busy life, his parents could not provide the support and approval their children craved.[8] Yet the school also held excitement for a curious eight-year-old. Phil's letters careened from topic to topic describing his adventures. "We had a fine sleigh ride yesterday," he wrote in February. "During the ride the carriage tipped over with Mary and the aunts in but no one was injured." And later: "We are going to play fort this afternoon . . . Charles Johnson is our captain as Bobbie is first lieutenant and I am a common, everyday soldier."[9]

The period of separation finally ended at the end of the spring term. Robert's and Mary's homesickness and Phil's repeated attempts to gain his parents' attention persuaded their parents that more direct parenting was needed. All of the children accompanied their parents to Washington the next year.[10]

During the short session of the 59th Congress, from December 1906 to March 1907, La Follette lived in Washington and the children stayed with Belle at Maple Bluff Farm, the sixty-acre estate four miles north of Madison that the La Follettes had purchased in the fall of 1905. Robert walked to school in Madison, and Belle taught Phil and Mary at home. La Follette missed his family, but Belle delighted in having the children with her. She found Phil a pleasure to teach, especially as he learned to harness his boisterous energy and "concentrate his thoughts." Life on the farm settled into a quiet and comforting routine. La Follette's presence in the house—except for Christmas—took the form of daily letters, which Belle read aloud to the children. They were very much like the later radio serials of the 1930s and 1940s, describing in vivid and heroic details the senator's daily battles with the powers in government. He recounted every speech and every encounter with political leaders and even provided detailed accounts of the weather and his travel plans.[11]

The senator occasionally wrote directly to the children themselves, and when he did his letters contained fatherly advice that could easily have come from a newspaper advice column. When one of the beloved ponies went blind in one eye, Phil dutifully reported it to his father. La Follette responded: "I am sure you did all you could for her and we have to bow our heads to the things we can't help and for which we are in no way to blame." La Follette also sought to imbue his children with a sense of responsibility and civic duty and made even the most mundane tasks take on political significance. "The work in school is preparation for the battle of life," La Follette wrote his sons. "Day by day you are forging the great fight." Phil's boyhood letters reflect the seriousness that his father sought to instill. He wrote of his plans to train the ponies for a circus and described the details of the farm business and his assessment of the hired help. Phil regularly reported his progress in school as well as in farm work, equating success in both areas with parental approval, and only occasionally complaining about the hard work ("I do not think Dad ought to make me read history," he grumbled).[12]

Belle also wrote regularly, telling of the children's progress in school. She was proud of Phil when he won a debate in school, but also noted how he could improve his schoolwork. She cultivated Phil's spirited imagination and interest in the dramatic. Belle cheerfully noted that for his tenth birthday Phil asked for a theatrical costume rather than a gun

like his brother, Robert. When La Follette sent a box of wigs and cos-
tumes a few weeks later, Belle recounted Phil's delight: "He was simply
overjoyed as he tried on the different wigs . . . he assumed the characters quite as a matter of course. I laughed til I cried."[13]

Despite Phil's energy and imagination, school proved difficult for
him, in part due to shuffling back and forth between Madison and Washington, in part due to his high-energy personality that made it hard for
him to focus on schoolwork. The children began school in Madison in the
fall of 1907. That December the family moved to a small house on California Street in Washington, and the children enrolled in schools there,
fitting in as best they could. This pattern would persist for the next three
years in order to keep the family together while Congress was in session.
This difficult educational environment made it hard for Phil to keep his
grades up, which made him worry about his parents' approval. In 1909,
for example, Belle described the scene when Phil brought home his
report card. "Poor little Phil looked rather pale the night he came home
with his report card—but he stood up bravely and I thought his courage
was worth a great deal more than 'marks.'" Writing and spelling were the
most tortuous subjects, and Belle made sure that Phil diligently worked
through his homework, not just to improve his grades but to learn discipline. Belle also interested Phil in subjects beyond farm work. After she
gave him a children's history of England, Phil became fascinated with
history and biography, a trait he would carry with him his entire life.[14]
Phil retained a great affection for Maple Bluff Farm all his life, and these
years—riding ponies and daydreaming of circuses—were certainly
among his happiest.

Life in Washington was never as idyllic. When Belle's father suffered
a stroke in the summer of 1910, she and Mary went to Baraboo and left
the children with La Follette in Washington. At first Phil enjoyed staying in Washington and in part took over his mother's role in the household. He promised to report twice a week "about the house and
everybody in it" and took great pride in planning the meals and going to
the market every day to buy food, which he kept under a dollar per day.
But when his father gave this responsibility to Nellie Dunn (one of the
three "hired help" the family brought from Madison), homesickness
overwhelmed him. "I am very homesick for you[,] Mary and the farm,"
Phil wrote his mother. "[I]t is afoly [sic] lonesome without you."[15] When
he learned that the congressional session would last longer than
expected, he broke down. "I have been crying all afternoon I am so
homesick, but never mind me with love to all, your son Phil."[16]

Being the son of a senator nonetheless provided wonderful opportunities for a precocious boy with an interest in politics. Phil had virtually unlimited access to the Senate chamber and often watched proceedings from the galleries. At White House receptions, the La Follettes' invitation usually contained a "blue card," which allowed certain of the president's guests to enter via the south entrance (thereby avoiding waiting in line) and wander freely among the rooms of the White House. During these receptions, Phil chatted with officials he knew and freely introduced himself to those he did not.[17] Phil took full advantage of his father's position in government and the subsequent connection with influential officials, which fostered in him an interest in political leadership and "great men." Napoleon was a childhood hero. Associates of his father, such as Joseph Beck, Herman Ekern, and Solomon Levitan, would later play roles in his own administration. Phil was on intimate terms with many of these people: Supreme Court Justice Louis Brandeis was "Uncle Louis," and Andrew Furuseth, the gruff head of the Seamen's Union, was "Uncle Andy." Phil particularly admired Brandeis and often turned to him for political and personal advice. Between 1914 and 1915, Phil began accumulating a sizable collection of autographed photographs, including those of Winston Churchill, Thomas Edison, Josephus Daniels, David Lloyd George, Ramsay MacDonald, and Kaiser Wilhelm II. Familiar with and impressed by political leadership from an early age, Phil relished moving in those circles.[18]

Despite this immersion in "political high school" and the close working relationship among the family, there was always some distance between Phil and his father, who was forty-two years older. Robert was always closer to his father than was Phil and without a doubt was the favored son on whom the elder La Follette's political ambitions rested. Worried when Robert's poor performance at the University of Wisconsin threatened to jeopardize a future in public service, La Follette warned his son to work harder, noting that "soon enough you would make a great candidate for Governor." La Follette never planned a career in politics for his younger son. Yet Robert was shy and quiet, and Phil's personality was, ironically, much more like La Follette's: full of energy, curious about everything, playful and dramatic. When Elizabeth Glendower Evans met the family in September 1909, she described the thirteen-year-old Phil as "volatile like quicksilver." "As a child and in my youth," Phil wrote years later, "my father did not dislike me, but I worried him."[19]

Although Phil had a distant relationship with his father, he and his mother were exceptionally close until her death in 1931. Belle, perhaps sensitive to the fact that Robert was always La Follette's favorite, often told Phil that at her first sight of him she had thought, "This is *my* boy." She frequently mentioned in her letters how much she enjoyed having Phil around the house and reminded him repeatedly how much she appreciated his work in school and his help in tutoring his sister Mary. Every year on his birthday, Phil wrote Belle a letter to express his affection and gratitude, often in surprisingly intimate terms. He looked to her for personal, professional, and political advice. She responded to his intellectual pursuits, encouraging him to read William James and Ralph Waldo Emerson, and was interested in his ideas as well. "I like to get your suggestions, too," she wrote him in 1913, "and know what you think about divorce and other questions in the current thought of the day."[20]

Though Belle provided her son with necessary emotional support, family separations continued to take their toll during his teenage years as he divided his time between Washington and Madison. He complained about La Follette's attempts to direct his studies, and he resented family separations. In 1911, after his parents considered leaving their children in Madison for a second long-term separation, Phil wrote a tentative note suggesting he and Mary travel alone to Washington but apologized for "butting into your affairs."[21] Correspondence from 1911 through 1914 reveals a seasonal pattern: summers on the farm in Baraboo were happy, while the school year, with its shifts between Madison and Washington, were difficult.

In addition to the continued stress of family separation, Phil began to worry about family finances. The financial strain of maintaining two homes and the rarely profitable *La Follette's Magazine* (the newspaper La Follette started in 1909 to promote his reform agenda) was a heavy burden on the La Follette family. In his journal Phil confided that "we are terribly hard up," and he wrote an elaborate will providing his parents an income of $6,000 a year and $3,000 a year for each of his siblings. His parents perhaps unwittingly encouraged this obsession. When they were in Washington and he in Madison, they urged him to spend money as carefully as possible, and his mother regretted that family finances were tight. La Follette even gave his sons expense books to impose the Victorian idea of value. Later, as a college student, Phil remained preoccupied with money and kept a detailed account of his expenses.[22]

The year 1914 brought an experience even greater than hobnobbing at the White House, an unintentionally well-timed trip to England in the summer funded by an inheritance from his Grandmother Case. Phil and his father's secretary, Nellie Dunn, arrived in Plymouth on July 31, 1914. They toured the southwest of England and arrived in London just as Europe began to prepare for war. The events prevented a planned trip to France, but armed with a letter of introduction to liberal Irish M.P. T. P. O'Connor, Phil was admitted to the House of Commons and witnessed the debate over the war bill firsthand. Later, Ramsay MacDonald visited him at their hotel to discuss the war.[23] MacDonald evidently impressed him because Phil reported back to La Follette that he was, like MacDonald, "very much pro-German." MacDonald pointed out that England had mobilized its navy and Russia its army even before Austria's ultimatum to Serbia and suggested that Russia had been planning to attack Germany for some time and that France and England were expecting it—ideas Phil was quick to endorse.[24] Patriotic as he might have felt, Phil had already begun to challenge popular opinion and to insist he was right. The war made Phil and Dunn, like most Americans traveling abroad, above all anxious to get home. In Phil, it also stirred up a patriotic streak that wasn't countered by his antiwar stance. "I am a mighty ardent American indeed," he wrote his family.

Phil's antiwar sentiments fell in line with his family's. Between 1914 and 1917, the La Follette family as a whole opposed any American involvement in the war, but like so many Americans, they saw the events in Europe as remote events that did not really affect the United States. Instead, they compared sides as if they were two football teams. Phil had already indicated his sympathy with Germany, largely due to his dim view of the English aristocracy, and his father and brother rooted for Germany simply because it was the underdog. Belle remained strictly neutral, while Phil's sister Fola was sympathetic to the British.[25] As the United States became more involved in the war, and as German U-boats sunk neutral vessels and British officials intercepted American mail, La Follette saw it as his own mission to keep the United States out of war. Convinced, as were many Progressives, that bankers and manufacturers were pushing the United States into a pointless conflict, La Follette worried that war would end the progressive movement and possibly even jeopardize democracy at home. This position was consistent with his long history as an insurgent, and he cut a heroic figure that greatly impressed Phil, especially when La Follette came under intense criticism from other political leaders, including Woodrow Wilson and Theodore Roosevelt.

In the fall of 1915, Phil entered the University of Wisconsin at Madison at the same moment La Follette entered the most difficult phase of his public career, his highly controversial antiwar period. La Follette's opposition to American involvement in the European war and Phil's separation from the family in Washington was not all negative, though: it actually provided the grounds for father and son to begin to understand one another. Like his childhood in general, Phil's college career was a mixture of the everyday and the political. He wrote his family frequently ("Phil will write no matter how busy he is," Mary remarked to Belle), and his letters would sound familiar to most college students today. He devoted considerable time to his fraternity, assured his parents he was working hard, asked for money, and pretended not to worry about his grades. Belle was particularly eager to hear from him. "Your letters no matter how short," she wrote, "are like a glimpse of you and I feel refreshed and strengthened much as I would if you had rushed in and given me a hug and a kiss, before hurrying off to school." She offered to send him a package of preaddressed postcards to make it easier to write.[26]

During the fall of 1915, Phil's relationship with his father began to change, due in part to physical distance but mostly to La Follette's recognition of his son's abilities. Despite having been in the infirmary with tonsillitis, Phil won the University of Wisconsin's freshman declamatory contest in February 1916. La Follette, in Madison to campaign against Governor Emanuel Philipp's university policies, stayed up late to hear the results. After waiting until past midnight for Phil to return home, La Follette was delighted to find his son had taken first place. The teary-eyed senator gave his son a bear hug, remembering his own triumphal return from an oratorical contest as a university student forty years earlier, an event that had made La Follette a campus hero. After Phil's similar success, La Follette regularly gave him tips on public speaking.[27]

Tensions continued, however, over money and over Phil's frequent plans to stay at the farm rather than in the city, and the two sometimes had serious arguments. La Follette returned to Madison after a brief trip to Washington on March 19, 1916, and they had a noisy argument that almost came to blows. The cause was the abrupt marriage of two of La Follette's employees, secretary Nellie Dunn and the managing editor of *La Follette's Magazine*, Fred McKenzie. When La Follette learned that they secretly had married without letting him know in advance, he took it as a personal betrayal. Phil spoke up in their defense, and La Follette grew even angrier. Phil stormed out of the house to sulk. In a letter to Robert, Phil raged that their father "seems to resent anything in the way of friendship from this kid of his, so he shall never see it in me again. . . . Dad's attitude makes it awfly [*sic*] hard to take his money to get through school with." Phil's uncle Robert Siebecker calmed him down, but Phil, ever cautious, was not likely to have done anything without careful thought. "I'll not do anything rash, spectacular or sorry for later," he assured his brother, "I take it mighty slow." A day later, Phil wrote a stiff letter of apology to his father.[28]

Disagreements continued, but La Follette also came to trust Phil's reports and suggestions on the political situation in Wisconsin. A recurring theme was the need for active leadership, to meet with people in person despite his frequent stays in Washington: "I feel that all of Dad's friends feel the need of his directing presence. They feel that he should get out amongst the people and get into close contact with them again." Later in July 1916, Phil again urged La Follette to campaign in the state where Progressives were having a difficult time coordinating their efforts. Phil himself began to do some of the planning. When six hundred North Dakota farmers visited the University of Wisconsin, Phil spoke to a number of them and interviewed North Dakota progressive reformer Lynn Frazier for the *Daily Cardinal*. He also began to spend more and more time in La Follette's Madison office, forwarding mail to the senator with suggested action.[29]

This trend of giving political advice to local Progressives continued into 1917 as La Follette's role as a leading opponent to American involvement in World War I grew. La Follette, so often at odds with congressional leaders, now courted hostility to an even greater extent. In March 1917, the Senate considered an administration bill that would have allowed American merchant ships to be armed. There were enough votes to pass the measure, which La Follette believed would surely bring war to the United States. He and a small group of other Senators—what Woodrow Wilson called a "little group of willful men"—filibustered the Armed Ship Bill while Wilson himself sat in the next room waiting to take the oath of office for his second term. Before the measure could even be voted on, the congressional session came to an official close on March 4, and La Follette's group had stymied the president and blocked certain passage of the bill. In organizing the filibuster, La Follette made himself the target not only of bitter criticism but also of threats of physical violence, and the Senate became a decidedly dangerous place. After receiving an anonymous tip that he would be assaulted on the floor, La Follette asked Robert to bring a revolver to the lobby of the Senate in case he needed it. La Follette supporter Harry Lane even readied himself to stab a hostile senator in the heart with a rat-tail file should the need arise to defend

Old Bob.[30] The public response to La Follette's position was neatly summed up by cartoonist Roland Kirby, who printed a cartoon in which La Follette and others were decorated with a large iron cross.

After Congress declared war on Germany, the abuse La Follette faced became increasingly vicious. Shortly after his vote against the declaration, the *Boston Evening Transcript* announced that "Henceforth, he is the Man without a Country." Students on several college campuses burned him in effigy. Such malice was not confined to the young. A few days after La Follette's impassioned antiwar speech, Senator John Sharp Williams of Mississippi challenged La Follette's patriotism on the floor of the Senate and called his address "pro-German, pretty nearly pro-Goth, and pro-Vandal, which was anti-American president, anti-American Congress, and anti-American people," an absurd charge against a leader who had built his career around reforms to make the government more responsive to the will of the people.[31]

Just as La Follette had begun to recognize his son's potential, Phil began to see his father as more than just another political leader. He remained optimistic (and naïve) that Secretary of State William Jennings Bryan and La Follette could forestall war, and in his mind his father grew in importance the more unpopular he became. "I have always felt that you were giving us kids a great deal more than any other man of our generation in the way of a great name to live up to," Phil wrote his father shortly after the Armed Ship filibuster. "[I]t will take an almost superhuman effort on any of our parts to even approximate living up to you." Though vilified for his "un-American" actions, La Follette became something of a model for Phil through his lonely and pugnacious stand. Phil found this image of the misunderstood patriot crying in the wilderness romantic. Ever in search of greatness, Phil despaired of being able to live up to his father's example. In a letter to his father written just after the filibuster, Phil struggled with the painful side of insurgency:

> I love you so much for your courage . . . but most for [your] fortitude which gives you the courage and the strength to do as you see without making you bitter. Oh I pray God that I may in some small way be worthy of you. I do so want to make my life worthwhile, but you have set an almost unattainable ideal for us. *But I'll do the best I can.*[32]

Phil now saw La Follette as a "world figure" who would inspire generations to come, and he hoped to live up to his father's insurgent legacy.

To distract himself from world events and to compensate for missing his family, Phil threw himself into schoolwork and social activities, including fraternity business, the Union board, the YMCA committee, and the Joint Debate Board. It was a season of loneliness, as his almost daily letters to Belle reported. Despite the declaration of war in April, he stayed on in Madison to manage the farm and keep track of the Wisconsin political situation. During the summer months he worked at *La Follette's*, for which Belle arranged a small salary. Both Belle and La Follette were anxious that the political climate not threaten Phil's education; they never obliged Phil by asking him to join them in Washington. In response to Phil's letter of March 1917, La Follette wrote, "I long to see you to talk things over with you," but then provided two pages of detailed instructions for the farm and further instructions for sending a package of clothes.[33] Phil was clearly impressed with his father's role during the national crisis, but he was as yet unsure how he himself fit into it.[34]

———•———

This personal insulation from world affairs changed rapidly during the later months of 1917, the most difficult and most significant time in La Follette's career, a time that made Phil feel the difficulty of insurgency firsthand. In September 1917, while delivering a speech to the Nonpartisan League in St. Paul, Minnesota, La Follette answered a heckler by acknowledging the hostile acts by Germany against neutral powers. The United States, La Follette declared, had "serious grievances" against Germany, but none worth declaring war over. The stenographer from the Associated Press misquoted him, however, and the next morning newspapers across the nation reported that La Follette told his audience that "we had no grievances against Germany." The response was immediate. Hundreds of editors condemned the senator without first verifying the story, and the Minnesota Public Safety Commission became the first of many organizations to demand his expulsion from the Senate. His colleagues abandoned streetcars and elevators when he got on, and the Madison Club's board of directors expelled him as a "disloyal citizen." Old rivals such as Theodore Roosevelt—who declared that La Follette should be shot as a traitor—pounced on this opportunity to denounce him. Even old friends failed to come to his defense. Former Secretary of State William Jennings Bryan asked La Follette to publicly retract his alleged statements, and the Minneapolis University of Wisconsin Alumni Club wired him collect asking him to resign. La Follette stubbornly refused to do either.[35]

In February 1918, the *Saturday Evening Post* printed a short story by Irvin S. Cobb in which a thinly disguised La Follette–like character named Jason Mallard thrives on the hostility of the press because it feeds his ego. A group of editors organize a complete boycott and refuse to print anything about him, and within six weeks, this silence drives Mallard to suicide.[36] Even in Wisconsin, La Follette was not safe from abuse. At the university—still under the presidency of La Follette's old friend Van Hise—an overwhelming majority of the faculty signed a round-robin petition condemning La Follette's actions. The legislature also debated a resolution to condemn his actions, during which Senator J. Henry Bennet compared La Follette to Judas Iscariot and Benedict Arnold. The resolution, drafted by conservative Republican Roy P. Wilcox, a first-term senator from Eau Claire, condemned La Follette for failing "to support our government in matters vital to the winning of the war." Only three senators voted to support La Follette.[37]

Despite Phil's initial bravado, his father's opposition to war made life in Madison increasingly difficult, and the events forced Phil to move beyond his admiration and support of his father and to make difficult decisions on his own over his role in both the war and in the Progressive movement. The most immediate question was over military service. In April 1917, the University of Wisconsin faculty passed a provision to allow students to substitute military drill for classes and receive credit toward graduation. Phil struggled to decide what he should do. He suggested to his parents that military drill would be preferable to the universal service bill then under consideration in Congress. Belle was furious, especially when she learned that the drill could not guarantee commission as an officer, complaining that "the Faculty had just assumed that they could turn the University into a training camp and gone wild without any thorough investigation of the law."[38] Phil also considered joining the French ambulance corps, which would also have prevented his being drafted. He wrote his parents that he did not want to go but that he could justify his efforts as saving lives rather than taking them. La Follette immediately wired him saying not to enlist, but Belle understood that Phil's musings were an attempt to sort out his opinions of the war and not a prelude to immediate action. She was pleased, writing to her son, "[Y]ou are thinking your problems through and through, over and over and arriving at a wise and workable conclusion." Although she noted that she was a pacifist, she said that if she were in Phil's place she would serve if drafted, and she encouraged him to make up his own mind. Eventually, Phil decided not to take the drill and tried to focus on his studies as much as possible.[39]

Phil's recurring impulse to enlist came from his intense desire to do the right thing. If drafted, he decided that he would go or else "go through life with the blot that [he] didn't stand behind the government [when] it needed us." Yet Phil despised the student-patriots on campus who refused to back up their words by enlisting. He also believed that the experience of having served would make him a more effective peace advocate when the war was over. Eventually, he decided that he should either volunteer or refuse—waiting to be drafted was hypocritical. He also decided that he would have more influence as an officer and could be more useful to the progressive cause after the war ended.[40]

Phil's thoughtfulness on the enlistment question pleased Belle, and La Follette was proud that Phil even survived "the earthquake that tore the university from its foundations and threw the faculty into hysterics." Simply staying at the University of Wisconsin became itself a political act. Phil went out of his way to talk to people about the war in an attempt to gauge public opinion; he initially believed that it was turning against Wilson and the war. He planned to stay at the university but promised to go to Washington if his parents wanted the family together. He again offered to "sacrifice anything to help along in the work," even though he preferred to "stay here in this war mad university of ours and sort of 'stick to my guns.'" From a distance, Phil continued to be deeply impressed by La Follette's unpopularity, the threats he received, and even the possibility of his arrest for sedition. He had often thought in the past that having a famous father made life too easy for him, and now this crisis gave him the chance to fight on his own: "[I]f I ever amount to anything of any account," he wrote his family, "it will be [due] quite largely to this crisis." Phil almost relished the hysteria because it made him feel as if he himself was a political leader.[41]

Nonetheless, life at the University of Wisconsin became increasingly uncomfortable as the fall semester wore on. President Van Hise dismissed a professor in the German department who joked about a colleague's liberty loan pin. Professor Carl Russell Fish spoke at a pep rally and denounced pacifists (and by extension, Belle) as traitors. The *Wisconsin State Journal* called Phil's fraternity house a "hotbed of sedition," prompting a fellow Beta Theta Pi member to remark at a meeting that Phil and his friends had better guard their tongues. After a friend suggested that Phil's views on the war had been influenced by the state's German population, he wrote the man a blistering letter (preparing and saving several drafts) in response to the insult to him and his family, which had opened a "deep gash" in their friendship. Finally, in December 1917 a group of fifteen to twenty students hanged and burned La Follette in effigy in front of the university library. Phil pretended not to be overly upset, but he was quite shaken. People in the street jeered at his sixteen-year-old sister Mary, calling her "the traitor's daughter." "During the war years," Phil wrote in his memoirs, "I never heard the name La Follette spoken in public places without flinching and bracing myself for some epithet."[42]

Even old friends, some of whom had joined those same La Follette family conferences that Phil had solemnly listened to years earlier, attacked the family. Returning to Madison from Washington after Christmas, Phil met UW professor John R. Commons, who demanded to know where Phil had gotten a five-dollar gold piece. When Phil told Commons the money had been a Christmas present from his father, Commons snapped, "No patriotic citizen would have gold in his possession in time of war." Still Phil clung to the belief that people would recognize the correctness of his father's position. He admitted that the student population was "pretty bad," but he argued that working people and farmers agreed with La Follette. If only La Follette would speak to the people, they would understand. "The people who do the talking in towns need some courage shot into them," he wrote. "And . . . Daddy is the only man that can do it."[43] Rather than becoming depressed and alienated from this hostility, Phil almost relished the bitterness his father faced. His experiences during the war years provided a rite of passage of sorts by which he could prove himself worthy of his father's legacy.

Despite the growing war hysteria, Phil was determined to pursue his studies and dropped most of his outside activities. Even then he brought his political battles into the classroom. His victory in the Joint Debate brought his father "great joy," especially since Phil's position was against the war and therefore "unpopular" and "unpatriotic." Unfortunately, the effort left him exhausted and ill at the exam period. He subsequently failed three classes. This brought a chiding letter from La Follette, who was dismayed at his son's poor health and scholastic difficulties:

> I would be glad to know just how you can handle your university work—it seems like a heavy load to undertake and pick up on those in which you failed. . . . <u>You have gone beyond all limits</u> in the things you have taken on extra. I do think for every con-

sideration you should let up on it. . . . I suggest that you figure on being obliged to do a <u>little better</u> than required <u>by the regulations</u> in order to "breast the tape."[44]

Phil's health problems continued—his doctors recommended that he cut back on his course load—and by March he was clearly unhappy at the University of Wisconsin. He wrote his father that the entire faculty was "looney" and suggested that he take his brother's job as La Follette's secretary if Robert, suffering from a complicated bacterial infection, was too ill. For the rest of the semester Phil repeatedly offered to come to Washington, although he did not want it to appear as if he was leaving because of the war. La Follette demurred, and Phil instead devoted much of his energy to the farm.[45]

Despite his clinging devotion to his father's beliefs and positions, Phil did at times disagree with La Follette and assert their differences. Unlike his father, Phil found the sense of crusade appealing and struggled to reconcile his visions of glory with his parents' pacifism and his own sense of insurgency. "I should like to wave my flag . . . I should like to be with my friends," he wrote. "But there is something within me, which keeps me plugging ahead along the road of mental discontent; of unpopularity and hatred from one's fellow men." While his father opposed conscription and other war measures as a matter of principle, Phil eventually decided to enlist in the army in early 1918, in part out of the desire for experience and in part to in some way share his father's hardship. "The life of an ambulance driver is hard," Phil wrote to his father in January 1917, when he was still considering enlisting in the ambulance corps, "but no harder than you have been living all your life, nor than I shall have to go through if I am to amount to anything." The "almost unattainable goal" set by his father still haunted Phil, and joining the humanitarian part of the armed forces would allow him to follow his father's path while at the same time asserting his own independence. It was not enough to manage the family farm while achieving a satisfactory scholastic record at the university. He anticipated his father's reaction, however, and pointedly asked him to read through his letter before passing judgment.[46] Phil had other reasons for enlisting, which he pointed out to his father: he could learn French while in Europe and form a more educated opinion about war. It would "bracen him up" in a way that studying at the university could not, and such an independent choice might win respect from his father. Phil may very well have been trying to assert his independence, but it was not until May 1918 that he actually enlisted in the officers' training program in Fort Sheridan, Illinois.[47]

Phil arrived at Fort Sheridan on June 2, 1918. He described army life in detail in letters to his family and took to the rigorous schedule of rising at five to drill all morning before afternoon lessons. "This business is good hard work," he wrote, "but it hasn't bothered me much so far." After basic training, the base commander sent Phil as "one of his very best men" to Norman, Oklahoma. He was commissioned a second lieutenant and reported to the Student Army Training Corps Unit at the University of Oklahoma. His job was essentially superintendent of employment, placing inductees in positions according to their skills (finding the "right place for every soldier") and supervising the payroll.

During his time in Norman, Phil exchanged regular letters with La Follette, now living alone in Washington while the rest of the family lived with Robert, who was recuperating from his illness in La Jolla, California. It was something of a turning point in their relationship. La Follette, lonely without his family, reported to Phil on the flu epidemic there and about his treatment in the press and inquired frequently and with great interest about Phil's responsibilities. In turn, Phil discussed his life in the army and his plans to enter law school. La Follette still offered advice—often tersely worded—to his son, as when he fired off this short note in June: "Phil—you spell accuracy with two c-s not acquracy the way you have been spelling it in your letters. Get a little pocket dictionary. Dad." Overall, however, it was a friendly, chatty correspondence with little of the tension that had marked their letters while Phil was in college. The two came to rapprochement for several reasons. First, once the war had started La Follette thought it honorable to enlist—he had no illusions about the nobility of the war, but respected volunteers' willingness to fight for their country. La Follette told Phil to make his own decision and at one point actually suggested a position in the Marines. Furthermore, both were separated from the rest of the family, and the correspondence comforted them. Had the war continued, there might have been renewed tension over Phil's enlistment, but the war lasted only one month after Phil arrived in Oklahoma. Although Phil had proven himself loyal to—and worthy of—his father's insurgent legacy, by enlisting in the army he also demonstrated a distinct independent streak and a willingness to challenge even the most immediate of authority figures. He had clearly demonstrated both his ability and his character, and La Follette began to look on him with much greater respect. Phil had grown up.[48]

After the armistice and without the steady stream of draftees, Phil's work at the Student Army Training Corps Unit began to wind down. He refused a reserve commission because he did not want the military to "have any strings on" him. Although eager to see his father in Washington and witness "history in the making," after his discharge on December 26, 1918, he traveled to La Jolla, California, where Belle, Robert, and Mary were still living. Despite still harboring ill feelings toward the University of Wisconsin, Phil was eager to finish his degree, and by the middle of January he was back in Madison adjusting to civilian life.[49]

Old hurts occasionally resurfaced. The refusal of the university prom committee to invite La Follette as an honorary guest in 1919 (as they did Senator Irvine Lenroot) set off a short-lived tempest in Madison. It was of little consequence but reminded Phil that insurgent politics carried an inherent unpopularity that never fully vanished. Phil wrote Belle that until then he had been feeling "flushed with my own meager success" in the army, but being back at the university reminded him that he (contrary to his hope) could not be both "popular/respectable" and a visionary. Events like the prom controversy were no longer things to endure but opportunities to grow. By the end of the semester, he again believed that people respected him, and that, perhaps, conservatives "feared" him.[50] Phil was even feeling confident enough to make light of some of the past irritation between himself and his father. He jokingly sent an itemized expense list for seventy dollars his father had recently sent him to demonstrate that he had wasted none, and he graciously accepted La Follette's suggestion that he cut back on smoking (he smoked a pack a day—La Follette sent him a pipe).[51]

Reimmersed in his academic pursuits, Phil left his dreams of flag-waving glory behind and returned to a "semi-monastic" life in Madison. He roomed with his old friend Joe Farrington, took classes at the university, and supervised work on the farm. He also began an informal discussion group reading "great books" such as the Bible and works by Emerson and Shakespeare. Despite some difficulty readjusting to academic life, he enjoyed his classes, particularly a philosophy class taught by Max Otto. Otto, in turn, enjoyed encouraging Phil's analytical bent. Once when Phil disagreed with Otto's interpretation of Emerson, Otto made him present his ideas formally to the class. Phil also spent time at *La Follette's Magazine*, urging his father to turn it into a publication aimed firmly at the working classes, just as *The Nation* was aimed at intellectuals and *Hoard's Dairyman* was aimed at farmers. He was restless, however, and unsure what to do with his life. At different times he

considered traveling to Europe to see the conditions after the war, joining the consular service, traveling to South America, or staying in Madison to work on the magazine. He had no difficulty confining himself to a
rigorous daily schedule of studying, reading, and exercising, but he was
bored, ready to leave the university and do something productive.[52] As
he finished up his final year at the university, he began considering what
career would best allow him to develop his talents and remain true to his
parents' progressive beliefs while giving him a way to enter public service.
Law school was his almost immediate choice.

By the time he returned from Oklahoma at the end of the war, Phil
had decided on law school as his immediate future task but was still
unsure where to go. Both of his parents had attended the University of
Wisconsin Law School. But Wisconsin Justice Marvin Rosenberry
advised him to study somewhere other than the university for at least a
year, since the practice of law in the state had become so simplified there
was little value in attending the university. Rosenberry, however, did
suggest that Milwaukee would be an excellent place to open a practice.
Phil considered Harvard, Columbia, and Georgetown, but in the fall of
1919 he enrolled at George Washington University in Washington, D.C.,
so he could be near his family, also back in Washington.

One of the positive effects of the move was that it allowed Phil to fos-
ter his growing relationship with his father. Rumors circulated that
La Follette had disowned his son for enlisting, but Phil was fully reconciled with his father and more than ever devoted to his political creed—
and perhaps even more radical. La Follette never questioned the
legitimacy of private property, but Phil was much more willing to consider
socialism—government ownership of key industries—than his father. This
flirtation with radicalism not long after the 1919 anticommunist raids led
by Attorney General A. Mitchell Palmer amused his friends. "I trust that
this letter will be forwarded to your place of incarceration," wrote his
friend Joe Farrington in November 1919, "for I am sure that the government did not overlook you in its most recent raid for Reds." Phil, in a style
much like his father's, wrote many letters to friends discussing his political views, often in a spirit of "knowing it all," according to Farrington in
response to Phil's arguments for miners' ownership of mines during the
coal strike of 1919. But Phil remained devoted to his father and his progressive creed. "So long as I live," he wrote him, "I am going to keep
scrapping for the same things you have, to the best of my ability."[53]

Law school suited Phil's temperament and work ethic. He enjoyed
studying law much more than he had his undergraduate degree, in part

because his energy was focused on only one topic. "I feel serious, purposeful, without 'grindishness,'" he wrote Belle shortly after starting classes. He worked hard his first year, to the point that Belle worried about him, especially when he took an extra class that made him late for dinner twice a week. "Phil sticks to his law faithfully," she wrote in February. "I am sure he is making good progress." But she could not help adding that "I like to think he is dancing and forgetting his work for awhile," while he was on a date.[54]

Phil allowed little time for socializing while in law school, but in the spring of 1920 he became engaged to a childhood acquaintance, Betty Head. She took a job in New York. Phil moved back to Madison to finish at the University of Wisconsin Law School in the summer of 1920, and so the two saw little of each other over the next year, except for a Christmas spent together with the La Follette family in Washington in 1920. She immediately impressed everyone, especially Belle. "It made me very happy to feel how deeply I could love her," Belle wrote Phil. "You have always been good to me Phil, I realize how much you care for your lifemate and how devoted you will be to her. You are fortunate in having won such a girl as Betty." This fortune did not last, however, due not least to Phil's treatment of his fiancée. On the morning she was to leave Washington, he slept late while she waited for him to take her to the station, an incident that produced a scolding from Robert. This incident was the first crack in Phil's and Betty's relationship, and after a few tortuous months, they broke their long-distance engagement in March 1921. Phil explained to Belle that there was simply nothing holding them together but mutual attraction and that he couldn't marry her unless they shared common ideals, goals, and interests. He and Betty had not been friends first and so could never be "utterly frank" with each other. Phil confessed that in this and other romantic relationships he had been unwilling to let go of his emotions.[55]

Back in Madison, Phil again plunged into a disciplined academic life, his chief source of human contact being letters to and from his family, which he wrote nearly every day. Despite his disinclination to be intimate and his immersion in law study, another student at the university found Phil "fas-kinating." This was Isabel Bacon, known to many as Isen, a University of Wisconsin undergraduate whom Phil had met in a Sunday evening discussion group known as the Walrus Club. Despite his penchant for flirting, she recognized and understood his high-minded seriousness and shared his political ideals; the two quickly became friends. "Who is this Isobel [*sic*] Bacon that seems to be taking some of

your valuable time?" Robert inquired in June 1921. "[O]ne of the ladies
. . . said just as she was leaving, 'I understand that Phil is seeing something (now what did she mean by that?) of Isabel Bacon and I want you
to know that she is a wonderful girl.'" After the recent disaster with Betty
Head, Phil may have been reluctant to introduce Isabel to his family
until he had made up his mind about her, but Isabel had no such reluctance. While Phil hesitated about jumping into another relationship,
Isen forged ahead and quickly overcame his doubts. The previous
November she had written to her family that she had sat next to Phil at
a literary meeting. "I'd surely like to vamp him," she confided. "We
talked on Russia and had a great time." The relationship proceeded
smoothly, and they became engaged in May 1921, just two months after
Phil's broken engagement to Betty Head. The quickness of the engagement didn't stop the La Follette family from warming up to Isabel when
they finally met in September 1921. Isabel also felt warmly toward her
future in-laws from the first meeting. After the visit, she wrote to Belle
to thank her for making her feel "immediately perfectly 'at home.'"
Robert thought her a "rare woman."[56]

Before they were married, Phil still needed some coaching to keep
his academic life and his closeness with his family from crowding out a
partner. In January 1922, Belle warned him that he must never appear
reluctant to express his feelings to Isabel, especially while among the
family, lest he seem indifferent. "I prize your spontaneous spirit," she
advised, "Don't <u>repress</u> it needlessly." His closeness with Belle certainly
must have also influenced his attraction to Isabel. Their relationship
reflected that of the elder La Follettes, which for forty years had been a
political partnership as well as a marriage. From the first, La Follette
and Belle were devoted to each other and shared a close and affectionate marriage. The two were also closely matched in intellectual temperament and political ideology. Belle, although shy and self-effacing, was
La Follette's equal in many respects. Belle regularly worked in
La Follette's congressional office and Senate office, corresponding with
constituents and reviewing his speeches. She was La Follette's most able
critic, and when they began *La Follette's Magazine* in 1909, she was a
weekly columnist, entering into the debates on suffrage and desegrega-
tion. She was also La Follette's equal on the stump, and she gave hundreds of speeches, not just on his behalf, but also for woman suffrage and
anti-lynching legislation. Belle did not neglect more traditional duties of
being a wife, however. La Follette's frequent illnesses and almost constant travel worried her, and she nursed him back to health on a number

of occasions and tended to his emotional needs. Yet if Belle preferred to remain in the more traditional role of supportive spouse than assume a public life herself, their marriage was one of equals, with both shouldering the burden of progressive insurgency.[57] Belle's daughter-in-law would take on many of the same roles in her marriage to Phil, which was also based on shared intellectual and political interests. Gifted in writing and communication just as her mother-in-law was, and devoted to the cause of progressivism, Isabel would come alongside her husband as an able critic of his work and his best ally and as the one person who could best gauge whether he was working too hard.

Isabel and Phil planned to be married when he was earning enough money, and in the meantime Isabel took a social work job in Bayonne, New Jersey. The relationship continued primarily through warm and affectionate letters, as they told each other about their work and thoughts on current events. In 1923, Belle arranged for Isabel to work at *La Follette's Magazine*, thereby incorporating her into the family enterprise and providing financial support. The couple planned to marry on April 14 in Chicago. Although they would not be married before their families—a not uncommon phenomenon before the end of the Second World War when large weddings became the norm—they did have their families' blessings. A week before the wedding, a barn fire at Maple Bluff Farm caused Phil to suggest postponing the wedding to summer or perhaps even fall. "We weren't planning on living in the barn, were we?" responded a thoroughly startled Isabel. They did not postpone their marriage date, but Phil still seemed to have a hard time believing it would happen. The day before the wedding, he wrote his family that he "in all probability" would be married tomorrow. The next morning, Phil and Isabel met in Chicago and were married by Dr. Eustace Haydon of the University of Chicago Divinity School. They left immediately for Maple Bluff.[58]

Belle was delighted that her daughter-in-law shared so many of her interests. In 1925, Isabel began lobbying the Wisconsin legislature to support the child labor amendment and followed the developments closely. She mirrored Phil's disgust with legislators who failed to live up to their supposed progressive ideals; she told Robert that they needed to clean out "the imitation and broken furniture" in the legislature. At *La Follette's Magazine* Isabel wrote editorials and laid out articles and eventually started her own column entitled "A Room of Our Own," in which she discussed current events from a "woman's perspective." Although Isabel initially consulted Phil on editorial decisions, she gradually took on more responsibility, and Phil had less and less to do with the management of the magazine. Belle encouraged her efforts and depended on her not only for magazine work (Belle seems to have distrusted the managing editor, Fred Holmes) but also as a researcher for the biography of her husband she had begun writing. Belle also insisted that Isabel receive a salary for all work she did, partly out of respect for her talents and partly because Belle knew firsthand about the necessity for women to demand equal compensation with men.[59]

Isabel did not try to share Phil's legal work, but she often went to see him in court and reported back to the family on his work and health. He was working "like a dog," she told Robert, "late nights, and you know how absorbed he gets when he has problems to work out." Phil's tendency to overwork was a trait he shared with his father and that had served him well during his years as a student, but it became increasingly problematic after his marriage. Phil's and Isabel's first few apartments were located in downtown Madison, and Phil took advantage of the location to walk to his office in the evenings and on weekends. La Follette was impressed with Phil's efforts but nonetheless warned him not to become too involved in his work. What Phil claimed was a temporary situation could easily become a lifelong habit, his father pointed out, and noted that he wished he could have lived that part of his life differently. It was ironic advice, since so much of Phil's career would be based on that of his father. For the next two decades the long hours continued, and Phil struggled to balance the demands of family and of his career, a struggle that became more problematic as Phil took on an increasingly important role in Wisconsin politics in the 1920s.[60]

CHAPTER TWO

Apprenticeship

During the same years that Phil La Follette completed his education, established a law practice, and settled into a comfortable domestic routine with Isabel, he served as something of an apprentice to his father. Those years saw a remarkable comeback for Old Bob. Despised in 1917, he nonetheless won reelection in 1922 and ran for president in 1924. Just as Phil's childhood had shaped his ideological view of the world, the period between 1920 and 1925 saw him take on an indispensable practical role in Wisconsin politics, acting as his father's intermediary in Madison and taking an active role in campaigns for his father and other Progressive candidates. Phil's political development and his father's career are closely intertwined. Working alongside his father, Phil learned the workings of everyday politics and demonstrated his capabilities as a public voice for Progressives. At the same time, he asserted an identity for himself distinct from that of the family, largely through his time as Dane County district attorney. He emerged as a rising leader of the Wisconsin Progressives.

Before he could take on a fully political role, Phil had much to learn from his father's experiences. La Follette's infamous 1919 libel suit and campaigns on behalf of Wisconsin and Minnesota Progressives in the early 1920s set the stage for his presidential race. At the same time they laid the foundation for Phil's emergence on the political scene. La Follette's triumphant reemergence as a major political figure was part of the vindication he sought after the end of the First World War, which had been a tense, traumatic time for the La Follettes.

By the armistice, change was already in the air. The Congress elected in 1918 was only narrowly Republican, and Old Bob found a curious reconciliation with the party that now suddenly needed his vote. After the Senate Committee of Elections and Privileges quietly dropped its investigation of his St. Paul speech, in which he had been misquoted and accused of sedition, La Follette once more walked the floor of the Senate unmolested. As the reaction against Wilsonian idealism took hold of the country, a sense of vindication and a renewed popularity dominated the last few years of his career. It was this sense of vindication that Phil absorbed as he took up politics in earnest, traveling with his father in his last campaigns. "I may never live to see my own vindication," La Follette told his daughter and son-in-law, "but you will."[1] La Follette did live to see it, and it proved to be Phil's most vivid image of his father.

La Follette's vindication began in the courtroom. Early in 1919, La Follette filed libel charges against the *Madison Democrat*, the *Wisconsin State Journal*, and the directors of the Madison Club. His old law partner Gilbert Roe (who had also represented him before the Senate committee) again represented him and examined the defendants in court—no witnesses could produce any evidence to support their charges of disloyalty. "It was gratifying," Phil wrote later, "to watch them squirm as, in effect, they ate their words." At the same time, however, he did not completely approve, comparing his father's actions to a boxer "yelping" to a referee rather than fighting back. Leaders, Phil believed, must be able to "take it." As he considered the implications of the libel suit over the following months, Phil began to see his father as a member of a political lineage that wasn't afraid to disagree with majority opinion. Phil regularly placed his father alongside other historic figures, such as Abraham Lincoln, Henry Clay, and Daniel Webster, who defended the right of Congress to define war aims and defended free speech during the Mexican War. He also pointed out David Lloyd George's opposition to the Boer War and William Pitt's and Edmund Burke's objection to the Revolutionary War. His favorite analogy was to John Bright, the British Member of Parliament who opposed the Crimean War but went on to a long career as a populist reformer and who became the subject of a popular biography by George Macaulay Trevelyan. Phil truly believed that La Follette was as popular as ever (based in part on the fact that he himself received no further ill treatment), but that the people needed encouragement in expressing their trust in him. He realized that the people needed leadership—individuals to educate, articulate ideas, and direct political action. He vigorously shared these views with family and friends in his correspondence. It was as much a matter of personality as politics.[2]

A personal sense of right was one thing, but La Follette quickly received acclaim for his courage in the political arena as well—his last campaigns confirmed his lasting, icon-like popularity and initiated Phil into the actual work of La Follette–style politics. The 1920 election, crucial in Wisconsin where conservative Republicans led by retiring Governor Emanuel Philipp had controlled the state since 1914, repeated the insurgent pattern set by Old Bob years earlier and marked the return to power of the La Follette forces. In July, La Follette endorsed John J. Blaine for governor for the Republican nomination in the primary election against Roy P. Wilcox, the state senator who had introduced the 1918 resolution condemning La Follette for failing to support the government and inciting sedition. Blaine won easily and went on to win the general election in November. Nine out of ten La Follette candidates also won nomination to the House of Representatives, although La Follette's candidate for the United States Senate, James Thompson, lost to incumbent Irvine Lenroot, a one-time La Follette ally. During the 1920 campaigns, Phil took an active part for the first time, delivering his first speech in the village of Rome in Jefferson County to about fifty people seated on planks supported by beer kegs in a kerosene-lit hall. It was an experience that showed Phil he had what it took to take the stage. "I found I could swim," Phil noted with uncharacteristic brevity.[3]

Although the 1920 elections proved that the spirit of progressive reform in Wisconsin had survived the war, it remained unclear how the Old Man himself would fare, and many of his advisors suggested he mellow his rhetoric in order to heal the wounds inflicted by his stand against the war. By the summer of 1921, however, it became evident that La Follette's vindication was at hand. On Saint Patrick's Day, La Follette delivered an address to more than three thousand members of the Ancient Order of Hibernians in Milwaukee in which he advocated the independence of Ireland. The message certainly suited his audience, and the cheering and applause interrupted him so often that it took twenty minutes for him to get through the first eight pages. He had, wrote Phil, who watched from the floor, "all the fire and zip which over-joyed all his friends and made his enemies fear he was going to live forever."[4]

A few days later La Follette faced a much tougher audience when he delivered an address on corporate influence in state legislatures sponsored by the People's Reconstruction League. It was his first address in

Madison in four years and the first in the recently completed capitol. His friends urged him not to mention the war, to let the hysteria recede, to strike a note of reconciliation—no one thought it wise to start a new fight. The large crowd gathered in the Assembly Chamber and gave him a warm welcome, and La Follette started the speech with the formalities of the day, graciously thanking the people of Madison for welcoming him back to his home. But then his demeanor changed, and he raised his right arm and barked out, "I am going to be a candidate for reelection to the United States Senate. I do not want the vote of a single citizen under any misapprehension of where I stand: I would not change my record on the war for that of any man, living or dead!" Silence filled the chamber for a moment, and then the cheering started. As Phil watched, his father received the largest ovation of his life for refusing to abandon his beliefs. One longtime political foe remained seated with tears running down his cheeks; "I hate the son of a bitch," he muttered, "but, my God, what guts he's got!"[5]

The dramatic speech in the chamber marked the beginning of yet another "Fighting Bob comeback" and also the beginning of his last campaign for the United States Senate. During this final phase of his career, La Follette became a left-wing icon, vindicated but largely powerless in the conservative political atmosphere in the 1920s. As a visible lieutenant of his father, Phil became a key figure in the Progressive movement not only in Wisconsin, but nationwide. Phil's role in the early 1920s was twofold: as a campaigner, he delivered rousing speeches and rallied the rank-and-file Progressives, and as the only family member actually living in the state, he acted as the field officer, providing reports on political conditions and popular opinion.[6] La Follette by now fully appreciated his younger son's immense talents: "Dad has wanted me with him every spare moment," Phil wrote his future wife, Isabel, in February 1922, as Phil helped his father prepare speeches for Milwaukee and Madison and plan campaign strategy with Progressive leaders in Madison.[7]

In 1922, Phil began to give speeches on behalf of the Progressives, encouraging local organizations that had become disorganized during the war. In March 1922, he traveled to Oshkosh, home of the most anti–La Follette newspaper in the state, to look over political conditions and to speak to a small group of La Follette supporters who were organizing for the Republican nomination. A few days later, he went to Janesville in Rock County, the most consistently conservative county in the state. In both places, he acted as the family's scout, investigating

Progressive strength and "meeting the folks," reporting back his findings to the family. In the spring and summer, Phil gave a number of campaign speeches for Progressive candidates around Madison and Milwaukee, and he took over Governor John Blaine's speaking itinerary when Blaine was called back to Madison to deal with state affairs. In August, a month before the primary, Phil often spoke a dozen times in one week. On August 11, he delivered six campaign speeches in Adams and Juneau Counties to crowds of one to four hundred during the day and to a crowd of seven hundred that night. When La Follette was called back to Washington, Phil took over his engagements in the central part of the state. He had a strong desire to "take it to the folks" and a knack for discerning which issues were unclear to voters and making them more salient. Throughout, he missed his family. Conscious of the strain the campaign took on his personal life, he wrote back to his Isabel, "please try to put up with me until this is over."[8]

Like his father, Phil bore up well under the strain of almost continuous speaking engagements while still working daily in his own growing law practice. "Phil made a wonderful campaign," Belle wrote to Isabel. "He lost weight, but he looks well. He made friends and won admiration wherever he spoke. There can be no question that it will bring him [legal] clients." By September, he had made more than two hundred speeches, cementing his position as a political heir ably suited to tour the state and oil the machine.[9] The end of the senatorial race delivered a spectacular victory to La Follette and the Progressives. In the Republican primary, La Follette won 362,445 votes compared to 139,327 to the other Republican candidate, William Ganfield. The lone Democratic candidate polled a mere 16,663 votes. It was the largest landslide in state history. La Follette carried districts that had consistently voted against him and won in every county but one. Moreover, the entire slate of Progressive candidates won nomination, and the future legislature appeared to be Progressive as well.[10]

Such a large victory in the primary guaranteed victory in the general election in November and freed La Follette to campaign for other Progressive candidates in other states. In Minnesota, the race was more personal than the usual conflict between conservatives and progressives. The conservative Republican Frank B. Kellogg, who had led the fight in the Senate to expel La Follette for disloyalty, faced an unlikely challenger in the Farmer-Labor candidate, a small-town dentist named Henrik Shipstead. La Follette's diatribes against Kellogg's political stance soon escalated to the level of national exposure, as his campaign on

Shipstead's behalf made national news. On November 1, La Follette and Phil went to Mankato to speak, but the Minnesota National Guard—citing his "war record"—denied them the use of the Armory. Phil and his father used a local theater instead, but the atmosphere remained tense. They arrived after dark at an almost deserted train station, and their hotel clerk told them that feelings were running high against La Follette—they could expect trouble.[11] Nonetheless, the evening went well. Phil spoke before his father, defending the six senators who voted against the declaration of war, and despite the early hostility of the crowd, he managed to win over his audience by the time his father arrived on the stage. According to a local reporter,

> [a]s usual it was announced at the outset that Senator La Follette had been detained, and that while waiting Philip La Follette, a son, would speak. Philip out-bobbed his father, got mixed up in his arguments and made two or three false starts, but succeeded in getting the crowd worked up into a frenzy by using some of Billy Sunday's methods.[12]

Old Bob went on to deliver a rousing address, castigating the grip corporations had on Minnesota through branch banks and chain stores.[13]

Just prior to the speech, La Follette had worried about how Phil would do: should he send a twenty-five-year-old to face a mob? When Phil delivered a powerful address that completely won over the crowd—the same speeches he had made that summer in Wisconsin—La Follette was delighted in his son. Later in their hotel room, La Follette embraced his son, tears streaming down his face. "You are *my* boy," he sobbed, unconsciously echoing Belle's oft-quoted remark.[14] The next evening, La Follette and Phil spoke in Minneapolis before a crowd of more than a thousand people. The father-son act continued with Phil warming up the crowd before his father delivered the main address, which contained an attack on Kellogg and the Minnesota newspapers as tools of the special interests. Although La Follette did not discuss the war, sixteen veterans escorted him into the auditorium, in tacit agreement with his record.[15]

On November 3, La Follette returned to St. Paul for the first time since his controversial speech in 1917. He spoke at the city auditorium, and crowds packed the streets for blocks trying to get into the already overcrowded building. The audience numbered more than twelve thousand with another ten thousand in the streets outside. Two blocks away, Kellogg addressed a crowd of twenty-five hundred.[16] As usual, Phil "thrilled" the audience for about ten minutes, while his father was "detained," to warm up the crowd. When La Follette finally got up to speak on his planned topics of the day, big business import tariffs, he could not help commenting on the irony of the situation and recalled his speech of 1917: "About five years ago I made a speech in this hall. . . . All that I then said has been demonstrated to be true, not one syllable of my utterance must or will I ever retract or modify in the slightest degree."[17] The audience roared its approval. La Follette continued his speech and then did something even more unprecedented. Encouraged by the approval of the crowd, La Follette struck personally at his own nemesis, Senator Kellogg: "God Almighty, through nature, writes men's characters on their faces and in their forms. Your senator had bowed obsequiously to wealth and to corporations' orders and to his masters until God Almighty has given him a hump on his back—crouching, cringing, un-American, unmanly." Belle detested such personal attacks, but La Follette, caught up in the mood of triumphant vindication, grinned at his son and said, "Your mother will give me hell for saying that about Kellogg."[18] Shipstead went on to win the race, and Kellogg, who had tried to remove La Follette from the Senate, was himself forced out of office—a clear vindication for La Follette and his supporters. Further, the November elections reduced the Republican majority in the Senate to eleven, so that the progressive Democrats and Republicans again held the balance of power. Old Bob had once again risen from political death to become a popular government leader.

The years after La Follette once again took his seat in the Senate up through his quixotic final campaign for the presidency continued the central themes on which Phil would base his political career. La Follette, as leader of the Progressive insurgents, held the balance of power in the Senate. He also increasingly fit his reputation as a radical: his antimonopoly rhetoric of 1924, although placing him squarely in the tradition of Lincoln and Jefferson, did little to debunk this popular image. Once again, La Follette's family was in the field supporting him, and Phil emerged as a key figure in the campaign. In March 1924, when La Follette came down with pneumonia, Belle and Robert worried about his health and urged him not to carry on with plans for a presidential campaign. La Follette waited until they had left the room and then quietly told Phil he would recover in a week and was determined to go ahead with his campaign. After having campaigned with him in 1922,

Phil understood his father's love of politics better than anyone. Phil also became critically important as the family's Madison agent, spending days with Progressive leaders like Governor John Blaine and Attorney General Herman Ekern, acting as an intermediary between the family and local leaders and offering his own advice.[19] Progressives in other states also used Phil as the contact for organizing a third party movement in their own states. Although Phil and Robert shouldered most of the work while La Follette was ill in March, Robert, also in poor health, spent most of his time trying to avoid involving the Progressive ticket with Communists, leaving Phil to do most of the organization and recruiting work.[20] That month, Phil and Governor Blaine filled in for La Follette when he was too ill to speak to a large campaign meeting in Chicago, where Isabel noted Phil's combination of folksiness with "youthful appeal." Phil wrote that "I was quite calm and cool inside with beaucoup [*sic*] steam built up, and I let them have some of it." He recognized, however, that the applause he received really belonged to his father.[21]

As the campaign heated up in June, both Phil and Robert continued to be key organizers for the Progressive ticket. On June 14, fifteen hundred delegates to the Railway Brotherhoods' meeting in Cleveland cheered them as they promised to keep up the fight. Phil also began to build his reputation as the more radical of the two brothers when he was quoted in the *Freeport* (Illinois) *Journal-Standard* in reference to the recent Republican convention, where the Wisconsin delegation's minority faction had been booed down. "They call us radicals. If being a radical is to be for human rights rather than for the dollar, if it is being opposed to a monetary system that takes milk from babies and feeds it to hogs, then I am a radical."[22]

As his father's campaign went forward, Phil continued to travel to speak to various organizations. Unlike his ventures two years earlier, he was often the featured speaker and not merely a warm-up act for his father. In April, he gave a speech in Illinois on behalf of progressive Republican Newton Jenkins for the United States Senate in which he denounced the Esch-Cummins law, which regulated railroad workers and which La Follette viewed as a measure greatly inferior to direct government management of railroads, and incumbent Senator Medill McCormick. "The young son of a noble sire," wrote one journalist, "seemed imbued with the same sort of enthusiasm for the progressive cause that has enabled his father to carry on. . . . He never hesitated nor minced words when attacking persons and practices which he claimed were undermining the government."[23] At the same time, Phil continued to work in Madison, lining up third district Progressive candidates for the Republican national convention and traveling around the Midwest and Pacific Northwest to set up La Follette-for-President committees in each state. His work was complicated by the fact that in each state petitions needed to be filed in order to get La Follette's name on the ballot, and each state had different regulations for doing so.[24]

As the actual campaigning got under way in September 1924, Phil took to the stump for La Follette, and newspapers across the nation couldn't resist comparing father and son. After a vigorous speech attacking the corruption of the Coolidge administration, Louis Seltzer of the *Cleveland Plain Dealer* commented on their similar appearance, noting that "Philip got his share of his father's ability as a talker." Seltzer described Phil's campaign speeches as self-effacing and credited his parents for his ability. He compared La Follette to Lincoln and Jefferson, a recurring theme in the campaign, but put his own twist on the comparison by noting that Lincoln in 1848 had opposed the Mexican War just as La Follette had opposed war with Germany in 1917.[25] Other writers commented on Phil's youth: in a debate in Chicago, he looked like "a college boy set to explain Einstein" but quickly roused the audience with "the same fiery enthusiasm that won his father the sobriquet of 'Fighting Bob.'"[26] In St. Louis, Phil again defended his father's role in the war and referred to the St. Paul speech that had almost led to his father's expulsion from the Senate. He impressed his family as well. His sister Fola thought he held his audience "in the hollow of his hand," and La Follette himself sometimes delayed his entrance on stage because Phil was doing so well.[27] La Follette was grateful for his son's assistance and apologized for taking him away from his law practice. "Phil dear boy," he had written his son in May, "I know how much you are sacrificing in all you are doing—for your dad—it is a great load you are carrying and I marvel that you are doing your work like a veteran campaigner. Whatever befalls we are going to make some history within the next year."[28]

In city after city, crowds thronged around the La Follette party and packed auditoriums. In October, as Old Bob began his great train tour around the country, Phil was his constant companion, often delivering the preliminary address before La Follette arrived on stage. These evening speaking events were in themselves a remarkable confirmation of La Follette's renewed popularity. His opening speech at Rochester attracted five thousand people; eleven thousand saw him in Chicago; and eighty-five hundred listened in St. Louis. In all three cities, parades escorted him from the railroad station. Most remarkable, however, was that most of his audience *paid* to hear him, either by way of an admission fee of between fifty cents and two dollars or by dropping money into a hat passed around during the evening. Such contributions provided the critically needed funds to allow the under-funded campaign to continue—it was a struggle that continued all through the campaign.[29]

With all of the burdens of his own work and his dedication to the cause, Phil occasionally groused at being an assistant rather than a leader. "It is always a source of irritation to me," he wrote Isabel late in 1921, "to be introduced as my father's son. I shall feel I have begun to make progress when I am introduced as <u>myself</u>. Not that I'm not deeply proud of Dad's name & reputation—I am: But I want to be true to my heritage from Father & Mother <u>by being worth what I may be worth</u>. On my own account. But that can come only with time."[30] Nonetheless, the war and campaigns of the early 1920s left a deep impression on Phil. He had seen his father burned in effigy and almost expelled from the Senate for disloyalty; a few years later, he saw the people of Wisconsin return him to the Senate by a huge margin and thousands of people actually paying to hear him deliver campaign speeches. Phil shared in this sense of vindication as he, too, felt the thrill of a captive audience.

In October 1924, Phil got to sample firsthand the hostility leveled at his father by conservatives when the president of the Iowa Agricultural College at Ames denied him permission to use the campus for his speech. As his father had done many times before, Phil ignored the injunction and spoke anyway. In the speech, he told his crowd that Ames's president would always be welcomed to speak at the University of Wisconsin. He also stated that he believed that most Iowans would vote for La Follette but refused to say so openly out of the fear that "their economic heads [would] be cut off by some of the local barons and dukes."[31] This was classic La Follette.

The 1922 and 1924 campaigns also gave Phil a level of notoriety in the national arena afforded to few people his age. Phil had gained more than just oratorical style and detailed knowledge of political activity—he had learned that leadership required one to make difficult and unpopular choices and that those would eventually be vindicated. His very political childhood and his fascination with leadership suggested a future, and his new abilities guaranteed it.

———•———

The elections of 1924 brought mixed results for Wisconsin Progressives in general and for the La Follette family in particular. Progressive

Republicans easily retained their hold on the state government, but in what would be his final campaign, La Follette lost his bid for the presidency. Phil's election as a Dane County district attorney—his first campaign as an actual candidate—did little to offset his father's defeat. As the family listened to election returns over the radio in the Executive Chamber in the state capitol with Governor John Blaine and his wife, Anna, the mood quickly turned gloomy. The La Follette ticket—although never expected to win—did not come close to fulfilling Progressives' expectations. La Follette and running mate Burton K. Wheeler of Montana carried only Wisconsin and none of the western states that Progressives had hoped to win.

The bitter national failure overshadowed local races, and Phil all but forgot that he was now the new district attorney of Dane County. It was indeed a forgettable victory. Phil ran unopposed for the Republican nomination and gave only a scattering of very conventional speeches on his own behalf. In Stoughton, in the southeastern part of the county, he promised to enforce the laws with total impartiality regardless of his personal opinion—a thinly veiled reference to the prohibition controversy that threatened to divide Progressives into wet and dry factions. Dane County was a Republican stronghold, and nomination in the primary guaranteed election in November, when Phil overwhelmingly defeated Democratic candidate Alvin M. Loverud. Phil was therefore able to spend almost all of September and October on the campaign trail with his father and returned only to check up on his own campaign in early November. Phil no doubt kept tabs on his race, but he focused his energy on the presidential bid. The *New York Times* mentioned his election as a curious side note to the national campaign, but locally he had a hard time making himself known in such a minor office. To many, he was just another "La Follette boy." After the election, the *Capital Times* printed his photograph under the caption "Young La Follette Winner, But Dad Loses on Tuesday." Unfortunately, even the most sympathetic newspaper in the state got his name wrong and identified him as Robert Junior.[32]

Phil's victory was overshadowed not only by his father's 1924 presidential bid, but also by his father's own campaign for Dane County district attorney in 1880. By the time of Phil's own election, the 1880 race had become legendary, largely through the efforts of La Follette himself. According to his 1911 autobiography, the twenty-five-year-old La Follette had decided to run for district attorney for the legal experience and for the business it would bring his new law practice. He also desired the position because it came with the munificent salary of eight hundred dollars. La Follette had been a mediocre law student at best (in an early court appearance he had to ask a colleague what "arraigned" meant), and it was common for young lawyers to start their careers in the role of prosecutor. The district attorney position seemed a logical next step.

According to his account, La Follette received a shock when the Madison postmaster and Republican political boss Elisha W. Keyes bluntly informed him that party leaders had already decided who the next candidate would be and that La Follette was "fooling away" his time in pursuing the office. Spurred on by this challenge, and counting on his popularity as an orator and the support of his university friends, La Follette canvassed the county and talked to farmers, promising to run the district attorney's office more efficiently and do all the work himself rather than hiring expensive assistants. The promise of efficiency and frugality resonated with the farmers still recovering from the depression of the 1870s and suffering through the transition from a farm economy based on wheat to one based on dairying. As he would do in all of his subsequent election campaigns, La Follette kept notes on almost everyone he met, especially those who expressed an interest in his campaign. Such organizing laid the groundwork for a formidable network of supporters and fed La Follette's reputation as a man of the people who seemed to know everyone. Despite Keyes's assertion that the decision had been made, La Follette was one of five candidates at the Republican caucus for the office, and there was no clear front-runner. After several tense rounds of balloting, delegates from his hometown of Primrose, Wisconsin, swung the vote in his favor after a moving speech by a Norwegian farmer named Eli Pederson, who referred to La Follette as "our boy." Buoyed politically and emotionally by this show of popular support, La Follette went on to win the general election by a scant ninety-three votes, and Keyes, in the words of John Dos Passos, "about fell out of his chair."[33]

Phil's campaign lacked such insurgent drama, but there were a number of similarities between these two victories separated by forty-four years. Both candidates were young and just out of law school. La Follette was twenty-five, and Phil was twenty-seven. The chief objection both faced was the charge of being "over-young."[34] The experience and professional exposure the post brought was attractive to two lawyers struggling to build a practice in Madison; being district attorney brought experience and reputation. Furthermore, in both 1880 and 1924, the incumbent district attorney was unpopular and chose not to run for reelection, which gave the challengers an excellent opportunity. In 1880

James Reynolds was notorious as an alcoholic who regularly visited prostitutes and failed to prosecute the tramps and vagrants (there were many after the economic depression that began in 1873) who so alarmed citizens of Dane County. In 1924, the incumbent district attorney, Theodore G. Lewis, had done little to investigate a series of murders in Madison's Greenbush neighborhood, reputed to be the county's center for the manufacture and distribution of illegal liquor. In retaliation for his lax record, the city council cut the district attorney's salary to eighteen hundred dollars a year—to which Lewis replied by choosing not to run in the next election.

Further, both La Follette and Phil strayed from their local races and took time to speak out on national contests. Just as Phil went on the stump for his father in 1924, La Follette joined other local Republicans in campaigning for presidential candidate James Garfield in 1880. At a rally in Paoli, Wisconsin, in October 1880, La Follette—in a wholly conventional speech devoid of insurgent rhetoric—urged his listeners to vote the straight Republican ticket and denounced the Democrats as the party of secession and states' rights. In sum, both La Follettes presented themselves as energetic young men who promised to work hard and vigorously enforce the law, and both showed promising futures. Thus in 1925, Phil began his political career on much the same path as his father had years earlier despite the popular image of La Follette's insurgent victory.[35]

As Dane County district attorney from 1925 to 1927, Phil quickly impressed the voters. Almost as soon as he was sworn in, Phil began to carry through with his promise to enforce law and order. He had outgoing district attorney Theodore Lewis stay on as special prosecutor in the trial of two men accused of the murder of a police officer, since Phil himself had little firsthand knowledge of the case. He instead chose to second-chair the case. He also became much more involved in the actual investigation of crimes, following the advice of his father. To do this, he arranged with the Madison chief of police and the Dane County sheriff to contact him as soon as their departments were called; he often arrived at the scene shortly after the police.

Phil's opportunity to prove his worth came almost immediately. Less than a week after he took office, Madison was shocked to hear that a young university French instructor had been shot by her deranged fiancé in a university boardinghouse. Phil was at the scene in less than an hour, but there was little investigation to be done—the assailant had shot himself fatally after attempting to murder his fiancée. After a few days, when the victim had recovered enough to tell the story, Phil dropped the whole case, convinced that the assailant's suicide meant that justice could not be served further. Rumors abounded about an anguished love affair and a broken engagement, and reporters sniffing scandal pressed for more information. Annoyed at the intrusion into the couple's private life and not wanting the district attorney's office to fuel a sensation, Phil refused to make public a number of private letters that contained the details of their affair. "We do not do [such things] in Wisconsin," Phil curtly told the police reporter. In these first few weeks in office, Phil had demonstrated not only how seriously he took his position, but also how seriously he took Wisconsin's reputation for progressive and incorruptible government.[36]

The abrupt end to this sensational case did not sit well with Madisonians. Murder cases were normally rare events, but in the previous two years, the tranquil university town had found itself in the midst of a crime wave. The center of this disorder was the neighborhood known as Greenbush, or more often simply "the Bush." This six-block area just south of the university was also called "Little Italy," and for good reason: almost all of Madison's Italian families lived there.[37] Since 1920, Greenbush had become notorious as the center of Dane County bootlegging. In 1922, police conducted regular raids and made many arrests, but in 1923 and 1924, the number of raids declined, and the results of police activity were disappointing. The police seemed not only incapable of curbing the bootlegging and violence, but unwilling to even try. In 1923, for example, police arrested nearly five hundred men for public drunkenness but arrested only ten for actually *selling* alcohol. Moreover, police seemed reluctant to patrol the area in part due to its violent reputation. Between 1913 and 1923 a total of six people were killed in Greenbush; in 1924 alone, there were a record twelve murders. Partly in response to this threat to law and order, the Ku Klux Klan enjoyed a brief moment of popularity in Madison. The Klan involved itself in liquor raids, and Mayor Milo Kittleson deputized a number of Klansmen after district attorney Theodore Lewis refused their help. William Evjue, editor of the *Capital Times*, denounced this false choice between the Klan and "the gun-toting Sicilian" and called for more aggressive enforcement of the law by the police and sheriff's office.[38]

When Phil became district attorney, there was a growing outrage over the high-crime area and a mounting distrust of legitimate law enforcement. Evjue, largely responsible for fueling the hysteria, proclaimed in another *Capital Times* editorial his "great hopes for the regeneration of this section in the fact that Phil La Follette and Glenn Roberts [Phil's assistant] are now working aggressively in the district attorney's office." Phil took the challenge seriously and immediately set out to clean up the Bush, using the same methodical and detailed planning that Progressives used to win elections. First, he met with the sheriff and the chief of police to coordinate patrol efforts and create a closer cooperation between the city and county forces. Then, on February 7, Phil and Roberts orchestrated the largest liquor raid Madison had ever seen, keeping it completely secret until the undercover raiders had already filtered into the neighborhood. At precisely 5:15 p.m., the police entered homes and shops, arrested sixteen people, and confiscated seventy-five gallons of moonshine. In order to demonstrate the new determination in the district attorney's office, Phil set the raids for late Saturday afternoon in order to prevent anyone from posting bail on Sunday, when no judges were available, ensuring that the accused had to spend at least one day in jail. Not until Monday morning could the accused go before a judge to post bond. Furthermore, during the hearings Phil demanded and received bonds set higher than the maximum fine in order to prevent anyone from merely forfeiting bail and skipping a court appearance. Despite their long weekend in jail, twelve of the sixteen arrested pled not guilty.[39]

This was the first step in a series of actions dedicated to completely ending the liquor traffic in Madison, and the raids continued for the next several weeks. On March 5, police captured three stills, and on March 23, they captured two more. As late as April, Phil was still using evidence gained from his initial raids to get warrants and conduct further searches. Raids continued sporadically over the summer months, and as late as August, police and sheriff's deputies patrolled the Bush armed with arrest warrants issued in February. Phil confidently told the press that those still missing had fled Madison in the face of certain prosecution. By the end of 1925, the district attorney's office had handled twelve hundred cases of making, purchasing, or selling liquor.[40]

Phil's efforts impressed his family but worried them at the same time. Robert wrote to him just before the raids began and voiced his concern: "Phil, [you] are tackling a tough bunch when you go after the murder-moonshine gang in Little Italy. They do not fight fair and their favorite method of communication is through the medium of sawed-off shotguns. You be damned careful how you prowl around alone." His father's former law partner, Gilbert Roe, conferred about the situation with the New York City police commissioner, who remarked, "That kid has guts." Phil was also working harder than ever. As a student, he had kept a rigorous schedule of reading and study that left little time for recreation. This same tendency to overwork manifested itself in his professional career as well. Phil always arrived early in the morning and frequently stayed up late going over evidence, or, if it were near an election, campaigning. This enthusiasm worried his family. "Phil looks tired," Robert wrote Belle in March. "I labored with him as best I could to take things easier, but you know how positive he is about everything concerning himself." Being "positive about himself" for Belle meant an almost reckless energy with which he threw himself into his work, never worrying that he might be risking his health. This was a familiar sight—she remembered the same energy and drive, almost to the point of exhaustion, that La Follette had demonstrated as an attorney and as a public official. Despite the concern, she and La Follette were proud of Phil's efforts. "I hope you feel the interest and prid[e] Daddy takes in your work," Belle wrote Phil in late April 1925.[41]

Phil denied wanting to use the office of district attorney as a political stepping-stone, but his term in office generated a widespread favorable public response. In the spring elections of 1925, every candidate for city council endorsed Phil's efforts, as did the former sheriff. The local branch of the Women's Christian Temperance Union passed a resolution praising Phil for his efforts to rid Madison of the "moonshine evil," as did Our Savior's Lutheran Church and First Congregational Church. Evjue of the *Capital Times* was particularly effusive in his acknowledgment, telling his readers that Phil had added "new laurels to the family name." He noted that Phil had no desire to become a dry crusader and sought only to stamp out lawlessness as public sentiment demanded. Throughout the spring, Phil accepted invitations to talk to local organizations about his views on crime and about the Greenbush situation. He was such a local celebrity that he even participated in the dedication of the new WIBA radio station. Despite the bully pulpit his office provided, Phil tried to avoid overstepping the bounds of district attorney and only spoke of his experiences. He did his best to avoid talking politics. Nonetheless, through these appearances, Phil—much as La Follette had done in the 1911 autobiography he wrote in preparation for his 1912 presidential campaign—developed a very carefully crafted image as a capable and honest public official who worked to enact the will of the people.[42]

This public image was inherently contradictory. Phil, well known for his thundering denunciations of authority and his insurgent rhetoric, was now the chief law-enforcement official of the county. As a firm believer in both the power of government and the sovereignty of the people, Phil was able to wrap up most of his work as detective and prosecutor in populist language and maintain his identity as a Progressive. He did this in two ways. First, he depicted Prohibition, a divisive issue among Progressives, as merely another law that had to be enforced equally and without favoritism. Law officials could not simply disregard the will of the people. Phil vowed, as he had told his audience in Stoughton, to see that "the laws are enforced speedily, justly, and with absolute impartiality." Phil thus stressed the democratic nature of his role to enforce the will of the people.

Second, Phil depicted the Bush as not just the center of bootlegging, but the center of a malicious and organized body out to harm regular citizens. Meeting in March 1925 with the city council, Phil emphasized the seriousness of the situation: "[A] vicious, criminal ring is in control of the moonshine industry in Little Sicily and . . . they are selling filthy, poisonous moonshine at profiteers' prices." Phil thus managed to include a number of progressive themes common twenty-five years earlier: sinister, organized business interests; profiteering; even—he held up a full moonshine bottle containing dirt, straw, and dead flies—impure and hazardous products. This was not at all unfamiliar since many Progressives of the early twentieth century campaigned against impure foods and drugs. Phil even made a call for democracy when he told the council that a majority of citizens wanted the Bush cleaned up and that fighting this popular will was a vicious gang of criminals. The leader of this organized gang, Tony Musso of Rockford, Illinois, had even gone so far as to offer Phil a thirty thousand dollar bribe if he would keep police away from Musso's businesses. Musso's offer was no match for Phil's stance against government corruption. Phil saw his role as district attorney—as he would later see his role as governor—as the administrator of the public will, working for public, not private interests.[43]

Phil went even further in his role as progressive district attorney in his willingness to challenge other authority figures over questions of crime in Dane County. When Judge August C. Hoppmann sentenced seventeen defendants arrested in the Greenbush raids, he reduced some sentences significantly from those that Phil had requested. Phil had recommended for those convicted a total of 132 months in jail and $10,600 in fines. Hoppmann's sentences amounted to only 46 months in jail and a mere $4,600. Phil, infuriated with the sentences, remarked to reporters that they "will not deter those who have made thousands of dollars in the bootlegging industry." Phil argued that the only way to end bootlegging was to make it unprofitable with definite prosecution and heavy fines; Hoppmann's fines amounted to little more than "license fees."[44] When Evjue chastised Hoppmann for hindering the efforts of the district attorney's office, Hoppmann claimed to be acting from a sense of judicial restraint to temper the demands of angry citizens. Hoppmann later won election in April by depicting himself as the role of a dispassionate and objective justice who refused to bow to popular pressure and ethnic prejudice by levying harsh sentences against Italians.[45] Phil also criticized Governor (and La Follette protégé) John Blaine for pardoning Harry Barry, sentenced to eight months for selling liquor. Despite Blaine's harsh words for "prohibition fanatics," Phil signed a letter challenging Blaine's pardon and provided a long list of reasons for the original sentence. In another case, Superior Court Judge Ole Stolen was disbarred after Phil uncovered evidence of bribery. In September 1926, Stolen admitted to Phil in a John Doe hearing that he had several loans due to people who lived in Greenbush, some of whom had been before him charged with bootlegging. A few months later, after the state supreme court began proceedings to remove Stolen, the *Capital Times* serialized Phil's cross-examination of Stolen. Stolen eventually resigned.[46]

Phil's activities as district attorney did not revolve solely around Greenbush. The district attorney's office also issued warnings to owners of rural dance halls that they would be prosecuted not only for selling alcohol but also for allowing people to drink on their premises. Phil also ordered the prosecution of anyone found in possession of alcohol, even if sober, and prepared to carry a test case all the way to the United States Supreme Court, though such a case never developed during his two years as district attorney. Phil likewise stepped up the enforcement of a ban on slot machines and other gambling devices and again used progressive language to justify his prosecutions, pointing to the large sums of money lost to unscrupulous business owners. With booming automobile sales, traffic violations also took up a great deal of time at the district attorney's office. The *Capital Times*, ever dedicated to badgering public officials, kept a running count of "vampire" drivers involved in hit-and-run accidents. After one well-publicized incident, Phil arranged to have several additional motorcycle police appointed to combat speeders.[47]

The *cause celebre* of Phil's tenure as district attorney, however, came in January 1926, when Rudolf Jessner shot and killed a police officer in Greenbush. Promptly charged with first degree murder, Jessner initially pleaded insanity. Later he claimed that he had been harassed by the police patrol for months because he was a Jew. He claimed he had acted out of self-defense when the police threatened to break into his restaurant. The defense highlighted this angle to gain sympathy with the jury and the public, especially after it was revealed that the police officers involved in the incident had been members of the Ku Klux Klan in previous years. In order to quash any charges of ethnic bias that would tarnish law enforcement agencies, Phil needed to prove Jessner's guilt beyond any reasonable doubt. The responsibility wore heavily on him, especially since Progressives in the past had often adopted a nativist, sometimes racist slant. Jessner's conviction was due in great part to Phil's five-hour cross-examination. He used a line of questioning that made it impossible for Jessner, a very intelligent man, to discern what he might be giving away until it was too late. In the end, Jessner unwittingly provided the testimony that convicted him. The case lasted until April, when the jury found Jessner guilty. Isabel came to court to hear Phil's closing speech, and she wrote to Belle that visitors to the courtroom were impressed by his speech and by his obvious sincerity and mastery of the facts. Another lawyer remarked that Phil had "trimmed"—that is, completely outperformed—the defense counsel. Immediately following the verdict, Phil and his partner, Glenn Roberts, caught a train to Chicago for a weekend's rest.[48]

The district attorney's office did provide Phil with ample legal experience, but it also brought him a great deal of public recognition, not only for his actions but also for his progressive views on crime. In describing his ideas on criminal behavior, Phil again demonstrated how he adapted his progressive heritage and insurgent rhetoric to new situations. In an address before the Madison Rotary Club in March 1925, he told his audience that law enforcement in Dane County was most impeded not by corruption among police nor by an unsympathetic public, but by the fact that there were simply too many laws on the books. With so many statutes, Phil argued, two people in the district attorney's office could not possibly keep up with all legal infractions and had to concentrate on only the most serious. Referring specifically to the Greenbush crime wave, he responded to charges that the Italians were inherently criminal by criticizing oppressive Americanization efforts and pointing out the number of innocent foreign-born residents who had already left, driven out by criminal activity. Greenbush, Phil said, was the center of an organized "murder ring," and the inhabitants were as much terrorized victims as was the general population of Madison. In stating this, Phil avoided easy excuses and stereotypes and stressed the difference between vigilant, impartial enforcement of laws and mindless ethnic harassment.[49]

In addition to criticizing the multiplicity and complexity of laws, Phil also argued that there were two kinds of criminals. Again he based his views on progressive ideology. "Cold-blooded" criminals, he said, acted out of a desire to profit at the expense of others. They calculated the potential gain against chances of conviction and played the law just as corrupt lumber barons and railroad magnates had tried to avoid regulation just a few decades before. The only sure remedy, Phil said, was swift and sure prosecution—the kind he emphasized as district attorney— to make this type of crime unprofitable. "Hot-blooded" criminals, in contrast, operated out of passion, in the heat of the moment and without any premeditation. For this reason, Phil argued, such crimes were almost completely unpreventable.[50] Like progressive reformers a generation earlier, Phil emphasized environment and proper social influence as the only means of preventing these crimes.

Phil's prosecution reflected the philosophy he laid out in his Rotary Club address. Although he prosecuted liquor distillers and sellers and demanded harsh sentences, he also acted more leniently to those whom he saw as victims of circumstance. When two young men were convicted of embezzling cash from Madison's Orpheum Theater, Phil recommended only four months in jail and restitution. He based this light sentence on their youth, the fact that it was their first offense, and their frank confession, but also because of their poor salaries. An employer, Phil told the judge, "who takes a youth of this age, without experience, [and] pays him to handle so enormous a sum of money without supervision, is partially responsible in putting such a temptation before an untrained, unsupervised, inadequately paid young man." In contrast, Phil recommended a longer sentence for a university student convicted of burglary, arguing that he had had more opportunities in life and knew he would be punished if caught.[51]

Phil brought his views to a larger audience when he delivered an address before the Wisconsin State Bar Association meeting at Kenosha in 1926. He told the assembled lawyers that the large number of laws made criminals out of petty offenders; his favorite example was the fact that a boy who takes a frog from his neighbor's pond is technically a burglar. Far more dangerous and more sinister, he told his audience, was the organized crime that menaced the county, out to enrich itself at the expense of the public—language similar to that used repeatedly by his father railing against the "vested interests." Phil's solution to these problems was for the district attorney to use discretionary powers to prosecute primarily those criminals genuinely out to harm the public and not those who merely violate "social regulations," like blue laws or traffic laws. The mark of a good district attorney, according to Phil, was not the number of convictions, but a low crime rate and few prosecutions. By operating with just this sort of discretion and judgment, Phil was stepping beyond the usual role of prosecutor and taking up some of the responsibility inherent in the city council and state legislature. He saw his role as chief law enforcer as one that combined legal interpretation with a built-in pardoning mechanism that allowed leniency for those defendants who were not perpetrators, but victims, of the system.[52]

Phil's reputation as a persuasive legal speaker and trial lawyer landed him several high profile cases during his tenure as district attorney. He traveled to Washington to argue for the Capital Times Company's right to operate radio station WIBA before the Federal Radio Commission. He also led a prominent investigation of alleged tax evasion by the "UW Co-op," a private business that used its name to suggest both an association with the university and a nonprofit status, neither of which it had. Most prominently, Phil was appointed as special investigator by the Wisconsin Supreme Court to examine alleged cheating in the state bar exam, held every spring in the Assembly Chamber. The case made headlines for nearly a month as Phil called dozens of witnesses to demonstrate how widespread plagiarized exams had become.[53]

Despite a quite positive public response to his two years as district attorney, Phil's future remained uncertain as he left office in 1926. He followed state supreme court justice Burr W. Jones's recommendation that two years was all he needed to learn how to be effective as a courtroom attorney. He certainly could have built up a highly successful law practice, even without the La Follette name; his frequent lectures and addresses to civic groups provided a splendid source of free advertising. His time as district attorney brought a great deal of exposure and almost universal accolades and led to his appointment on a number of major cases. Despite his success at law, however, Phil's future remained uncertain as he tried to develop a career that could both support his family and further the progressive cause. Of monumental importance in these deliberations was the death of Robert M. La Follette in June 1925.

———•———

La Follette had never been in good health, suffering frequent collapses since the 1890s and spending months at sanitariums trying to recover his strength. Indeed, his health and age were issues of grave concern during the 1924 campaign, and the family forced him to rest between campaign stops to ensure that he did not appear too fatigued on stage. His health deteriorated rapidly during the spring and early summer of 1925. Despite his optimism, the weakness brought on by heart disease kept him confined to bed. On June 18, 1925, just a few days after his seventieth birthday, Bob La Follette died of a heart attack in Washington, D.C. His family surrounded him as he died, and they escorted his casket back to Madison, where an elaborate funeral was held in the capitol rotunda.[54]

In the months following La Follette's death, one question remained at the forefront of the progressive agenda: who would take La Follette's place in the Senate and as leader of Wisconsin's Progressives? Phil was an obvious choice. Throughout his time as district attorney, Phil continued to act as his family's Madison agent in matters both political and trivial. Often he acted as a go-between for his father and Governor Blaine, whom Phil had started to see as too ambitious, interested only in promoting his own political fortunes. Phil also arranged numerous conferences among Progressive leaders in Madison. His role increased when La Follette died, and he took on the added responsibility of overseeing Belle's interests in Madison. Belle wrote frequently, often directing that certain items be shipped to or from Maple Bluff Farm or requesting money. Phil directed the sale of a portion of the estate that ultimately resulted in Belle's financial independence. He was also named "Wisconsin Editor" for *La Follette's Magazine* and worked with publisher Fred Holmes in both editorial and financial matters. All of this was in addition to his law practice.[55]

But his continued role as Wisconsin agent for the La Follettes after Old Bob's death didn't mean Phil would inherit his father's mantle. Taking up after his father meant going against the elder La Follette's deepest wishes. La Follette had long envisioned a political career for his oldest son, expecting Robert to run for governor in his own lifetime and increasingly delegating to him important tasks such as managing his reelection campaign in 1922 and shepherding a tax bill through the state legislature. The rest of the family, however, did not share in that speculation. Robert himself had no love for campaigning or for the grassroots organizing that his father thrived on; he was more comfortable as his father's secretary and office manager. Moreover, Robert had suffered a variety of debilitating ailments for years that left his health fragile; at times he was bedridden for months. For these reasons, especially after Phil's performance on the 1924 presidential campaign tour, the younger son seemed to be the heir apparent. Even Robert recognized this: "Phil has such a wonderful future before him," he wrote Fola in 1918. "He will amount to so much and I will never amount to anything." All family members had been active in La Follette's 1924 campaign, but since Phil was the most public figure, the Progressive faithful in Wisconsin also thought of him as the logical successor. "There has been a good deal of speculation in recent years," wrote one follower in 1922, "as to who in the La Follette faction, if anyone, was of sufficient size to take the place of Sen. La Follette when the time comes for any reason that he must relinquish the leadership of the Progressive Republicans in this state. It has occurred to me that it may quite possibly develop that the junior member of your firm [Phil La Follette] may be the man we shall have to look to."[56]

But this "logical" choice for succession wasn't recognized by the elder La Follette, who had never officially relinquished leadership to either of his sons. As a consequence, the question of succession, particularly of his seat in the Senate, hung in the air for months. The almost universal choice to finish his term in the Senate seat was his widow, Belle. She was recommended by more than just sentiment. La Follette's "wisest and best counselor," Belle had frequently gone on the campaign trail and the lecture circuit as well as helping her husband in his work as governor and senator. What's more, she was a graduate of the University of Wisconsin Law School. Telegrams flooded Governor Blaine's office urging him to appoint her to fill out La Follette's term or to support her candidacy in a special election. Not all the messages were from Wisconsin: people from as far away as Idaho and New York urged Belle to become a candidate. Although Belle was certainly qualified, politicians in Wisconsin had more nefarious reasons for desiring her election. They assumed that she would fill out the term and then retire from politics, leaving the seat open in 1928. "All politicians," Phil later wrote, "were for her. With Belle Case La Follette elected for that short term, the field would be wide open for one and all in 1928."[57] Belle, however, declined the honor, citing her lack of desire to enter the political arena. Rather, she said, she wanted to dedicate herself to writing her husband's biography. "I know from long experience," she wrote to her supporters, "the exacting demands, the ceaseless strain of public service. At no time in my life would I ever have chosen a public career for myself. It would be against nature for me to undertake the responsibilities of political leadership."[58]

Belle having declined so graciously, her sons became the most obvious candidates, formidable for their experience and for their parentage.

Phil had immediate support from several fronts. Just after La Follette died, Oswald Garrison Villard, editor of *The Nation* and a longtime La Follette supporter, telegraphed Governor Blaine urging Phil's appointment to the Senate: "If compatible with your own plans I earnestly suggest your giving temporary appointment as senator to Philip La Follette. His ability warrants it and the appointment would gratify the millions who voted for his father and would hearten progressives throughout the country. I earnestly hope that before long the two senators will be yourself and Philip La Follette." Another correspondent argued that Phil was the choice of most Wisconsin Progressives and worried "that if Robt. Jr. runs he will forever put out of consideration the other boy who seems to be the more aggressive." Many politicians favored Phil for the Senate seat, but the La Follette family made Robert the designated heir in his own right, and not just to hold the seat until 1928, when Phil would be old enough to run. After her husband's death, Belle, who had always viewed Phil as "her boy," became much more protective of Robert. She insisted that he would take over his father's career and urged Phil to find another career so that he would not compete with his brother. There was, however, one insurmountable obstacle: Phil's age. In 1925 he was only twenty-eight, and for once his youthfulness worked against him; the Constitution requires senators to be at least thirty years old. Within a month of La Follette's funeral, Robert announced his candidacy, and Progressives rallied around his campaign for the special election in 1925.[59]

This was not, however, the end of Phil's political aspirations. Despite the fact that he could not run for senator in the special election, rumors continued to emerge about Phil's elevation to higher office in 1926, when he would be eligible to run (he would be thirty by the time he was sworn in). Only a few months after he began working as district attorney, word circulated that he was using the office as a stepping-stone and planned to run for state attorney general or even governor in 1926. Phil laughed at these rumors and pointedly denied using his office merely to advance a political career. Nor was his rumored future confined to Wisconsin. "I have noticed the discussion of your fair name," college friend (and brother-in-law) Ralph Sucher wrote him a few months before the 1926 fall election, "in connection with the senatorship." Irvine Lenroot was up for reelection that fall, and a number of Progressives thought Phil should run. The rumors also became a matter of national interest. After Fighting Bob's death, Wisconsin politics remained a nationally important topic, and the *New York Times* commented on the unusual possibility of the two

La Follette brothers representing the same state in the Senate. A number of local newspapers boomed him for the Senate, beginning with the *Fennimore Times*. Several readers wrote in to the *Capital Times*, urging Phil to run and pointing to him as the best candidate to defeat Lenroot. Others worried that a loss in the primary would ruin his future career and jeopardize the progressive movement both in Wisconsin and nationwide.[60]

Phil was thinking seriously about his future at this time, but it wasn't on such a large scale as his supporters assumed. His concerns were more local, and they weren't confined to politics: what career should he follow after his term as district attorney ended? Although a legal career in Madison seemed promising, he and Isabel were not sure they wanted to remain in Wisconsin. In the fall of 1925, Phil wrote to Gilbert Roe in New York for advice on whether to stay in the state or leave. Madison offered no large financial returns, Phil complained, and although he had received valuable experience as district attorney he had made no money. Furthermore, Phil argued, he had established an identity separate from his father's and saw no real reason to stay. To Ralph Sucher Phil despaired that he was "not progressing as he should" and wondered where he fit in with the Progressive cause. Phil considered several options: a lucrative job with a California law firm, relocating to Chicago to build a law firm and become involved in Illinois politics, or entering academics as a legal scholar and professor.[61]

The last option seemed especially promising. Phil began lecturing at the University of Wisconsin Law School in 1926 at the invitation of Dean Harry Richards. The course met twice a week, and Phil managed to fit it into his already manic schedule. Phil had always had "a hankering to teach" and quickly established himself as a popular and effective teacher. A few years later, University of Wisconsin president Glenn Frank would offer Phil the deanship of the law school, causing Phil to write more agonized letters seeking advice. He viewed both the deanship and public office as teaching, or in his words "educating the public," although university teaching was much more secure. He wrote to Louis Brandeis—"Uncle Louis"—complaining that he would have to choose between politics, a law practice, or teaching. For Phil, it was a great philosophical question: how could he best serve the Progressive cause?[62]

Phil worried that a legal career—either as practicing lawyer or professor—would be too confining and could possibly remove him from the popular audience he believed was necessary to progressive reform. Campaigning and teaching both exhibited a touch of the dramatic. For a time, Phil worked on the Chautauqua lecture circuit, traveling from town to town with other speakers to provide education and entertainment to small-town Americans in the years before radio became common. He was also following in the footsteps of his parents: both La Follette and Belle had been part of the circuit in the 1890s and early 1900s. In January 1927, Phil signed a contract with the Redpath Lyceum Bureau to deliver thirty-one lectures in July and August. He had considered the lecture circuit for some time and even before La Follette's death had written his father for advice on what organization he should work for. Redpath billed Phil as a "headline attraction," but Phil found the audiences were tougher than he liked—few really wanted to hear the lecture, and Redpath barred politics or other controversial topics. It paid well, however: Phil earned $250 a week traveling around the Midwest, lecturing most often on crime. Writing home almost daily to Isabel, he remarked that despite the unenthusiastic audiences, the Chautauqua was like "a cross between a college and a circus."[63]

Progressive politics, law practice, and the lecture circuit were not the only influences on Phil's career; he also had a family to support. Though Phil's and Isabel's relationship was one of equals in many ways, the household roles each expected of the other were purely conventional. Phil was the breadwinner; Isen ran the house. "From the beginning," Phil later wrote, "Isabel and I had a financial understanding: she was to have the check for family finances on the first of the month. It was to be my job to see that that check came on time and also my prime responsibility to say how much that check was to be. It was her prime responsibility to spend within that amount."[64] In the spring of 1926, a son, Robert M. La Follette III, was born after a somewhat difficult pregnancy. Isabel suffered from nausea for most of it and was confined to bed for several weeks, so Phil usually prepared her breakfast before dashing to his office. He began to curtail his late nights working, staying at home and reading several books a week. Belle had suggested the baby's name (Mary's son was also named Robert), but Phil got permission from his brother before making his son Robert's namesake. (A second child, Judith, would be born in December 1928, and a third, Sherry, in 1936.) Phil and Isen found a house on the west side of Madison after Robert was born, no longer within walking distance to Phil's office, but one from which the children could walk to Randall Elementary School and West High School.

In the two years following La Follette's death, Phil was pulled in a multitude of competing directions. Family and law vied with politics, and politics continued to shape him as many called for Phil to succeed his father as leader of the Wisconsin Progressives. But Phil also had a hand in his own future during these years. He created a distinct political identity for himself and gained a national reputation on which to build his later career. This identity was of course based very closely on his father's political philosophy. While retaining a close affinity with La Follette's politics, Phil at the same time sought to shape his personal life quite differently than the family in which he had grown up. Both these decisions—political and personal—would shape his later career. In the years between 1927 and 1930, Phil would remain an important part of Wisconsin politics as he struggled to decide what his future would be and how he would make his mark on the Progressive movement.

WHi Image ID 30174

From 1900 to 1906, while his father was governor, young Philip La Follette spent his days playing near the governor's mansion on East Gilman Street in Madison, seen here about 1904.

WHi Image ID 30380

A formal portrait of Fighting Bob La Follette taken in Madison by E. R. Curtiss in 1906, La Follette's first year in the U.S. Senate.

WHi Image ID 30384

Belle Case attended the University of Wisconsin, where she was the star pupil, with Robert La Follette, who almost did not graduate. Although she disliked public life, she provided crucial support for La Follette, assisting in his legal work and providing political advice.

WHi Image ID 30382

As a child, Phil (seated, in front of Robert Jr.) formed an exceptionally affectionate bond with Belle. Like her husband, Belle had high expectations for their children, but she encouraged Phil's independence and creativity and provided political advice until her death in 1931.

Pets—both ponies and dogs—were a large part of Phil's childhood. In 1906, shortly after his father moved to Washington, Phil soberly reported to him that the family dog, Scotchy, had been shot by police after it contracted rabies and was found wandering Madison's sixth ward.

WHi Image ID 35042

WHi Image ID 29987

Despite the demands of a political career, the La Follette family found time for recreation and a few memorable vacations. Even then, the line between family and politics blurred, as Fighting Bob's associates often joined the family. From left: Fighting Bob (in dark hat), Bob Jr., Netha Roe, Mary, Belle, Gilbert Roe, unidentified boy, young man labeled in family album as "Joe," and Phil.

WHi Image ID 35044

In 1906, Robert La Follette purchased eight Shetland ponies, and his three younger children began raising and selling ponies. The care of the ponies, left primarily to Phil and Robert, became another way in which the La Follettes instilled a sense of responsibility in their children.

WHi Image ID 27038

La Follette's time as a United States senator meant the family divided its time between Washington and Madison. Belle and the children sometimes remained in Madison while the Senate was in session, but La Follette was happiest when his wife and children were with him.

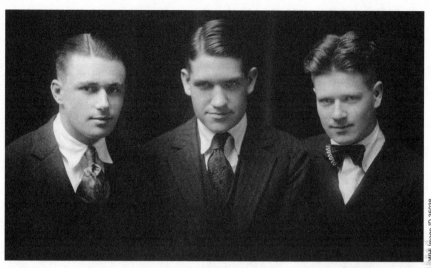

WHi Image ID 35038

After enrolling at the University of Wisconsin, Phil joined the Beta Theta Pi fraternity and became close friends with Joseph Farrington (left) and Ralph Sucher (center). Farrington remained a lifelong friend and often provided political advice. Sucher married Phil's sister Mary, but the marriage ended in divorce.

WHi Image ID 35040

Despite his father's controversial opposition to American participation in World War I, Phil himself (shown here at right) enlisted in the army in 1918. He was commissioned a second lieutenant and stationed in Norman, Oklahoma, at the headquarters of the Student Army Training Corps.

WHi Image ID 30151

Isabel Bacon met Phil while she was an undergraduate and he was a law student. She wrote her parents that he was "quite a flirt." Although Phil suffered an attack of cold feet, the two were married in 1923, forming a solid partnership that weathered political and personal crises.

WHi Image ID 11128

During the 1920s, Madison's Greenbush neighborhood (shown here in 1911) became notorious as the center of bootlegging and organized crime. Phil's hands-on approach as district attorney alarmed his family, who warned him against entering the area to investigate crime. The district attorney's office conducted regular raids in Greenbush and dramatically reduced liquor trafficking in the city.

WHi Image ID 30350

Phil accompanied his father for most of his 1924 independent presidential bid. Only a few years earlier, the family had been jeered and harassed because of La Follette's opposition to World War I. In 1924 La Follette was greeted by cheering crowds.

WHi Image ID 6907

At the insistence of Governor John Blaine, the family listened to the 1924 election returns on the radio in the Executive Chamber of the state capitol rather than at Maple Bluff Farm. Although La Follette lost his presidential bid, Phil won election as Dane County district attorney. From left: Isabel La Follette, Anna Blaine, Phil, Governor Blaine, Old Bob, and Young Bob.

WHi Image ID 28380

La Follette had been in ill health for some time, and his death in 1925 was not unexpected. After his death, his casket was brought back to Madison, where it lay in state in the capitol rotunda. Approximately 50,000 mourners came to pay their respects to the fallen leader.

WHi Image ID 35036

Phil married Isabel Bacon in 1923. Their first son, Robert M. La Follette III (seen here with Phil and grandmother Belle), was born in 1926. There was some hesitation over the name: Phil wanted to name his son after his father but worried that his yet unmarried older brother would object. Robert did not.

CHAPTER THREE

The Ghost at the Banquet

By the mid 1920s, it had become conventional wisdom that the Progressive faction controlled Wisconsin government and that Fighting Bob La Follette controlled the Progressive faction. Again and again, newspapers and magazines meant more than just where he was from when they referred to "La Follette's state." Yet these accounts tended to give La Follette more credit than he deserved. Despite charges of bossism, La Follette never had full control of the Republican Party. By the time of La Follette's death in 1925, Wisconsin Progressives were already badly divided over a number of issues; the tenuous thread that held them together was La Follette's success. Although he seldom exerted direct control, his electoral popularity among the voters was such that his endorsement and support were invaluable. Potential candidates sought his support and shaped their issues on that support. After 1925, without this sort of "ideological bossism" to hold it together in policy and strategy, the Progressives degenerated into a collection of squabbling, mutually distrustful cliques. A generation of politicians who had subordinated their own ambitions to La Follette's leadership suddenly found themselves fighting for the throne, each trying to convince Wisconsin voters that *he* was the legitimate heir of Fighting Bob. It was by no means clear that Robert and Philip would become the standard-bearers for the Progressives. The 1920s was a critical period in which the La Follette sons solidified their control over the faction and became significant political powers in their own rights. This process began with Robert winning election to the United States Senate in 1925 and winning reelection in 1928. While Robert focused on national issues and quickly made a name for himself as a thoughtful and dedicated politician, Phil worked in Wisconsin to keep the Progressive faction united. The struggle to keep Progressives cooperating required Robert and Philip to work closely with each other, and for the next decade fraternal harmony prevailed.

After Robert M. La Follette's death, Phil and Robert had to deal with a Progressive faction that had never been as cohesive and solid as observers believed. La Follette dominance dated to the 1890s, but it had been a continual struggle for him. He exerted a strong grip on the coalescing Progressive faction for two main reasons. First, La Follette was a popular orator who was willing to tour the state rallying voters around Progressive measures. Second, he was a skilled organizer who recruited supporters from the state to the township level. He was capable of articulating ideas (often developed by others) and generating support for them. This combination won elections—local or regional leaders who had no statewide prominence themselves recognized the value of allying themselves with him. As a factional chief, however, La Follette tolerated no dissent from what he saw as progressive dogma, and he equated challenges to his authority with corruption and betrayal. He also recognized that his popularity was a key factor holding Progressives together. At times he acted accordingly when it appeared that personal disagreements might threaten Progressive goals, which he often equated with his own personal success.

In 1905, for example, the election of a U.S. senator threatened to split the Progressives. La Follette had promised to deliver the vacant Senate seat to the wealthy Marinette lumber baron Isaac Stephenson, who had financially supported La Follette since Stephenson's senatorial ambitions had been frustrated in 1899 by the election of former Wisconsin senator Joseph Quarles. La Follette planned to rally his supporters around Stephenson when the legislature met to elect a senator. In early 1905, however, La Follette received word that another Progressive, William D. Connor, had begun lobbying for the election. Two Progressives fighting for the same seat threatened to divide Progressive votes and possibly to elect a Stalwart, but La Follette continued to back Stephenson. To his dismay, La Follette learned that many legislators refused to vote for Stephenson and swore they would elect Quarles again if it appeared that the legislature would deadlock. La Follette met with Connor, who claimed to have enough votes to control his own election and defeat any reform legislation as well if La Follette did not support him. Such a threat was more than La Follette could stand, and, unable to force the election of Stephenson, he announced his own candidacy. Such a move guaranteed the election of a Progressive and maintained Progressive harmony, but it alienated Connor and made Stephenson decidedly more wary. By claiming the Senate seat for himself, La Follette demonstrated that he would allow no insubordination and asserted for himself the leading voice of the Progressive faction.[1]

Such sway over Progressives and over voters had its limitations, however. The 1906 campaign for governor again fractured Progressive ranks, and La Follette was unsuccessful in getting his candidate elected. In 1902, La Follette's lieutenant governor, James O. Davidson, had been added to the La Follette ticket to garner support among Norwegians, a large ethnic group that had been taken for granted in previous elections as unwavering Republican voters. La Follette and his closest associates regarded the genial and popular Norwegian as a political lightweight, competent for the nearly meaningless office of lieutenant governor but by no means a strong party leader. La Follette expected Davidson merely to fill out the remaining year of his term, but Davidson had other ideas and announced his own candidacy for reelection. La Follette met with his law partner, Alf Rogers, as well as Herman Ekern and James A. Stone; together they decided not to support Davidson, claiming that he was too uneducated and too friendly with conservatives to lead the progressive cause. He was also unlikely to follow La Follette's advice and would not be aggressive in pursuing a progressive agenda. La Follette instead backed Assembly Speaker Irvine Lenroot of Superior, Wisconsin, a loyal supporter. Lenroot had been largely responsible for getting much of the progressive legislation through the assembly and had proven himself to be a skillful party leader. La Follette could trust him to keep up progressive momentum in the state and also defer to his leadership. Lenroot was also a Swede, which La Follette hoped would maintain votes among Scandinavians. Despite careful planning, the ploy did not work. La Follette could rely on Norwegians to vote for a Progressive in the Republican primary, but faced with a choice between a Progressive Norwegian and a Progressive Swede, ethnic pride won, especially in the years immediately following Norwegian independence from Sweden. Moreover, Davidson attacked La Follette for attempting to name a successor, and he gained the support of a number of Republican moderates who saw him as a figure who would return harmony to the party. Davidson won nomination for governor by a large majority, and, adding insult to injury, Connor, the would-be U.S. senator, was nominated for lieutenant governor. These two incidents demonstrate the difficulties facing the Progressive faction during La Follette's ascendancy. La Follette could unite Progressives behind himself, but trying to transfer the unity to another candidate often proved disastrous.[2]

The Progressives survived the split between La Follette and Stephenson, Davidson, and Connor, but even more than "desertion" by these supporters, La Follette worried about the rise of Francis McGovern, the Milwaukee Progressive who was elected governor in 1910. McGovern had built a base of support almost totally independent of La Follette and was a potentially serious rival. This wariness ruptured into an open and acrimonious split in 1912, when McGovern's delegates to the national Republican convention entertained an alliance with Theodore Roosevelt's forces to wrest the presidential nomination from William Howard Taft. Such a deal—or even the suggestion of such a deal—enraged La Follette, who wanted the presidency for himself and saw Roosevelt's candidacy as a betrayal by his supporters. The central issue, however, was not merely whom the Wisconsin delegation would support for president, but rather about how much control La Follette would have over Wisconsin politics. When Lenroot joined McGovern in campaigning for Roosevelt, La Follette broke with him also. He could not stand to have any one, no matter how close a friend, challenge his authority in politics or his interpretation of progressivism.[3]

As these schisms suggest, La Follette was not the all-powerful boss critics claimed him to be. He was able to keep the Progressive faction united some of the time, but at times the older politicians who had already been in public service before his election as governor resisted La Follette's leadership. The establishment of a primary election law complicated the matter even further. Before the time of open nomination, La Follette could have quietly cobbled together a coalition and united behind one candidate. After the law was passed, he had to depend on his public endorsement and support by campaigning. When nominations were up to the public, he could find no way of keeping Progressives united without appearing to select one candidate over another, thereby tarnishing his image as the crusader for the popular will. La Follette also demanded unquestioned loyalty, which these older, more experienced politicians were reluctant to give him. As time went on, younger politicians without statewide recognition and with no large geographical base made the Progressive faction somewhat easier to control. Milwaukee was the exception and produced two major political figures wholly outside La Follette's influence: Progressive Francis McGovern and conservative

Emanuel Philipp. Progressive disunity was costly: Philipp won the 1914 primary over La Follette supporters State Senator William Hatton and Assemblyman Andrew Dahl, and Progressives lost the governor's chair for the first time in fourteen years.[4]

By the 1920s, La Follette's organization had been effectively "purged" of those who were unwilling to subordinate their ambitions to their Progressive leader. Every county had loyal La Follette supporters, but almost all of these were younger than La Follette and were more than willing to defer to his leadership in return for being part of a successful movement. In the late teens and early twenties, young political hopefuls such as John Blaine, Henry Huber, Herman Ekern, and Joseph Beck became part of the La Follette movement as they rose up through the legislature or state agencies. Because La Follette's influence was sought by many, he was in certain instances forced to choose between candidates, often a difficult decision. In 1920, three candidates sought La Follette's support for the nomination for governor in the Republican primary: Beck, Blaine, and Lieutenant Governor Edward Dithmar. All had progressive credentials, and La Follette met for weeks with Progressive leaders trying to get them to come to an amenable agreement. Eventually Beck, after meeting with both Phil (who personally favored Beck) and La Follette, withdrew in the interests of Progressive harmony, but Dithmar announced his candidacy despite his promise to await advice from other Progressive leaders. As a result, La Follette backed Blaine in the primary despite his initial intention of supporting him only for attorney general. Even then the fear remained that multiple Progressive candidates could result in the nomination going to a conservative.

Such dissent among the ranks was problematic as it was common and was part of the political baggage Phil and Robert inherited as they prepared to take the reins from their father in the years before his death. As La Follette shifted his focus from state to national politics and spent time nursing his health in various hospitals and spas in his later years, he began to depend more and more on Robert and Phil to lead the Progressives at the local level. But as Phil and Robert tried to corral local Progressives, they often faced normally loyal supporters who did not like to be bossed by "the kids." Not until 1929—four years after their father's death—were they able to assert their control of the faction.[5]

Progressive factions were not the only issue the sons of Bob La Follette had to deal with. Several pertinent issues divided the Progressives in the

1920s, many centered around Governor John Blaine, who was the most public face of local progressivism at the time but proved to be a difficult ally to the La Follette regime. The most dramatic of these was Prohibition. Instead of settling the question once and for all, the Eighteenth Amendment only exacerbated the battle between "wets" and "drys" that threatened the cohesiveness of the Progressive faction. Some Progressives believed that Prohibition was a crucial reform measure; others saw it as an unwarranted assault of the government on individual liberty. Governor Blaine was an avowed wet, and so providing legislation for the enforcement of Prohibition became a political crisis and to some extent reflected a split between some Progressives who favored strong Prohibition measures and other Progressives who were uncomfortable with the effort to influence private behavior. In the spring of 1921, the state legislature passed an enforcement bill introduced by Assemblyman Alexander Matheson of Rock County. It passed the assembly in a close vote of 53 to 44. Although it was not a precise rural/urban split, the strongest support for the bill came from the rural southern and western parts of the state, predominantly Yankee and Norwegian in population. The entire Milwaukee delegation voted against it, as did the representatives from Madison, Green Bay, and Kenosha, but the representatives from the cities of Superior, La Crosse, Appleton, Oshkosh, and Fond du Lac voted in favor of it. The representatives from the rural and small-town areas of Douglas, La Crosse, Taylor, Clark, Marathon, and Juneau Counties all voted against it. It was much the same in the senate: southeastern senators opposed it, central and western senators supported it. This is, of course, only a rough way to gauge public opinion, but it is suggestive: although the vote was somewhat dependent on urbanization, it was complicated by ethnicity. The parts of the state with larger German populations (except conservative portions of the Fox River Valley) opposed the bill, and those areas of the state with large Scandinavian or Yankee populations supported it. Progressives, rather than having a single cause to rally around, found themselves on both sides of the issue, divided by geography and ethnicity.[6]

There was no question where Blaine stood, and he infuriated dry Progressives by vetoing the Matheson Bill. Referring to the Anti-Saloon League, he declared that it had been drawn up by "a dictatorial lobby" that "bludgeoned members into acquiescence." Although he acknowledged the dangers of illegal liquor, Blaine criticized the bill because it made no provision to penalize unlawful purchases and because it was unnecessarily long and complicated. Instead, Blaine wrote his own bill and had it introduced by Senator Herman Severson of Wuapaca, Wisconsin. Known as the Severson Act, it ultimately passed both houses, though dry Progressives continued to complain about lax enforcement and unsympathetic appointments. They opposed Blaine for the rest of his time as governor. For his part, Blaine refused to risk losing support from voters by advocating further modification of Prohibition enforcement laws. In the next session, he was, however, spared the embarrassment of having to act on another measure that would have repealed the Severson Act. On June 7, 1923, the "Tucker Bill," introduced by Milwaukee Socialist Herman Tucker, a strong opponent of Prohibition, was approved by the assembly. The bill created controversy because of its outright repeal of enforcement laws. Moderate wets wanted legislation that would move more cautiously toward repeal but were unable to unite Progressives to prevent the vote, and the measure passed 47 to 43. The measure died in the senate, but the issue continued to fester throughout the 1920s: drys complained about a lack of enforcement, wets urged repeal, and moderates tried to duck the issue.[7]

Progressives bickered over other conflicts between urban and rural interests as well, most notably road construction. In June 1923, Blaine vetoed a bill that established a two-cents-per-gallon tax on gasoline, with the proceeds earmarked for road construction and improvements. Three-quarters of the funds would have been used for the state highway system, which would have benefited those living in the cities connected by the system and by the growing resort industry in northeastern counties. Blaine pointed out in his veto message that there were almost seventy thousand miles of unimproved roads used primarily by farmers to transport their products to market. As written, the proceeds of the tax would fund only one-seventh of state roads. Nonetheless, senators representing those areas with unimproved "farm-to-market" roads were so desperate for the funds that many of them voted to override the veto, an action that failed.[8]

A much more divisive issue, and one in which the La Follettes became covertly involved with little success, was the formation of a new tax bill in the 1923 session. At the heart of the issue was the disparity between property and income taxes. When the original Wisconsin Income Tax was enacted in 1911, most Progressives believed that it would eventually replace the property tax, which had become problematic due to underassessment of real estate, the property tax's failure to consider one's ability to pay, and the easy evasion of personal property tax. In order to maintain local revenue that depended on taxes on real and personal property, the income tax law included a personal property tax offset; that is, receipts for payment of personal property tax at the local level could be used to reduce assessed payments on income tax at the state level. This dramatically reduced the funds generated for the state through income taxes. Between 1912 and 1921 a total of $78,000,000 of income tax was assessed, but only $41,311,336 was paid in cash—the rest was eliminated by the personal property tax offset. Many Progressives in the legislature wanted to eliminate this offset and shift the burden of taxes to income rather than to property, arguing that revenue would be generated more fairly on the basis of one's ability to pay, which would in effect transfer the source of revenue from rural areas to cities. Given the agricultural depression of the early 1920s, this was a politically explosive issue: repealing the offset essentially redistributed wealth from urban citizens to rural citizens. Those who benefited most from the offset were corporations that paid personal property taxes on equipment and stock, although some of the largest and wealthiest farmers benefited as well.[9]

Blaine himself supported a repeal of the property tax offset, but wary of the voting numbers of the urban southeast, he did not take the lead on the issue. Instead, the first shot in the battle came from two Progressive Republicans, Senator (and erstwhile Blaine supporter) Herman Severson of Waupaca and Portage Counties and Assemblyman John Dahl of Barron County, both of whose constituencies were largely made up of small farmers. They drafted a compromise measure that would have maintained the offset, repealed taxes assessed for education, and funded state aid to schools through a surtax on large incomes. This was a traditional progressive approach to the problem, but Blaine refused to support their plan and had his own bill drafted and introduced by Senator Charles Hanson. This was a disaster for Progressives, who nominally controlled both houses but were unable to pass a tax bill. Blaine had his supporters in the legislature kill the Dahl/Severson Bill, but on June 9, 1923, the senate defeated the Hanson Bill 19 to 12. Dahl promised to rally Progressives around a compromise, but it looked unlikely that any revision would be made. The next day, another Severson tax bill was defeated 16 to 15 after Senator George Staudenmayer broke ranks from the Progressives. On June 14, an omnibus compromise bill, agreed upon by Blaine, Dahl, Severson, Hanson, Herman Ekern, and Robert La Follette, was introduced. It passed the assembly easily but again died in the senate due to Progressive defections. Phil and Robert tried to engineer some kind of compromise in order to avoid a Progressive embarrassment, and they sent frequent telegrams to La Follette, who was staying in the Battle

Creek Sanatorium. What infuriated them was that Progressive legislators seemed to be disagreeing for petty reasons: "[T]he constant jockeying for position has tried my patience to the limit," Robert complained. Two uncooperative Progressive senators, William Titus and Eldo Ridgway, particularly earned their ire, and an infuriated Robert suggested that they should try to "eliminate" them in the next election.[10]

The tax affair frustrated Robert and infuriated Phil, who from early on laid responsibility for the debacle squarely with Blaine, whom he thought had "not exercised the leadership that is so essential to a governor." Rather than trying to build a compromise at the last minute, Phil thought that he, Robert, Blaine, and a few other key players should have promulgated a bill and then rallied the Progressive legislators around it through conferences and public speeches. Itching for a fight, he also scorned those senators who seemed uneducated on the issue. Despite Phil's reservations, the La Follettes continued to support Blaine after Lieutenant Governor George F. Comings announced that he would run in the Republican primary against Blaine. Comings was a credible threat. He had support from the Farmer-Labor Party and dry groups and could expect to run strong in rural areas, especially since Blaine was unable to deliver on his promise of tax reform. He also claimed support from "leading Progressives," including Senator Dahl, Secretary of State Fred Zimmerman, and Congressmen Henry Allen Cooper, John Nelson, and John Schafer. Neither Phil nor Robert was eager to support Blaine, the most likely nominee, but La Follette endorsed him nonetheless, eager to maintain as much influence in the state as possible during his presidential campaign, which kept him effectively out of the Wisconsin scene. Blaine defeated Comings in the primary, but his margin of victory in the general election was much narrower than it had been two years previously: Blaine received 76 percent of the vote in 1922 and only 52 percent in 1924. Despite their support, Blaine was a difficult ally. He opposed Henry Huber's candidacy for lieutenant governor, and Phil thought Blaine campaigned too much on the wet issue, which would only exacerbate the split among Progressives. The La Follettes spent much of the summer of 1924 trying to hold Progressives together.[11]

La Follette wanted to maintain friendly relations for another reason. The University of Wisconsin Board of Regents was about to begin a search for a new president, and the La Follettes had a proprietary interest in making sure the "right" candidate was selected. They wanted someone who in their view would live up to the great legacy of John Bascom, who had transformed the university from a poorly funded and backward

academy into a significant seat of learning and instilled in his students a
sense of social responsibility. Phil was particularly anxious that the president be one who would carry on the progressive nature of the university. In
late 1923, he had suggested that they should work on getting Roscoe
Pound, Alexander Meikeljohn, and Robert Morss Lovett as president,
dean of the College of Letters and Sciences, and dean of men, respectively.
Belle confided that she had more interest in the selection of the UW president than of the U.S. president and suggested it was just as important. In
Madison, Phil sounded out regents and was dismayed to learn that Superintendent of Public Instruction John Callahan opposed Lovett because
Lovett was clearly a liberal, and Callahan, Phil thought, was at heart a conservative. It was up to Blaine to appoint a committee to conduct the search,
and the makeup of the board and his selection would influence whom the
committee recommended. Blaine, however, delayed appointing a committee, which infuriated La Follette, who by this February 1925 letter to the
family had lost patience with him:

> Blaine is giving us a double deal on this all important matter.
> Herman [Ekern] writes that he proposes to put through the elec-
> tion of a president with the Board half-stalwart so as to show he
> is keeping politics out of the university. When did he become so
> good? He has made politics of [Wisconsin] civil service—the
> insurance commission, the charitable and penal institutions and
> now he is making politics of the election of a university presi-
> dent—by angling for the stalwarts who have dragged the univer-
> sity through the political mire for ten years. He is riding to a fall
> that is liable to break his neck.[12]

After Blaine had assured the La Follettes that the Board of Regents
would take no action on appointing a president, Phil believed they had
been double-crossed when the board unexpectedly empowered a committee to make its choice. He fired off an angry letter to Robert, who forwarded it to his parents with his own summation of Blaine's behavior:

> The man must be mad to have played such a game as this over a
> matter about which he knew there could be no compromise.
> Apparently the trimming down which he got at the last election
> has not had an efficacious effect upon his ego. . . . In fact I
> should like to pare it down in his own estimation to the point
> where it will once more serve him as the country lawyer he is and

I suppose was intended to be. Perhaps fate is scoffing us now for attempting to stretch him beyond his normal point of elasticity.[13]

The conflict over the selection of a university president and the fights in the legislature over tax and other issues suggest how tenuous the Progressive faction really was in the early 1920s. These incidents also serve to reiterate that by 1925, La Follette's political leadership was handled largely through Phil and Robert. As La Follette worked in the Senate, campaigned for president, and recovered from illness, Wisconsin Progressives experienced his "directing presence" (as Phil once called it) largely through his sons.

When La Follette died, many of his faithful supporters were reluctant, because of personal ambition or skepticism, to defer to the next generation. The factional division loosed by their father's death haunted the La Follette brothers for the rest of the 1920s and seriously threatened their authority as political leaders and their power as elected officials. Although the family had determined among themselves that Robert would run for his father's seat in the United States Senate, the interfamily harmony that prevailed did not extend to other followers of the late Fighting Bob. Those closest to the family agreed that Robert would make the best candidate, but other Progressive leaders throughout the state were less sure. O. B. James, editor of the *Richland Center Republican and Observer,* noted that Old Bob La Follette had worked his way up to the top. "It would be an injustice to Young La Follette to start him at the top and kick him to the bottom. Young La Follette is a nice young man, [but] has done nothing to distinguish himself from others." Or, as the Socialist Victor Berger grumbled, "The Senatorship is not a hereditary monarchy." Moreover, there was a plethora of potential candidates who had worked for the progressive cause in the legislature and in Congress and believed themselves deserving of the office. Governor Blaine received hundreds of letters and telegrams boosting one candidate or another. Some wanted Henry Allen Cooper, the old Progressive warhorse from the second congressional district, arguing that he had served long enough in the House and deserved promotion to the Senate. Several urged General Billy Mitchell, a native of Milwaukee, who as a popular hero could draw support from all quarters. A few (including Clarence Darrow) hoped that Wisconsin would send a woman to the Senate and suggested Portage author and university regent Zona Gale.[14]

It was up to Blaine to call a special election to fill the vacant seat, and for a time it was unclear just what he would do. Phil and Robert did not trust him after their frustrating experiences with the tax bill and with the university presidency. Blaine and Old Bob were not on very good terms, and Blaine seemed ready to claim the Senate seat for himself. Clearly Blaine was considering his options. After having served three terms as governor, the next logical step was the United States Senate, and it was common knowledge that he planned to challenge Senator Irvine Lenroot in the Republican primary in 1926. Among the letters and telegrams arriving daily in his office were many urging him to run now. One of the most vocal supporters was lawyer Frank Morgenroth. He urged Blaine to run and reported that none of the Progressives he talked to favored Robert as a candidate. A run by Robert would promote only the interests of the family, he argued, and not the progressive movement. For the first time, some Wisconsin Progressives began to consider a movement without the La Follettes, and some thought this was Blaine's best chance to assert himself. Philip Lehner, a lawyer in Tomahawk, Wisconsin, demanded that the governor not give in to sentiment— Robert did not have the ability to win the nomination, nor was he quali- fied to be senator. Older Progressives, Lehner continued, did not take him seriously, and a loss in 1925 would jeopardize Progressive chances in 1926. Another correspondent, Harold Shannon, urged Blaine to move quickly but cautiously: "While we accept that it would be unfortunate for you to advance your own interests vigorously, we are nevertheless cog- nizant of the well-managed propaganda the purpose of which is to defeat your 1926 purposes, and the further patent fact that 'junior' is at present without his own organization and has not been thoroly [sic] 'sold' to the state, in his own right." Blaine wanted very badly to be senator, and the argument that Robert's candidacy imperiled his own future career—and the progressive movement itself—carried real weight. He delayed call- ing a special election, however, until he had a better sense of his options and of his support.[15]

Not until August did Blaine call for a special election. He set the primary for September 15 and the general election for September 29. Some observers believed that the delay would diminish the emotional impact of the election and work against Robert.[16] These dilatory tactics alarmed some Progressives around the state who feared yet another split in their ranks would allow conservatives to win the seat. Several informed Blaine that they thought him the best candidate but urged him to "settle the matter" with the La Follette family. Blaine, who was likely aware of the La Follettes' mistrust, refused to arrange any conferences among Progressives that might threaten his own advancement. To the surprise of not a few Progressives, Blaine eventually came to a decision that produced an unlikely alignment with the La Follette clan. After meeting with Robert in August, he decided to stick to his plans to challenge Lenroot in 1926 and came out in support of Robert. Clearly some agreement had been reached, even if Blaine merely received assurances of Robert's support for 1926. Although Blaine did go on the stump for Robert, his support was lukewarm: he spent more time attacking Lenroot than he did promoting the actual candidate! In response, Lenroot, traveling the state in support of the Stalwart Republican candidate, concentrated his fire on Blaine, denouncing him for trying to wrap himself in La Follette's mantle.[17]

By the time the Senate campaign got fully underway in August, there were several candidates, but the central figure was the ghost of Old Bob. Stalwart Republicans backed Roy P. Wilcox, the former state senator from Eau Claire who had introduced the resolution to censure La Follette in 1918. Wilcox, out to reassert conservative control of the party, demanded that Robert run not as a Republican but as an independent as his father had done in 1924. Also running as a Republican was former governor Francis McGovern, who still nursed a grudge over his frustrated senatorial ambitions in 1914. He ran as the anti–La Follette progressive candidate, pointing to his accomplishments as governor and stressing his experience, which was certainly beyond any of the other candidates, in order to legitimize his claim. In the Socialist Party, John M. Work repeatedly claimed that *he* was the only real Progressive; his chief issue was the need to curb the power of the courts, and he reminded voters that this had been a major part of La Follette's presidential platform in 1924. Robert's own platform was simply to continue the policies of his father; he offered, essentially, "more of the same." This time, however, the rapprochement between the La Follettes and Blaine provided conservative Republicans with their strongest weapon: an attack on the "Madison Ring." Wilcox, McGovern, and Lenroot all attacked what they saw as a dictatorial clique trying to control the Republican Party. They accused those closest to La Follette—Blaine, Robert La Follette, and Ekern—of attempting to put their own choice in the Senate without consulting other party leaders by capitalizing on public sentiment. Who led the ring was never clear, but critics repeatedly implied that it was made up of illegitimate usurpers. Even after his death, La Follette continued to define Wisconsin politics.[18]

Once again, Phil hit the campaign trail, this time in support of Robert. Still serving as district attorney, he traveled around southern

Wisconsin, giving speeches in the evenings after working all day in his office or in court. He vigorously defended his brother's abilities. In Portage he answered charges that Robert was too young and inexperienced and drew on his own military experience to give weight to his words. "The younger generation," he told his audience, "will have to fight the next war and bear the burdens. It seems to me that it would be a good thing to have in the Senate a man who reflects the point of view . . . of my generation." He went on to rail against Calvin Coolidge's "economy measures" and Treasury Secretary Andrew Mellon's tax policies. While pointing to the future of the progressive movement, he also resembled the elder La Follette, who had used any opportunity to denounce those in power. Phil saw these campaign speeches as not only a way to convince people to vote for Robert but also a way to educate supporters about important issues and rally voters around "the cause." In Janesville, he spoke to a crowd of about six hundred with great effect. "Phil La Follette," wrote the reporter for the *Janesville Daily Gazette*, "was full of fire [and] of enthusiasm for the progressive cause and backlashed at Senator Lenroot with determination that was remindful of his father. Seldom did he mention the name of Wilcox but he did have plenty to say about Coolidge, Lenroot, Mellon, Wall Street, and J. P. Morgan." In so doing, Phil demonstrated the belief that politics and teaching were very much the same. Above all else, he sought to *educate* the voters: if they only knew the truth, they would vote the right way.[19]

Phil's enthusiasm, however, belied an underlying worry: although Phil himself was an excellent public speaker, Robert had spoken to large groups only a few times and had never given a campaign address. It was unclear if he would be able to articulate an agenda and convince voters that he was not merely trying to capitalize on his name. "We shall have a stiff campaign," Phil wrote his wife, "but I believe Bob has the inside track." But even Phil hedged his bets: "We might get an awful surprise." McGovern's candidacy worried him, in particular, because he had been a popular and productive governor and could attract votes from Progressives who doubted Robert's ability. Phil's fear was that the overall vote would be light, which would sap progressive strength in sparsely populated rural areas and allow more conservative elements to put McGovern, who could depend on strong support from Milwaukee, over the top.[20] Robert delivered his first campaign speech in Stoughton, a small town southeast of Madison in rural Dane County. His speech was not bad, but definitely not up to family standards. His mannerisms and gestures seemed awkward, and his voice did not project well. Phil's and

La Follette's old law partner Alf Rogers gave Robert much advice, and after some coaching and much practice he became, according to Phil, "a forceful and eloquent speaker."[21]

What's more, Phil's worry about an "awful surprise" proved unfounded. In the primary, Robert quashed his Republican opponents, winning 56 percent of the Republican vote and beating his nearest opponent, Wilcox, by nearly 100,000 votes. Robert went on to win the general election winning 68 percent of the total cast in a five-way race. There was little need for detailed analysis of the results: supporters still loyal to Old Bob rallied to his most obvious successor.[22]

Progressives wasted no time celebrating Robert's victory and immediately began making preparations for 1926. Senator Lenroot was up for reelection, and Blaine eagerly anticipated capturing his seat. The La Follettes, despite a tacit understanding that they would support Blaine, remained unsure whether he was the best candidate and kept their eyes on the horizon for another potential candidate behind whom they could throw their support. Not only did they distrust him, they doubted his qualifications to be a senator. Even Belle, who hated to make personal comments, noted that one of his letters to the family "read as though he had softening of the brain." Although he had been elected governor three times, Blaine was not nearly the popular figure he considered himself to be; a sizable block in the state senate had worked against him, and even after La Follette endorsed him in 1924, a number of prominent Progressives had refused to support him. Early in November 1925, Robert wrote Phil asking him, Alf Rogers, and Ekern to "keep an eye out for the right man for the job here." Rumors persisted that Blaine was out to "knife" Robert once he was safely in the Senate. Nevertheless, after three terms as governor—longer than La Follette had served—Blaine believed it was his turn. Having patched up his differences with the La Follettes, Blaine jumped into the fray and began aggressively campaigning against Lenroot—action that spurred the La Follette brothers to search all the more aggressively.[23]

The search for a candidate for governor was far more difficult than either Robert or Phil expected. Their father's choice for a possible senatorial candidate before his death proved to be a hazard, not a help. In the early 1920s, La Follette had suggested Attorney General Herman Ekern as a candidate, and Ekern was certainly qualified. He had served as attorney general for four years, had been a Progressive leader in the legislature, had headed the state Insurance Commission, and had a national reputation as a lawyer. He had also been totally loyal to La Follette and had worked untiringly in the legislature and behind the scenes often at the expense of his own business. Unfortunately, Ekern was a poor campaigner. He maintained a home in Madison and offices in Chicago and traveled all around the country on business. Phil had a difficult time getting him to stay in the state long enough to campaign for more than a few days at a time. Despite Ekern's regular, and over-confident, assurances that all was well, Robert kept urging him to take to the stump, warning him that others would make themselves well known before he even got started. Belle noted that although Ekern was good at working for others, he had real difficulty in campaigning for himself. In April, Ekern finally began making speeches before formally announcing his candidacy that summer. The La Follettes were relieved, but Ekern proved to be both an ineffective speaker and an ineffective organizer. Phil, therefore, took on much of the burden of prodding him to action and accompanying him on the stump and also took on much of the burden of writing the Republican platform after Ekern neglected the task. Working on the campaign was particularly difficult: there was little enthusiasm for Ekern. Moreover, Blaine and Ekern did not get along, and Blaine did almost nothing to support his fellow candidates, a violation of the usual custom of Progressive candidates promoting each other during their own speeches.[24]

Ekern's candidacy also exacerbated charges against the Madison Ring, which once again threatened a split among Progressives. The La Follettes' effort to put through their personal choice for governor and their continued management of the campaign irritated other Progressives who saw the brothers as upstarts. When one potential candidate for attorney general, G. M. Sheldon, heard rumors that he would be "passed over" because he had not consulted "the La Follette boys," he fired off an angry letter protesting the continued control of the Progressive faction by a small group of Madison insiders. Although he had "accepted the dictation of the late Senator La Follette," he was "not prepared to accept dictation from any other quarter." Sheldon threatened to announce his candidacy and make the best fight he could with or without La Follette backing. The "multiplicity of candidates" frustrated Phil, who believed that it would divide Progressives, allow the election of a Stalwart, and dishearten longtime Progressive supporters.[25]

Dissension among Progressives also led to backlash against Ekern, and anti–La Follette forces rallied around an unlikely figure: Secretary of State Fred Zimmerman. Zimmerman, a gregarious and popular

Republican, had been a La Follette supporter for years, but he had never actually done enough to earn the wrath of conservatives as Ekern had. Prior to La Follette's death, rumors circulated that La Follette had wanted Zimmerman to run against Blaine for the Republican nomination for the Senate in 1926, leaving the governorship for Ekern. For his part, Phil thought very little of Zimmerman. Being secretary of state was not a challenging job, he noted, and Zimmerman was "vastly inferior" to Ekern in terms of ability and leadership. Zimmerman, however, had a few important credentials in his favor. He was acceptable to Stalwart Republicans, who recognized that he would not swing hard for progressive principles like Ekern. He was also well known and good at promoting himself. "Apparently there isn't a church or other small organization that he has passed up," wrote Isabel. "He certainly is a good handshaker." As secretary of state, he was responsible for issuing automobile licenses and other state records and so had instant name recognition. Zimmerman tried to capitalize on La Follette's name as well, telling voters repeatedly that he was the only one loyal to the principles of La Follette and railing against the "Madison Ring." He frequently compared his campaign to that of La Follette's 1890s crusade against the party bosses. Most effectively, he trotted out an alleged commendation from the dead master: "I have known Fred Zimmerman for twenty years and he has always been right." Despite demands that he reveal the source of this quotation, he never did, and Ekern supporters insisted it was false.[26]

To bolster Ekern's flailing campaign and to promote Progressive unity, Phil again went into the field to campaign and, as he put it, "meet the folks." In the summer of 1926, he went on tour with Ekern and other candidates, and again he spent most of his time talking about national issues. In Manitowoc on August 10, after Ekern delivered his own address, Phil spoke to the crowd opposing U.S. entry into the World Court and attacking Lenroot's Senate record. "The youngest son of the late Senator," wrote one reporter, "displayed some of the fiery oratory that made his father famous and was unsparing in his denunciation of the present republicans at Washington." Throughout the end of July and into August, Phil kept up a busy itinerary, often giving ten speeches a week in addition to his normal duties as district attorney. On the whole it was a frustrating experience. In September, Phil declared that Ekern was "devoid of the elements of leadership" and his campaign needed to be run completely by others.[27]

The time Phil spent in the field on behalf of Ekern did not pay off. In September, Ekern lost the primary to Zimmerman. He received 178,252 votes to Zimmerman's 215,546. Two other Stalwart candidates received only 67,000 between them, indicating that Stalwart support for Zimmerman had contributed significantly to his victory.[28] Ekern ran well behind the rest of the ticket: Lieutenant Governor Henry Huber received more than 200,000 votes, Treasurer Sol Levitan received nearly 260,000, and Attorney General John Reynolds received 201,000. As a result, La Follette supporters thus won all of the statewide offices but lost the governorship—a great blow to the Progressive faction. Blaine went on to win nomination to the United States Senate by a slim margin (the result was in doubt for several days), but the primary election was disheartening to the La Follette family. Shortly afterwards, Blaine, Ekern, Robert, and Phil held a conference to decide whether the Progressives should attempt to field an independent candidate in the general election. Older members wanted Phil to run, believing that the name alone would wrest the victory from the renegade Zimmerman. Eventually, they decided against the idea, wary of the financial costs of a futile third-candidate campaign, and Zimmerman went on to trounce his opponents in the general election. The election set a worrisome precedent: a candidate could claim some connection with La Follette to his own advantage, even if other Progressives opposed him.[29]

Zimmerman wasted no time in exercising his new authority, and his actions suggest an attempt to build a personal political machine. The day after the election, he fired the assistant secretary of state, Robert Siebecker, La Follette's nephew (son of Wisconsin Supreme Court Justice Robert Siebecker and La Follette's sister, Josephine). After he was sworn in as governor, Zimmerman denied a request by Attorney General Reynolds to retain Ekern as state counsel in a complex suit with the state of Illinois over Lake Michigan water rights. He then demanded resignations from several Blaine appointees. His own appointees included Ole Stolen, state humane officer, whom Phil had worked to disbar for corruption a year earlier. This wasn't his only "defection" from the progressive cause. As Zimmerman grew closer to the conservative wing of the party, it became apparent that he was abandoning all pretenses of being a Progressive: he even stopped using the "endorsement" from Old Bob, visited with President Coolidge in Superior, and called for the nomination of Herbert Hoover for president. Newspapers—particularly the *Capital Times*—hounded Zimmerman throughout his term as governor, charging corruption in the state highway department and dredging up evidence that he had been a member of the Ku Klux Klan. In his two years as governor, he issued 129 pardons, more than Blaine had in six years, and Evjue accused him of pardoning political supporters. Even moderate Republicans could no longer stomach the governor. Walter

Goodland, who edited the *Racine Times-Call* and had little affection for the late La Follette, urged Republicans to abandon Zimmerman. Convinced that Zimmerman would hang himself if given enough rope, the La Follettes began seeing hope in the next round of elections. Indeed, so much rancor developed in the capitol that Zimmerman could not govern effectively, and the 1927 session of the legislature turned out to be the longest to date, even though it accomplished little.[30]

In the aftermath of the 1926 elections, Phil recognized the need for greater unity, and as Zimmerman bumbled his way through his term, Phil and a few other Progressives organized to prevent a repeat in 1928. This was more difficult than it appeared. Progressive leaders had to walk a tightrope between two extremes: they had to maintain a united front but also had to avoid anything that smacked of bossism, especially among out-of-state Progressives. The Stalwarts' charges against the "Madison Ring" still echoed as the Progressives laid their plans for the 1928 elections.

The obvious gubernatorial candidate for Progressives to rally around was Ekern. He badly wanted to run again, but Phil and Robert knew it would be a tough race against an incumbent governor and bluntly told him that they would support him only if he dedicated at least three months to campaigning in the state. They had been disappointed in his lackluster campaign in 1926, even though he was "the perfect candidate on paper." In the early months of 1926, Phil talked to Ekern for hours, but he refused to make such a commitment. Phil and other Progressive leaders agreed that it was better to back one candidate—even if he lost—who would lead an aggressive and thorough campaign than a qualified but absent Ekern. This was important for two reasons. First, an energetic campaign, even if unsuccessful, would lay the groundwork for the future, and Progressives needed at least some momentum. Second, Robert was up for reelection, and they could not afford to have a less-than-dedicated candidate dragging down the ticket. Phil and Robert needed someone who could carry his own weight in the governor's race.[31]

The field of potential candidates, however, was not great. In the legislature, Harry Sauthoff, who represented Dane County in the state senate, had been a loyal follower of La Follette for several years, serving as Dane County district attorney and as Blaine's secretary before being elected to the state senate in 1924. Phil thought him promising but believed he lacked experience for immediate nomination. Furthermore, Sauthoff was a virtual unknown outside of the Progressive stronghold of Dane County. There was also two-term Lieutenant Governor Henry Huber, who had won national recognition for his speech in the state senate defending La Follette's war record. He had the recommendation of having been elected twice to statewide office, but he was also nearly sixty years old. He did not actively pursue nomination.[32]

State Treasurer Solomon Levitan did not pursue the nomination either, but he was virtually a declared candidate by the summer of 1927 because of his popularity both in the press and in public opinion. He had been elected treasurer three times and in 1926 was the highest vote getter on the Republican ticket. Levitan had a sterling reputation for honest and efficient administration and had been a loyal La Follette follower since the 1880s. Both the *Milwaukee Journal* and the *Wisconsin State Journal* boosted Levitan, although they admitted that he might split Progressives and open the way for a conservative nomination. The *Wisconsin State Journal* was especially lavish in its praise, noting that he was acceptable to all factions, although the first choice of none. The newspaper began boosting his candidacy in part to restore Republican harmony and in part to scare Blaine and the La Follettes. Levitan himself knew he could win, and he was the only candidate that Zimmerman feared running against. The Levitan boom uncharacteristically surprised the La Follettes: "I have been reasonably sure Sol had it in mind to run," Phil wrote Isen, "but did not expect he would begin so hasty." He was another example of a popular candidate who might win but might not pursue Progressive policies as aggressively as Phil and Robert wanted.[33]

Had any of these candidates seriously pushed his own interests, the Progressive faction would have totally collapsed. Only a lingering sense of loyalty to the ghost of Old Bob kept Progressives united, though as the newspaper reports implied, no one candidate was fully supported by the faction. A choice still had to be made, however, and the La Follettes finally decided to support Congressman Joseph Beck for the nomination. Beck was first elected to the House of Representatives in 1920 after having served as chair of the Wisconsin Industrial Commission. He had wanted to run for governor in 1918, but La Follette had persuaded him to withdraw in favor of Blaine. In 1920, La Follette supported him in his race for the Republican nomination to Congress, and he had defeated John Esch. Beck remained loyal to La Follette and was willing to sacrifice his own interests in the interest of Progressive harmony. After he introduced a resolution into the House opposing a third term for President Coolidge, Ralph Sucher remarked to Phil that Beck was "the only member of the delegation who has exhibited any guts for a long time." Loyalty and nerve were exactly what the La Follettes wanted, but Beck was in other ways not a very attractive candidate. Although Phil considered him qualified to be a university professor, Beck appeared to others as something of a hayseed. His sloppy dress and constant tobacco chewing suggested a local lawyer at most, not a fourth-term congressman. Yet because Beck was willing to work hard to secure the nomination and had been unflinchingly loyal to La Follette, Phil and Robert decided to back him.[34]

Having made their decision, the La Follettes had to convince Progressives to support Beck, and they had to do it without alienating any dissatisfied Progressives. In October 1927, sixty Progressives met at Maple Bluff Farm to plan for the spring elections. The purpose of the meeting was twofold: they would select delegates to the Republican National Convention and plan for a December conference of Progressives in Milwaukee to endorse candidates for the 1928 primary. Still sensitive to charges of bossism, the La Follettes waited to see whom the others supported before coming out for Beck. There was "an overwhelming feeling" that the best candidate would be former U.S. Representative and longtime La Follette supporter Edward Voight, but he adamantly refused. Levitan, despite favorable newspaper coverage, was not a popular choice among the Progressives: many thought he was not qualified, and others thought he was too interested in advancing his own standing. Apart from the general appearance of a political lightweight (he had said nothing on the major state issues), Levitan was also too much of a "character."[35] Levitan kept the matter tense for a few months by neither confirming nor denying the rumors of his candidacy.

Further muddying the waters was continued agitation for Phil to make the run himself. Letters to the *Capital Times* appeared frequently calling for Phil to run. Even the stolid *Wisconsin State Journal* acknowledged this possibility: "Phil La Follette, probably the unanimous choice of his faction should he run. Intellectually radical, keen and clean, now standing on the first rung of a ladder which he has chosen to climb from the bottom, behind him an unimpeachable record." Phil was pleased with the rumors but was unwilling to leave his law practice; Belle was unreservedly opposed to his candidacy. Another motivating factor in not running came from the Progressives themselves, who were alarmed at the possibility Phil might announce his own candidacy. Blaine, ever cognizant of the political winds—and ever distrustful of Phil—fretted over renewed charges against the "Madison Ring" and opposed any mention of Phil as a candidate. Blaine believed that Phil's candidacy would cause a political revolt in Wisconsin and jeopardize Progressive seats in the legislature and in Congress. It would also be, according to Blaine, an affront to the legacy of La Follette, who had built his career on the right of the people rather than the party leaders to choose candidates. Any attempt, he wrote Robert in November, "by the family to capitalize on the name La Follette would be a betrayal of the services and sacrifices of Senator La Follette, the Senior, and that the Progressive movement did not mean that there is any patrimony in public office." Although Robert immediately wrote to Blaine to assure him that Phil would not run, there was some insight in Blaine's alarmed letter. Robert's renomination to the United States Senate was by no means a sure thing, and both La Follettes wondered if voters would balk at "too much La Follette" on the ticket.[36]

Having decided nothing at the Maple Bluff conference, Progressives from around the state went to the Milwaukee conference in November 1927 unsure of what would happen. One hundred delegates met to decide whom they would endorse for state offices and also to decide whether or not to endorse Nebraska Senator George Norris, a longtime progressive Republican and close friend of the La Follette family, for president. Phil went as a delegate from Dane County. Levitan also attended, not as a delegate but in order to sound out other delegates about a potential candidacy, hinting that he could be persuaded to run with or without La Follette support. Most observers, unaware of the La Follette preference for Beck, thought Ekern might be endorsed. Phil remained a possibility but an unlikely one, according to the *Green Bay Press-Gazette*: "Only an almost unanimous demand from the conference that Philip La Follette be substituted for Ekern would be accepted by La Follette as a call for his candidacy."

Next to deciding a gubernatorial candidate, Prohibition remained the most divisive issue. Ekern was a well-known dry, and Milwaukee area delegates were unlikely to support a dry candidate. Levitan, a dry, marked time, waiting to see what would develop before either declaring his availability or stepping aside.[37]

The delegates met in a closed executive session, chaired by Robert, on the first day of the conference and quickly decided whom to endorse as candidates for the delegates-at-large to the National Republican Convention election in April. Robert, Blaine, Zona Gale, and Theodore Kronshage were endorsed. The delegates also agreed to face the Prohibition issue squarely by advocating reform but not to make it the center of their platform. In his keynote address, Robert denounced Zimmerman as having betrayed Wisconsin voters and being a tool of the Stalwarts and the Klan. Robert stressed harmony, and Blaine announced that he was in total solidarity with the La Follettes. At the executive session it was also announced that Levitan would not be a candidate. Levitan's friends claimed that he "would do nothing that would harm the La Follette cause." Four names were presented to the delegates for governor: Huber, Phil, Ekern, and Beck. The rural second and sixth districts backed Ekern, but Milwaukee delegates would not accept an Ekern candidacy under any circumstances. Having disposed of a potential Levitan candidacy, the convention adjourned for the day, leaving the question of a candidate still open.[38]

Cracks in the Progressive harmony began showing the next day when balloting began to endorse state officers. The convention unanimously endorsed the current officeholders, Huber for lieutenant governor, Levitan for treasurer, Theodore Dammann for secretary of state, and John Reynolds for attorney general. The contest between Ekern and Beck, however, resulted in a tense, four-hour deadlock. On the first ballot, Beck won 40 to 39, but supporters of Ekern demanded a recount, and the second ballot produced a 39–39 tie. It appeared for a time that Ekern had enough votes to win, but when he was called before the convention to give his views on Prohibition, he reinforced wet delegates' opposition to him. Finally, Phil announced his support for Beck, basing his decision on Ekern's poor showing in 1926, after which Blaine and Robert also announced their support. Beck finally won the endorsement 35 to 33, after which the convention voted to make the decision unanimous. Despite all their efforts to make the Progressive endorsement both democratic and harmonious, the La Follettes could rally their troops behind a candidate only by an open announcement of their support.[39]

The Milwaukee convention succeeded in endorsing candidates for the primary, but it also produced a storm of controversy that underscored how fragile the Progressive faction was. Clearly there were pockets of strength beyond the La Follette family's influence. Levitan and Ekern both had strong support among Progressives, and Blaine had declared his solidarity with the La Follettes only after he was assured that Phil would not be a candidate. And Madison wasn't the only area of power: the Milwaukee delegation remained an important consideration since any candidate needed to succeed in the city to win the state.

After the November meeting, many delegates returned home convinced that they faced defeat with Beck leading the ticket. Conservative newspapers blasted the hypocrisy of the Progressives for dictating the choice of a governor in a secret convention and denounced the deliberate snub of Ekern and Levitan. The editor of the *Antigo Journal* argued that the secret sessions of the conference violated the spirit of Old Bob, who had condemned such behavior in the Republican Party. "If anyone can reconcile La Follette, the bitter enemy of the secret conference, with the tactics of his followers of the present day," he wrote, "they can overlook more than we can." Rumors circulated that Blaine had engineered the convention in order to prevent Ekern's or Phil's endorsement and that the La Follettes went along with him to secure his support for Robert's reelection. Others speculated that the La Follettes backed Beck as a guaranteed loser to leave the way open for Phil in 1930, claiming that Ekern or Levitan might have served for six years, leaving Phil out of politics until 1934 or forcing him to run against Blaine in the senatorial primary in 1932. Evjue dismissed the rumors as an attempt to drive a wedge between Progressives and create divisions that did not really exist. The results of the convention, however, were clear. Without Fighting Bob present to command the party—by respect or by force—the Progressive forces disintegrated into several factions with no clear leader, requiring a great deal of diplomacy and maneuvering to keep everyone together.[40]

Yet factional division was not the only problem facing Progressives that year. They had lost the nomination in 1926 because they were divided, but they lost in 1928 because they fielded a ridiculously weak candidate against a strong conservative candidate, Walter J. Kohler. Kohler was a plumbing magnate who had carefully cultivated his image as a beneficent industrialist who treated his workers fairly and who built a self-named company town just outside of Sheboygan. "Kohler of Kohler" also had wonderful name recognition—voters all over the state saw his name every day when they used a Kohler toilet. Kohler spent much of his own money on the campaign, sending agents into every county and printing thousands of placards with his picture on it. After the disastrous administration of Zimmerman, moreover, Republicans could point to Kohler as a business-minded and efficient administrator. He also proved to be an excellent figure for disgruntled Progressives to rally around. One former La Follette supporter from Beaver Dam wrote that he "was always a sincere admirer of the elder La Follette and gave of my time and money in his campaign, but I contend that those who pretend to lead in his place today are not worthy to step in the footprints of so grand a man as Robert M. La Follette, Sr." Kohler also played on the farm crisis of the 1920s by mailing a thinly veiled campaign circular, *The Wisconsin Citizen*, to farmers all over the state promoting his candidacy. Evjue denounced Kohler's spending almost daily in the pages of the *Capital Times*, claiming that Kohler would spend over $100,000 on the primary. Evjue also charged that Kohler's employees were coerced into supporting their employer.[41]

Not even the La Follette campaign machine could counteract the exorbitant spending by the anti–La Follette Republicans, known since the days of Fighting Bob as Stalwarts. Progressives—including the popular team of Henry Huber and Solomon Levitan—traveled around the state delivering speeches and urging voters to support Beck and other Progressive candidates. Phil outdid himself in touring the state, addressing picnics and fairs, and denouncing Zimmerman, Kohler, and Coolidge. In August, he delivered daily campaign speeches in the evening.[42] As in previous years, he attracted crowds of several hundred in rural areas and impressed listeners with his thundering denunciations of opposing candidates. In Manitowoc, Phil spoke to the crowd of a few thousand for two hours, displaying "probably more oratorical power than even possessed by his father." Belle was particularly impressed with the campaign, telling Robert, "How proud and happy Daddy would be to know you were both carrying on the good fight as you are." But it was not enough. Kohler won the nomination with 224,421 votes to Beck's 203,359 and Zimmerman's 82,837. Beck did well in the rural north and west of the state, winning 37 of 71 counties, but Kohler's domination of the more urban areas of the east and south carried the day. Zimmerman again played spoiler, sapping enough votes from Beck to give Kohler the victory. As in 1926, Progressives lost because they fielded a weak candidate in a three-way race.[43]

The brightest spot in the 1928 election was Robert's overwhelming reelection to the Senate. His platform was much as it had been in 1925: he promised to continue the work of "our great leader," denounced the administration, and reached out to farmers and laborers. The voters evidently approved. He won the primary by a two-to-one margin and the general election with 86 percent of the vote. Such was his confidence in his election that after the primary he virtually shut down his campaign and spent his time in Minnesota, North Dakota, and Montana campaigning for Progressive congressional candidates. Robert's reelection had two significant effects. First, it confirmed his stature as the leading Progressive and as the senior senator of Wisconsin and guaranteed that his opinions and endorsements would carry much greater weight. It gave him greater seniority in the Senate and demonstrated his ability to be elected in his own right, and his fellow senators looked on him with respect. Second, his victory reinforced his national reputation, already strong after his nationally broadcast address to the Republican National Convention, when he presented the minority platform. As one reporter noted, "He had absolved himself of two grievous charges: that he was young and a famous man's son."[44]

After 1928, Robert spent most of his time on national issues and tended to neglect Wisconsin politics. For Phil, this meant that he had primary responsibility to maintain the Progressive political structure and to hold Progressives together, but this became increasingly difficult to do without actually being a candidate. These difficulties would spur Phil to take the matter more firmly in hand by becoming a candidate in 1930 as the only sure means for the Progressives to recapture the governor's chair.

CHAPTER FOUR

Republican Victory

In October 1929, Belle La Follette received a letter from journalist Lincoln Steffens. Years earlier, in 1904, Steffens had made then-governor Robert La Follette Sr. into a nationally recognized reformer when he published "Wisconsin: A State Where the People Have Restored Representative Government—The Story of Governor La Follette" in *McClure's Magazine*. When he started work on the article, Steffens had expected La Follette to be a "charlatan"; instead, Steffens had been deeply impressed by the state's progressive reforms and had become one of the family's closest friends. The La Follettes had even accompanied Steffens on his 1923 trip to the Soviet Union. Now, twenty-five years later, he commented on their children: "I have seen Fola and Young Bob this summer, and I have heard a lot about Phil. You and Bob bred true." Nonetheless, he was impatient. "Some of you seem to have bowed a bit to the reactionary propaganda that there should not be two La Follettes in the Senate (or anywhere)," he wrote. "I want to see Phil also go to the Senate or beyond." Steffens suggested that Belle prod Phil to pursue a public career more aggressively.[1]

Steffens's was not an isolated comment; rumors that Phil would run for office popped up regularly in the late 1920s. In November 1925, the *Milwaukee Sentinel* reported that Phil planned to run for attorney general in 1926, and the *New York Times* described rumors that Phil would run against Governor John J. Blaine for the Republican nomination to the United States Senate. The suggestions that Phil run for the Senate created a stir because it would have led to the unprecedented situation of two brothers representing the same state. One reader of the *Capital*

Times in late March declared that Phil should run because he could unite the Progressives better than any other candidate and suggested that he would be an even better senator than Robert. Progressives in Monroe County actually endorsed Phil as an independent candidate for governor in 1926 and collected two hundred dollars for his nonexistent campaign. Not everyone was so enthusiastic. Blaine still felt threatened any time Phil's name came up in connection with a political office. The editor of the *Wausau Record-Herald* sneered at the "draft Phil" movement: "The State of Wisconsin is learning that there are men within its borders of great executive ability entirely outside the La Follette family." Nor was this speculation entirely confined to the state. Phil appeared on the October 2, 1928, cover of *Time*, and an article in *World's Work* speculated on his political future.[2]

Phil deliberately remained silent on the possibilities of a future in politics. Part of this reticence was because he hadn't made up his mind. Money matters worried him, and while growing up he had been very conscious of the precarious financial position his family had endured. He wanted to build up a stable law practice to provide a steady income for his growing family, and he relished his teaching position at the university law school. For a time he had contemplated a long-term academic career after University of Wisconsin President Glenn Frank offered him the deanship of the law school in 1929. Yet Phil remained dedicated to "The Cause" and traveled around the state in 1929 and early 1930 to speak on behalf of the Progressive candidates and at the invitation of community groups interested to hear about his experience as Dane County district attorney. The speeches were not overtly political, but they did serve to keep his name before the public while he considered his options and assessed the political climate. Phil talked about the need for participation in government, political reform, and the menace of chain banking. To Progressives, the sudden presence of "chain banks," local branches of national banks, seemed an ominous sign of the growing power of financial monopoly. Chain banks could draw capital out of small towns, Progressives asserted, and if one branch failed, depositors in another city or state might also lose their savings. Driven by Progressive editors such as William Evjue of the *Capital Times*, chain banking was a popular issue that Phil would use in his first campaign for governor. At the same time, he "met the folks" and chatted with local Progressives, building a strong support base. From mid-February to mid-March, he spoke in Eau Claire, Rice Lake, Oconto, Mineral Point, Westby, twice in Milwaukee, and several times in Madison. Phil worried about the strain politics would place on his family, and he undertook such a taxing schedule only because Isabel and the two children spent the winter months in Biloxi, Mississippi, after the children had been exposed to tuberculosis. Without his family nearby, he easily slipped back into his bachelor habit of long hours of work and frequent travel to political meetings. At the same time, he gave no clear indication of his plans, worrying about charges that he was trying to capitalize on his name.[3]

The election of Walter J. Kohler in 1928 had serious implications for Progressives. Although they had been successful in other races, the future of the faction was unclear. Robert had won a huge victory, sending him back to the United States Senate, and Progressives had retained four of the five partisan state offices: Henry Huber as lieutenant governor; Theodore Dammann as secretary of state; John Reynolds as attorney general; and Solomon Levitan as treasurer. Of these, Reynolds was the youngest at fifty-two, and although each was an experienced officeholder, none had the inclination to lead the charge against an already popular governor. Reynolds was the most qualified, but he had his heart set on a seat on the Wisconsin Supreme Court. Blaine still held much clout in the party, and although he was unwilling to give up his Senate seat, he was also reluctant to give his support to a potential future challenger in an attempt to unseat the governor. The conventional wisdom was that it would be impossible to beat Kohler, and so candidates for the nomination tested the waters cautiously. Levitan hinted that he would be available for a draft nomination, and Assemblyman Charles Perry began making speeches on public utilities and chain banking. By the summer of 1929, however, the political situation puzzled Phil and others because there was little about which they could criticize the governor. Kohler had come through the legislative session without having raised any issues a Progressive candidate could use against him, and he remained popular with the public. Phil thought that Kohler's campaign in 1930 would be a repeat of 1928: noisy and colorful, but with no real issues on which Progressives could debate him. This was the best argument he could find for his candidacy—he believed it was necessary to fight to keep the Progressives united, and he began to acknowledge that he might have to run in order to forestall another weak campaigner as in 1926 and 1928.[4]

A lawsuit to oust Kohler from office also had muddied the political waters and put Progressives in a difficult spot. During the 1928 primary campaign, *Capital Times* editor Evjue had begun railing against Kohler for trying to buy the election by spending large amounts of money in violation of the corrupt practices act, predicting that the campaign would spend over $130,000, far beyond the $3,000 legal limit. The charges eventually sparked a John Doe hearing in Madison, and attorney Fred Wylie filed a petition with the state supreme court to order the secretary of state to remove Kohler's name from the November ballot. The court refused. In December, a special investigator charged that various organizations had spent, with Kohler's knowledge and consent, well above the statutory limit of $3,000 during the primary. Under the terms of the corrupt practices act, any citizen could file a petition with the attorney general to begin proceedings to nullify Kohler's election. A few days later, Attorney General John Reynolds received just such a petition, signed by Evjue, Phil, Assemblyman Alvin C. Reis, and Dane County District Attorney Glenn Roberts. Phil's name was the first on the complaint, giving the case its official name: *State of Wisconsin, ex rel. La Follette v. Kohler*. Evjue pursued the matter with glee, but Phil was much more reluctant, afraid that the Progressives could end up looking like sore losers at best and as participants in a coup d'etat at worst. On January 26, 1929, Reynolds announced that his office would prosecute Kohler and appointed Walter Corrigan of Milwaukee and Harold Wilkie of Madison as special prosecutors.[5]

Kohler denied the charges and claimed to have spent only about $2,700 on his campaign. He denied any knowledge of other money spent for advertising or promotional material. The event threatened to set off a constitutional crisis: if the governor were removed, Lieutenant Governor Henry Huber would assume the office, but if the court retroactively removed Kohler from either the primary or the general ballot, then the office might devolve onto Joe Beck or Albert Schmedeman, the Democratic candidate. Kohler's lawyers countered that the corrupt practices did not apply to the governor because the only mechanism for removing a sitting governor was impeachment and trial in the state senate as laid out in Article Seven of the state constitution. The investigation sputtered along, and Phil, anxious to have the matter settled quickly, urged Wilkie to begin action. In July, Kohler was served with the summons to appear in Dane County court. Kohler's lawyers won the first two rounds of court proceedings: they had the venue changed from Dane to Sheboygan County, and they convinced circuit judge James Wickersham to grant their motion to dismiss on the grounds that the corrupt practices act did not apply to a sitting governor.[6]

Wilkie appealed to the state supreme court, which on February 4 ruled that the corrupt practices act *was* constitutional and *did* apply to a sitting governor; the court ordered Kohler to go to trial. Although an apparent victory for Progressives, the decision was tainted by the makeup of the court. Only four justices (the bare minimum required for quorum on the court) ruled on the case: Justices Chester Fowler and Oscar Fritz recused themselves because they had been appointed by Kohler, and there was one vacancy. Three of the four ruling justices had significant Progressive connections: Charles Crownhart had been appointed to the bench by Blaine, Walter Owen was Crownhart's law partner, and both were La Follette supporters from Superior; and E. Ray Stevens had been appointed to the ninth circuit court by La Follette. Only Chief Justice Marvin Rosenberry seemed above the political fray. The ruling provoked anger from conservative Republican leaders. The *Chicago Tribune* declared that the state had become a La Follette fiefdom and that the supreme court was merely trying to keep out of office those who challenged the ruling dynasty. Sensing these political winds, Kohler opted not to appeal the decision and instead chose to defend himself publicly in an open courtroom. Phil himself continued to have doubts, writing to Isabel that the short-term effects were hard to guess: "There is the element of sympathy and etc. that always goes with a defendant in any case, plus the factor in this one that practically every newspaper in the state is misleading its readers with colored stories of the entire case, making Kohler out a victim of cheap politics, etc." Phil acknowledged the need for challenging the election, but he was concerned that the political fallout would hurt Progressives.[7]

Even though his name led the list of petitioners, Phil had little direct involvement in the case and was actually in Europe at the time the initial summons was served. Nonetheless, the trial was popularly viewed as a battle between the governor and his challenger apparent. The trial began in late April, and the prosecution had to prove that Kohler knew what was being spent. Although Kohler denied that he or the Kohler company coordinated campaign expenditures, he proved to be an evasive and occasionally bumbling witness. Yet any attempts to discredit the governor's testimony were undone by the actions of the judge. Judge Gustave Gehrtz ruled several times against the state, effectively eliminating all evidence that Kohler had any agency in the expenditures. The jury found the governor not guilty, bringing to a close almost two years of doubt as to his legitimacy. The end result seemed to make Kohler look even more unbeatable.[8]

Kohler's victory in the trial and his emergence as a popular governor hampered by partisan politics assured that Phil would run for the nomination. No other Progressive was willing to challenge Kohler, and to have been seen as one of the initiators of the court case and then declining to run would have made Phil appear to be something as an opportunist. These politicized conditions were not, however, the only factors in the 1930 election. The Great Depression was just beginning to make its mark on the Wisconsin economy, and Phil, as a Progressive candidate committed to the needs of the people, was the right man at the right time to address these looming concerns.

Phil's candidacy occurred against the backdrop of the Great Depression. Wisconsin's newspapers paid remarkably little attention to the Wall Street Crash in 1929, and it took more than a year before the seriousness of the economic decline began to sink in. In late 1929 and early 1930, the press and government agencies stressed the temporary nature of the economic downturn and focused almost exclusively on the unemployment problem. The Wisconsin economy, like that of the nation as a whole, was already weakening well before the crash, although its relatively diversified economy withstood the Depression better than other midwestern states. The underlying problem was increased efficiency in industrial production that allowed $300 million more in value to be produced in 1928 than in 1920, but with industry employing only an additional thousand workers. At the same time, Wisconsin's population increased 11.7 percent, mostly due to natural population increase, and most of this increase was in cities; rural counties generally lost population. Several industries were in decline during the 1920s, including lumbering, railroading, agriculture, and mining, and so the shift in population occurred with a greater reliance on manufacturing for employment. Milwaukee alone absorbed two-fifths of the population increase, and the rest occurred in smaller industrial cities such as Eau Claire, Chippewa Falls, Appleton, Janesville, Beloit, and Oshkosh. Only two cities, Superior and Ashland, both dependent on shipping, lost population in the 1920s.[9]

The retrospective focus on the abrupt increase in unemployment in 1929 obscured the fact that industrial employment was shaky even before the economic contraction began. During the 1920s, agriculture in the state was already in decline, as were lumbering and mining, both crucial to the northern part of the state. The economy's increasing dependence on one economic sector meant that the economy was more vulnerable to sudden fluctuations. Even manufacturing itself was not wholly stable, and employment had been slack in five years out of twelve between 1920 and 1931. This situation was made even more tenuous by the increased numbers of persons seeking industrial employment. By one estimate, there were 155,000 more employable persons in cities in 1930 than in 1920, but the number of actual industrial jobs increased by only 1,000. In the summer of 1929, a gradual decline in employment began as Wisconsin factories employed 15,000 fewer workers than in the summer of 1923, the peak year of employment for the decade. This trend in unemployment was independent of expansions and recessions and was due mainly to increased efficiency. As one anonymous manager noted in 1931, "The depression will come to an end, and we will be able to call our men back. But what is going to become of these poor devils who are being displaced by machinery and the shutting down of plants?" In 1929, there were almost 3,000 fewer factories in Wisconsin than there had been in 1919. Many factory owners had fought competition by expanding their operations, thinking they could reduce per-unit cost, but those factories unable to implement increased efficiency simply closed. This often created a ripple effect across communities. In one city, the employees from a closed factory had $450,000 invested in homes, many of which were lost to mortgage foreclosures or tax sales. The dramatic population spike at the end of the 1920s exposed a long-term trend toward higher unemployment and indicated how vulnerable many putatively well-off communities actually were.[10]

It was not just manufacturing that was affected by the Great Depression. Wisconsin agriculture declined also, although not as sharply as in other states; two decades of planning and diversification lessened the impact of the Depression on farms. Wisconsin produced a greater variety of crops than other midwestern states and also benefited with better livestock, marketing, and dairy production, led by the University of Wisconsin Extension, the State Board of Agriculture, and county agricultural agents. Rural areas of the cutover (the northern third of the state was virtually deforested in the lumber boom between 1880 and 1910), however, suffered significantly more than other areas. By 1920, energetic promotion and colonization efforts had led to the establishment of twenty thousand small farms, around two million acres total, in marginally arable soil. Some of these farms in the lower tier of counties (Marathon, Clark, Chippewa, Eau Claire, Portage, and Waupaca) prospered, but most provided only marginal returns on the at times herculean efforts to clear the land of stumps and rocks. These farms had boomed during World War I but provided diminishing income through the 1920s. Since much of the land was mortgaged to local banks (the average cutover farm had one thousand dollars worth of buildings and one hundred dollars worth of machinery), foreclosures reduced available cash in small towns as well. Long before the crash, farmers often found themselves unable to pay property taxes, further endangering local economies. In 1921, one million acres in seventeen counties were delinquent in property taxes, and this figure increased to two and a quarter million in 1922. Although the state had made efforts at reforestation by reducing taxes on acres of land growing trees, the problem of local economic infrastructure remained. Farm income remained stagnant, and property tax delinquency continued to rise. One town in Taylor County did not even have enough money to print election ballots and pay poll workers during the 1930 election.[11]

In the early 1930s, economist Edwin Witte estimated that Wisconsin's unemployment in 1930 was about 5.5 percent, but there was significant variation among industries. According to a 1931 study by economists Don D. Lescohier and Florence Peterson, manufacturing was hit hardest and suffered most acutely from unemployment, at 8 percent in April 1930. In 1929, Wisconsin manufacturing had employed on average 264,745 persons each month for $352,490,893 in wages. By 1932, this had dropped by more than half to 116,525 persons and $141,797,338 in wages. Salaried officers employed by manufacturing fared somewhat better, dropping from 50,516 to 37,892 persons, a 25 percent decrease, and from $130,913,267 to $72,002,298, a 45 percent decrease. The small Wisconsin automobile manufacturing industry was perhaps hit hardest: half of its employees had been laid off by the summer of 1930. The printing industry was better off than many but still lost 12 percent of its workforce between August 1929 and July 1931. This was the result of a steady demand for tissue products, newspapers, and book stock provided by Wisconsin's woodlands. Food industries (flour milling, canning, and milk products) remained stable, but hotels and restaurants cut their workforce regularly during 1930. The building trade also suffered severe declines and by 1931 had laid off 40 percent of its combined workforce. Overall, the unemployment figures were grim: in April 1931, 160,000 persons were looking for work.[12]

Governor Kohler's response to the unemployment problem was cautious. In late 1929, he called an informal meeting with representatives of the Industrial Commission, the University of Wisconsin Department of Economics, and the Wisconsin Conference of Social Workers to discuss the statistics compiled by the Industrial Commission that documented the increased unemployment in the summer and fall. This gathering recommended that the governor establish an official committee to encourage employers to maintain employment levels through hour reduction and to maintain wage levels. This recommendation was made on the assumption that the nation was facing another recession (the short decline after World War I was the most recent) that could be waited out and coped with effectively through business cooperation. Nonetheless, Kohler took no action. On April 9, 1930, this group again met and repeated its request. This time Kohler did appoint a task force, the "Citizens' Committee on Employment," which met between July 10, 1930, and April 10, 1931. Similar to the informal gathering the previous fall, the committee was made up of business owners, labor leaders, UW economists, and social workers. The limited perception of the extent of the Depression is indicated by the fact that farm and service workers were not represented. The committee's operating agency, the Bureau of Unemployment Research, was established through the Industrial Commission on September 1, 1930, and headed by University of Wisconsin economist Don D. Lescohier. It was funded by $13,500 from the state emergency fund. Lescohier's bureau quickly began an extensive study of unemployment and relief in the state.[13]

While the Citizens' Committee got itself under way, Kohler called a meeting of mayors, county supervisors, and employers on November 14, 1930, to discuss relief efforts. Thirty-eight cities and twenty-four counties sent representatives, and the meeting passed several resolutions. First, it declared that unemployment existed due to worldwide economic depression. Second, caring for unemployment was a local issue, and local committees should be set up to deal with the problem. It did, however, recommend the creation of a state agency to coordinate local efforts. Again, the immediate problem was unemployment, not economic contraction, and it was considered an entirely local matter.[14]

Meanwhile, Kohler's "Citizens' Committee" went about its work gathering data, and in November 1930 it released its recommendations for local government. The committee urged towns and cities to increase their relief budgets and make relief operations more efficient, to move forward with public works, to spread available work among as many persons as possible by eliminating overtime, and to establish a centralized public employment office. As with the meeting of local governments, the committee demonstrated its limited vision by focusing on the local relief of unemployment, stressing above all else administrative efficiency. Even its bolder efforts were scuttled by the state and federal governments; the committee made plans for an enlarged and improved state employment office, but the legislature appropriated no funds for it. President Hoover vetoed a measure introduced by Senator Robert Wagner of New York that would have financed such public employment offices. The committee's recommendations for business, released in February 1931, were equally superficial. The committee urged businesses to maintain pre-Depression wage levels, to spread available hours among as many employees as possible, and to increase production. All of these recommendations, however, were predicated on the expectation for recovery by 1931. The committee's recommendations backfired. By advising businesses to do almost exactly what they were least likely to do, the committee guaranteed that its recommendations would be ignored. Far too many businesses, not sharing the committee's optimism, did not cooperate and continued to reduce wages and hours, discharge employees, or close plants, thus nullifying the efforts of the committee and a few of the more public-spirited business owners who sought to bolster purchasing power and consumer confidence.[15]

As time wore on, however, it became evident that not only were most businesses unwilling to comply with these suggestions, but local governments also found themselves completely overwhelmed by the crisis. During the 1920s, Wisconsin county, municipal, and state governments combined spent an average of nearly $848,000 each year on relief. In 1930 alone, the total spent reached $2.2 million, with an additional $400,000 spent by private agencies. During the winter of 1930–31, a number of cities and counties began make-work programs, often in the form of projects that were begun ahead of schedule to provide immediate jobs. Other cities had work done by hand rather than by machine in order to provide additional jobs. Yet there was significant variation among communities. Eau Claire spent $15,000, but nearby Chippewa Falls spent only $6,500. Kenosha spent $109,000, but Green Bay spent only $5,000 for relief efforts. Moreover, not only was the number of relief applicants growing, the available funds were shrinking. Property taxes plunged due to lower assessment and—more alarmingly—to delinquency. During 1929, the statewide delinquency rate was 5.5 percent. This increased to 7.7 percent in 1930, to 11.1 percent in 1931, and to 17.6 percent in 1932. By 1933, more than one quarter of all Wisconsin property holders were delinquent in taxes.[16]

Faced with dwindling resources and ballooning demand, local government struggled with providing adequate relief. Most counties depended on both government and private charities, although in some cases, the private agencies found themselves pinched because they had lost money in the stock market. Associated Charities, for instance, had to turn over its cases to an already financially strapped Chippewa County. A number of cities depended on make-work projects to fund city building and maintenance projects. Both Sheboygan and Beloit undertook city improvement programs early, and Two Rivers specified that all workers employed on its projects had to be on relief—their pay was forwarded to the welfare office and credited to their payments. The city of Superior spent part of its relief funds to build a municipal golf course, which required mostly hand labor. Douglas County hired men to cut trees to build a barn for the county asylum, selling the surplus lumber to raise funds. Although some municipalities were creative at handling the crisis, others failed completely. The city of Oshkosh ignored the problem and actually reduced its funding for relief. It eventually committed $50,000 to a program for reclaiming shoreline from Lake Winnebago. Milwaukee County, with the largest population and hardest hit by the Depression, spent the most on relief. Two public and five private agencies increased monthly spending from $1,100 in 1929 to $4,700 in 1930. In April 1931, the county set aside $100,000 for work in county parks, specifying that men on relief had to be hired and that payment was made partly in cash and partly in provisions. But even then there were limits: each laborer was limited to thirty days employment for fifty cents an hour. The city of Milwaukee undertook $600,000 of make-work programs, including playground and sanitation work. Between January and April 1931, the city and county combined spent over a million dollars on relief work.[17]

Not only was there variation in the amount of relief provided, the administration of relief also fluctuated. Some counties employed professional social workers; others used, in the words of one report, "methods used in the Middle Ages." Prior to 1931, Oshkosh kept no records whatsoever for its charitable office. In another city, each applicant had to appear before a committee to testify to his or her condition. In counties where relief was administered at the township level, each town chairman determined the amount of relief and who qualified. The cost of administration also varied widely depending on the methods employed. If a city or county agency simply provided cash, the cost of food and milk for a family of five for one month was thirty-eight dollars, but if an agency purchased food in bulk and handed out boxes to families, the cost was only about eighteen dollars. The cost of coal, clothing, and shoes likewise varied. Rent was a particularly vexing problem: some cities refused to provide any money at all for housing, although some cities provided housing for the elderly. Superior was unique in that it actually constructed shacks for homeless men. In locations where both city and county offered relief, there was often friction between governments, and private agencies often turned over cases to government agencies after a limited period, which caused further tension between agencies and public officials. Few public agencies employed professional social workers, and there was seldom cooperation among private and public relief organizations.[18]

A 1931 study by Don Lescohier made a number of recommendations for the administration of relief. An adequate, salaried staff was necessary to avoid inefficiency and waste. Public and private agencies had to coordinate their efforts to prevent duplication of cases, and detailed, confidential records had to be maintained. Yet even by this time, the movement of the state into the business of relief caused concerns and indicated the political boundaries in which Progressives had to operate. Could a state agency oversee a large program, or would professional social workers be needed in order to prevent politicians using the money to reward supporters? There was also widespread fear of the establishment of the "dole system," in which the government simply allocated tax revenue to fund payments for the unemployed. This system brought to center stage the troubling question of how families would be affected by government charity. Receiving a monthly cash payment was the most expensive form of relief, but it was also the most confidential. The most efficient way, distributing boxes of food, was the most public. It was also the most evident to children, a fact that worried Lescohier: "One wonders what the effect in future years will be when thousands of these children have grown up with the consciousness and expectation that it is customary practice for the government to feed large numbers of families." The final recommendation was based in this grim realization that relief could become a long-term problem. Progressive proposals were based on Lescohier's recommendations: prolonged cases should be supported by tax-supported, public agencies and should be in the form of work, not doles.[19]

Against this backdrop of increasing unemployment and local crises in relief expenditures, Phil finally decided to run for governor. Phil continued to make public speeches throughout 1929, and, while these presentations were almost always nonpolitical, progressive principles were never very far under the surface. In May 1929, he spoke to the Wayland Club of the First Baptist Church in Madison, urging his young audience to develop an interest in government as a means to reform society. A trip to Europe in the summer of 1929 kept Phil off the stump for a few weeks, and when he and Isabel returned, they discovered that their children had been exposed to tuberculosis. Isabel took Robert and Judy to winter in Biloxi, Mississippi, away from the Wisconsin winter. Their absence depressed Phil, but it also provided the opportunity to devote more time to his speaking schedule. During the first three months of 1930, Phil traveled around the state, visiting Rotary or Kiwanis clubs as far away as Rice Lake, Stevens Point, and Eau Claire. Politically, Phil gave no indication of his future plans, but privately he was already thinking about running for governor. He still had not made up his mind, and he was especially worried over how the voters would react to "too much La Follette." Kohler's popularity, too, scared away other potential candidates, and Phil worried that without a viable standard-bearer, the Progressives would have to sit out the election. In January 1930, he wrote to Isabel in Biloxi: "Nothing is settled. We are really just marking time and letting the situation develop as political currents [show] a natural trend. There may be a change in the situation—but at present it continues as it has been for the past six months: a general feeling among our people that I should be a candidate. . . . I see no reason for altering my present attitude, which is simply awaiting events—with my mind open—and without commitments either way."[20]

Some Progressives, however, were unwilling for Phil to take on Kohler. Blaine, still distrustful of Phil and by no means eager for his career to develop, speculated that four candidates from Dane County for the constitutional offices was too many, obliquely suggesting that Phil should wait. The speaker of the assembly, Charles Perry, who had recently broken politically with the governor, announced that he was "available," but the Wauwatosa lawyer had tenuous Progressive credentials and had been in and out of politics sporadically for years.[21] Alf Rogers did not want Phil to get involved in politics until he had built up some "financial competence" through his law practice. The editor of the *Marshfield News-Herald* thought Phil would be a bad choice because of the apparent inevitability of Kohler's reelection and suggested that Phil wait until 1932.[22]

Progressives were not the only ones waiting for a candidate to announce. Phil thought that most of the conservative Republicans were convinced that he would be a candidate, and Kohler's refusal to declare himself a candidate for reelection worried them.[23] Nonetheless, rumors of a "draft Phil" movement continued to dominate the political columns of the state, provoking some editors to speculate as to why Progressives seemed so eager to sacrifice Phil to Kohler's inevitable reelection when there were many other younger Progressive leaders around the state who could make a creditable campaign.

Yet none of these Progressives stepped forward to challenge Kohler. Even Alf Rogers admitted that 1930 was Phil's best chance to run: "It happens that right now," he told Phil, "no other Progressive leader wants to run—hardly anyone thinks Kohler can be beat—so the way is open for you as it may never be again." The requirements for a Progressive candidate were indeed stiff. To challenge Kohler in the primary required a candidate who had statewide name recognition, could unite the disintegrating Progressives around a single candidate, and was willing to campaign at a frenetic pace. This disqualified Fred Zimmerman, who had burned his bridges with Progressives in 1926; Herman Ekern, who had no stomach for a prolonged campaign; and Joseph Beck, whom many Progressives considered too rural. Moreover, even if the Progressives' candidate failed, they at least needed someone who could weld them together and reinvigorate the lackluster county organizations. If Progressives were to learn from the mistakes of 1926 and 1928, Phil was the ideal candidate. One mistake they had learned from was the disastrous 1927 Milwaukee conference. Rather than having one statewide meeting of Progressives, which would open Phil to charges of being the candidate pushed through by the "Madison Ring," Progressives held smaller conferences in each state senate district. As these one by one began to endorse him, his candidacy began to appear more and more like a draft.[24]

As Phil "grew into" the idea of running, he looked to his closest political advisors: his family. In April, Phil, Robert, and Belle met in Atlantic City to discuss Phil's campaign strategy. All three had by then decided that his candidacy would be best for the progressive movement and that he should run, but they decided not to announce Phil's candidacy until after nomination papers had been circulated and filed. The delay gave Phil the time to prepare his announcement and quietly plan the campaign while still maintaining the image of a draft as local organizations lined up behind him. Writing the announcement caused considerable debate within the family. Immediately after reading the first draft, Belle "hit the ceiling" and telephoned him from Washington to tell him that she was sending his brother-in-law Ralph Sucher to Madison to help. Sucher, Mary's husband, covered Washington news for the Associated Press. Belle also demanded that Isabel work on it as well. When Isabel protested that she lacked political judgment, Belle told her, "You are an intelligent woman. If what Phil writes does not appeal to you, rest assured it will not appeal to others." Phil, Isabel, and Ralph worked on the document at Maple Bluff Farm in June until everyone was satisfied with it. Phil also followed a practice of his father by drafting his personal platform. After consulting with other Progressive leaders and legislators, Phil sent the draft of his platform to Belle, Robert, and Ralph, now back in Washington, to work on. As always, a La Follette campaign was a family affair.[25]

Phil's announcement, after much family editing, reaffirmed continued devotion to the memory of the elder La Follette. "The fortune of birth does not entitle any candidate to the support of a single voter," it read. Nonetheless, Phil clearly stated that he felt a special obligation to "uphold the noblest traditions of a great public office and to render to all the people of Wisconsin the best that is in me in faithful service." The rest of the announcement could have served in 1900. It claimed that the incumbent administration was in league with "selfish interests." It called the progressive years the "greatest victory for representative government in half a century."[26]

Phil claimed that his name offered no special privileges, but he was more than willing to capitalize on its enduring reputation, especially when it balanced his young age. His announcement reminded the faithful that Wisconsin was not won without struggle and that he was willing to fight for "that faultless progressive State government which prevailed from 1900 to 1926." Those who had worked for Old Bob were quick to point to Phil's lineage as well. Daniel Grady, former president of the University of Wisconsin Board of Regents, grandly claimed that Stalwarts did not fear Phil's youth but the "blood that courses in his veins."[27]

Phil's platform offered a few new planks, but it was firmly rooted in the progressive traditions of the elder La Follette. The platform denounced "monopoly" and called for a firmer corrupt practices act, the direct primary, initiative, and recall, all items espoused by La Follette twenty years earlier. It also called for public hydroelectric power to compete with privately generated electricity and expand service into rural areas. It promised to shift the tax burden from property taxes to income and inheritance taxes, a long-standing Progressive demand. As a direct slap to Kohler, the platform contained a plank vowing to strengthen the corrupt practices act. Old progressive ideas were updated to combat the Depression as well: public works, conservation projects, and road improvements. All of these, however, reflected a rural bias of Fighting Bob's movement. Publicly owned electric power with lines reaching into the rural areas was aimed specifically at farming communities that still had no electricity. On Prohibition, the platform waffled, as had La Follette himself: it called for the enforcement of the laws but also for a national referendum to decide the question of repeal. It promised support for dairy farmers and a ban on oleomargarine, a synthetic butter substitute that farmers perceived as a significant threat to their livelihoods. The platform's weakest section dealt with labor and unemployment; it advocated no specific policy and weakly denounced the Kohler administration for not doing enough. Yet it offered only a vague pledge to do something about unemployment, and some liberals wondered how effective the campaign or the platform could be. The *Milwaukee Journal* editorialized that the problems of the Depression "cannot be cured by the program and the philosophy of the elder La Follette." Even Alf Rogers sensed the weakness of the Progressive campaign and remarked that the concrete examples of the 1928 campaign expenditures and the chain bank issue were "Manna from Heaven."[28]

One of the few really new planks dealt with chain banking, and that issue became the centerpiece of Phil's campaign. During 1929, Wisconsin newspapers were filled with almost daily reports of small, local banks being swallowed up by a large chain based in Milwaukee, the First Wisconsin National Bank. Progressives decried this as a loss of local autonomy and yet another example of how the "money trust" was subverting democracy. This resonated particularly with farmers, not well off in the 1920s, who saw consistently low prices due to obscure and alien "market forces." Evjue, in particular, rode this hobbyhorse on the pages of the *Capital Times*, running regular stories of small-town banks merging with the chain, adding to the concentration of wealth in a few hands. Phil adopted the matter as well, giving him a single, relatively simple issue that he could rally Progressive forces around, and, more importantly, with which he could attract hundreds of people who had never voted Progressive before. In doing so, he followed the example of his father, who always picked one or two major issues to center his campaign around.[29]

Phil opened his campaign for governor on July 15 with a speech at Sauk City. Despite the fact that Belle had advised him against anything that appeared like a "whirlwind tour," that was precisely what Phil's campaign was. In the next two months, Phil would give 261 speeches around the state. His daily schedule regularly included two speeches in the morning and two in the afternoon, often to crowds of around two hundred; an early evening conference with local leaders; and a late evening speech to an audience of between two thousand and five thousand. At

Sauk City, Phil set the tone for what would become his standard presentation. He railed against chain banking, blamed the Depression on the policies of Hoover and Kohler, denounced the Smoot-Hawley Tariff Act (which made it harder for American manufactured goods to be sold abroad), and castigated Kohler as a servant of the "monopolies." From there and for the next two weeks, Phil traveled around the north-central part of the state, touting Progressive accomplishments of the past and boosting local candidates.[30]

University of Wisconsin philosophy professor Max Otto had reminded Phil to emphasize the fact that he represented a cause, and the content of Phil's speeches left no one in any doubt of that fact. His attacks on Kohler were traditional in that he did not blame him personally for failing in a time of crisis but rather characterized him as the latest in a long line of Stalwart Republicans more interested in preserving the wealth of the few. The Depression was just the latest manifestation of that line. "The American people today," Phil told an audience in Milwaukee that September, "are being squeezed tighter and tighter between two vices. On the one side is the monopolization of wealth in the hands of a few and on the other the inequitable tax burden on the many. Until these two forces are broken up, real prosperity cannot return." The key to winning, Phil thought, was to convince as many undecided voters as possible, using the Depression as compelling evidence that his father had been right all along. He remained convinced that if enough people "saw the light" the Progressives could reinvigorate democratic government. He also recognized the importance of jump-starting local leaders, and he held informal meetings with them so that they could maintain interest and enthusiasm until election day.[31]

With all the Progressives in the field for Phil, it was sometimes unclear who the real candidate was. Both senators stumped the state. Robert's speeches emphasized not the accomplishments of the candidate for governor—there really were not any—but instead defended the record of Wisconsin Progressives in general. He compared this campaign to La Follette's in 1900 and listed the number of reform measures adopted nationally that were first introduced by the Wisconsin delegation to the Republican national convention. The nearest to the present that Robert came was a discussion of the Progressive platform, itself very reminiscent of the 1924 national platform. In one campaign speech, Robert even neglected to name Phil as the candidate for whom he was speaking! Blaine likewise came out swinging for the Progressive record. Beginning in mid-August, Blaine attacked Kohler and Hoover (in his mind, the two were nearly synonymous) as millionaires who ran the state and national government solely for the benefit of big business. Having made his reputation as a cost-cutting governor, Blaine denounced Kohler as "the most extravagant governor that state has ever had," while at the same time blaming him for withholding money for state construction. When he did get around to mentioning Phil, it was to assure his listeners that youth was no handicap—hardly a ringing endorsement. If Blaine appeared less than enthusiastic about Phil, he probably had his own political future in mind. Blaine was still reluctant to see another rival in Progressive ranks, and a loss in the primary would most likely have ended Phil's political career. Moreover, most reporters favored Kohler to win, and a popular, two-term governor would be in an excellent position to run for Blaine's seat in the Senate in 1932. One reporter for the *Milwaukee Journal* noted that "Mr. Blaine's effort reads more like the opening speech of Senator Blaine's campaign for reelection . . . with Gov. Kohler as his opponent." Other familiar names also took to the campaign. Former governor Francis McGovern, dismayed at the amount of money the Kohler campaign spent in 1928, announced his support for Phil, despite the fact that he had broken with La Follette in 1912 and had run against Robert for the Senate in 1925. Herman Ekern and Joseph Beck, passed over in 1928 and 1930, gamely went into the field to deliver a few addresses for Phil, stirring up the chain bank issue.[32]

Most significantly, Isabel took a major part in the campaign, participating fully in her husband's political life for the first time, albeit somewhat reluctantly. When she asked Phil in 1930 who was going to run his women's campaign, Phil replied to a startled Isabel, "You, I guess." The Progressives had traditionally made a point of courting the support of women, and in the past Belle had organized the effort. In 1928, however, she had recruited only a few women to work on the Beck campaign, and now she was wrapped up in writing her husband's biography. Although Isabel protested that she knew too little about the issues and had no idea how to organize such a campaign, she eventually agreed. This was in part because there was no active political network of women available to Progressives—the League of Women Voters was dominated by conservative Republicans, and the American Association of University Women focused on educational, not activist, issues. Isabel accompanied Phil around the state but had a hard time recruiting volunteers: even if husbands were supportive, she found that their wives did not go to the mass meetings that the Progressive speakers specialized in. Isabel then took a different approach. Rather than trying to get women out of their homes, she brought the speakers to them. A local woman volunteered to have a small gathering at her home, and campaign headquarters supplied a speaker—almost always a woman—to address them on the issues of the campaign, tailored to emphasize how Progressive policies would allow families to buy more food or have a more stable income. Usually the meetings took place in the living room, but larger crowds sometimes gathered in the basement. As was customary, the "hostess" usually provided refreshments, but Isabel discouraged this out of the fear that poorer women would be unwilling to participate. These meetings usually lasted about an hour, and the speakers often found themselves questioned more vigorously than was the case at large outdoor gatherings. The idea quickly took hold, and Isabel was out most of the summer taking care of the "greater housekeeping of the state." Isabel's social status and financial position made this participation possible: she left the children in the care of their housekeeper.[33]

Yet Progressive speakers simply could not get themselves out from under the shadow of Old Bob. Those speaking on behalf of Phil frequently referred to "the democracy of Robert M. La Follette," which infuriated the Kohler forces who tried to emphasize Phil's youth and inexperience by referring to him as "the young man" or "the second son."[34] At times this became silly: in Centuria, a band of Ojibwe made Phil an honorary chief, "Rising Sun."[35] In Sheboygan, he was introduced by Oscar Huhn, an old friend of his father, as if an old-timer could legitimize his presence in the governor's hometown. Zona Gale declared that he was "a man of the future who has been grounded in the best of the past."[36]

The Kohler forces at first tried to be dismissive of the Progressive efforts. Conservative newspaper editors pointed to the lack of specific proposals offered by Phil and accused him of trying to capitalize on his name. They were harsher on Blaine and on Robert, who seemed to be fighting completely different—and nonexistent—battles unrelated to the gubernatorial campaign. By early fall, however, conservatives were more worried and began to lose their tempers. Kohler referred to Phil as a "whippersnapper." Gerhard Bading, former mayor of Milwaukee, pushed for the nomination of Kohler and became particularly vituperative of Phil and the Progressive organization: "This youth . . . has nothing of accomplishment in any field which would entitle him or justify him to request, at this time, that the citizens of Wisconsin place him in the governor's chair. His sponsors are a clique of self-seeking, tricky politicians who meet behind closed doors in Madison and determine who are to be the candidates for various offices." The charge was actually fairly close to the truth: Phil ran not on his own record but on the record of the Progressives of the past thirty years. Despite his protests that his name did not mean he deserved to be elected, it did make him a virtual "prime-minister" of the Progressive faction.[37]

If the campaigners tried to play down the La Follette name, observers of the race, both state and national, could not help but comment. After Phil's announcement in July, the *New York Times* noted that although his name was "long magical in Badgerdom," he would have to stand up on his own merits. *The Nation*, which had enthusiastically supported La Follette's presidential campaign in 1924, remained doubtful: "The La Follette machine has its back to the wall, and so it has brought out its biggest trump." Nonetheless, the key to success, the editors argued, was for Phil to emphasize a program significantly different from Kohler's. A September issue of *Labor* included a four-page special on the campaign, comparing it to La Follette's campaigns in the 1890s.[38]

Overall, it was a very well run campaign that avoided the problems that had plagued Progressives since 1926. The faction united behind the strongest possible candidate, one who was willing to campaign vigorously and meet endlessly with local leaders to build up the Progressive network. The interest thereby generated resulted in a large primary turnout: 663,238 voters participated in the Republican primary in 1930; in 1928, there had been only 514,065, and in 1926, there had been only 460,842. These two elements, a united Progressive faction and an energetic campaign, led to the nomination of a Progressive for governor for the first time since 1924 as Phil defeated Kohler 395,551 to 267,687.[39]

Once nominated, Phil coasted to an easy victory on November 8 over Democrat Oscar Hammersly, 392,958 to 170,020, carrying every county but Sheboygan. He quickly turned his attention to formulating his administration's policies on relief and unemployment, and to do so he relied on traditional progressive ideas. He had already begun this process in drafting his personal platform, which became the official Republican platform after his nomination. As it was during Phil's campaign, the platform was a mix of the old and the new. It praised Wisconsin's record in progressive government and offered specific examples in stringent language of what had to be done to continue the struggle. It called for public hydroelectric power to compete directly with private power companies and to extend electricity to rural areas. It demanded the strengthening of the corrupt practices act, tariff revision, increased reliance on income and inheritance

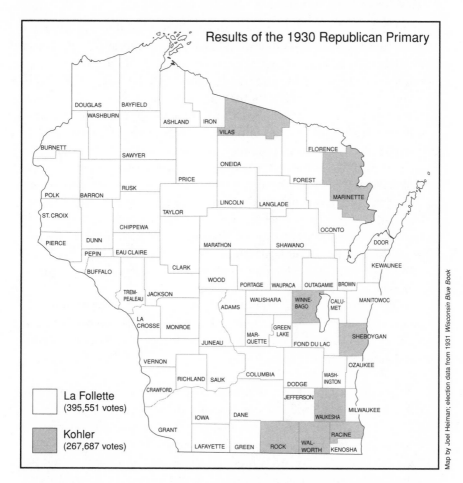

Results of the 1930 Republican Primary

La Follette
(395,551 votes)

Kohler
(267,687 votes)

Map by Joel Heiman; election data from 1931 *Wisconsin Blue Book*

taxes for revenue, and the elimination of chain banks. There was only a passing mention of the current Depression in a call for public works for the unemployed. It closed with a ringing salute to the "inspired and inspiring leadership of Robert M. La Follette."[40]

After the breakneck pace of the campaign, Phil took a two-week vacation in California visiting Fola and George Middleton to catch up on his sleep and relax. On his return to Madison, Phil wasted no time in beginning to develop a state program, and the first step was to assess the state's financial situation. Under the recently passed Executive Budget Act, the governor-elect held budget hearings before taking office. These hearings lasted nearly six weeks, and Phil asked all departments to submit their budgets and an explanation of their services and costs prior to the hearings. He also began working with Progressives in the legislature to divide responsibility for research and drafting measures. His intention was to prepare all the bills that would fulfill the platform pledges before the legislature even met, creating a closer working relationship between the executive office and legislature than had existed in years. He thereby also firmly asserted his role as a party leader to keep Progressives working together. University of Wisconsin economist and assemblyman Harold Groves worked on tax bills, and Senator Orland Loomis drafted amendments to the corrupt practices act. Conscious of his reputation as a radical, Phil also arranged meetings with nongovernment officials to seek advice and give reassurances that the young governor was not out to wreck them. He discussed his plans for eliminating grade crossings (where railroad tracks intersected with roads) with the presidents of railroads operating in Wisconsin and the banking and financial situation with bank presidents. Both meetings were successful and cordial, and the new governor looked forward to a productive legislative session and widespread public support for his measures.[41]

By the time of his inauguration on January 5, the economic downturn appeared much more serious, and Phil, fresh from his conferences with economic and business leaders, acknowledged the difficulties ahead in his inaugural address:

> As a state and a nation we have astounded the world in production. Our energy and brains have shown the world how to produce the necessities and luxuries of life in sufficient quantities to satisfy the needs of all our people; but in the midst of abundance of agricultural and industrial production we have want and suffering. Unless we can solve the problem of the distribution of this abundance—unless we can stop hunger and hardship in all of this plenty, we will be the actors in the greatest tragedy of human history.

Nonetheless, Phil still viewed the current problems in the context of traditional progressive views of the economic system. The natural result of continual monopolization and domination of business interest was a breakdown in prosperity and purchasing power. He went on to recall Wisconsin's pioneering role in political and economic reform and promised that the state would "again assume leadership in sound, effective and constructive solutions to the greatest economic problems that have confronted mankind." In other words, the Great Depression was a startling new event only in its severity, and Progressives knew how to fix the system.[42]

Progressives wasted no time. On January 7, a group of railroad executives met with Phil and agreed to a plan whereby their companies would pay 40 percent of the cost of constructing railroad overpasses. On the fifteenth, Phil addressed the legislature and outlined his agenda. In addition to the grade crossing elimination program, he called for revisions in the income tax system and the highway construction program (both to relieve property tax payers), a new labor code, and a public power program. He also proposed two plans for governmental reform: first, the creation of an executive council, and second, changes in the primary election law that would allow a candidate who received an absolute majority of all votes cast to automatically win the general election. The next day Progressives began introducing these bills into both houses. Phil's message received much praise from the state newspapers. Most editors agreed that in general the Progressive agenda was a rational and scholarly approach to the Depression. Change, it seemed, was in the air.[43]

The most striking thing about Phil's message was not the provisions he advocated (most of these were expected) but the way he put the current economic problems into a historical and ideological context based on the frontier thesis advanced by Frederick Jackson Turner, which argued that the presence of a frontier had shaped American character, making the United States more democratic and offering more economic opportunity. Reverting back to his days as a law school lecturer, Phil told the legislature that the goal of politics was to guarantee freedom and opportunity. In the nineteenth century, according to Turner's interpretation of American history, this opportunity was guaranteed by the existence of the frontier, where "men were free to bundle their families into covered wagons and move west to a new freedom and a new opportunity." But, Phil noted, this easy escape allowed the economic and political systems to remain stagnant and prevented them from "adapting to changing needs and changing conditions." The Progressive movement was a response to this condition, it had been working for thirty years to adapt to new circumstances, and as the speculation of the 1920s burst, the plutocrats had come to roost. The government's task, he charged, was to continue the Progressive movement to meet the current situation—not a new situation, but the latest in a series of economic downturns that threatened the autonomy of individuals. "Have we, from our forty years of experience, any wisdom to contribute, or is our message obsolete?"[44]

The application of the frontier thesis to the Depression was not exactly a new idea. As early as 1918, sociologist Robert Tudor Hill in *The Public Domain and Democracy* had argued that the end of the frontier meant that a shift was needed from individual effort to collective enterprise. This theme had been picked up by public intellectuals such as Charles A. Beard, Stuart Chase, and other left-leaning academics, who argued that the inevitable economic decline had only been delayed by the development of mass production, the world war, and the expansion of consumer credit in the 1920s. This concept of economic maturity was later incorporated into political rhetoric by Hugh Johnson, Henry Wallace, Harold Ickes, and ultimately Franklin Roosevelt. But Phil's use of the frontier thesis in his address was its first appearance in such a formal political forum and the first time it was accompanied by a collection of concrete proposals.[45]

Phil's message to the legislature outlined the Progressives' proposals. Many dealt with the Depression only tangentially and were designed to make government more efficient and responsive to the public will. Phil called for the creation of an Executive Council made up of representatives to the assembly, senators, and citizens appointed by the governor. The council would represent different interests—business owners, organized labor, consumers—to research economic problems such as unemployment and loss of purchasing power and advise the governor. He also suggested revision in the election law to allow the immediate election of any candidate who received a majority of all votes cast in a primary election without having to go through a general election. Phil also proposed a new labor code, highway relief bill (to reduce property taxes), income tax revision, the railroad crossing elimination program, and an ambitious public power program. Issues that had been key in the campaign, such as chain banking and direct relief to the unemployed, Phil chose to defer to later. The general reaction to the message was remarkably positive. Stalwarts, perhaps having braced themselves for something more confrontational, respected the "sincerity" and "scholarly-ness" of the address. Normally conservative newspapers like the *Milwaukee Sentinel* and the *Janesville Gazette* thought it moderate and fair.[46]

While Phil hosted frequent conferences with them, the Progressives began to advance their program in the legislature. It seemed that the Progressives would be successful, and newspapers around the state made much of the fact that for the first time in ten years the governor and the legislature were in fundamental agreement on important issues. The Progressives controlled the assembly by a large majority, and it appeared that they would control the senate by one vote after a normally Stalwart senator, Peter J. Smith of Eau Claire, announced that he would support the administration.[47]

The administration's early months were indeed remarkably harmonious. As the legislature began scheduling hearings on Progressive bills, Phil sought the cooperation and support of a variety of interest groups and solicited opinions from experts. He sent copies of the public power bills to university professors (including James Landis, Felix Frankfurter, and David Lilienthal) and arranged group meetings with Wisconsin manufacturers. The cooperative effort brought quick results: by early January, the governor and the railroad presidents had worked out a grade crossing elimination program to provide work, with 60 percent of the cost borne by the state to eliminate seventy-one crossings. The first contract was signed on January 20, 1931. This seemed to bode well for the fate of Progressive bills in the legislature as well. Progressives had a large majority in the assembly, and shortly after the legislative session began, it appeared that they would control the senate as well. With the cooperation of two Socialists and a Democrat, Progressives elected Herman J. Severson president pro tem.[48]

As long as this era of good feelings prevailed, Phil thrived in his job as governor. He arrived in his office by 8:30 in the morning and usually poked his head out the door to greet visitors throughout the morning. In the unusually informal office, it was common for the governor to discuss matters of state while sitting on the edge of a table swinging his feet. Politicians sometimes found the familiar atmosphere off-putting, and one senator took to calling Phil "Little Lord Fauntleroy." Isabel wrote to Belle that although he worked often until late in the evening, he was having a "marvelous time. It would gladden and amuse you to see his imagination at work on a thousand different matters. I can see how he was when he was little!"[49]

The honeymoon continued with the budget message, delivered to the legislature on January 29, 1931. Phil recommended an overall cut of almost $15,000 from the previous biennial budget of $56,895,996, including a cut of over $800,000 from the University of Wisconsin and Normal Schools. He also urged an end to automatic salary increases for state employees and had a few days earlier discussed with the director of personnel the reorganization of state agencies to reduce expenses. He did recommend, however, increases for the court system, the forest cropland program, and charitable and penal institutions. A call to public service permeated his message as he declared that salary should be based on performance and service and warned the university, in particular, against adopting an "acquisitive spirit" in recruiting faculty. The Progressives, Phil assured the legislature, remained committed to service and education, but he warned that "we can never afford unproductive enterprises." In his call for efficient and dedicated public service, Phil hit on what had been a sore point for years. Albert O. Barton, the Madison writer and La Follette biographer, later told him that there was often a "torpor" in state agencies because of divided responsibilities. "There is widespread feeling too," he added, "that large numbers of university men are overpaid and 'should take some cuts like the rest of us.'" Phil later reduced his own salary by 20 percent and convinced the Board of Regents to reduce administrative salaries at the university, including that of an annoyed President Glenn Frank, but he mitigated the cuts somewhat because no state salary under $3,600 would be reduced.[50] Not everyone was pleased with the call for fiscal contraction. Phil's friend and former professor Max Otto reminded Phil that not all may feel as deep an affection for the state: "[A] man may show his social interest elsewhere as well as Wisconsin . . . [and] is no less socially minded because he prefers $5000 to $4000." He warned Phil against "economic myopia." The president of the university local of the American Federation of Teachers also protested against the insinuation that the faculty was overpaid.[51]

By grasping for middle ground, Phil also began to produce critics on both his right and his left. In late January 1931, regular letters began appearing in the *Capital Times* from old supporters of the elder La Follette disparaging Phil's comfortable working relationship with bankers and manufacturers. "A Taxpayer" criticized Phil's no raise policy as dictatorial, but "A Red" argued that the Progressives' proposals did not go far enough.[52] Despite the generally receptive mood, some of Phil's proposals generated a great deal of criticism. The proposed change in the primary election law (an obvious slap at the ineffectual Democrats) drew a sharp rebuke from the president of the Jefferson Club of Milwaukee: "[I]t will not only surely eliminate what is left of the Democratic Party [in] Wisconsin . . . but it will also prevent an effective expression of that large body of voters of Wisconsin who are from time to time most justifiably dissatisfied with the Republican candidate for president." Another writer suggested that the proposal would eliminate the important "watchdog" function of the two-party system.[53]

Despite having a clear leader in the governor's office and a united front in the legislature, the cry of "politics" continued to bedevil the Progressives. Although the appointments of David Lilienthal (who gave up a twenty-thousand-dollar salary to take the job) and Theodore Kronshage to the Railroad Commission were quickly and unanimously confirmed by the senate, the appointments of Joseph Beck to the Agriculture Commission and Herman Ekern to the Emergency Relief Board were more contentious. The two previous, unsuccessful candidates for governor received appointive positions from the successful one, and regardless of how qualified they were (and no one criticized their qualifications) it simply looked bad. Phil defended his appointments by asserting his right to appoint those sympathetic to the laws they were to administer. Progressives also had to deal with the perennial supreme court candidate John Reynolds. Reynolds had been attorney general since 1927 but had run against incumbent justice Chester Fowler in April 1930, lost, and then ran for reelection as attorney general, even though Progressives had begun to line up behind Alvin C. Reis. Now, in February 1931, less than a month after taking his oath of office, Reynolds announced his candidacy against Fowler, who was running for a full ten-year term. Uncharacteristically, Phil gave only lukewarm public support to Reynolds and privately remarked that his candidacy was "ill-considered." Phil stayed out of the fight in order to preserve Progressive harmony and stay out of politics for a time. Reynolds lost on April 7, 1931, and did not run for the court again.[54]

Progressives scored early victories in getting their program through the legislature. The Emergency Highway Relief Bill passed the assembly on March 18 and the senate on March 24. The legislature also approved the creation of the Executive Council. The various parts of the public power program also passed, including the joint resolution calling for a constitutional amendment allowing the state to operate power plants, except for the Loomis Bill allowing municipalities to acquire their own utilities, which died in the senate in June. And at the end of June, Phil signed into law the state Labor Code, written largely by Senator Thomas Duncan. In July, Phil appointed Duncan his executive secretary, a controversial move that placed an influential member of the legislature in the governor's inner circle. Progressives also succeeded in enacting a tax on oleomargarine, income tax revision, and the reorganization of the Railroad Commission into a strong Public Service Commission. It was the shortest legislative session since 1909, but the chief issues of the 1930 campaign remained unresolved: chain banking, unemployment insurance, revision of the corrupt practices act, and unemployment relief. By the end of the session, however, it became apparent that the Stalwarts were unwilling to allow the Progressives to get everything they wanted. Conservatives, led by Walter Goodland of Racine, regrouped and defeated a number of bills, including those for relief.[55]

By the end of the session, Phil, too, became less conciliatory toward the Stalwarts and more strident in his public statements. In another message to the legislature on June 4, 1931, he scolded the members of the legislature for not doing more. He promised to veto any tax bill that would force relief to be funded through property tax, especially while income from dividends remained untaxed. He specifically mentioned chain banking restrictions, unemployment insurance, and general relief as subjects that needed to be taken up. Isabel also joined Progressives in attacking Stalwarts, delivering a radio talk in early August in which she outlined the Progressive accomplishments and chalking up the session's failures to the "continuous pounding of lobbyists." The honeymoon was over.[56]

It was widely believed that Phil would call a special session of the legislature to meet sometime in the fall, and he did plan to do so provided there was enough time to study the issues properly. In the meantime, Phil returned to the stump giving not overtly political talks, but speeches that stressed the same themes he had during his first months in office. In Milwaukee on July 6, he discussed the need for "equality of opportunity." The next day he addressed a 4-H convention in Madison on "citizenship." And in Manitowoc he told a crowd of a thousand people that unemployment could be cured in the same way that industrial accidents had been reduced: through cooperation between employers and employees, guided, he did not need to say, by Progressive legislation.[57] Again and again, Phil stressed the need for greater equality of wealth, not just as an immediate solution to the Depression, but to correct a long-term trend of monopolization and centralization of economic power. The Internal Revenue Service in 1930, he told students at Florida's Miami University,

> reported more swollen incomes than in any year, except the period of war profiting. The greatest earnings in the history of the world have been reported, yet there is not a man in contact with the merchant, the small manufacturer, the farmer, or the mass of workman [sic] who is not aware that for a year in some cases, and for five years in others, the mass of our citizens have been having difficulty in making both ends meet, and keeping out of the clutches of bankruptcy court.

Yet in another speech in May, Phil defended Wisconsin's record of providing service financed by a fairer tax system than in other states. In an address before the annual convention of the National Association of Retail Grocers in Milwaukee in August, he told his audience that no one individual could solve the Depression, but cooperative effort could redistribute the wealth the country produced. To end the Depression required a greater equality of wealth, and this required an active government curtailing unfair business practices and fairer taxation. By September, Phil had become even more strident. In a speech at Fond du Lac on Labor Day, he gave some chilling statistics that indicated the underconsumption of the vast quantities of goods produced by industry. He went on to recount the technological displacement of workers and the frightening result: the fewer people needed to produce manufactured goods, the fewer who were able to buy them. He praised the legislature's work so far, especially the Labor Code, but he insisted that the government had to use its power to redistribute wealth and thereby equalize purchasing power. He repeatedly used World War I as an example of how quickly and efficiently the government could mobilize the nation and claimed the only thing holding the government back was lack of political leadership.[58]

Phil also made clear that these abstract ideas would be enacted in state policy. When the legislature's interim committee on unemployment met with him, he told them that the wealthy "must come to the rescue of the situation." In an October conference of industrial leaders in the executive office, he bluntly told the assembled business leaders that the practice of trying to revive the economy by restoring confidence had failed and that public confidence in both government and business was collapsing.[59] Business leaders, however, began to dig in their heels once Phil was no longer actively courting their support. The Wisconsin Manufacturers Association promised to fight any restriction of hours and any compulsory unemployment insurance plan. Fred Clausen of Horicon, president of the Van Brunt Manufacturing Company, dissenting from the interim unemployment committee's recommendations, opposed any unemployment insurance and the eight-hour day. While Phil received criticism from business leaders, he also faced hostility from the Wisconsin Socialist Party. Powerful in Milwaukee, the party promoted its own solution to the Depression: immediate relief, unemployment insurance, a five-day week, and a six-hour day. To conservatives, it appeared as if Phil had suddenly taken a sharp left turn. It promised to be a stormy special session.[60]

While Phil was planning the special session, the La Follette family went through a horrible summer of personal tragedy. On July 25, Phil left for a six-day cruise to Nova Scotia, telling a reporter that he needed "six days of sleep"; on his return he suffered an infected foot that kept him bedridden for days. Just after Phil returned from his vacation, Robert and Rachel lost their first baby shortly after its birth. Then, still grieving the loss of its youngest member, the family lost Belle on August 19. Three days earlier, she had undergone a routine medical checkup in a Washington hospital. During a proctoscopic examination, the device inserted by the doctor tore her colon, which soon became infected. Robert and Phil were both in Madison at the time and raced to their dying mother's bedside. Robert took the train to Washington; Phil, delayed by a treatment for his foot, followed in a chartered plane. They found her conscious, but within a few hours she died from peritonitis. Her funeral was held at the State Historical Society in Madison on August 21, and her children escorted her to her resting place next to Old Bob in Forest Hill Cemetery. It was a devastating loss for Phil, who had relied on Belle for emotional support throughout his life; at a critical time in his term, he also lost his most insightful political observer. Belle's death brought to the surface the introspective aspect of his personality and left him depressed for months.[61]

On November 17, Phil called for the legislature to meet on the twenty-fourth in special session. The governor specified what the legislature was to consider: unemployment relief, unemployment compensation, a tax bill, and legislative reapportionment. It was apparent that it would be a difficult session. Robert sympathized with "the tremendous strain" but noted that Phil was making a great impression in Progressive circles. "My only fear," he cautioned, "is that you will go beyond your strength, and I beseech you to husband your energies as much as possible under the circumstances." To draft his message to the legislature, which he called "the hardest job I've had yet," Phil retreated to the relative tranquility of Maple Bluff Farm. When he finished with an initial draft, in late November, he sent it to Robert and Ralph Sucher in Washington for comment. Robert wryly predicted that it would make the wealthy "holler," and Ralph wrote that it reminded him of Belle's writing in its emphasis on practical things.[62] It was certainly the most important speech in his career. It was also one of his most strident. In what he called "the greatest domestic crisis since the Civil War," Phil told the legislature that Americans were divided into two groups: those who favored collective action to meet the emergency and those who opposed action in order to preserve their own wealth and privileges. He summed up what he had been telling audiences for the past few months. Monopolistic business practices had led to ruinous maldistribution of wealth that now threatened the political and economic health of the nation. He proposed four "courses of action" that could be taken: public ownership, business self-regulation, long-term economic planning, and redistribution of wealth through taxation. These were radical propositions, but the specific proposals were somewhat less grand. Phil recommended $16.5 million in direct relief to be administered by the state and by local governments and financed by increased taxes on large incomes, gifts, and inheritances, compulsory unemployment insurance, and reorganization of the banking system. It was assumed that the bills would be amended during debate, but as he ended his address he urged his supporters to hold fast. He told them that they would be assailed as communists and anarchists for their part in "the age-old struggle of mankind to build a better world."[63]

On one level, Phil's closing words were meant to brace reluctant senators, but the entire message was clearly aimed at a much broader audience. The Associated Press and the Scripps-Howard wire services picked up the story and reprinted excerpts from the message widely. Phil became something of a darling among Progressive intellectuals, and Wisconsin again became a state to watch. *The Nation*, always eager to admire a La Follette, repeated its central ideas and urged governors of other states and President Hoover to read it carefully. Louis Brandeis sent a note of congratulations, and Charles Beard remarked that "[i]n the history of American public documents there has not appeared a more important or reasoned state paper."[64] After two years of depression, a vigorous call resonated with a public disenchanted with the lack of ideas from the federal government. "Jobs—not doles. Work—not charity. That is Wisconsin's idea of solving the problem of unemployment," trumpeted journalist Frazier Hunt in January 1932. Hunt interviewed Phil and described him in an article as a kind of political philosopher who pursued a middle ground between traditional American values of individual action and more radical ideas of collectivization. During lunch at the university, the governor told Hunt that his state was "unalterably opposed" to communism: "The whole Wisconsin idea is based on *individualism*—the rights, fortune, chances and opportunities of the individual. We're opposed to anything and everything that works against the individual."[65] By defusing the red menace up front (as La Follette had done in the 1920s), Phil could lay claim to traditional American rhetoric and turn it on its head. Progressive government was not, as Stalwarts claimed, out to take away rights, but to ensure them for all citizens equally. He went on to speculate that either the federal government could act to redistribute purchasing power through tax policy or that businesses themselves could work together "to clean its own house." Either way, Wisconsin could be an experimental state in developing public policy. Alternatively, Phil acknowledged, the federal government could continue bungling through with "half-baked, piecemeal legislation." Pursuing such a middle ground, of course, left Progressives open to attacks from both the right and the left, but the very idea of directed and rational government action attracted a great deal of attention.

The difficulties encountered by the Progressives in June at the end of the last session, however, only got worse. The Stalwarts were able to organize the senate and elected Milwaukee Senator Oscar H. Morris as president pro tem, a startling defeat for the well-respected Herman Severson. After most of the administration bills had been introduced (including a $16,750,000 relief package), Socialist members demanded more. Milwaukee mayor Daniel Hoan, also a Socialist, opposed the relief bill because it would take more from wealthy Milwaukeeans than it returned to the city's poor. Business and industry groups, including the Milwaukee Association of Commerce and the Wisconsin Manufacturers Association, also publicly denounced the relief plan. Public hearings in the senate attracted some three hundred spectators, and numerous business leaders testified against increased taxes and the unemployment insurance bill, melodramatically claiming these measures would ruin their businesses. Others claimed that companies just needed time to develop their own plans or that their workers did not really want relief. Unlike the last session, the Stalwarts were from the beginning much better organized. "The Stalwarts are moving heaven and earth to beat our program," Phil wrote Robert. "Old timers say there has been nothing like it in years." During debate, Stalwarts proposed several amendments, including proposals to reduce the total relief sum to $5 million and to have the funds distributed solely by local governments rather than by a state agency. On December 19, the senate finally killed the relief bill and then passed a substitute introduced by Philip Nelson of Maple. The Nelson plan, later revealed to have been written by a business lobbyist and introduced by Nelson before he had even read it, provided for $6 million of relief funded by a tax provision that would not have produced nearly enough revenue to provide the appropriation; the state would have had to rely on property taxes to make up the shortfall. Progressive senators held together, but tempers flared. Stalwarts delayed again after the Christmas recess through a series of parliamentary maneuvers, including a call of the house that took up an entire day. When one member called Phil a Socialist, Senator Walter Polakowski retorted that Phil "couldn't be an office boy in the socialist movement." When Senator Walter Hunt demanded to know what the Stalwarts were stalling for, Thomas Duncan quipped that there must be some disagreement among lobbyists. The next day, sensing that the conservative members of the legislature would not budge, Phil began preparing a new bill, believing that the real objections were to the sheer amount of relief.[66]

Although Phil decided to propose a compromise bill that would pass both the senate and the assembly, he kept swinging at the Stalwarts to keep public opinion on the side of the Progressives. On January 5, 1932, he delivered another address to the legislature. He recited figures to demonstrate that the need for relief was only growing and berated the legislature for not providing anything at all. He reiterated in some detail his insistence on raising revenue through income tax rather than property tax. Then he attacked the senators themselves: "I am convinced that the conservative majority in the [s]enate is displaying a dangerous and reckless disregard for the basic safety of the state in refusing to grant adequate funds for the relief of the hungry and for the overburdened property taxpayer." He promised to veto any provision that depended on an increase in property taxes to fund relief payments or work projects. The next day, the assembly quickly passed the new administration relief bill 73 to 15, but the opposition to it was now led by Speaker Perry, who objected to Phil's address and the blunt statement of what he would and would not sign. In the senate, Walter Goodland declared Phil a dictator during a speech that referred to the administration's proposals as "ridiculous" and "objectionable." The *Milwaukee Journal* compared Phil to King John at Runnymede as well as to George III and Mussolini. The war for relief continued in the media. Phil broadcast an address on Milwaukee radio station WISN to promote Progressive arguments for relief. He urged listeners to contact Milwaukee Senators Daggett, Morris, and Gettelman and urge them to back the administration bill. Isabel joined the battle, writing a long column describing the view from the senate's visitors' gallery and the many letters she received from the unemployed.[67]

In the end, the stormy session ended in compromise. The relief bill that was passed provided $8 million, "far less" than Phil considered necessary, but raised "in a fairer fashion" than Stalwarts had wanted, by a surtax on 1931 incomes and a limited dividend tax, the Stalwarts having blocked a general tax on corporations. Phil signed a two-year tax on chain stores, but nothing was done on chain banking. A plan to stabilize industrial employment and wages failed even after some Progressives declined to support it, and legislation to enforce an eight-hour day died after it had been loaded with thirty amendments and a $10 million farm subsidy.[68] The most significant result of the special session was the enactment of the Unemployment Reserves and Compensation Act, written largely by University of Wisconsin economist Harold Groves. Unemployment compensation was not a new idea—Henry Huber had introduced a similar bill regularly since 1921, and Groves had discussed the idea extensively with Paul Raushenbush and Elizabeth Brandeis. Its passage was a mix of intense effort and compromise. Communists and business leaders joined hands against the measure; Raushenbush and Brandeis lobbied recalcitrant senators (in one case using a Catholic priest to convince a conservative Milwaukee senator). Public hearings drew many to speak in favor of the bill, including one farmer who told the senate that he thought the bill would mean more money for workers to buy his dairy products ("Now I have to go home to milk the cows," he said as he finished his statement). Manufacturers had opposed the bill in the past, claiming they preferred to develop their own, voluntary plans. Phil disarmed their argument, announcing that the bill would contain a proviso making it null if 200,000 (later amended to 175,000) workers were covered under such voluntary plans by 1934. Such a proviso meant that now few could oppose it without appearing callous to the suffering of the unemployed.[69] Yet the bill was not as radical as its opponents claimed. It operated on the progressive idea that employers must keep the welfare of their workers in mind as well as their own profit. The bill did not simply provide a government stipend to the unemployed—doles were anathema to Progressives as well as Stalwarts. The act allowed—and expected—a great deal of individual responsibility on the part of employers. Rather than one gigantic pool, each employer of ten or more workers contributed 2 percent of payroll to a separate, state-controlled account; to encourage employers to maintain employment, the company could reduce its contribution to 1 percent when the account reached $55 per employee and stop altogether when it reached $75 per employee. Relief payments that dropped the account below these levels required contributions to begin again. Unemployed workers could draw up to ten dollars a week from their employer's account for up to thirteen weeks. Phil signed the bill on January 28, 1932.[70]

When the legislature adjourned in February, Progressives had accomplished a number of long-standing goals. The state had also become a model for innovation in dealing with the crisis. Phil and others confidently looked forward to a second term and an increased majority in the senate, leading to even more far-reaching reforms. Events in the spring, however, would knock Progressives out of office and reshape Wisconsin politics.

CHAPTER FIVE

The Progressive Party

In early 1932, the Wisconsin Progressives emerged from the legislative sessions intact and with a remarkable record. The legislature had passed a major relief bill, a program for unemployment insurance, and a tax program that shifted much of the financial burden from small property owners to those with large incomes. The Unemployment Compensation Act in particular was groundbreaking, and its passage reinforced the Progressives' greatest rhetorical tool: while the federal government did nothing, Wisconsin—led by Progressives—could develop and implement innovative policies to deal with the economic crisis. Just as important as the Progressive faction's renewed reputation was the Stalwarts' shifting public image. Instead of appearing as thoughtful questioners of new untested programs, an image they had carefully crafted for years, they instead seemed like blustering lackeys of big business, poised to oppose any relief plan at all. Stalwart intransigence reinforced what Progressives had been saying for years: the Stalwarts were out to protect the wealthy. Even more important than their legislative success, Progressives had framed the debate in their favor, forcing the Stalwarts to engage in a fight over how much relief rather than whether there would be any relief at all.

Governor Philip La Follette in particular had benefited from the Progressives' success. His vigorous public statements on the Stalwart senators' reluctance to pass a relief bill combined with his own populist image (he had cut his own salary to five hundred dollars a month) underscored his sympathy with the unemployed. In February 1932, he met with Charles Dawes, president of the Reconstruction Finance Corporation, to discuss the establishment of a state agency to manage Wisconsin banks' applications for loans; even the arch-conservative former vice president seemed willing to take Phil's advice. By summer, conservative Republicans would be afraid to run anyone against him, and his political future seemed bright. Progressives looked forward confidently to a second term and more relief measures and reforms.[1]

With the legislature adjourned, Phil and the Progressives began focusing on national issues. In March, he and Robert delivered a joint address sponsored by the *Washington Star* and nationally broadcast on the radio by NBC. Phil gave a characteristically dramatic speech comparing the Depression to being lost in the forest. He iterated themes now familiar to Wisconsin voters: twenty-five years of predatory business practices had so badly concentrated wealth that the entire economic system was in danger of collapse. He pointed to Wisconsin's history of political and economic reform but, foreshadowing his growing interest in a national role, noted that "Progressives of Wisconsin recognize that no single state can alone solve our problems."[2] Since February, Wisconsin Progressives had also been booming Nebraska Senator George Norris for the Republican presidential nomination; Phil had nearly worn himself out attending district delegate meetings and urging Robert and Senator John Blaine to arrange some speaking dates of their own. Like the NBC address, the progressive Republican platform was particularly vocal in denouncing the "tyrannical power" of special interests and called for economic planning, unemployment reserves, public works, a public power system, and tax reform. Progressives had controlled the Wisconsin delegation at almost every convention since 1904, and they looked forward confidently to making trouble for President Herbert Hoover. Although his duties restricted his schedule, Phil delivered several speeches on behalf of the Progressive candidates in the western and southwestern part of the state.[3]

Despite recent successes, Phil was worried and returned from a February speaking tour in the plains states "less sanguine" about the future. Rumors began circulating that former governor Walter J. Kohler would run against Phil for the Republican nomination for governor. Because he had virtually disappeared after 1931, Kohler was not at all associated in the public mind with the Republicans, who had discredited themselves during the special session by opposing the unemployment compensation and unemployment relief bills. And then there were the Democrats. Governor Franklin Roosevelt of New York was the front-runner for the Democratic presidential nomination, and he, too, had a national reputation as a reformer and successful governor. The La Follettes, however, were skeptical. Phil's brother-in-law Ralph Sucher remarked that it appeared that Roosevelt could not be stopped. "No doubt," he wrote Phil, "he is honest, with fine impulses, and is a charming gentleman, but he was a shouter for the war and the League . . . [and] asks for a blank check from the voters in the primaries." Sucher assured Phil that a strong Democratic candidate would not hurt him personally, but Phil was less sure. On March 16, the North Dakota primary produced a record Democratic turnout in a state that had been solidly Republican and one of the strongest areas of support for the elder La Follette. In Wisconsin, the Democratic primary was generating much interest because the state party was closely split between supporters of Roosevelt and former nominee Al Smith. The national Democratic Party contained both conservative and progressive elements, and a candidate like Roosevelt who called for a greater effort to address the Depression could draw from La Follette's voter base. The political landscape was changing, and it was by no means clear how the Democratic resurgence would affect the Progressives in general and Phil in particular.[4]

Conservative Republicans were also preparing to "get Phil." On February 11, the *Uncensored News*, a weekly tabloid edited by former *Capital Times* reporter William Dawson, had begun circulating in Wisconsin. The publication resembled a newspaper only superficially: it printed rumor, innuendo, and complete fabrication in order to discredit the La Follettes and other Progressives. The first issue included headlines such as "La Follette 'Gang' Get Rich in Politics," "Phil Stalls Relief for Unemployed," and "Socialist Is in Love With Phil's Plans." The front page featured a cartoon depicting Phil, William Evjue, and Herman Ekern as drunken pirates cavorting around a treasure chest labeled "Profits of Radicalism." An open letter to Isabel demanded to know if it was true that she had used one thousand dollars of state money to purchase a dozen goblets for the Executive Residence. Such attacks may not have been convincing, but they kept anti–La Follette sentiment stirred up while Stalwarts regrouped. A libel suit would have been difficult because it was not clear exactly who financed its publication or directed its content. Moreover, a libel suit would have drawn the *Uncensored News* additional publicity. Even Progressives who dismissed the *Uncensored News*'s hysterics were concerned over growing discontent over taxes and cost of government. This was the conservatives' most potent argument: blaming the Progressives for high taxes. Despite Phil's own salary cut and his efforts to reduce government expenditures, the money for relief had to

come from somewhere. Progressives were successful in protecting property tax payers, which sat well in rural and small-town areas, but Stalwarts were preparing to raise the cry of higher income taxes in urban
areas, where Progressives had always been vulnerable.[5]

Phil became even more worried after April, when the Roosevelt candidacy produced an astonishing turnout of voters in Wisconsin's Democratic presidential preference primary. In 1928, only about 110,700 primary
voters had voted on the Democratic ballot; in 1932, the number jumped to
185,000. The total Democratic vote in the 1930 gubernatorial election was
only 170,000.[6] Although the increase in the number of Democratic votes
between 1930 and 1932 was not great in and of itself, the location of the
increases was significant. The greatest percentage increase occurred in
Milwaukee County and in the northwest, where Progressives had always
run strongest. In some of these counties the Democratic vote more than
doubled. At the same time, the vote in the Republican delegate race
declined from 240,297 in 1928 to 228,734 in 1932. The Republican vote
for governor in November 1930 had been nearly 393,000.[7] Those areas
where the Republican vote decreased, moreover, corresponded to the
areas where the Democratic vote had increased most sharply: Milwaukee
and the northwest. To Phil the implication was obvious—normally Progressive voters had participated in the Democratic primary. Isabel
reported to Fola that "our" Democrats had returned to their party to vote
for Roosevelt and that "our people" had a low turnout. Some political
observers suggested that there was really little for Progressives to worry
about, since voters could vote for a Democratic president and a Republican governor, thus allowing Roosevelt supporters to vote for Phil. This
assumed, of course, that Phil would be nominated in the primary—a result
that Phil was finding increasingly unlikely.

Progressives went into the summer campaigning season in what was for
them an unusual position: they had to defend the La Follette administration's policies and not just attack the Stalwarts. Phil invited reporters to
a series of "off-the-record" dinners at the Executive Residence in an
attempt to make the press more sympathetic. In May, he went on the
stump to accuse Stalwarts of raising "false issues." He defended the
state's deposits in the failed Capital City Bank, an organization in which
he and other Progressives held stock, by pointing out that there was actually less state money in it than when Kohler had been governor. In
response to Stalwart criticisms of higher taxes, Phil urged people to total

all their utility bills for an entire year, which he promised would be more than what they paid in taxes. He also read lists of well-known Stalwarts who seemed to be dodging their "fair" share of taxes, including Lucius Niemann, the owner of the *Milwaukee Journal*, who in 1930 paid only $1,212.59 in taxes on an income of over $1.25 million.[8] To organize Progressives, Phil planned meetings in each congressional district to line up support for his platform and "for the purpose of laying foundations for proper organization for the legislative fight." At the meetings Phil and other Progressives discussed the charges made by conservatives, explained their response, and planned future legislation. These strategy sessions, usually attended by between 350 and 500 supporters, served not only to unite Progressives behind legislative candidates but also to give them all the answers to the attacks made against the administration. These meetings buoyed Phil's spirits somewhat, but he sensed a general spirit of discontent. He noted to Robert in May that national economic conditions were worsening: "Unless something drastic is done . . . I doubt if things will hold together."[9]

In June, Phil and other Progressive leaders gathered with supporters from around the state in Madison to get their stories straight. More than four hundred campaign speakers gathered at the Lorraine Hotel, where a parade of state officials laid out the facts to the troops. Harold Groves told the audience that taxes were actually $10 million less than in the last year of the Kohler administration. Defending state salaries, Phil reminded them that the members of the Public Service Commission earned $9,000 less than the three chief officers of Madison Gas and Electric, and that four officers of the Neenah Paper Company made more than the seven supreme court justices. "When you go hunting," he quipped, "go where the ducks are." Joseph Beck recited the ways in which farmers were benefiting from La Follette administration policies. William Evjue, recalling the motto Fighting Bob had chosen for his own newspaper in 1909—"Ye shall know the truth and the truth shall make you free"—promised that the Progressives would run an "educational campaign." Simply by laying out the facts, he argued, campaign speakers could not fail to convince the voters to support Phil.[10]

Isabel again took on a major role in the fight, editing what became the Progressives' bible for the campaign, the *Progressive Campaign Textbook*. It opened with the platform of the progressive Republicans, which stated bluntly that the Depression had been caused by decades of concentration of wealth and was "a greatly accentuated phase of this contest" between the people and the special interests. It denounced the Hoover administration for failing to provide relief, revive purchasing power, or halt deflation. At the state level, the platform called for continued lowering of property taxes (and thereby lower taxes overall), shifting more of the state revenue to income taxes and new taxes on dividends. The platform included nods toward agriculture and, to a lesser extent, industrial workers, promising strict enforcement of the oleomargarine licensing laws and efforts to reduce hours of employment and maintain wage levels. It made special mention of Progressives' public power program. In short, it promised more of the same, highlighting the accomplishments of the 1931–32 legislative session and denouncing the "reactionary" senate. Nowhere did the platform mention the late Robert M. La Follette. The Progressive faction had come of age and was now underscoring its own accomplishments rather than the personality of its founder.

The textbook also included an extensive, catechism-like section outlining the hard questions local leaders and campaigners would face and the appropriate answers. ("Who was responsible for the depression?" No one person, but mainly business leaders and Stalwart Republicans.) Other questions responded to charges leveled at Progressives. The book defended the relief bill as fair to industrial communities because the higher burden in those counties falls on the wealthy. It promoted the fact that the grade-crossing elimination program had constructed ninety-one overpasses and employed 11,076 workers. And on and on, providing detailed information to refute Stalwart charges that the La Follette administration spent more than Kohler and that taxes were higher. Every campaigner could carry the slim volume in his or her pocket.[11]

As the textbook predicted, the Stalwarts relied on arguments against high taxes, expanding government, and ineffective relief. The grade-crossing elimination program in particular became a favorite target. The use of machinery reduced the number of jobs, Stalwarts said, and it brought too many strangers into local communities. One village had a banner stretched across a street proclaiming, "We've had our Phil." Others called the overpasses "Phil's roller-coasters."[12]

Neither conservative Republicans nor Democrats wasted time in preparing campaigns for the 1932 gubernatorial elections. By the end of May, four Republicans had announced their candidacies: Assembly Speaker Charles Perry, U.S. Marshall James Tittenmore, Milwaukee businessman Howard Greene, and Colonel Frank Scheller. The elephant behind the curtain was former Governor Walter J. Kohler. On May 24, he announced that he would not be a candidate for governor. Republican leaders supposedly wanted him to run for the U.S. Senate against Progressive John Blaine, but Kohler remained silent. He did not say that he would refuse a draft. Stalwarts had an even easier time lining up campaign issues. Residents of Milwaukee complained loudly that the city paid more in income taxes than it received in state aid. Greene was vociferous in his speeches. Despite a rash of budget cuts in May, he denounced extravagant government. "The state," he declared, "is overrun with the tax gatherers of these Pharohs [*sic*]."[13]

In early June, the Stalwarts met in Madison to write their platform and endorse candidates. A brief moment of levity occurred when Madison Mayor Albert Schmedeman welcomed the gathering, noting that his past experience as a diplomat made him well suited to the task but telling his audience that the next governor would in fact be nominated the following week at the Green Bay Democratic convention. In his keynote address, Greene depicted the Stalwarts as the defenders of individual rights against a cold-blooded political ring. The platform reflected this hostile tone, denouncing "inflated" state government and "failed" relief measures and promising to cut taxes, encourage business, and reduce the number of state agencies. Kohler did not attend the convention, and after a frantic day of trying to reach him in New York City, the convention chair received a telegram from him in which he said he would accept the endorsement if it were offered. The Stalwarts promptly endorsed Kohler; the other candidates withdrew. The convention also endorsed Harry Dahl of La Crosse for lieutenant governor, Senator Ben Gettelman of Milwaukee for secretary of state, Levi Bancroft for attorney general, and Elmer Samp for treasurer.[14]

Wisconsin Democrats met a few days later and took exactly the opposite approach. Rather than endorsing specific candidates, the convention endorsed all Democrats running. This included three candidates for the United States Senate, four for governor, two each for lieutenant governor and secretary of state, and four each for attorney general and treasurer. This was a remarkably shrewd move: a lively and contested primary would keep Democratic voters from participating in the Republican primary and so generate support for the eventual Democratic nominee. The platform adopted was almost as conservative as the Stalwarts' platform. It called for locally administered relief and voluntary industrial cooperation. The platform also denounced government waste and "excessive regulation," included only a vague promise of "fairness" to agriculture, and made no mention whatsoever of industrial labor.[15]

Unsurprisingly, the developing hot issue was taxation. As the Great Depression forced more and more property into arrears, Phil tried to cope

with the situation by sending questionnaires to all county treasurers solic-
iting information on financial conditions. A week later, on June 13, he
called on county officials to postpone real estate tax sales from July 1 to
October 15. His motivation may have been partly political, since there
was a growing tax revolt developing in some western counties. On June
15, some three thousand farmers from Juneau, Sauk, Monroe, Vernon, and
Columbia Counties collectively refused to pay any property taxes unless
they were reduced. They demanded cuts in the number of state employees and the university. One news service reporter noted that the tax
notices produced "an anguished howl," and he predicted that the chief
issue in the Republican primary would be taxation.[16]

On July 6, Phil announced his candidacy for reelection and issued
his personal platform. It was a pugnacious document that repeated much
of what had become familiar: monopoly of wealth, selfish business interests, and intractable Stalwart senators were all singled out as villains. The
remedies were also familiar. His platform called for lower property taxes,
reduction of hours of employment, relief, and public works. It also highlighted the Progressives' accomplishments in the past two years, including the labor code, unemployment compensation, and utility regulation. It
especially defended the tax policy and stressed the fact that property
taxes had been reduced. Compared to the Stalwart and Democratic platforms, it took much more radical—and more concrete—stands on policy.
As in the progressive Republican platform adopted prior to the presidential primary, there was no mention of Fighting Bob. Nonetheless, the language was reminiscent of the late senator: "If we stand today on the brink
of a precipice it is due to this wicked and selfish prostitution of the
agency of government for the relief of the rich and ignoring the poor." On
July 7, Lieutenant Governor Henry Huber, Secretary of State Theodore
Dammann, and Treasurer Solomon Levitan announced their candidacies,
and two days after that, Progressive State Senator Leonard C. Fons of Milwaukee announced his candidacy for attorney general.[17]

On July 18, Phil opened his campaign in ninety-degree heat in Sauk
City and was on the defensive from the very start. This first speech was
a defense of the administration's tax policies, and Phil reminded listeners that since he had been governor, property taxes had actually been
lowered. He traveled through central Wisconsin in the sweltering heat,
swigging orange juice to keep his voice, regularly attracting crowds of a
few thousand. In the city of Adams he cited several local farmers by
name and indicated that their taxes were lower than they had been the
previous year. In Auburndale he denied that Progressives had driven

away business, and in Neilsville he specifically advocated eliminating the exemption of dividends from income tax. As he continued into northern Wisconsin, he continued to emphasize property taxes but also stressed recent conservation efforts and public works. Sizable crowds continued to attend his addresses, but discontent was in the air. In Rhinelander, a United States Senate candidate and editor of the anti-La Follette *Ashland Press*, John Chapple, tried to break up one of Phil's speeches and was physically thrown from the hall. Other candidates began campaigning later in July, including Huber, Levitan, and Blaine, all of whom promoted the relief efforts of Phil's administration. Despite the tension, Phil enjoyed being on the road and delivering speeches, arguing with hecklers, and meeting young Progressives.[18]

Isabel, too, leapt into the campaign to a much greater extent than she had in 1930. Although she did not give the same outdoor speeches before large crowds as other campaigners, she did make a special effort to reach women. Her first extended trip took her to the north-central part of the state. In one small town she told a crowd of two hundred, mostly women, that the state "should be as important to a woman as her home; it is merely greater housekeeping for a larger family." The work was particularly rewarding to Isabel, whose efforts in 1930 were now making it much easier to attract women to Progressive meetings. Again these meetings often occurred in homes rather than in public buildings, and the enthusiasm was such that when the power went out at times, the audiences usually believed it to be a deliberate act by the power company to put a stop to their sessions. This was also a much more personal campaign for Isabel because she had witnessed firsthand how Phil and others had driven themselves to exhaustion in their efforts to, in her words, "generally lift ourselves up out of the depression," and now she had to defend them against often quite petty attacks. She herself had been maligned in the *Uncensored News* for supposed extravagance. The women in Isabel's audiences tended to ask questions about her life and her own experiences in the progressive cause, but she seldom lacked answers even for difficult questions on the Progressive platform or policies.[19]

The Stalwarts began their campaign in early August, and Walter Kohler quickly showed a great deal more fire than he had two years previously. In Beaver Dam, he denounced the Progressives for their "dishonest government" and promised to expose all the "broken promises," particularly the chain bank issue. He snidely referred to the grade crossings as roller coasters and asserted that the La Follette administration had done nothing to end unemployment. The attacks continued.

Throughout his campaign, Kohler used phrases like "orgy of spending" and "professional politicians." Both were familiar charges against the Progressives, but against the backdrop of the Depression, they carried new weight. Again money was spent freely on Kohler's behalf, some sixty-two thousand dollars by one *Capital Times* estimate.[20]

Phil tried to respond to the Stalwart campaign—and to its charges—with traditional insurgent rhetoric. He told one Milwaukee crowd that the Stalwarts were interested only in their own well-being, a charge that carried particular weight when the next day a *Capital Times* reporter revealed that eight Republican businessmen had donated more to Kohler's campaign than to charity. "The millionaires who live in Fox Point, in Chenequa and in River Hills," he joked to a crowd of about nine thousand in Milwaukee, "of course want relief to be a local problem. They are willing to care for all the unemployed millionaires in their midst!"[21]

Democrats watched gleefully as Progressives and Stalwarts swung at each other, and the Democratic candidates could not resist throwing gasoline on the fire. Schmedeman repeatedly denounced the "rule of factions" and urged Democrats to resist the temptation to vote in the Republican primary in order to be done with the bitter factionalism once and for all. Milwaukee attorney William Rubin in turn denounced both factions as "professional office-holders"; given the Democrats' record in the past thirty years, they could rightly claim to be amateurs. Democrats in fact spent more time attacking the Republicans than they did their primary opponents. Late in the campaign, rumors began circulating that anyone who intended to vote for Roosevelt in November *had* to participate in the Democratic primary; Phil and others devoted much of the last days of the campaign trying to squash the rumor.[22]

Despite the Progressives' best efforts and confidence, the primary results shocked liberal leaders and editors nationwide. In the Republican primary on September 20, Progressives lost the nomination for governor, lieutenant governor, attorney general, and treasurer; only Secretary of State Dammann squeaked out a thin victory. The total vote in the gubernatorial primary was nearly 900,000, a record turnout for the state. Of this total, 734,459 votes were cast for Republicans: 414,575 for Kohler, and 319,884 for Phil. Even more shocking was incumbent Senator John Blaine's loss to John Chapple, whom even Stalwarts found distasteful, by a scant 10,000 votes. Conservative newspapers heralded the results as a triumph of common sense over class warfare. The *Milwaukee Sentinel* bluntly declared that Phil lost because he was openly hostile to manufacturers and industrialists and because his "class prejudice led to unfair taxes on the wealthy." Evjue blamed—as he had in 1926 and 1928—a dirty fight of misinformation by the Stalwarts, funded by tens of thousands of dollars in unreported spending. He added a new twist and rebuked the defections of thousands of Democrats who had voted for Progressives in the past, leaving the election to Kohler.[23]

Evjue's observation was essentially correct. The total vote cast in the Democratic primary was 131,930. In 1930, the vote in the primary had been only 17,040. The dramatic increase, foreshadowed in the April delegate election, was caused by two related events. The first was the emergence of Franklin Roosevelt as the Democratic presidential nominee; his likely victory over Herbert Hoover created renewed interest in the Democratic Party throughout the state, even in the staunchly Progressive northwest. Additionally, in 1930 there had been only one Democratic candidate running for governor, but in 1932 there were three, all very attractive candidates sensing national victory, and all of the other state offices were contested as well. This Democratic revival cut into Progressive totals, costing Phil nine northern and western counties that Progressives had almost always carried. The industrialized eastern counties, crucial to Progressive victory in 1930, saw a similar jump in Democratic turnout. Between the 1930 and 1932 primary, the Democratic vote increased from 10.4 to 27.0 percent in Portage County, from 2.2 to 18.6 percent in Outagamie County, from 4.8 to 34.3 percent in Kewaunee County, from 3.3 to 18.6 in Milwaukee County, from .93 to 12.7 in Racine County, and from 4.8 to 21.6 percent in Kenosha County. The industrial lakeshore counties had been crucial to Progressive victory in 1930, and in those same counties in 1932 Democratic voting increased the most. Kohler solidly won the Republican primary. In short, the FDR-inspired revival drew votes from Progressives in agricultural areas and even more strongly in urban and industrial areas.[24]

For Phil, the first La Follette to lose a nomination since 1898, it was a humiliating defeat, and the governor's office seemed like a funeral parlor for the next three and a half months. The day after the primary, his sister Mary wrote to remind him of the excerpt from *Invictus* that had hung in their father's room for so many years: "It matters not how straight the gate, How charged with punishment the scroll. I am the master of my fate, I am the captain of my soul." This was probably of very little consolation. The big question was what Progressives would do next. Phil told reporters that more important men than he had lost elections but promised that "I am enlisted in the Progressive movement for life." The struggle, he promised, would continue. Some Progressives immediately

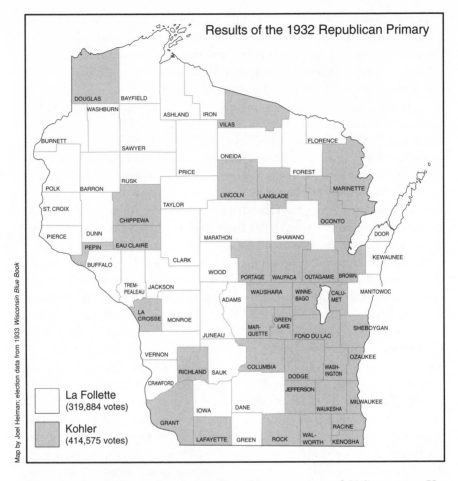

Results of the 1932 Republican Primary

DOUGLAS BAYFIELD
WASHBURN
ASHLAND   IRON
VILAS
BURNETT
SAWYER   FLORENCE
ONEIDA
PRICE   FOREST
POLK   BARRON   RUSK
LINCOLN LANGLADE   MARINETTE
ST. CROIX   TAYLOR
CHIPPEWA   OCONTO
PIERCE   DUNN
PEPIN   EAU CLAIRE   MARATHON   SHAWANO   DOOR
BUFFALO   CLARK   KEWAUNEE
WOOD
TREM-   JACKSON   PORTAGE WAUPACA OUTAGAMIE BROWN
PEALEAU   WAUSHARA   WINNE- CALU- MANITOWOC
ADAMS   BAGO   MET
LA
CROSSE   MONROE   GREEN
MAR- LAKE   SHEBOYGAN
JUNEAU   QUETTE   FOND DU LAC
VERNON   OZAUKEE
RICHLAND SAUK   COLUMBIA   WASH-
CRAWFORD   DODGE   INGTON
JEFFERSON   MILWAUKEE
IOWA   DANE   WAUKESHA
GRANT   RACINE
LAFAYETTE GREEN   ROCK   WAL-   KENOSHA
WORTH

☐ La Follette
(319,884 votes)

■ Kohler
(414,575 votes)

Map by Joel Heiman; election data from 1933 Wisconsin Blue Book

began urging independent campaigns for governor and U.S. senator. Yet most realized that another campaign and probable defeat would only hurt Progressives' long-term prospects, and so Progressives decided to focus on the legislative races. Progressives looked forward to controlling the assembly and to having some influence in the senate, where they counted on fifteen of thirty-three votes, including two Socialists and one progressive Democrat. Phil continued to campaign on behalf of Progressive candidates. At a rally at the capitol in early October, he pledged his support to them and expressed his willingness to speak on their behalf. "Although defeated," he told the crowd, "I am not going into a coma." Up until election day, he stumped the state for Progressives and even ventured into Illinois to speak on behalf of Franklin Roosevelt when George Norris fell ill and had to cancel his engagement.[25]

On election day, November 8, Progressives received an even more disturbing blow. They had been convinced that they would maintain a majority in the assembly and at least some presence in the senate, but again the Democrats stole their thunder. They not only elected a new governor, Albert Schmedeman, they swept all of the constitutional offices except secretary of state, electing fifty-nine of one hundred representatives and seven senators; only twenty-four members of the assembly would return, the greatest turnover in decades. Many of the new Democrats in the assembly came from areas that had been staunchly progressive for years, including seventeen from northwestern districts that had been represented by Progressives in the last session of the legislature. Milwaukee's delegation now included fifteen Democrats, three Socialists, and two Republicans, whereas in 1931 it had been eight Socialists, eight Republicans, and only one Democrat. Both of Kenosha County's and all three of Racine County's seats switched from Republican to Democrat. Wisconsin's congressional delegation would be made up of five Democrats, four progressive Republicans, and one Stalwart Republican. President-elect Roosevelt had long coattails.[26]

As Progressives and Democrats alike got over the shock of the 1932 election results, Phil considered an intriguing new possibility: a federal appointment. Shortly after the election, an article by Ernest K. Lindley appeared in the *New York Herald-Tribune* suggesting Phil as a potential secretary of the interior. Between his election and inauguration, Roosevelt made a special effort to maintain the support of progressive Republicans. Phil had joined a number of other prominent Progressives in supporting Roosevelt, including Hiram Johnson, George Norris, and Bronson Cutting. In assembling his cabinet, Roosevelt eventually included progressive Republicans Harold Ickes as secretary of the interior and Henry A. Wallace as secretary of agriculture, and Phil was on the short list for a similar appointment. Phil was skeptical of the "cabinet business." He agreed with Robert that if Roosevelt's overtures to Progressives were genuine then they should support the president-elect's decision "to take the Progressive course." Phil had met Roosevelt for the first time that April and had a generally favorable impression, but he had thought him somewhat superficial, lacking both a clear understanding of the causes of the Depression and the intellectual rigor Phil thought necessary for political leadership. Phil also speculated that Roosevelt was simply trying to lock in Progressive support for 1936 when the Republicans might nominate someone more liberal than Hoover. Although Phil

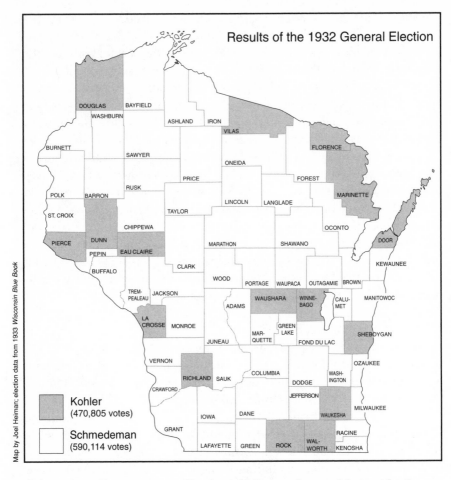

Map by Joel Heiman; election data from 1933 *Wisconsin Blue Book*

Results of the 1932 General Election

Kohler
(470,805 votes)

Schmedeman
(590,114 votes)

did not actually expect an offer, he told Robert he would consider it very carefully. He promised his brother that he would not consider any position without first conferring with him, Cutting, and Norris.[27]

In the final months of Phil's term in office, a time in which things were, as he put it, looking bleak, a new opportunity presented itself. James Causey of Rockford, Illinois, an old admirer of Phil's father and friend of the La Follette family, invited Phil and Isabel to dinner. Causey had amassed a small fortune in a Colorado brokerage firm. At dinner, he suggested that Phil and Isabel go to Europe for "a real exploration into the facts and minds of Europe." Phil could, Causey explained, easily pay for the trip by writing a series of articles for syndicated publication in newspapers, and Causey offered to advance him the necessary funds. After discussing the matter during their drive back to Madison, Phil and

Isabel decided to take his offer. Soon they had rented a house on the west side of Madison, arranged for their housekeeper to take care of the children, and were prepared for a long European trip. As Schmedeman and Roosevelt prepared their administrations, Phil wound down his, which became particularly difficult during the last few weeks. "The last couple of days have been trying emotionally," he wrote Mary while waiting in his office to escort Schmedeman to the capitol rotunda for his inauguration. "People coming into the office all stirred up, tears in their eyes and etc. It has been more of a strain than I anticipated." The day of inauguration, Phil and Isabel left Madison to spend a few days with the family in Washington before traveling to New York to sail to Europe on January 5.[28]

Another purpose of the trip to Washington was to confer with Robert and other Progressives about potential cabinet positions. Phil remained unconvinced that Roosevelt would really pursue a progressive course, and he did not want to participate in an administration with which he was not in total accord. In New York, he met with diplomat (and later first American ambassador to the Soviet Union) William Bullitt, who thought that Progressives faced a "grave crisis" in Roosevelt. He also talked for an hour with Colonel Edward House, Woodrow Wilson's political manager. House was vague but talked at length about the need for young Progressives to support Roosevelt's administration. Phil encouraged this line of thought but remained noncommittal. He wrote Robert that he thought it unwise for Progressives to "put its eggs in F.D.R.'s basket" unless Roosevelt would seriously apply his administration to relief and reform. On this Phil was adamant; it wasn't enough for Roosevelt to get Progressives, the Progressives had to be sure they had "got" Roosevelt. Phil left on his trip determined that unless Progressives were convinced that Roosevelt was willing to take their advice seriously, it would be unwise to join his official family.[29]

Despite Phil's hesitancy, representatives of Roosevelt continued to court him, although not very energetically. On January 9—after Phil and Isabel had sailed—Robert received a telegram from Roosevelt's future secretary of the treasury Henry Morgenthau Sr. requesting a meeting with Phil. Colonel House, evidently, had not informed Morgenthau of his meeting with Phil, which angered Robert. "It seems very poor work on the part of Roosevelt's staff," he wrote Phil, "to let you slip through their fingers. Certainly House must have known you were sailing and if Roosevelt wanted to see you why didn't he say so[?]."[30]

The *La Fayette* departed New York on January 5, and for most of the weeklong voyage Phil worked, pounding away on a portable typewriter, on addresses he was to deliver at the London School of Economics, the English-Speaking Union, and the Royal Institute of International Affairs. Phil and Isabel disembarked at Plymouth at 4 A.M. on a drizzly Friday the thirteenth and caught an 8:25 train for London. Phil recorded his detailed observations of Great Britain: the dole system, the public figures he met, even the cost of dinners (Sat 14: "dined Italian Restaurant Soho—9s."). It was enlightening to learn how European nations coped with the Depression, and he interviewed as many government officials and intellectuals as he could. He also shared with audiences his views on world politics and how Wisconsin had dealt with the economic crisis. In his address on British-American relations to the English-Speaking Union on January 17, he stressed the importance of facts over sentiment, noting that the "hands across the sea" appeal was no longer effective given the economic conditions in the United States. Phil's observations of British life reinforced his earlier belief that although British liberals were discouraged and divided, the Depression seemed to be affecting Great Britain less than it was the United States. This he ascribed to the dole system, which he reasoned had kept purchasing power strong despite declining production. "Whatever may be the merits one way or the other, America [also] has come to the 'dole,'" he wrote in his diary, "but it is a combination of private charity and public grants, with the advantages of neither and some of the bad features of both." His experiences in Great Britain reinforced his belief in the desperate need to expand purchasing power in the United States.[31]

On January 24, Phil and Isabel left for the continent and after stopping briefly in Brussels continued on to Germany, which everyone in Great Britain had told Phil was the center of the European situation. Phil toured the industrial city of Essen, including nitrate plants, which he thought could be duplicated at Muscle Shoals. In Berlin, they visited the museums and got caught in a massive demonstration by the Socialist *Arbeiter Partei* (the back-and-forth political shouts reminded him of Wisconsin-Minnesota football games). The orderliness of the crowd impressed him, and he thought it belied the popular image of Germany as a nation on the edge of chaos. Things took an uglier turn a few days later when an ill President Paul von Hindenburg appointed Adolf Hitler chancellor; in celebration of the event, Nazis held a rally in front of the French embassy and sang patriotic war songs from the 1870s. Despite the "critical and dangerous" atmosphere, Phil met with several local officials about unemployment and financial difficulties. He also spoke at length with Karl Brandt, the head of the Institute for Agricultural

Co-operatives about the comparative agricultural conditions in the United States and Germany. Conservative and reactionary forces in Germany had outmaneuvered and divided liberals, much as Phil believed they had in Great Britain, and he worried about the consequences. The political situation, especially the suppression of free press, was so unstable that Phil stopped writing letters for ten days until he had left Germany, and even then he noted that he would be more frank about his observations in person. He and Isabel left Germany with a disturbing vision of how the Depression could fuel people's fears, and how those fears could then be manipulated by reactionary leaders.[32]

From Berlin, Phil and Isabel traveled through Poland to Moscow. All along the rail route, Phil was astonished at the vast numbers of soldiers and everywhere the energy of people "moving to and fro, from office to house, from shop to store, and back again, without getting just what they want or expect." Food prices meant that most people had little to eat, and every village they encountered seemed on the verge of crisis. He saw both a vision of what the Depression could do to the United States and an untapped market for American produce and manufactured goods. His observations were not far off. Within a year, collectivization would decrease Russian agricultural production to the point of mass starvation.[33]

Phil's Europe trip was punctuated by regular updates from Fola on the developing Roosevelt administration and Phil's potential role in it. In late January, newspapers began reporting that Montana Senator Thomas Walsh would be named attorney general and either Phil or Bronson Cutting would be offered the Interior Department. Alf Rogers, Fola wrote, cautioned that Interior offered few opportunities for public service and too many for political entanglements. Phil generally agreed with Cutting's course—that he would not accept an offer unless another Progressive were included in the cabinet—but he went even further. In Europe he was seeing how reactionary forces had let the Depression become increasingly critical until people had no choice but between far left and far right, at which point they usually opted for what best offered order. He suggested that "it will be for the best if it works out that none of us are in his cabinet, and are left free to use this year to organize ourselves into a closer and more definitely organized group." The image of a divided and powerless Progressive organization suddenly seemed a realistic, if desperate, possibility. Nonetheless, Phil recognized how difficult it would be to decline an offer for a cabinet post, and he wondered if he should avoid writing anything on—or even visiting—the Soviet Union lest he become too controversial. Fola advised him that he should rely on reporting the facts on such an important issue, as "Daddy" had in 1922. After Phil had left the Soviet Union, newspapers began reporting that Roosevelt would offer him the ambassadorship to the Soviet Union, although such a post would have removed him from the domestic scene, a move perhaps intended to be something close to a Siberian exile. In early February, after a few days in Italy (including an audience with Pope Pius XI), Phil received a telegram from Robert urging Phil to return to the United States to meet with Roosevelt personally. They cut short their trip and embarked for the United States. Isabel returned to Madison, and Phil remained in New York in order to finish his articles and visit the president in Washington. The articles were syndicated and appeared in Wisconsin and national newspapers, giving Phil a reputation as an insightful observer of foreign affairs.[34]

Progressives in general and the La Follette family in particular were anxious to see if Roosevelt would push Democrats along a liberal course, but they were wary of a new liberal leader from outside the progressive Republican circle that had dominated liberal thought since 1918. In late February, Roosevelt called Robert to sound him out on the possibility of Phil accepting appointment to either the Federal Trade Commission (FTC) or the Power Commission. Thomas Duncan, Phil's former secretary, surprised Robert by suggesting that Phil accept, noting that 1934 would be a bad year to run for governor with Robert running for reelection to the U.S. Senate. Phil briefly considered the FTC, but he decided to decline since it would have meant giving up politics. The Power Commission was attractive, but he worried that the post would be purely administrative with no opportunity to push for a public power program.[35]

Phil and Robert finally met with Roosevelt on March 21, 1933. Phil went into the meeting remembering his earlier impression of Roosevelt's habit of appearing to agree with whatever he was hearing rather than sifting contradictory information and reaching his own conclusions. Meeting at the White House a year later was different. During the first part of the meeting, the three discussed relief, Robert prodding the president for quick action to meet the immediate needs of the unemployed, especially since legislatures were in session and would need to pass bills for matching provisions. Then Roosevelt asked Phil to report on Europe. Phil told the president that he was most concerned by how the Depression had made the continent dangerously unstable; he suggested that war might break out at any time and disrupt domestic recovery. He pointed to the million shabby huts built by the destitute outside of Berlin as a measure of the desperation. He also suggested that recognition of the Soviet

Union by the U.S. government would provide a vast market of 165 million people for American agricultural surplus, despite Soviet officials' repeated requests for heavy machinery. Finally, after listening attentively to Phil's description but giving no indication of his own plans, Roosevelt got to the point of the meeting. Phil later wrote that the president "was very anxious to have me join his administration . . . and he wanted to know what I was interested in." The president suggested the Power Commission, some kind of national transportation position, the Federal Trade Commission, or public works administrator. Phil's response was carefully thought out and respectful. He told Roosevelt that the president might need friends in the future and that he could be of greater service "formulating" public opinion, and there were many who were better suited to administrative tasks. Phil promised to keep in touch with the president: "May we leave it for the present that as the battle lines form in the months ahead, if I can help you in a *real* fight, call on me?" [emphasis original]. Despite this rebuff of the president, and Phil's sense of being underwhelmed, their relationship remained friendly.[36]

The La Follette brothers' visit to the White House renewed public speculation as to Phil's appointment to the cabinet or some other federal post or as ambassador to the Soviet Union. "I only called to pay my respects," Phil told reporters, "that's all I can say." He did, however, promise to make his views on the Soviet Union known in a speech to the Foreign Policy Association of New York later that month. Phil spent the next several weeks in New York writing his articles on European conditions for the Hearst Press. Although he refused to discuss his meeting with Roosevelt, he announced that he would return to Madison to resume his law practice. The *Capital Times* reported that Phil's decision not to take a post in Washington resulted in part from his wish to remain in Wisconsin and work on relief at the state level. The other reason— not reported by the *Times*—was that he was unwilling to be swallowed up in the first liberal administration in twelve years and was "skittish" about Roosevelt's lack of a coherent program, which differed vastly from Phil's custom of advancing only carefully developed and researched proposals.[37]

Phil returned to his neglected law practice and spent the rest of the year lawyering, delivering public lectures, and conferring with Progressives on their political future and the Roosevelt administration. He traveled to Washington in May to discuss public works bills sponsored by Robert and Bronson Cutting, but he was discouraged by the smaller amounts proposed by administration officials. Progressive leaders continued to discuss their future throughout 1933; state leaders dropped by Phil's office regularly, and Phil spoke at meetings around the state, each preceded by a conference of local leaders.[38]

Despite the cordiality of his meetings with Roosevelt, Phil began to speak out against some aspects of Roosevelt's New Deal programs, which struck Phil as uncoordinated and contradictory. In the first three months of Roosevelt's administration, Congress passed an abundance of legislation to respond to the Depression. For immediate relief of the unemployed, Congress passed the Federal Emergency Relief Act, which provided $500 million to state and local agencies. The National Recovery Administration (NRA) attempted to restore industrial production and to end unfair competition by supervising the creation of "production codes" regulating labor conditions, wages, and prices. The Agricultural Adjustment Act (AAA), which established the Agricultural Adjustment Administration, attempted to raise farm prices by subsidizing farmers' production cuts. Many Progressives approved of Roosevelt's vigorous action, but others, like Phil, remained skeptical that the programs would be anything more than a temporary solution.

In late September, in an address to Waukesha businessmen, Phil denounced the administration's economic policies, particularly the Agricultural Adjustment Administration's practice of cutting production when people were hungry. He declared that the Soviet Union or China could easily absorb the surplus and pay farmers for their produce. He also attacked relief measures that paid the unemployed to do nothing, which did not solve the fundamental problems of the Depression. In Los Angeles, he debated with Lincoln Steffens on the question "Can Democracy Function in America?" In an interview with the *Los Angeles Illustrated Daily News*, Phil bluntly gave his views on the economic system:

> Call it the profit system, or what you will, the fact is that an economic organization under which 1 per cent of the population get 60 per cent of the income cannot maintain itself under modern conditions. In labor as well as in the so-called professional occupations we have ceased to be the nation of self-sufficient individuals that we were in 1893. If 1 per cent of the population get 60 per cent of the income in bad times, economically speaking, there simply is not enough money, not enough purchasing power left among the other 99 per cent to keep the industrial machine running.

He went on to say that the NRA, or any recovery agency that depended on the cooperation of business, could not adequately redistribute wealth to restore genuine prosperity. While Steffens announced that the United States could take either the road to communism or the road to dictatorship, Phil recalled what he had seen in Europe and insisted that if only the wealthiest nation on earth pursued a more equitable distribution of its resources, economic well-being could be restored and democracy ensured.[39]

In Santa Fe, New Mexico, Phil was even more strident in a speech in the chamber of the state house of representatives. He again iterated his stand on the need for expanded power of consumption in order to keep up with mass production. He praised Senator Cutting's efforts toward greater relief measures, and he advocated a public works program "large enough to put every unemployed man to work," funded by increased inheritance and income taxes. He saw no need for government to borrow, either: "We ought to begin milking the pocketbooks of the few men who have cornered billions of dollars of this country's income and let up on the milking of the pocketbook of the American people." In Rochester, New York, at the Associated Academic Conference in October, he told reporters that the New Deal was a mixed bag. The Civil Works Administration, the temporary New Deal agency that funded nearly $1 billion in work projects for the unemployed, was the only part that he believed had returned any purchasing power to the unemployed, and he thought the NRA was a good "shield" against "cutthroat competition" but did little to solve the fundamental problem of the maldistribution of wealth. He praised Roosevelt for "ingenious and sincere" efforts but urged him to be "ruthless" and not compromise in his actions toward decentralizing wealth. By December, Phil had organized these criticisms into specific proposals: public works, rehabilitation of capital equipment, federal loans for capital investment, and old-age pensions. His speeches also began to take on a more optimistic tone. Rather than stressing the dire consequences of failing to act, he began to stress the bright future possible if the United States took on the challenge seriously. These remarks, however, did not cut him off from the administration. In December, he met with Treasury Secretary Morgenthau and discussed "the administration's failure to produce results that reached the mass of the people." By the beginning of 1934, however, Phil still had his doubts about Roosevelt and was unsure if Progressives should continue to support the president or forge their own way.[40]

Early in January 1934, Phil worked with University of Wisconsin economists to produce three bills for Robert to introduce in Congress: one to aid railroad workers, one to aid dairy farmers, and one to aid public schools. Phil advised Robert to introduce them quickly with a good public statement. At the same time, Phil advised Robert to wait on introducing a new public works bill because the administration, he said, would water it down to the point that it was ineffective, and worse, Robert's name would be linked with it and its failure. Phil confidentially noted to Isabel that during a January meeting with Robert and Senators Robert Wagner and Bronson Cutting, Roosevelt had remarked that he thought the Depression was about over and planned to begin laying off workers on federal projects in February.[41]

Phil's impatience with Roosevelt was heightened by the worsening conditions in Wisconsin. Unemployment in Wisconsin had decreased slightly throughout 1933 but began to increase in the fall and winter of 1933–34, hovering between 20 and 25 percent below average. At the same time, the state's Public Welfare Department reported that the amount of money spent on general relief had ballooned from just over $2 million in 1932 to almost $19.5 million in 1933. Much of this increase came from the Federal Emergency Relief Administration. Wisconsin received its first grant of $2,074,861 in July; the state also began receiving Civil Works Administration (CWA) projects and other New Deal federal aid. The state legislature also established the Wisconsin Emergency Relief Administration (WERA) in April 1934 to help cope with the massive distribution of the state and federal aid. In April 1934, 14.2 percent of the population living in areas eligible to receive state and federal funds (approximately 83.8 percent of the total state population) received direct relief. In January 1934, just under sixty thousand cases received aid; in April this had increased to ninety thousand. Geographically, the counties worst off, according to a 1935 survey by the WERA, were all in the north and west; cutover counties accounted for twenty-one of twenty-five of the poorest counties. The implications were stark: despite dramatically increased federal and state spending, unemployment and poverty persisted. Phil, always sensitive to public opinion, reported that although people generally appreciated Roosevelt's efforts, they did not understand the expenditures and were becoming restless. Farmers, he noted, became bitter against the AAA, and the CWA had produced friction in almost every community. As farm income continued to drop, there was a noticeable shift in population to towns and cities, and even greater tax delinquency on property—26.6 percent in 1933.[42]

Two episodes in particular underscored the restiveness endemic to both rural and urban Wisconsin at this time. Dairy farmers, never very prosperous even before the Depression, faced declining prices for milk used for cheese and butter production, down to 85 cents per hundredweight from two dollars in 1929. The farmers' anger was directed at milk buyers and dairies, which still showed sizable profits on dairy products. Supposed abuse by this "milk trust" brought forth several organizations, including a branch of the Farm Holiday Association, a national organization that had sponsored farm strikes and other forms of direct action throughout the Midwest. The most radical of these organizations was the Wisconsin Co-operative Milk Pool, which in 1933 had sixty-seven thousand members and was led by Walter M. Singler. Singler called for stable prices of $1.40 per hundredweight, and the Milk Pool was able to shut down small cheese and butter factories in the Fox River Valley in February 1933. The Pool tried to expand the strike to other regions as well by picketing, blocking roads, and dumping milk; sheriff's deputies often broke up such roadblocks with clubs and tear gas. Governor Schmedeman's timid response was to suggest that dairies begin offering one dollar per hundredweight, but in May farm leaders called another strike. The governor ordered an embargo on twenty-one counties where strike sentiment was strongest. Adjutant General Ralph Immell offered twenty-five hundred National Guard troops to sheriffs and offered to supply them with tear gas. Several bloody confrontations occurred between farmers and deputies, particularly in Waukesha County, where the "Battle of Durham Hill" became notorious when soldiers with bayonets broke up a blockade. The strike ended on May 19, but an even bloodier conflict arose in November when at least seven cheese factories were bombed before striking farmers gave up. The 1933 milk strikes cost the state $170,000. Although short-lived and with little real consequence, the sight of state troops firing on desperate farmers chilled the state and reinforced people's sense of desperation.[43]

During the tumultuous early 1930s, discontent was not restricted to rural areas. In July 1934, more than 1.3 million worker-days were lost in the state because of strikes, double the number of any previous month in that year. Milwaukee saw only six strikes in 1933 but withstood forty-two in 1934. Tensions between manufacturers and employees continually bubbled under the surface, but the passage of the National Industrial Recovery Act in 1933 brought these to a boil as workers took advantage of Section 7(a) and asserted their legal right to organize. The most spectacular example was the strike at the Kohler Plumbing Company in

Kohler, Sheboygan County. Years of paternalistic management and a reputation for humane capitalism did not protect the company from a vicious confrontation. After owner and former governor Walter J. Kohler refused to recognize the new AFL Federal Labor Union No. 18545, the union voted to strike. On the morning of July 16, 1934, a thousand pickets blocked the entrances to the factory and kept out most of the employees. On July 27, the relatively peaceful strike became a riot when village deputies armed with shotguns broke through picket lines and began to tear down camps. A night of battle ("ghastly terror" according to the local newspaper) left two strikers dead and forty-seven wounded. Governor Schmedeman called in the National Guard to restore order, and peaceful picketing resumed the next day. The worst violence was over, but the Kohler strike dragged on until 1941. It is a stretch to imply that Wisconsin was on the brink of anarchy in 1933–34, but it is clear that widespread discontent erupted into violence when people were pushed by militant leaders or angered enough by unsympathetic officials.[44]

By 1934, the deterioration of conditions in Wisconsin, the resurgence of the Democratic Party, and continuing doubts about Roosevelt's understanding of the Depression and his lack of dedication to a progressive program forced Wisconsin Progressives in new directions. The impetus for a new political organization came not from the La Follettes—Phil was traveling extensively on speaking engagements to build up his almost exhausted bank account—but from another ousted official. Thomas Amlie had suffered the same fate as Phil: he had lost his bid for reelection to Congress from the first district in the Republican primary to Stalwart George Blanchard. Amlie was perhaps the most radical of Wisconsin Progressives; he firmly believed that capitalism itself was dying and that Roosevelt could at most postpone the inevitable. Like Phil, he believed that the frontier had allowed Americans to escape hard times by relocating to available lands. Since such relocation was no longer possible, Amlie believed the boom-and-bust economy would only increase the disparity of wealth, and he argued that only a quick and thorough shift to socialism could save the nation from economic ruin. After Amlie delivered an address along these lines to the League for Independent Political Action in Chicago in September 1933, many liberal intellectuals were persuaded to form an independent political organization, the Farmer-Labor-Progressive League. Amlie had high hopes of using a regional party to unite rural and urban producers to influence national policy, but in order to start in Wisconsin, he would need the cooperation not just of the farm organizations and labor unions but also of the La Follette–led Progressives.[45]

Amlie and Phil spoke frequently, and after a political meeting in Kenosha on September 30, it is likely that the two privately discussed at length the possibility of a third party.[46] Phil shared many of Amlie's concerns over the direction of the New Deal and was receptive to the idea of a third party for liberals disenchanted with Roosevelt. Indeed, Progressives had been flirting with the idea for years and in fact were already organized much like a party. Phil believed that the time was "propitious" to form a new movement that would "cut away from old political methods and old political slogans." Nonetheless, as dedicated to the cause and as fascinated with new ideas as he was, he believed that his brother's reelection was critical to the whole progressive movement and did not want to do anything that might threaten his chances. For the rest of 1933, Amlie continued to discuss the idea of a third party with political supporters, and for the time being Phil let him lead that effort.[47]

In early February 1934, Phil began planning a meeting of Progressives in Madison to discuss the formation of a new party and to gauge support. Representatives from each county were invited, as were incumbent Progressive officeholders and representatives from farm, labor, educational, veterans,' and women's groups. Invitations went out on February 22. A smaller group met at Maple Bluff Farm on March 2 to iron out as many differences as possible before the large group gathered the next day. One of the biggest obstacles was Robert, who remained uncertain about the new party, fearing it would be taken over by radicals who had no real grasp of the situation. He also worried that voters would be reluctant to abandon the two major parties even in order to support a popular candidate. Nonetheless, he took no stand, doing nothing to promote the idea of a third party and little to hinder it but raise questions. Others doubted the advisability of a third party. More than half at the gathering argued against a formal break with the Republicans; the most vocal among them were Theodore Dammann, John Blaine, and many of the older Progressives, particularly those who had survived the 1932 election. Phil, reluctant to argue against Robert publicly, worried about what would transpire at the conference. Evjue chaired the conference the next morning at the Park Hotel. Robert took no position and told the delegates that it was their decision and he would not argue one way or the other. Those who attended the conference had in fact made up their minds already, and as the county roll was called, it became clear how widespread interest was in a third political party. Despite vigorous opposition by Dammann and others, two-thirds of the county delegations favored a new party. Not surprisingly, the strongest support came from farmer and labor groups, especially the state Federation of Labor, the Farmers' Holiday Association, and the Co-operative Milk Pool. In his closing address, concerned about maintaining the support of those who opposed the move, Phil stressed the need for Progressive unity, an issue more critical than it had been in the 1920s. The Madison convention established a committee, chaired by Phil, to begin proceedings to formally establish a new party. After the convention, Robert, despite his refusal to take a public stand, was furious at the results and threatened to drop out of politics altogether. According to Isabel, he believed the leadership belonged to him by virtue of his hard work in Washington, and he resented the "hijacking" of the progressive movement by more radical groups. Phil, however, was more sanguine and was convinced that the movement was "spontaneous" and a mandate for Robert and himself. Amlie was also pleased. "I am satisfied," Amlie later wrote, "that the convention in Madison last Saturday is going to result in the formation of a new party in Wisconsin. Under the leadership of Phil La Follette, I am sure that this party will go completely to the left." Assuming leadership of the new party came naturally to Phil, but he worried that his actions and Robert's vacillation might hurt both politically. The brothers continued to support one another, but their different attitudes toward the party would fester for the next twelve years.[48]

The political landscape reshaped by Roosevelt in 1932 presented the nascent party with its first problem: how would the president react to a third party? His endorsement would be invaluable, Phil reasoned, if Robert ran as a third party candidate. It was clear that the president's blessing would be of little help if Robert ran as a Republican, but it might convince Democrats to vote against their party's candidate. Another problem was recruiting candidates. Phil himself was reluctant to run for governor just yet—although he badly wanted to—because he feared it might jeopardize Robert's chances of reelection if two La Follettes ran on the same ticket. As he had in 1930, Phil worried that voters might balk at "too much La Follette," and he knew which of the two of them was the more popular. It appeared for a time that former senator (and former governor) Blaine might return to the state and run for governor, an idea that Phil liked because it would generate interest in the party and give leaders a greater sense of direction. In early April, Blaine visited the state for a "look-see" to get a sense of his chances. What is more, there were still lingering doubts as to the party's viability. The Roosevelt administration continued to pressure Robert to run as a Democrat, promising not only Roosevelt's support but also his influence to ensure that Robert ran unopposed in the primary. Phil had to keep arguing with him about the necessity of a third party. And what would the Stalwarts do? Phil sensed that they were much less active than at any previous time, and he feared that they might throw their support to conservative state Democrats and make the Progressive separation meaningless.[49]

In the meantime, Phil continued to deliver addresses on the economic state of the nation, reinforcing his role as a left-wing critic of the New Deal. "This generation," he told a gathering of the Chicago Bar Association, "holds in the palm the fate of civilization." In late April at the University of Chattanooga, he told a reporter that the Depression was a "disease," and he complained of the propaganda that relied on business conditions to evaluate economic well-being. "Look at the pocketbook of the American people. There has been no material change for the better. . . . Unless a change for the better puts something in the pocketbooks of the people there will be consequences."[50]

The biggest obstacle to the formation of a new party, however, was neither Roosevelt nor a lack of candidates but rather the vague legal requirements for obtaining a party line on the ballot. Phil had warned Progressives of the legal obstacles, and Secretary of State Dammann, who opposed the creation of a new party, interpreted the law strictly and set a high requirement for the number of signatures on a petition for ballot status. Dammann also required primary winners to run as independents in the general election. Phil then became part of a committee to petition the state supreme court to clarify the requirements. This was a smart decision, since it would short-circuit any further legal challenges that might have prevented the new party from actually participating in the fall election. In mid-April, Phil, supported by the attorney general, submitted briefs to the state supreme court. The court appointed Madison attorney William Spohn to argue for the other side, and he submitted his brief shortly afterwards. How the court would respond to the question was by no means clear. The law was sufficiently vague to allow multiple interpretations, and six of the seven justices had been appointed to the bench by conservative governors—five by Kohler. Amlie thought the court would decide in the Progressives' favor: "After all, this is the time when dictators are springing up everywhere, and as a matter of principle the Supreme Court ought to do everything in its power to make it possible for the people to express themselves by way of the ballot box."

The court reached its decision quickly and affirmed Amlie's faith in democracy. On May 1, the court declared that a new party can achieve ballot status if a petition is signed by at least one-sixth of the total presidential vote in the last election in at least ten counties. The new party could then run an entire ticket, including county, state, and federal races. This cleared the legal path for the Progressive Party but still left some problems. Phil noted that the numerical requirement was possible but not easy; the ruling would also mean that because only one set of nomination papers was required, almost anybody could run in the primary. Accustomed to having firmer control over Progressive candidates, Phil worried that there was a "risk that a lot of poor candidates would be in the primary." For the first time, however, there was a clear way to resolve Progressive factional disputes, and the Progressives could focus their strength on the general election.[51]

A Progressive convention was called for May 19 in Fond du Lac to formally organize the new party. Phil and Evjue took the lead in organizing it, but the whole enterprise threatened to break free of their control before it even met. Just a few days before the scheduled conference, Phil learned that some of the older Progressives planned to ignore the momentum for a new party and run a Progressive slate of candidates headed by Dammann in the Republican primary. Such a move would have split Progressives among two parties rather than uniting them into one. Although a majority of county delegations supported a new party, some opposed it and were ready to contest the decision; other delegations simply made no decision at all. Throughout May, Phil sounded out leaders and made his arguments. When the convention met, the opposition was vocal but exerted little influence. Two separate delegations arrived from Milwaukee County, one opposed to and the other favoring a new party. After some dispute over which was the legitimate representative of Milwaukee, compromise was reached and both were eventually seated—one group representing Milwaukee and one as "delegates at large." All delegations were invited to speak, and it quickly became evident that Phil had correctly gauged Progressive sentiment: only seven counties registered their opposition. The strongest came from Milwaukee. Milwaukee attorney Fred Wylie and Dammann spoke vociferously against breaking with the Republican Party. Dammann complained of "steam-rolling" and suggested that the party would struggle to get enough votes to win a three-way contest. In the early afternoon, the convention voted 252 to 44 to form a new party. The next question was what to call the party, and this time, Phil and Evjue took a firmer grip on the proceedings. They staved off advances from the more radical delegates, led by Federation of Labor President J. J. Handley, who proposed the name "Farmer-Labor Party." Phil gave an impassioned speech defending the use of the familiar "Progressive" and arguing that the party was to be open to all, not just farmers and laborers. The convention then voted overwhelmingly to adopt that name. Robert stayed away until late in the proceedings and delivered a lackluster speech declaring he would run on the party's ticket. He had decided to support the Progressive Party largely for Phil's sake, but he would complain about campaigning for the party and left the management of the party to others. Robert's lack of enthusiasm would irritate Phil, but the importance of fraternal loyalty and the safe Senate seat usually papered over any hurt feelings. The meeting adjourned immediately after, frustrating Amlie's and others' attempts to draft a platform, a motion that Evjue ruled out of order. That task was deferred to a later meeting, and the delegates appointed a state Progressive Central Committee to supervise the petition drive, chaired by Phil.[52]

The Progressive Party came into existence at the Fond du Lac convention, but it was still uncertain of its identity. Phil was clearly in charge and was perhaps the only figure the radical Farmer-Labor groups trusted enough to lead the party in a properly radical direction. Handley and the other leaders of the Wisconsin Federation of Labor got over their disappointment over the name of the party and deferred to La Follette leadership. Some farmer groups, however, continued to insist on a formal declaration of principles. To placate them, Phil urged Robert to develop his own personal platform, which the party could then adopt. This, too, would allow the La Follette forces to keep ahead of the movement. As the petition drive got underway, a group of radical Progressives led by Amlie, Appleton attorney Sam Sigman, former congressman George Schneider, and former state senator Anton Miller established a statewide association of liberals called the Farmer-Labor-Progressive League (FLPL), a political organization that would develop platforms and endorse candidates—everything that the Progressive Party had not yet done. Even though the organization never intended to develop into *another* party with ballot status, the FLPL did gather support from various farm and labor groups and threatened to undo the balance Phil had made between old-time Progressives and younger, more radical members. Phil wanted little to do with the organization, but he did agree to address its state convention on June 30. This was alarming, as Isabel noted: "This is a very ticklish situation as it will make a split in our ranks. . . . This group is friendly to Phil and would stick with us if Phil would run for governor as he is 'radical' enough to suit them." Not yet a month old, the Progressive Party was developing factions.[53]

Fortunately, Phil's hand was greatly strengthened by the results of the petition drive. In early June, the petitions were sent out to Progressives in each county, and Phil wrote to leaders in thirty-five counties to remind them of the petition's importance. By June 5, the committee had received 16,000 signatures; a week later the total was 95,000. The court required only 10,000 from ten counties, and when party leaders filed the petitions with the secretary of state, there were more than 122,000. This was twice the number of votes Schmedeman had received in the Democratic primary in 1932. The areas that responded most quickly were the north and west, traditional La Follette strongholds, a fact that furthered Phil's influence in the party. Secretary of State Dammann promptly certified that the Progressive Party would have a place on the ballot in the September primary election.[54]

While the petition drive was winding down, the question of candidates became more pressing. The Progressive Central Committee discussed informally preparation for a declaration of candidates and considered endorsing candidates in early June, well before the primary election. There was considerable opposition to Dammann and a few others because of their outspoken opposition to the party, but for the leadership to express favoritism in the form of an endorsement would have exacerbated the divisions within the party. For this reason, when the Central Committee met again on June 24, it voted unanimously against endorsing a slate of candidates and instead encouraged all prospective candidates to file papers for the primary election.[55]

On June 30, Phil had to convince the three hundred delegates attending the FLPL meeting that endorsing all of the candidates on the same ballot was the wisest course of action. To do so, he dusted off the Progressives' most powerful oratorical weapon: the image of Robert M. La Follette Sr. In his speech Phil described the Progressive Party as the culmination of a mass movement of people who demanded change. In the past, he said, the handicaps of the Republican Party forced Progressives to endorse a slate of candidates before the primary in order to prevent Stalwart victory. Now that Progressives had their own organization, such endorsement was unnecessary and actually contrary to the battles fought by Old Bob against the party bosses in the 1890s. He urged unity and called on all leaders to allow the rank and file to resolve personal and factional disputes through an open primary. He quoted his father to drive home the point: "The supreme issue is the encroachment by the power-ful few upon the rights of the many." He also called on Progressives to stay on the middle road, denouncing the Socialist Party's call for collective ownership that would deprive farmers of their individual farms. Phil knew his audience, and his speech was effective. He stayed around and chatted with the delegates until the meeting approved a platform, including planks for public ownership of utilities, old-age pensions, public works, and cooperative marketing—issues that would be acceptable to all Progressives.[56]

Phil left the meeting feeling very pleased with himself. When Fola and George returned to Maple Bluff Farm from a movie, they found a smug Phil sitting in the living room sipping a cool drink. "He seemed to feel," Fola wrote, "that the conference had gone very well, and by some questioning we overcame his modesty sufficiently to be able to deduce he had made a ten strike with his speech." His address had united older Progressives as well as the more radical behind the icon of Old Bob and clearly articulated the party's goals, thereby calling the troublesome FLPL to heel. Robert was also relieved with the concrete declaration of the history and purpose of the progressive movement, especially since it indicated that the La Follette family was clearly in control.[57]

Phil had good reason to be pleased. He had kept the FLPL loyal to the Progressive Party, and at the same time those who had initially opposed the new party had begun to change their minds. Both Adjutant General Ralph Immell and Secretary of State Dammann issued statements announcing that they would stand by the decision of the Fond du Lac convention. Fred Wylie announced his candidacy for attorney general, and even former Blaine supporters were swearing loyalty to the new party. Yet a nagging doubt remained regarding the candidate for governor. Immediately following the formation of the party, it became conventional wisdom that Phil would not be a candidate. Phil himself was disinclined either to announce his candidacy or to flatly refuse the nomination; instead he remained silent and awaited developments. Robert, Isabel, George Middleton, and Ralph Sucher all opposed his running for governor. Isabel noted in her diary that it would be risky for Phil to run because

> if the ticket is defeated it will be interpreted as Phil's fault for butting in and interfering with his brother's chances because he is so anxious to hold office again; if Phil should be defeated and Bob elected Phil would be damaged as a leader; if Phil were

elected and Bob defeated Phil would be responsible for Bob's defeat—i.e., whatever the result Phil would be the goat.

In other words, Phil had everything to lose and very little to gain. At the end of June, Phil was still not ready to run for governor; he was far too worried that his candidacy would hurt Robert's bid for reelection, and it was an article of faith that Robert's presence in the Senate was critical for the national progressive movement. Nonetheless, Phil refused to take himself out of the running once and for all.[58]

By the end of July, however, progressive sentiment abruptly shifted, and even those who opposed Phil's candidacy began to see it as the party's best option. In part this was because other progressive leaders refused to step forward for the nomination. Amlie demurred for financial reasons, although he had already set his heart on reclaiming his old congressional seat. He thought Phil would make the best standard-bearer, but he, too, worried that "the opposition would perhaps seek to wage the campaign on the family issue." Both Phil and Amlie wanted a liberal to run, perhaps Harold Groves or William Rubin, but publicly Phil continued to do nothing to encourage any kind of boom on his behalf. He did, however, deliver several addresses to progressive groups in which he denounced the AAA's restriction of production. When Robert asked Phil to draft a statement to the effect that he would not run, Phil refused, concerned that he might be the only viable candidate. In mid-July, Robert hosted a series of meetings with Progressive leaders at Maple Bluff Farm and was startled to learn how many wanted Phil to run. Even Amlie saw the strategic value, since Phil could unite Progressive voters; he feared that left-wing Farmer-Labor groups might advance a candidate and stir up active opposition from older Progressives who had originally opposed the party. Phil believed that if Robert clearly stated that he did not want Phil to run, the boom would end and Robert could then endorse someone like Groves or former state senator Harry Sauthoff of Madison. By the end of July, even Robert was convinced that an active gubernatorial campaign, behind which all Progressives would rally, would actually help his own reelection efforts. Phil quietly began having his nomination papers circulated, still waiting to see if another viable candidate would appear.[59]

In early August, as the deadline for nomination filing neared, public speculation became more intense. The very fact that Phil refused to commit himself one way or the other discouraged other potential candidates, none of whom wanted to risk facing him in a primary election. Several county organizations passed resolutions in support of his candidacy, and as a draft movement developed, Phil continued to play coy. In a public letter to one of the Progressives circulating nomination papers he noted that there was still time for another candidate to file, and he was willing to step aside if the "family issue" appeared it would hurt the ticket. A short while later, Phil's candidacy received a boost from an unexpected source: Franklin Roosevelt. On August 9, the president stopped in Green Bay amid widespread speculation about what he would say regarding the political situation in Wisconsin. With typical flair and cleverness, Roosevelt praised both Governor Schmedeman and Senator F. Ryan Duffy, the Democrat elected in 1932, as well as Robert, all of whom were seated behind him on the platform, in a tacit endorsement. He said nothing of Phil, which was widely regarded as a "slap on the wrist" of the not-yet candidate who had spent much of the past year publicly criticizing the administration. Yet the presidential benediction made Robert's reelection a virtual certainty, thus eliminating the leading argument against Phil's running. As the deadline loomed, William Rubin's nomination papers were filed with the secretary of state, but Rubin withheld a formal declaration of intent, which was necessary for his name to appear on the ballot. Finally, on August 14, after both Amlie and Groves again refused to run, Phil declared his candidacy and filed completed nomination papers signed by twelve thousand voters. One other candidate, Henry Meisel of Waukesha, also announced he would run for governor in the Progressive column, but the outcome was in no doubt. In November, the Progressive ticket would be headed by La Follette and La Follette.[60]

Once he decided to enter the race, Phil "sweated blood" over the type of campaign he should make. Shortly after filing his nomination papers, he went on vacation in northern Wisconsin to consider his options. His early speeches, delivered before the September primary, contained some familiar themes (redistribution of wealth, the concentration of power) but also some new ones reflecting the new party. In Augusta and Mondovi, he told crowds that there was no longer any distinction between Republicans and Democrats and that the real political cleavage was "between those who believe that government policies shall be shaped to favor a special few and those who believe they shall be designed to give economic justice and security to the masses." He cited the 150,000 signatures on the petition for a new party as evidence of this sentiment. As he moved into the southern and eastern parts of the state, he lightened up a little and specifically exempted Roosevelt from his attacks, partly because Robert intended to campaign on a pro–New Deal platform, but also because he believed that people were generally discouraged and needed a more positive message. Attacking the president was also politically foolish. Phil continued to attack state parties, however, and declared that the Republican Party was "satisfied" with Schmedeman and that there was little difference between Republicans and Democrats. In Milwaukee, he deliberately lauded the president but encouraged voters to reject the reactionary Democratic Party of the state. Republican candidate Howard Greene called attention to this and tried to make Phil appear hypocritical, but Phil's tactic seemed to work. By attacking the party and not the president, Phil diffused the argument that a Progressive state administration would be unable to work with a Democratic president, and he also subtly suggested that Roosevelt himself was not completely in charge of his own party. And there was still the millennialist vision that he invoked so effectively: "It is up to you and me," he told an audience in Ashland, "to decide whether we are going to make this world a better and finer world for us and our children or whether we are going to follow the blind and stupid leadership of the reactionaries backward down the road of human progress and lose the achievements of the past 300 years." Toward the end of the primary, Phil continued his defense of the formation of the new party as necessary to ensure a liberal victory. He urged Progressives to vote in the primary despite personal friendship or local loyalties, and he encouraged nominal Democrats to do likewise. In one speech he declared that Progressives offered the only home between the reactionaries and the "wild-eyed extreme of communism." When conservatives tried to hit Progressives as the "Party of La Follette," Phil declared that the Progressives were the only party to leave the endorsement of candidates solely to the voters.[61]

Phil issued his personal platform on September 15. His earlier speeches in this primary had been quite general, but now he offered specific proposals. As he had in the past, he framed the platform as a formal explanation of the Depression and the required remedies. He based the platform on six general principles and phrased them as a declaration of rights of every citizen: a right of worship and speech assembly; a right to work for just compensation; a right to receive publicly supported education; a right to economic security in old age; a right to bargain collectively; and a right "to live under a government strong enough to suppress the lawless, wise enough to see beyond the selfish desires of the moment, and just enough to consider the welfare of the people as a whole." Education and collective bargaining were old Progressive issues, but this new civics lesson phrased them as "rights" on the same level as those guaranteed by the first amendment and gave them new militancy. The platform was thereby radical enough to appeal to farmer-labor groups without alienating professionals or older Progressives. The platform went on to advocate twenty-two specific proposals, including public works, a marketing organization for farmers, old-age pensions, public ownership of utilities, increased school aid, and government-owned central banks. Phil spent the last week before the primary traveling around northern Wisconsin, promoting Progressive unity and reminding voters that they had a great opportunity in leading the rest of the nation into a grand political realignment.[62]

The results of the primary were a foregone conclusion. Phil defeated his opponent, Henry Meisel of Waukesha, a disabled navy veteran running on an anti–New Deal, tax-cutting program but who gave no campaign speeches, 154,454 to 7,520. Schmedeman beat William Rubin 166,001 to 41,985, and Republicans nominated Howard Greene narrowly over former governor Fred Zimmerman. All of the other state offices except secretary of state were contested, so there was much interest in the primary. The Progressive primary election in seven of ten congressional races was contested, as were sixteen of eighteen senate races and eighty-one of one hundred assembly races. Publicly, Progressives were pleased with the results. Phil told reporters that the primary vote was "highly encouraging." "Phil is Elated," ran one headline. Privately, however, Progressives—the La Follettes in particular—were worried. Phil had hoped for an overwhelming victory, but the combined Progressive gubernatorial vote was 60,000 below the Democratic gubernatorial vote, and only 13,000 higher than the Republican vote. Phil himself ran second to Schmedeman, so the key question was where the non-Schmedeman Democratic vote would go. The overall vote was light, so the Progressive Party was by no means doomed, but it did mean a lot of heavy campaigning before the election. The hoped-for overwhelming victory never came, and it was evident that the Progressives would have a hard fight to gain a plurality of the state vote. Milwaukee County was particularly worrisome: Phil had run third behind Schmedeman and the Socialist candidate and only 6,000 ahead of Howard Greene.[63]

After a few days' rest, Phil picked up the campaign in Monroe County on September 25. His speeches again stressed two major themes: the need for redistribution of wealth as a remedy for underconsumption and the need for Progressive unity, since the Progressive Party offered the only real alternative to the reactionary parties and the equally dangerous Socialists and Communists. The Progressives had relied on denouncing the Republican administration, and now they had to justify the formation of a new party. Phil accordingly characterized the Republicans as the party of the rich and the Democrats as the party of "time-serving politics" and "payroll politicians," as reactionary and hostile to Roosevelt as the Republicans were. He also denounced Socialists, who, he craftily told rural voters, wanted to "collectivize" agriculture. All parties met in convention in Madison on October 2 to draft platforms, and the Progressive Party largely followed Phil's lead. He provoked laughter by noting that the Progressives had already knocked the Republicans out of the capitol and would do the same to the Democrats in November. (The party with the largest vote in the primary met in the Assembly Chamber, and the party with the next largest vote met in the smaller Senate Chamber. Having run third, Republicans had to find quarters outside the capitol.) Phil read the party platform, which was almost identical to his own. He urged Progressives to hold together and to take their role seriously: "You and I hold in the hollow of our hand the fate not only of ourselves but of civilization itself. . . . [I]f we do the job that is here to be done, [this time] will go down in human history as the greatest age in which man has lived." Buoyed by Phil's vision, Progressives left the convention ready to fight.[64]

Nonetheless, Phil was not enthusiastic about his chances. He believed firmly that Robert would be reelected but thought "there was an extremely good chance that he [Phil] will get licked." Progressives sent representatives all over the state to gauge their chances. Distressed farmers, they found, had given up telephone and newspapers and had even given up gasoline to drive to meetings—the Depression had taken a heavy toll on enthusiasm for the Progressives. Isabel had expected an active movement by Progressive women as in 1932, but she found the work discouraging or even "sliding backwards." Some professional groups also seemed to have lost their past enthusiasm for Progressive candidates. Phil's reference to an "acquisitive spirit" among some teachers and university officials who viewed education simply as a means of earning a living rather than as a socially productive endeavor returned to haunt him as the *Milwaukee Journal* criticized his record on education, noting the drop in school aid between Kohler's term and his. The "general apathy" he perceived among voters forced Phil to campaign more strenuously than before, and in October he began delivering regular radio addresses to boost his support among urban voters, to generate more enthusiasm, and to defend the Progressives' record. As in 1932, he reminded voters that his administration had lowered taxes, enacted public works and unemployment insurance, and advanced public ownership of utilities. He also denounced the "silk-hatted bandits and frock coated robbers" who had siphoned off wealth from farmers and workers. During the last address before the election, he even bluntly attacked Schmedeman, despite having let up on him after the governor had suffered the amputation of a gangrenous leg (worth 30,000 sympathy votes, by one estimate). Phil described the governor's administration as "reactionary to the core." He demanded to know why it had killed attempts for public utilities, diverted gas and license tax revenue from road repairs, and "chloroformed" the old-age pension act, all while the Roosevelt administration was pushing for similar measures on a national scale. Again and again, Phil promoted the idea that the Progressive Party was more in step with Roosevelt than the state Democratic Party and offered the only real way out of the Great Depression.[65]

The strategy worked: Robert was easily reelected to the senate, and Phil won a close race for governor. At first glance it seemed that the Progressive Party had enjoyed a phenomenal success. It had elected a United States senator, governor, secretary of state, seven congressional representatives, twelve state senators, and forty-six representatives to the assembly. But the vote was close. Phil beat Schmedeman by only 13,626 votes; he carried most of the northern and western counties, building up enough of a margin in those areas to make up for the fact that he lost all the Fox River Valley and most of the industrial lakeshore, the two most populous regions in the state. Moreover, personality played an important part. Democrats reelected the incumbent lieutenant governor, treasurer, and attorney general over Progressives who had never held statewide office. Of the seven representatives, five had been elected to that office before (two were incumbents), and the other two had been state senators from their districts. Of the twelve state senators, ten had served in the senate previously, and two had been members of the assembly. Of those Progressives elected to the assembly, only eighteen were serving their first term in the legislature.[66] Nonetheless, for an organization less than six months old, the Progressive Party had already reshaped the political landscape and sat poised to reinvent state government.

Much of the Progressive Party's success was due to Phil. The third party depended on a delicate balance between new, radical supporters and longtime Progressive supporters. These two groups bickered about candidates, platform planks, and even the very name of their party. The

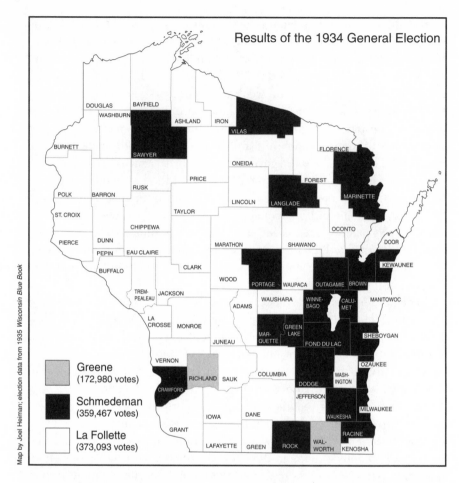

Results of the 1934 General Election

Greene
(172,980 votes)

Schmedeman
(359,467 votes)

La Follette
(373,093 votes)

Map by Joel Heiman; election data from 1935 *Wisconsin Blue Book*

only thing holding them together was continued loyalty to the La Follette family, and Phil was the only candidate who could keep the party united, both by his record and by his willingness to aggressively campaign throughout the state. The party's continued success would likewise depend on Phil's ability to maintain Progressive unity in the legislature and to convince the public of the soundness of Progressive measures.

The La Follettes were close as children and remained close as adults, supporting each other through political losses and personal crises. When Mary's husband—Phil's college friend Ralph Sucher—left her, the family rallied to protect her and her son. From left: Mary, Phil, and Fola.

WHi Image ID 35022

WHi Image ID 35043

For La Follettes, vacations were never really vacations. Phil regularly embarked on trips after campaigns, like this fishing trip to northern Wisconsin with Robert (left), but they always included a great deal of work, either preparing for the next term in office or writing articles for newspapers.

WHi Image ID 32437

After a great deal of consideration, Phil declared himself a candidate for governor in 1930. He embarked on a whirlwind campaign, delivering more than 250 speeches in two months, and defeated incumbent governor Walter J. Kohler for the Republican nomination in September.

When Phil began his campaign for governor, reporters frequently compared his stump style to his father's. Phil had actually campaigned for his father in 1922 and 1924 and engaged in the same highly dramatic and physical oratory.

Phil called the legislature into special session in November 1931 to deal with the crisis of the Great Depression. His academic leanings were apparent in his message to the legislature, which outlined the principle causes of the Depression and recommended a course of action. During the special session, the legislature enacted the first unemployment compensation program in the nation.

WHi Image ID 19103

Although Phil (right) and Robert worried that Wisconsin voters might balk at "too much La Follette," both were reelected to their respective offices. Phil served three terms as governor, and Robert was elected to the United States Senate in 1925, 1928, 1934, and 1940.

Phil always considered himself more an administrator than a legislator, and he took great satisfaction in managing state affairs during his first term as governor. He eagerly embraced the economic challenges of the Great Depression, and Wisconsin again became known for innovative government.

WHi Image ID 19372

Milwaukee Journal, August 8, 1934

Out to Welcome the Roosevelt Special

Pulitzer Prize–winning cartoonist Ross Lewis criticized Phil and other Progressives on the pages of the *Milwaukee Journal*. In this cartoon, Lewis suggests that Roosevelt had good reason to be wary of Phil.

WHi Image ID 16128

Phil and Isen wanted their children to be raised as free as possible from political life. Yet because politics so consumed his time while Bob, Judy, and Sherry were children, Phil's relationship with them was distant. By the time he returned from the army, the children were nearly grown. From left: Judy, Isen, and Bob.

WHi Image ID 35035

Phil ran for governor in 1934, 1936, and 1938 as the candidate of the Progressive Party, a third party formed when Progressive La Follette supporters abandoned the Republican Party. In all of his campaigns, Phil viewed his job primarily as an educator: if the people simply knew the truth, then they would vote Progressive.

WHi Image ID 35033

Being a politician left little time for family. Although Phil was devoted to his children, his official duties, extensive campaigns, and involvement in national affairs meant that he was an often-absent father. He had endured similar separations from his parents when his father went to the U.S. Senate. From left: Robert III, Sherry, and Judy.

Milwaukee Journal, October 12, 1937

'Heil, La Follette!'

Republicans and Democrats—and some Progressives—complained about Phil's aggressive management of the legislature during the 1937 special session. Events in Europe provided cartoonist Ross Lewis and other critics a chilling comparison.

WHi Image ID 35032

In probably the biggest blunder in Wisconsin politics, Phil tried to organize a third party—the National Progressives of America—nationally as he had done in Wisconsin. His energetic oratory, however, took on a sinister quality when seen against the ridiculous symbol of the NPA. The circle-and-x was meant to imitate a voter's mark on a ballot but was instead ridiculed by some as a "circumcised swastika." The NPA failed, and Phil lost his bid for reelection.

WHi Image ID 35027

After he returned from Europe in 1939, Phil (third from left) took on a new cause: keeping the United States out of the war in Europe. His isolationism alienated him from other liberals, with whom he often debated on nationally broadcast radio programs. Because these debates were conducted in front of a live audience, Phil was able to use his ability to play a crowd to match wits with figures from the Roosevelt administration.

Growing up on a farm left a deep impression on Phil, and he maintained a fondness for country life as an adult. Just before World War II, he purchased a farm in northwestern Dane County. Isen and the children were less than enthusiastic about the endeavor.

WHi Image ID 35030

WHi Image ID 35029

The strenuous life of a farm family during the war wore heavily on the family during Phil's overseas service. He returned for occasional visits, but the responsibility for running the farm fell hard on Isen and the children.

CHAPTER SIX

A Stolen Utopia

In January 1935, Phil became governor for the second time. Much had changed in the four years since he last took the oath of office. Although Old Bob La Follette remained a compelling icon, new figures now influenced Wisconsin politics. President Franklin D. Roosevelt's candidacy in 1932 had cost Phil the governorship and forced Progressives to form their own party as a means of keeping liberal forces united. However, establishing a clear identity in the 1930s was even more challenging than it had been in earlier years. As much as Progressives squabbled among themselves in the 1920s, opposition to conservative Republican presidents had at least provided them a sense of purpose that was greatly diminished by the New Deal.

Also frustrating to Progressives was the fact that opposition to the president placed them in company with liberals whose radical agenda was much farther to the left than their own. Although both Wisconsin and Minnesota produced successful third parties that advocated a more ambitious reform plan than Roosevelt offered, the appearances of Charles Coughlin, Huey Long, Charles Townsend, and Upton Sinclair posed more controversial challenges to Roosevelt. All bore superficial resemblance to Old Bob and to a lesser extent Phil. Like Phil, Coughlin frequently criticized the reductionist policies of the New Deal. He turned from an enthusiastic supporter to a perpetual faultfinder, making some of the same arguments that Phil did against the Agricultural Adjustment Administration and the National Recovery Administration. By 1934, Coughlin, too, began calling for national political realignment and created the National Union for Social Justice, a proto-political party advocating nationalized utilities and monetary reform. His physical collapse in 1936 just as he began to deliver an address endorsing Union Party presidential candidate William Lemke removed him from the public eye, but he left a lingering impression of what an "American Fascist" might look like.[1]

The ideas of Dr. Francis Townsend also bore superficial similarities to those of the Wisconsin Progressives; Phil's call for redistribution of wealth was echoed in the demands of the elderly California physician, who created a national movement by promoting a monthly pension for everyone over sixty. Supposedly, if the sum (which fluctuated between $150 and $200) was spent in one month as planned, it would generate an economic recovery. Although an old-age pension was a part of the Progressive platform, it was intended to be aid to those who could no longer make a living themselves, not an economic fix. When Townsend teamed up with real-estate promoter Robert Clements, the simplistic plan became a sensation. Townsend clubs sprang up across the nation, especially in the West and Midwest, and in January 1935, John S. McGoarty introduced the plan in the House of Representatives. Even after the passage of the Social Security Act, Townsend's followers remained a significant political force.[2] There was an important difference between this scheme and Progressive ideas: Townsend's plan was predicated on the idea that the nation had too few jobs and too many workers. Progressives argued just the opposite, that there were enough potential jobs for everyone. Phil repeated again and again that there was always socially productive work to be done—as in his grade-crossing elimination program—provided society was willing to pay for it. Creating employment was more important than just providing relief.

By far the most prominent Depression-era demagogue—and perhaps the most dangerous to Progressives—was Senator Huey P. Long of Louisiana, whose career somewhat resembled that of the late Senator La Follette. In 1918, Long was an undereducated but intelligent lawyer who bucked the political bosses to win election to Louisiana's Railroad Commission. In 1928, he was elected governor after a campaign that took him all over the state, denouncing the corporations that all but controlled Louisiana. His term as governor did see reform that benefited the poor, but the price was a virtual one-man government and a political machine that enriched Long and his supporters. In 1932, Long took his country bumpkin shtick to the U.S. Senate, where he quickly infuriated almost all of his colleagues. By 1935, he had broken with Roosevelt as much for personal reasons as political, and he had converted his vague calls for redistribution of wealth into a national organization with a mailing list of 7.5 million. The Share Our Wealth organization frightened Democratic leaders who worried that a Long candidacy in 1936 would cost Roosevelt the White House. Such a possibility seemed very real until Long was assassinated in the Louisiana state capitol in September 1935.[3]

Phil and other Progressive leaders thought very little of these figures but recognized their potential power among Wisconsin voters, especially since their slick marketing seemed to make up for their lack of well-developed programs. In late 1934 and early 1935, *The Progressive* ran cautious stories on Long, reprinting the infamous Hodding Carter and Gerald L. K. Smith articles from *The Nation* (published just weeks earlier) and covering the conflict between Hugh Johnson and Long. Subsequently, several letters appeared in *The Progressive* praising Long, and at one point editor William Evjue noted that Old Bob, too, had been called a demagogue. One admirer of Old Bob wrote to Phil personally, saying, "I have written Senator Long whose speeches in the Senate have appealed to many of us, and expressed faith in the platform of the Progressive Party as good material for a [national] third party." Father Coughlin's "sermons," both praising and criticizing the New Deal, appeared regularly, especially those that suggested the time was right for a new party. Progressives had frequently advocated the necessity of pensions for the elderly, so Townsend was a trickier figure to deal with, and Progressives generally responded by pointing out how unworkable his scheme was. Former Legislative Reference Library chief Edwin Witte argued that the plan would result in inflation, and other Progressives noted that the financing was through a sales tax—anathema because of its regressive nature.[4]

A syndicated newspaper story appeared in June 1935 lumping the La Follettes ("The Rover Boys of Politics") with these figures and noting that they were the only ones capable of uniting radicals and New Dealers. Despite superficialities between the proposals of Long, Coughlin, Townsend, and the Progressives, critical difficulties prevented any alliances. Progressives—Phil particularly—spent weeks and months researching policy and loaded their public speeches with facts and figures, a habit often practiced by La Follette himself. Working with University of Wisconsin faculty had produced the first workman's compensation law and unemployment insurance. Phil spent months preparing his work plan, itself built on years of study. "Start to talk about redistribution of wealth," wrote Evjue in *The Progressive*, "and you immediately set people thinking about the Huey Longs, the Dr. Townsends and other enthusiastic people whose desire for a reshuffling of the world's goods outruns their sense of what is practical."[5]

Practical things were very much on Phil's mind as he took office. As he worked with Progressives to develop a workable plan to provide work for the unemployed in the state that would function independently from federal relief programs, political considerations bedeviled him. Progressives still remained factious, and the farmer-labor members continued their attempts to push the party in a more radical direction—one that threatened to upset the united front Progressives had shown in the 1934 elections. Phil also faced the delicate tasks of working with a president whose policies he did not agree with, preserving Progressive unity, and avoiding comparison to Roosevelt's demagogic detractors. It was a difficult set of responsibilities, and Phil was only partially successful: although he developed a relief program distinct from the Roosevelt administration and kept Progressives united behind it, his efforts to gain public support made him vulnerable to charges of demagoguery and dictatorship and ultimately caused the Wisconsin Works Plan to fail.

After victory in the election, the governor-elect planned to hit the ground running and, as he had done in 1931, began preparing an ambitious legislative program. Phil and Isabel left for a short vacation in Bermuda, and then Phil embarked on a short national speaking tour to raise some quick funds. On his return to the state, it became apparent that his first task must be to wring more financial assistance from Washington in order to relieve the ever-present unemployment problem. During his campaign he had charged that the Democrat-controlled legislature not only had failed to appropriate enough money to adequately fund relief, but it also had not appropriated the minimum amount required by the Federal Emergency Relief Administration (FERA) to qualify the state for federal funds. As a result, the state would have to return $8 million to FERA. In addition to securing federal funds, Phil planned to push the Roosevelt administration to develop new means of combating unemployment. He told the Allegheny County (Pennsylvania) League of Women Voters that relief could be only a temporary measure—real recovery would come only from socially productive work. "I don't mean going out and building little bridges along the roadside," he added. "I mean really constructive work." As what would become the Works Progress Administration began to take shape in Congress, Phil had in mind a more far-reaching work program to promote economic expansion.[6]

For the time being, Phil promised FERA chief Harry Hopkins that he would request only an additional $5 million in relief funds from the legislature in order to fulfill Governor Albert Schmedeman's pledge of cooperation. In return, FERA would not demand the return of the funds already spent. Getting support from the Roosevelt administration was perhaps the easiest part of this job, since FERA officials never had been pleased with Schmedeman's administration; when she came to his office, FERA official Lorena Hickok found Schmedeman frightened of a radical uprising and "afraid to go home." Moreover, Schmedeman and state Democrats had infuriated many in the state (and in the Roosevelt administration) by cutting spending on education, enacting regressive changes to the tax code, and removing David Lilienthal from the Public Service Commission. Phil's promise of an immediate appropriation of the relief grant would return Wisconsin to the federal government's good graces and allow him to experiment with a new works program that would provide a practical example of what he believed Roosevelt should do.[7]

Early in December, Phil and Robert met with Roosevelt at the White House. Roosevelt received the brothers cordially, especially Robert, who had supported the New Deal less critically than Phil and now hoped to convince the president to go even further. After discussing legislation for the upcoming congressional session, Phil strategically laid out his suggestions for a new works program. First, he reminded the president how Wisconsin Democrats had allied themselves with Republicans in the past and how Progressive support in 1936 would be vital to the president's reelection. After discussing election politics, Phil asked Roosevelt if he would be willing to let Wisconsin develop its own plan for work relief and opt out of the federal programs in exchange for a cash grant. The president responded that under legislation he was developing, there would indeed be room for such independent state programs. Phil promised—at the president's request—to keep him personally informed of the details and left the meeting confident that Roosevelt would cooperate with the Progressives freely, especially since the president seemed worried about his own political future. Phil thought the meeting a success, although some doubts remained. "[T]he meeting with FDR was quite satisfactory," he wrote Isabel from New York the next day. "It was more than that *if* he comes through on all he indicated. Time alone will tell that."[8]

Phil threw himself into the development of the new program, requesting the Wisconsin Regional Planning Committee to compile a list of work-relief projects that the state could undertake. His ultimate goal was to eliminate all relief payments in favor of actual work projects that would provide long-term benefits to the state. The State Planning Board was in the midst of developing work projects, and Phil had the board's work incorporated into the works program. His secretary, Thomas Duncan, developed a plan to finance the program, and Adjutant General Ralph Immell assembled factual and administrative details. Phil hoped to have a more complete program planned for the president by January 15, a plan, as he described it in his memoirs, "to end the awful business of relief for the able-bodied."[9]

At his inauguration, Phil all but abandoned his theoretical analysis of the Depression that he had emphasized in his first term and instead promised "bold, concerted action." Mindful of his experiences of European dictatorships, he assured the state that there need be no choice between democratic government and economic recovery, that Americans could choose economic security without sacrificing democratic government. Anticipating criticism of excessive executive leadership—and charges of unconstitutional governmental action—he reminded the state that Lincoln, whom he described as "the most faithful servant of the Constitution in American history," violated the provisions of the Bill of Rights in order to preserve its spirit. This was quite a departure for the former law school lecturer; Phil had never shied away from vigorous leadership, but his 1935 inaugural address indicated that he saw the Depression as a crisis as great as the Civil War and one that warranted unprecedented government authority that must not be hampered by "outdated" customs of government. He was more mature, less bookish, and his trip to Europe had reinforced his belief that executive power could be used either to secure dictatorship or to ensure democracy. He wanted Wisconsin to demonstrate that people could enjoy both economic security and political freedom.[10]

Such sentiment did not bode well for a harmonious relationship with the state legislature. Phil sent his budget message to the legislature in late January, noting a shortfall of nearly $9 million for the coming biennium, while at the same time urging increased aid to schools and increased wages for "lower paid state employees." The question of securing federal relief funds was postponed for two weeks because of a lingering dispute over federal funds granted during the Schmedeman administration. Phil described the problem to the legislature, quoting a letter he had received from Harry Hopkins in which the FERA head firmly requested that the state pay its share of the $55 million spent on relief in the state over the past two years as had been agreed with Governor Schmedeman. The former governor denied any such arrangement, and Democrats balked at appropriating the $5 million Phil requested, which was to be financed by higher taxes on incomes, dividends, gifts, and utilities. Although he was willing to use strong-arm tactics with the legislature, Phil was very conscious of public opinion; the day after his message to the legislature, he delivered a radio address in which he carefully outlined what his spending priorities were, why the state needed additional funds, and how that money would be raised. Until this dispute was settled, the federal government was unlikely to finance the works plan.[11]

As Phil continued to work with his advisors on the Wisconsin Works Plan, participating in endless conferences and putting in sixteen-hour days in the office, its future in the legislature was already in doubt. After receiving Phil's proposed budget for 1935 on January 9, both houses of the legislature spent the first several days of the session passing resolutions (relating to, among other pressing matters, an investigation of relief administrators, the conduct of the Board of Control, U.S. participation in the world court, and communism at the University of Wisconsin). Democrats and Republicans, both unwilling to see a major Progressive victory, united in attempts to delay as much as possible.[12] Not content to await the legislature's verdict, Phil immediately began a concerted effort to rally the public behind the $5 million spending measure. On January 23, he delivered another radio address from the Executive Chamber; far from his usual hell-raising stump style, the address was much like Roosevelt's now-familiar fireside chats. Phil explained carefully that the state had not paid its fair share for relief and outlined his budget goals, including funding old-age pensions, restoring school aid that had been cut in 1933, funding the eight-hour day at charitable and penal institutions, and providing living wages for state employees. Republicans and Democrats continued to stall by proposing numerous amendments, and Phil again took to the airwaves to force the legislature to act. He became increasingly irritated by the delay, publicly referring to the legislators as "lazy" and demanding passage of the $5 million appropriation, emphasizing the inefficiency and expense of the current relief system. The assembly finally passed the appropriation on February 15; the senate, preoccupied with an investigation of the Board of Control and hunting communists on the university campus, passed the appropriation on February 28.[13]

Phil and other Progressives—most notably his executive secretary, Thomas Duncan—continued to develop the Wisconsin Works Plan, and the governor went to great lengths to cultivate public support for the program. In doing so, Phil not only reaffirmed Wisconsin as a state at the forefront of innovative policy, he also articulated a national liberal critique of the New

Deal. On March 8, Phil gave the most significant statement of his ideas to date over a national radio broadcast. The central theme of the address was that although immediate relief payments were humane, such a policy could be only a stopgap measure until general prosperity returned. Government's role, he argued, should be to increase the wealth of the nation, and the only way to do that was through work. "We in Wisconsin not only believe," he told listeners, "we know there is plenty of work for the people of this state." He described conservation projects, including reforestation and repairing erosion, repairs to homes and private buildings, highway construction, and rural electrification. Such work, funded by local, state, and federal money, would eventually produce a return in higher tax receipts from more prosperous citizens. Progressives naturally hailed the idea as yet another instance of the Badger State forging ahead, and even normally conservative voices were cautiously supportive. The *Wausau Record-Herald* and the *Milwaukee Sentinel* applauded the emphasis on work. Even Oshkosh's staunchly conservative *Northwestern* declared that the address "was filled with good sense and practical thought."[14]

As historian John Miller has noted, this was a major shift in Phil's approach to the problems of the Depression. During his first term, he had emphasized the need for redistribution of wealth, an old Progressive theme, and advocated that the state fund relief payments through taxes on large incomes, inheritances, and dividends. By 1935, he was convinced that this was no longer enough and began calling for state and federal programs that would promote economic expansion.[15] Such comments troubled some federal administrators, including FERA's Howard Hunter, who told Phil, "Honestly I cannot help but feel a little worried about some of the rather brutal things you say." Despite such unsupportive sentiments, Phil remained adamant that the relief administration was not functioning satisfactorily.[16]

In the meantime, the administration's budget bill languished in the senate, where members discussed the pros and cons of a single-chamber legislature, a pension for former Governor Schmedeman, and a bill requiring taverns to provide butter and cheese for every twenty-five-cent lunch. The federal agencies had no such preoccupations, and good news continued to come from Washington. On March 18, Harry Hopkins approved an additional $2.45 million in relief funds for the state, and on April 7 the new federal works bill allocated $20,104,000 for road construction in Wisconsin.[17]

In April, furious at the legislature's lack of progress on the budget and under tremendous strain in working out the details of the works plan, Phil attempted to spur the senate to action by actively campaigning on behalf of Progressive candidates running for two vacant seats in the senate. In a typical speech in Platteville, Wisconsin, Phil, sharing his father's penchant for inflating local issues into matters of universal importance, called the current session "a crisis in the world's history." This time the technique worked. The special elections added two Progressives to the senate, bringing the total to thirteen out of thirty-three. A few days later, the senate passed twelve bills, and later that month, the joint finance committee recommended a reduction of only $400,000 for the state budget. The legislature finally passed the budget in May.[18]

As the legislature dithered over the budget bill, Phil spent much of late April and early May in Washington discussing the works plan with administration officials in an attempt to get their approval before he presented the work bill to the state legislature. Robert kept "constantly in touch" with Harry Hopkins, who seemed supportive, but he worried that Roosevelt would not go along with the Wisconsin Works Plan. On May 3, Phil met with Hopkins and Secretary of the Interior Harold Ickes to discuss the plan in detail and spent a half hour at the White House with Roosevelt, Ickes, and Hopkins. None commented publicly on the meeting, although everyone was receptive. Ickes thought it a "well-thought out plan" and noted that all were in favor of it, especially since the federal money eventually would be repaid. At a press conference, however, Roosevelt—worried about alienating Wisconsin Democrats by seeming too cozy with the Progressives—attempted to downplay Phil's role in creating the bill, commenting that work on the plan had first begun under Schmedeman and that Phil had gone "over the plan and of course made certain minor changes." Roosevelt, too, referred to it as "a good piece of workmanship." Phil continued to meet with members of the administration, including Secretary of Agriculture Henry Wallace and presidential advisor Rexford Tugwell. University of Wisconsin Law School Dean Lloyd Garrison sent his encouragement to Phil through Isabel: "Camp right on the ground until you come away with what you want."[19]

The frequent meetings in Washington fueled public speculation over what the plan would be and how much money the state would receive from the federal government. Hopkins and Ickes gave confidential assurance of the president's support before Phil left Washington on May 11, and Phil returned to Madison and immediately began contacting members of the legislature and the editors of principal daily papers. On May 17, the president formally approved the plan, subject to the enactment of the appropriate legislation. The timing could not have been better:

Phil made his first substantive public remarks on the program at the anniversary celebration of the Progressive Party at Fond du Lac on May 21. In an address both forward-looking and self-consciously historical, he described the plan as the latest in a long line of accomplishments by Wisconsin Progressives. On May 22, the Wisconsin Works Plan was introduced in the state legislature.[20]

The Wisconsin Works Plan was an ingenious and ambitious economic program based on intensive surveys and research conducted by the State Regional Planning Committee. As Phil had discussed with Roosevelt at their first meeting, rather than including the state in the federal relief administration, the federal government would provide a lump sum payment of $100 million to the state to implement its own programs. The federal money would be used to set up the Wisconsin Finance Authority (WFA) (modeled on the Reconstruction Finance Corporation, the federal agency created under Herbert Hoover to lend money to failing businesses and banks) to receive federal money and administer the works program. Articles of incorporation for the WFA were filed with the secretary of state the same day the legislature received the bill. Capitalized by the federal grant, the WFA would issue its own banknotes in denominations of one dollar and five dollars, to function just like regular currency, to be used for payroll on the work projects and acceptable as payment for taxes or state fees. A state appropriation and local bonds exchanged for WFA notes would also finance the administration of the program. The use of the notes offered a modest inflationary boost to local economies and also provided a means of tracking how wages from work projects were spent. The state appropriation would be funded by taxes on dividends, chain stores, and inheritances, thereby including redistribution of wealth. The creation of the WFA as an independent corporation was necessary because the state was constitutionally prohibited from borrowing money; Milwaukee attorney Ralph Hoyt prepared a detailed brief on the constitutionality of the WFA. Aware that such a behemoth administrating work projects and issuing its own money would raise public anxiety, Phil began a series of radio talks to explain the program. He emphasized the efficient and cost-effective way in which the program would put people to work, thereby beginning an economic recovery and expansion. A committee of newspaper editors assembled a question-and-answer booklet that was sent to newspapers across the state.[21]

Alarm people it did. In the senate, both Democrats and Republicans balked at increasing taxes on incomes to fund a vast state appropriation for an independent corporation run by La Follette appointees issuing its own currency independent of legislative budget oversight. Once the legislature created the agency, it would be run by gubernatorial appointment and could spend money independently of legislative appropriations. Republicans derided Phil as a would-be dictator and accused him of trying to emulate Louisiana Governor Huey Long by amassing far-reaching personal control. Roland J. Steinle, chair of the Milwaukee County Republican committee, grumbled that "[i]f Phil La Follette's private corporation . . . is permitted to expend $209,000,000 of the tax payers' money without the direction of the legislature, it will make him the boss of the north." *Milwaukee Journal* cartoonist Ross Lewis depicted Phil adjusting his necktie in a large mirror over the caption "Gov. La Follette Meets with the Wisconsin Finance Corporation [*sic*]." Phil knew better than to let conservatives dominate public discourse at such a critical point. On the radio and in person, he urged the senate to pass the bill, stressing the benefits of a state-run program rather than one bogged down in the federal bureaucracy. He also emphasized the need to provide employment to all, outlining seven large projects ready to go and just awaiting federal financing.[22]

Democrats, goaded by U.S. Senator F. Ryan Duffy, charged that the Wisconsin plan had already cost the state money since the state stood to receive a larger share of the congressional relief appropriation if it was under the federal administration. In Milwaukee, Harold Ickes denied this and praised the plan. Despite this support from administration officials, Phil continued to argue that the state could do a better job alone than under federal control. While speaking to a meeting of cheesemakers in Madison, he criticized the Agricultural Adjustment Administration and federal relief agencies in general: "For the past five and one half years . . . we have followed this policy of reduction, and have found ourselves confronted with the problem of a shrinking market. There is no way out unless we restore our national income." Phil also delivered another radio address explaining more projects that the works plan would undertake, hoping to increase public support by providing concrete examples. Isabel, too, took to the airwaves, delivering a detailed explanation of the bill and describing the construction projects that would be funded. The campaign evidently had an effect; citizens of Sheboygan began circulating petitions, eventually garnering sixteen thousand signatures, urging Democratic Senator Harry Bolens to vote for the bill, and six hundred spectators packed the hearings before the joint finance committee.[23]

The bill gained support as well from a number of state and federal officials. Wisconsin Democrat and chair of the Federal Deposit Insurance Corporation Leo T. Crowley praised the plan, as did Wisconsin Federation of Labor general counsel Joseph T. Padway and several business groups. During the joint finance committee hearings, the only really strenuous opposition came from the Wisconsin Manufacturers Association, headed by Fred Clausen, who opposed anything petitioned by Progressives as a general principle, and the Wisconsin Bankers' Association, which objected to the WFA warrants, or circulating scrip, in the fear that they would drain off banks' other assets. Despite these objections, the finance committee recommended passage by a vote of nine to two.[24]

The bill did not fare as well once it was reported out of committee, as senate Democrats grilled Thomas Duncan for two hours on the program's financial details. The provisions for taxation and warrants raised the most concern. The taxation issue exacerbated a long-standing complaint from some urban leaders that the cities paid out more to the state in income taxes than they received back in relief or work projects.[25] Milwaukee mayor Daniel Hoan, a Socialist and member of the Farmer-Labor-Progressive Federation, also opposed the warrants because he feared the notes would flood the city treasury, making it unable to make out-of-state purchases. Phil tried to allay these fears by denying that the WFA warrants were scrip—that is, temporary emergency currency; he instead described them as "certified checks" and promised that at all times the WFA would be more liquid than any other bank in the state. Because the warrants could be used to pay state income taxes, Phil insisted that they would remain in circulation at par until they were retired in twenty years.[26]

The assembly passed the bill, but the senate voted nineteen to fourteen to indefinitely postpone consideration, effectively killing the Wisconsin Works Plan as well as Phil's hard work of the past several months. The next evening in his now weekly radio address, Phil emotionally discussed the vote, speaking directly to the unemployed, merchants, educators, students, and the elderly in an unusually sarcastic tone, his bitterness apparent. "I had hoped tonight," he said solemnly, "to be able to tell you that . . . Wisconsin would lift from your threshold the fear of poverty." He described in concrete terms the work projects that the bill would have funded and then grimly noted that "the Wisconsin State Senate, by a vote of 19 to 14, refused to accept the one hundred million dollars offered by the federal government and to enact the necessary legislation to carry the Wisconsin program into action." He read the names of those who voted against it, urged people to contact their senators directly, and promised to fight on. The next day local Progressive leaders announced recall efforts aimed at those who voted to kill the bill, and Phil began a ten-day speaking tour into those senators' home districts. His emotion was genuine. He was bitterly disappointed that the senate had ended what he saw as the only way to end the Depression. He believed that he had been given a great commission by the people of the state and by the president only to be stopped by a few representatives allied to selfish interests.[27]

Progressives did not give up. In order to make the bill more palatable to its critics, Progressive leaders in the assembly divided the bill into two parts (administration and financing) and eliminated the controversial warrant provisions. While the legislature took up debate on the amended bill, Phil began his tour on June 18, speaking at the Milwaukee South Side armory in a predominantly Polish part of the city. A crowd of three thousand roared its approval when Phil urged them to "convey your wishes to your senators." One senator, Arthur Zimny, was actually there and was booed as he quickly left the meeting only to be cornered in a tavern by angry constituents. Phil's trip continued through Kenosha, Racine, Oshkosh, and Appleton. The Oshkosh gathering was particularly large, with more than three thousand packed into the auditorium and a thousand more outside. Phil continued to berate the senate, especially since none of its members had advanced an alternate plan to replace the failed works plan. He believed that the heart of progressive government was to carefully research public problems and develop legislation to address those problems. By doing nothing, the senate had abdicated its duty and failed to live up to Wisconsin's tradition of cooperation between academics and politicians to solve creatively modern social problems. The speaking tour generated a great deal of excitement but ultimately failed to sway the senate; in a wild session on June 28 with scores of the unemployed in the galleries, the senate voted seventeen to sixteen to indefinitely postpone the bill again. As the governor remarked bitterly the next day, "Seventeen members of the state senate slammed the door in the face of you thousands of men and women . . . in need and out of work." Never had Phil been so angry. He was humiliated that the state, so long a leader in public policy, was simply following the lead of the federal government.[28]

With his grand Wisconsin Works Plan scuttled by the senate, Phil went back to Washington. He discussed Wisconsin's share of funds from the new Works Progress Administration (WPA), and he turned over project materials assembled for the Wisconsin plan for the agency's use. Wisconsin was now on the same footing as all other states, with state and municipal projects directly funded and supervised by the federal relief bureaucracy. Commenting on the situation, Roosevelt remarked to reporters (again giving primary credit to former Governor Schmedeman) that the projects anticipated under the Wisconsin plan would form the basis of the WPA work in the state.[29]

The defeat of the works plan put Phil in a bitter mood that was exacerbated by the large amount of work still pending in the legislature, including the state budget. After its defeat, the works plan seemed a lost utopia, stolen by a handful of conservative senators. "This great opportunity," Phil commented over the radio, "for you and for Wisconsin was denied us by the votes of seventeen senators." He went on to note that the federal program meant not just less, but long-delayed, aid. He also complained about the legislature's failure to pass either a tax or a budget bill. A few days later, again addressing his audience via radio, his criticism became more strident: "A coalition between reactionary Republicans and reactionary Democrats has pursued a general policy of procrastination, obstructionism and selfish partisan politics unequaled in the history of the state." Not until early August did the senate pass an appropriation bill, although it failed to pass a tax bill that would adequately fund the appropriations. Phil continued speaking against the senate around the state through September, goading the senate to act or adjourn (one senator compared his actions to a woodpecker on a tin roof). He also delayed making a number of key appointments until after the legislature adjourned to prevent battles over senate confirmation. Finally, in the middle of September, the senate passed an adequate tax bill and adjourned, at 262 days, the longest session of the legislature to date.[30]

The rest of the Progressive program, less prominent but also important, was also defeated, due in part to Phil's confrontational radio addresses and speaking tour, which united opposition against the "wild man of Madison." Long-standing Progressive proposals, including the referendum (to allow voters to decide on legislation) and initiative (to allow voters to initiate legislation), a constitutional amendment to allow municipal public power, a bill to aid unions in labor disputes, and a bill to impose moratoria on mortgages were voted down in the senate. Angry and discouraged, Phil left for a two-week vacation in Bermuda before making a short speaking tour of New York, during which he continued to criticize New Deal policies that reduced agricultural production and forecasting third party victories in states in 1936 and 1940. Not willing to give up on his more immediate concerns, he also continued lecturing around the state on the failed works program in an attempt to marshal public opinion behind the Progressive cause.[31]

Adding to the wearing pace of his daily routine in office was a series of personal difficulties that strained the larger La Follette family. In January 1935, Mary's husband, Ralph Sucher, announced that he was leaving her for Nellie Dunn McKenzie, a longtime family secretary. The family was shocked, and Mary was devastated. A divorce was arranged, but at first Ralph was regularly delinquent in child support payments. Fola arrived in Washington to help Mary find a job, which proved far more stressful than anticipated: "[E]very few days," Fola wrote Isabel in May, "something seems to break which creates a problem to be dealt with." Phil, who had always been protective of his younger sister, worked to arrange financial support, continually regretful that he could not do more.[32] Fola had her hands full as well, working to finish the biography of her father begun by her mother years earlier. Both Ralph and Nellie had been working on it when they left the country, and its unfinished state was "a terrible blow" to her. She remained in a state of near panic for months. For Phil, this meant a further financial burden in subsidizing the research and writing. For Isabel, it meant research missions for Fola's work in Madison.[33]

Resigned to the state's participation in the same federal relief bureaucracy he had often criticized, Phil tried to make the best of the situation. The Wisconsin Emergency Relief Administration was reorganized into the Department of Public Welfare (within the Industrial Commission from December 1935 to February 1936, then as a separate department). He also arranged for Adjutant General Ralph Immell to be appointed state WPA administrator, much to state Democrats' annoyance.[34] Federal relief officials got used to the governor badgering them about inadequate relief or poor administration. These complaints—not really new—took a more bitter tone because of the failure of the works plan. "The federal program," Phil told one correspondent, "is entirely too small to take care of the unemployment needs of the state. It affords hardly any consideration for the person who is not on relief. The whole picture," he was quick to add, "would have been different if the Wisconsin program had been adopted.[35]

The shift from a state-run to a federally run works program also placed a strain on the relationship between Phil and President Roosevelt. Although their meetings were always cordial, the two had an uneasy working relationship. Phil had spent much of his 1934 campaign arguing against New Deal policies, and his central argument for the Wisconsin Works Plan was that the state could plan and administer a program more efficiently and more effectively than could the federal government. Roosevelt, in turn, was troubled by the new Progressive Party and the repeated rumors of a national effort that would cost the Democrats the White House in 1936 or 1940. In February 1935, Roosevelt wrote Edward House, former advisor to Woodrow Wilson, noting that Progressives liked the idea of a third party even if it was defeated because it would "cause a complete swing to the left before 1940." These suspicions seemed to be confirmed when during a White House conference that summer Phil suggested Roosevelt suspend all relief programs and then tell the nation that he was merely doing what the "businessmen of the country" wanted. A division of liberal forces was a distinct possibility; both Wisconsin and Minnesota had strong third parties, and Phil thought similar movements were possible in other midwestern and northeastern states. Worried as Roosevelt was over a potential liberal challenge, the president also had practical politics to consider, and the Wisconsin Democrats were not happy. Local party leaders were dismayed at the president's public cooperation with Phil and angry that patronage seemed to flow more freely through Progressive members of Congress. Roosevelt's comments to the press on Wisconsin or the Progressives were always evasive, and he repeatedly mentioned Schmedeman as the originator of the employment programs.[36]

At the same time that Roosevelt fretted about his political future, Phil continued to be coy about third party organization in other states or nationally. Such reluctance irritated some members of the Progressive Party who saw the state party primarily as a means of a national political realignment that would see liberals from both Democratic and Republican parties unite into a new organization. Meeting on November 30 and December 1, representatives of the Progressive Party, the Socialist Party, the Farmer-Labor-Progressive League, labor unions, and farmers' organizations formed the Wisconsin Farmer-Labor-Progressive Federation (FLPF), an umbrella organization that would unite liberal forces in the state and endorse candidates. Despite the fact that the Progressive Party had been formed out of an intention to unify Wisconsin liberals, the Progressive executive committee decided to send twenty-five delegates but told them firmly that they were not authorized to participate in framing a party declaration or platform. Nonetheless, this is precisely what the convention decided to do, and in doing so they broke sharply with the late La Follette by boldly calling for the abolition of the capitalist system and the implementation of "production for use."[37] Phil—and many Progressives—refused to join the organization, although his most visible aide, Thomas Duncan, was one of its chief organizers and was instrumental in having the Socialist Party give up its ballot status in favor of endorsement of FLPF candidates. The organization was essentially a political party that would not have its own column on the ballot but would endorse FLPF members running on other tickets, whether they were Progressive, Independent, Farmer-Labor, or Democrat.[38]

Phil repeatedly noted widespread sentiment for a national third party but remained mercurial about actually supporting one. *The Progressive* ran frequent and enthusiastic reports on growing party movements in other states, and shortly after his election Phil himself reported on the "tremendous interest" in the east and south. His first months as the ranking officeholder may have cooled his enthusiasm somewhat, for at the first anniversary of the Progressive Party gathering he emphasized the need for slow, grassroots support. Alfred Bingham, editor of *Common Sense*, was convinced that Phil would not support a new national party that would unite Wisconsin Progressives, Minnesota Farmer-Laborites, and other local liberal organizations. Yet when reporters wrote that Phil was trying to forestall third party activities, he called them into his office to assert that he supported national realignment as strongly as ever.[39]

Clearly Phil wanted such a national movement, but he was determined that its leadership come from the established Progressives, especially those who had worked with his father, including Senators William Borah of Idaho, Burton Wheeler of Montana, George Norris of Nebraska (all friends and allies of Fighting Bob), and, of course, the La Follette brothers themselves. Although he was willing to let more radical groups stir up the public (and he certainly wanted them to support the Progressive Party), he kept a safe distance to prevent the Progressive Party from drifting too far from the mainstream. This required keeping the FLPF in check and ensuring that third party efforts continued to be most closely identified with the La Follettes.[40] When the Farmer-Labor Political Federation (a national organization that grew out of the League for Independent Political Action, formed in 1929) held a conference in Chicago in July 1935 for the purpose of promoting a national organization, the La Follettes all but ignored it. Phil was "ready and anxious" to further a national third party, he wrote Seldon Rodman, Bingham's colleague at *Common Sense*, but he recalled the lack of success Progressives had in 1924 and emphasized how complicated practical matters would be in setting up organizations in all states. To another correspondent, he was more blunt: "I wish that some of these third party enthusiasts would devote more time and energy toward meeting some of the real and practical problems than in making high sounding speeches." Since 1920, the La Follette family had been the recognized leader of the legitimate, if somewhat theoretical, third party, and Phil did not want to abdicate that position to any group that could not advance specific proposals as Wisconsin had.[41]

———•———

Throughout the rest of his second term, Phil continued to follow his own course, to the discomfort of the Roosevelt administration and to the irritation of the more radical third party enthusiasts. In January 1936, he delivered several addresses in New York and Pennsylvania critical of the New Deal, in which he continued to argue that the administration viewed the Depression as a problem of overproduction rather than underconsumption. He advocated a more rational public program to increase purchasing power by federal efforts to fuel economic expansion; expansion was critical to full recovery, particularly since Phil opposed continued government borrowing to fund relief and work projects. The governor was thinking in terms of long-term economic planning, not just temporary expediencies.[42]

Nonetheless, 1936 was a presidential election year, and Phil realized that he had most to gain by steering a moderate course and supporting Roosevelt. In March, a group of WPA employees from the Fox Valley arrived in Madison to demand a sixty-dollar-a-month salary rather than the forty-eight-dollar prevailing wage in the area and to air other grievances with the relief administration. Failing to get a satisfactory response from WPA administrator Ralph Immell or state officials, the workers occupied the assembly chamber, issued denunciations of the WPA and of Phil ("a wishy-washy liberal"), and refused to leave. Phil listened to their grievances (and gave them a thirty-dollar check for food) but after ten days ordered the police to evict them from the capitol. The entire episode was a great strain because it played upon his own conflicting impulses: he was sympathetic to their demands but was unwilling to take their side against the WPA or to challenge public opinion. To have publicly sided with the strikers would have been an even greater strain on the uneasy alliance with the White House. After a brief holiday in Central America, Phil returned to Madison to begin planning the fall campaign. He faced one obvious issue: the failure of the legislature to enact his works plan. His position between the New Deal and more radical elements in the state placed him in a difficult position: he needed to articulate a clear identity separate from Roosevelt (lest he become too much a "me-tooer") but more moderate than farmer-labor groups. As he had in the past, Phil borrowed heavily from his father to give the clearest arguments to date about why the Progressive Party offered the best response to the economic upheavals facing the state and the nation.[43]

After much consideration, Phil refused to advocate the immediate formation of a national third party and instead chose to back Roosevelt. He did so for more than just purely political reasons. True, the president's popularity and apparent closeness certainly could not hurt his reelection efforts, but Phil also perceived a growing influence over Roosevelt and thought that he might push the president to pursue a more aggressive relief agenda. In the summer of 1935, Phil and Robert met with the president in Washington and later in Hyde Park. In Washington, Robert was particularly blunt when Roosevelt supposed that his silk-stocking social friends would support his reelection. "Mr. President," Robert responded, "if you crawled to New York on your belly, they would welcome the opportunity to kick you in the teeth." A shocked Roosevelt responded that "if you say so I must believe it." In August, the brothers discussed the coming campaign with Roosevelt and brought along Phil's secretary, A. W. Zeratsky, who provided Roosevelt with a blueprint for a form-letter campaign that Phil had used in 1934. Moreover, there seemed little need to challenge Roosevelt in 1935 and 1936. At the president's urging, Congress passed the Emergency Relief Appropriation Act in the spring of 1935, the largest single appropriation at that time, and set up the WPA as a preliminary means to replace relief with productive work. In August, the president, with Robert at his side, signed the Social Security Act, based in large part on the Wisconsin unemployment compensation program. Progressives knew Roosevelt was a winner, but he also seemed to be steering a more progressive course.[44]

A series of U.S. Supreme Court decisions also rid the New Deal of the programs Phil found most distasteful and forced Roosevelt to be the more aggressive reformer Phil wanted him to be. In May 1935, the court struck down the NRA, and Roosevelt suddenly threw his support behind the Wagner labor bill, a banking reform bill, and a "soak-the-rich" tax bill, all liberal reform efforts that he at first had distanced himself from. In 1936, the court struck down portions of the AAA. Even Roosevelt seemed to be using the same rhetorical flourishes as La Follette, especially when he denounced "economic royalists," invoked divine justice, or condemned the menacing power of wealth.[45] Roosevelt wanted Progressives' assistance as well. In August, he recruited Robert to chair a committee to organize Progressive support throughout the country; the conference that endorsed the president borrowed heavily from Wisconsin Progressives in both membership and ideology. In his public addresses, Phil urged all liberals to support Roosevelt, telling one audience that although he did not support everything the president had done, he was convinced that "the people are going to vote for the sanest liberal leadership offered to them."[46] With the new burst of activity, the New Deal had moved closer to the platform of the Wisconsin Progressive Party, and this allowed Phil to politically and philosophically support the president as a national leader sympathetic to the ideals of Old Bob himself.

With the president as an ally, the Progressives looked confidently to the election in 1936. The primary election indicated the party's strength: Democratic candidates received a combined 146,767 votes; Republican candidates, 166,155; and Phil, unopposed for renomination, 178,134. The FLPF refused to endorse Phil because he was not a member, but the organization had no other viable candidate and so made no endorsement for governor. Theodore Dammann, the only other statewide incumbent, received 169,495 votes. Six candidates for lieutenant governor received 163,954 votes, and three candidates for treasurer split a total of 175,192 votes. Of the seven Progressives in Congress, only one faced a challenge in the primary, but in the three seats held by Democrats, twelve Progressives ran. In one hundred assembly races, sixty-four Progressive nominations were contested, as were eight of the sixteen senate seats up for election. Complete slates of Progressives were nominated in all counties. Without a campaign of his own, Phil stressed the need for high Progressive turnout generally, and he encouraged participation in the primary by emphasizing the history of political innovation in Wisconsin and by castigating both Republicans and Democrats as hopelessly reactionary. Progressives had made history, he told crowds of voters, and they, too, could make history by voting for the party at this critical point.[47]

Both the Democratic and Republican nominees for governor based their campaigns on attacking Phil. Democrats nominated Arthur W. Lueck, a Beaver Dam attorney. Lueck and the Democrats, having endorsed Roosevelt in their platform, could not easily campaign against relief efforts in the state, but Lueck did attack Phil's administration. Relief and education, Lueck claimed, had become too politicized, and he warned one audience of "queer political notions."[48] Republicans nominated Chippewa Falls attorney and businessman Alexander Wiley. The Republican strategy was much more straightforward than that of the Democrats: to link the Progressives generally and Phil particularly to communism and argue that Progressive policies had raised taxes and driven business from the state but had done nothing to end the Great Depression. Toward the end of the campaign, Wiley became more desperate. He charged that federal relief money had become an immense slush fund with which to reward loyal

Progressives with jobs and that the Progressives had concentrated too much power in Madison. At the same time, an anonymously published "newspaper" called *Wisconsin Facts* began circulating in Madison and repeated various anti–La Follette stories and innuendo. Ashland editor John Chapple printed and distributed *La Follette Road to Communism: Must We Go Further Along That Road?*, a hardcover book that purported to link Progressives to the "godless communism" supposedly destroying the university and depicted Phil as a political charlatan out to make a fortune at public expense. These charges convinced no one.[49]

Phil's strategy was twofold: to align with Roosevelt and attack both the state parties. The latter was familiar territory for Progressive campaigners, but the open endorsement of an incumbent president was almost unprecedented. In July, Phil refused to endorse the administration whose policies he had been critical of, but it was conventional wisdom that Phil would back Roosevelt. Nonetheless, he was slow to do so and at first he gave the president only indirect support. "Don't blame Roosevelt for ineffective public works," he told a Wisconsin Rapids crowd in mid-September, "blame the seventeen reactionary state senators who turned down Roosevelt's offer to hand over $100,000,000 to the state." Later that month, Phil referred to Kansas governor and Republican presidential nominee Alfred Landon as "devoid of constructive proposals for the nation's welfare." By the end of September, Phil formally endorsed Roosevelt during a speech in Milwaukee, calling him the only candidate behind whom all liberals could unite.[50]

For the next six weeks, Phil traveled the state urging voters to elect a Progressive legislature and blaming the failure of his relief program on the now-infamous seventeen senators. He promoted the Progressives as the only party that offered any real choice for the future and urged the party to stay united.[51] The plea for unity was aimed not just at voters who might be tempted to vote a straight Democratic ticket with Roosevelt at its head, but also at candidates. The dissatisfaction of the more radical farmer-labor elements who wanted Phil to move further to the left remained intense. When Progressives met to draft a platform, delegate Henry Ohl proposed a fairly innocuous "production-for-use" plank, and Phil objected on the grounds that it was too vague and would only confuse members of the public as well as alienate farmers who had little sympathy for the class struggles. The convention followed his lead and voted the plank down by seventy to twenty-nine; almost the entire Milwaukee delegation voted for it. With no candidate of their own, the FLFP members had to go along with the La Follettes.[52]

Progressives held together through Election Day and had reason to be pleased with the outcome. They won forty-eight of one hundred seats in the assembly (effective control when cooperation with a few liberal Democrats was added) and sixteen of thirty-three seats in the senate, all five constitutional officers, and seven of ten congressional seats. Phil himself received 46 percent of the vote (Wiley received 29 and Lueck received 22), a dramatic increase from the 39 percent he received in 1934. But the election also showed some ominous signs for the future. Unlike 1934, when Democrats had run a close second, the Republican Party clearly indicated its position as the second party when it gained seats in both houses of the legislature at the expense of Democrats. Of the seven Progressive congressmen, three races were much closer than in 1934; in another race, the Progressive candidate ran a weak third.[53] Roosevelt carried the state by more than 400,000 votes, running about 229,000 ahead of Phil; Roosevelt's total indicates that he had solid support of both Democrats and Progressives but that Democrats would vote for their own candidate for governor. Even though the president never endorsed Phil and declined repeated invitations to campaign in Wisconsin, the day before the election, Phil and Robert had sent a telegram of congratulations to Roosevelt, noting that "every progressive in America is proud of you." A few weeks later, Roosevelt congratulated Phil on his reelection: "Let's keep up the good work."[54]

Shortly after the election, Netha Roe, the wife of La Follette's old law partner Gilbert Roe, wrote Phil a note of encouragement: "I hope you're planning some rest, or at least a spree, for there is little rest ahead. As I see it, Roosevelt's election is not so much a victory per se as averting a great calamity." Phil did indeed take her advice, but in typical fashion the "rest" was a short working vacation to Europe. Phil and Isabel visited Scandinavia, where Phil met with the prime ministers of Norway and Sweden. Sweden particularly impressed him with what he saw as "a near duplication" of the failed Wisconsin works program, a glimpse of what might have been. Prime Minister Per Hansson and Professor Gunnar Myrdal confirmed Phil's beliefs in the importance of providing work for the unemployed as a means of ensuring a prosperous and democratic society. "The experience of these countries," Phil noted, "has demonstrated that you cannot have prosperity without supplying useful work to a very substantial part of the population." Buoyed by his trip and impressed with Sweden's "middle way," Phil returned to Madison for the budget hearings determined to push a comprehensive works plan and make Wisconsin again lead the nation in progressive government.[55]

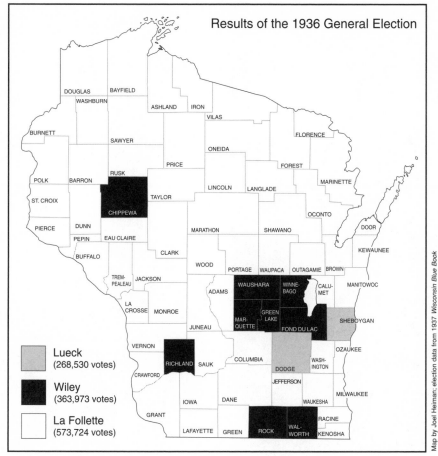

Results of the 1936 General Election

Lueck
(268,530 votes)

Wiley
(363,973 votes)

La Follette
(573,724 votes)

Map by Joel Heiman; election data from 1937 *Wisconsin Blue Book*

CHAPTER SEVEN

Third Term Controversies

On a hot June day in 1938, eight hundred people gathered for a memorial service in Forest Hill Cemetery on the west side of Madison. It was an unusually large crowd, especially considering the deceased had been there for thirteen years. The service, a memorial to Robert M. La Follette held annually since his death in 1925, had become a quasi-religious pilgrimage in which the faithful renewed their dedication to their departed leader. The year 1938 was a critical one for those loyal to the Progressive cause; only a few months earlier La Follette's son, Governor Philip F. La Follette, had capped a tumultuous legislative year by announcing the formation of a national Progressive Party to carry on the progressive movement. Congressman Gerald Boileau pronounced the late senator's blessings on the new enterprise:

> The spirit of the late Sen. Robert M. La Follette is with us in this cause and is urging us to pursue the course he advocated in his lifetime. He has shown us the way. . . . His record, his accomplishments and his declaration of principles are immortal. He lives today in the hearts and in the memory of millions of men, women and children throughout the land. We must move forward with him. He is not dead, he is just away.

Phil attended the service, sitting on the grass beneath a large tree. Afterward he and Isabel hosted an open house at the Executive Residence.[1]

In the years since his death, La Follette had rapidly moved from being a liberal icon to an almost prophetic figure: his writings became sacred text and his career almost a gospel. Progressives in 1938 clung to the conviction that his beliefs would be enshrined in a national political victory with the same seriousness that fundamentalists clung to the hope of a second coming of Jesus Christ. People repeated anecdotes about La Follette as if they were Bible stories. His battles and actions had become mythical, infused with a single-minded pursuit of democracy and equality.

La Follette's career, of course, was not as pure and unblemished as people remembered; he had engaged in a number of controversial actions, and at times his actions seemed to contradict his principles. In 1894, for example, he had urged his congressional colleague Nils P. Haugen to run for governor as the anti-machine candidate because he himself was unwilling to do so. In 1904 he had arranged for the Republican convention to be held in Madison at the University of Wisconsin gymnasium, where barbed wire and university football players prevented the seating of non-accredited delegates. In 1905 he had easily engineered his election to the U.S. Senate. Most famously, he led a filibuster of a bill to arm merchant ships in 1917, despite the fact that the bill would have passed Congress easily if brought to a vote. Throughout his career, La Follette had seen himself as a popularly anointed champion of democracy, and when convinced he was right, he was not afraid to use tactics similar to those he denounced as undemocratic. Nonetheless, he remained a popular figure, well loved by Wisconsin voters.[2]

Phil had always been keenly aware of his father's dedication and the people's affection for him. As a boy and young man he personally witnessed demonstrations of La Follette's stature in Wisconsin. He had seen how faith in democracy could excuse, or at least justify, controversial actions, and to live up to his father's legacy, he believed that he, too, had to take controversial actions and trust in his ultimate vindication.

By the summer of 1938, Phil had withstood a number of such controversies. During his third term as governor, he had been unable to enact the ambitious works plan that had nearly passed during his second term, and he had been rebuked for his involvement in the dismissal of University of Wisconsin president Glenn Frank, his appointment of political allies to important state positions, his reorganization of the state government, and heavy-handed dealings with the legislature. Most significantly, his supposed personal ambitions had become apparent when he launched a national Progressive Party with an eye toward the White House in 1940. Denounced as a dictator by enemies and doubted by his allies, Phil nevertheless believed his actions were necessary to hold together Progressives and would ultimately be vindicated by his dedication to making democratic government more efficient and responsive to the will of the people. In 1938, however, he would badly misjudge both public opinion and the cohesion of his followers; his actions would bring about his own political downfall and the decline of the Progressive Party.

———•———

The troubles began almost immediately upon Phil's return to Madison in December 1936, with the movement to fire University of Wisconsin president Glenn Frank. Phil had clashed with Frank several times in the past. Shortly after his election in 1930, while he was preparing the state budget, Phil had requested that former regent Theodore Kronshage examine Frank's proposed university budget; because reduced tax revenues and increased relief costs demanded tighter state budgets, Frank's request for $9.1 million—almost one million more than in the 1929–31 biennium—was an obvious target. The day before the public hearing, Kronshage "cross-examined" Frank for three hours at a private meeting at Maple Bluff Farm. While Phil found Kronshage's questioning "devastating, calm, cold, and relentless," he was astonished at the university president's lack of understanding of the budget; during the grilling, it became clear that Frank had not followed through on his earlier promises to eliminate "dead wood" from the faculty or implement other efficiencies and had actually increased salaries in an almost arbitrary fashion. The next day at the public hearing, Frank's humiliation continued for another six hours. After the hearings, Phil, surprised that Frank had not taken any measures to improve his presentation before the hearing, recommended a budget that cut funding for the university by $500,000. Throughout his first term he continually pushed the university to cut costs and salaries for administrators, including Frank's. Phil also met with the Board of Regents to warn them about what he considered Frank's poor administration.[3]

The hostility continued as Frank's and his wife's comparatively lavish lifestyle irritated the La Follettes and others keenly aware of the hardship brought by the Depression; the Franks tried to ingratiate themselves with the La Follettes, who remained aloof from the social-climbing university president. Aside from his meeting with the Board of Regents, however, Phil had done nothing about the situation in either his first or second terms because he was preoccupied with his legislative program and the never-ending demands of leading the Progressive Party. He also did not want to appear to be influencing the operations of the university too directly, especially since Frank had complained to some that the Progressives wanted to use the university as a "propaganda machine." Early in 1936, after giving Frank plenty of time to improve his administration of the university, the board took matters into its own hands. President Harold Wilkie came to the executive office to discuss the university situation; Wilkie told the governor that he and at least two other regents thought Frank had managed the university badly and had to be replaced. The next day, regent Dan Grady, Superintendent of Public Instruction and *ex officio* regent John Callahan, and Wilkie met with Phil. Callahan agreed to meet quietly with Frank to suggest he resign. Callahan, however, failed to get a letter of resignation or a firm statement out of Frank, and Frank, now aware of a movement against him, immediately began contacting other regents to gain their support. As Frank prepared for a confrontation, Phil had Wilkie delay action until after the 1936 elections lest the fracas overshadow other, more important issues. The entire matter simmered until after the election and then exploded in December of that year.[4]

On December 7, 1936, Regents Wilkie and Clough Gates met with Phil, determined to force the issue of Glenn Frank's resignation at the Board of Regents meeting two days later. Gates and Wilkie told the governor that they would inform Frank privately before the meeting that the board would not renew his contract. When they did so, Frank feigned astonishment and asked that he be allowed to resign. Gates and Wilkie agreed to wait until the December 16 meeting and allow Frank to find a new position. Recognizing that it was a mistake not to get such a promise in writing, Phil warned Gates and Wilkie that Frank would put up a fight; in the interim the Frank case became major news. It came as no surprise that Frank did not offer his resignation on December 16. Instead, Wilkie made a formal presentation of charges against Frank, and a public hearing and board vote was scheduled for January 6.[5]

The incident was a severe blow to Phil's reputation. Isabel filled two scrapbooks with newspaper clippings almost all hostile to the governor, who overnight became a villain to academics across the country who resented any hint of political control over a public university. Letters and telegrams defending Frank flooded the executive office, requiring extra secretarial help. The most damaging effect of the episode was not that longtime friends and supporters like Fred Holmes and Zona Gale turned against Phil, but that the public at large was so ready to believe that Phil had instigated Frank's ouster in order to control the university and eliminate a potential political rival (Frank had been boomed as a liberal

Republican presidential candidate for 1936). The implication was that Phil's ambition was a threat to academic freedom; observers pointed to Louisiana governor Huey Long's interference with Louisiana State University as a precedent.[6]

Phil worried that the affair would undermine support for his legislative program, and he attempted a resolution before the UW Board of Regents met in January. Based on a suggestion from educational reformer John Dewey, he proposed a faculty referendum on Frank's tenure, but several professors as well as College of Letters and Sciences Dean George Sellery talked him out of it, noting that not everyone had all the facts and that such a referendum would only divide the faculty. On December 21 Phil tried another solution and asked Harvard president James B. Conant to chair an independent commission to investigate the matter; Conant, however, declined to become involved. Either of these proposals would have ratified the decision to remove Frank, thereby relieving charges of unfounded meddling by Phil or his appointees to the Board of Regents. Having decided that Frank's removal was in the best interests of the university, Phil refused to back down, but without further ideas he would, Fola wrote, "simply have to sit and take it on the chin." Robert, too, was sympathetic: "I can imagine what it is like in Madison these days— having to talk about it from morning til night—or be talked at." Two days after Phil's inauguration, the Board of Regents voted eight to seven to dismiss Frank. Again this proved controversial: all eight regents who voted for dismissal had been appointed by Phil. Throughout the affair, Phil had refused to make any public statements until after the board had made its decision, but on January 8, well aware of negative public sentiment, he released a statement defending his involvement. The governor, he said, was responsible for all state agencies and would be abrogating his duty to the people if he did not do what he thought best for the university; he outlined his arguments against Frank's management and blamed Frank for injecting politics into the matter and placing his own career above the university's welfare. Shortly afterwards a group of six hundred university students marched to the capitol to protest Frank's firing and demanded to see the governor; he met with them in the Assembly Chamber for a short time and listened to their opinions, but he refused to be swayed.[7]

The Glenn Frank episode left Phil physically and emotionally exhausted at a critical time: although the Progressives had working majorities in both houses of the legislature, continual factionalism jeopardized enactment of any Progressive legislation. Shortly after the legislature convened on January 13, Phil circulated his budget message; like the 1935 budget it contained three schedules with varying appropriations, a "self-balancing" mechanism whereby expenditures would automatically adjust to reflect receipts.[8] Soon thereafter, legislators introduced other major Progressive legislation, including a labor bill modeled after the National Labor Relations Act. The bill defined unfair labor practices (discriminating against unionized employees, blacklisting, and interfering with an organizing drive, among others) and established a powerful three-person labor board with the authority to conduct investigations and arbitrate labor disputes. Phil, who praised the bill as a means to promote industrial harmony, went to great lengths to smooth over opposition to it, meeting with labor officials and business owners in mid-February. Industrial centers along the Lake Michigan shore had been plagued by often violent labor confrontations, not only between employers and unions but also among competing AFL and CIO unions. The labor board was critical in maintaining industrial peace. After several delays, the senate passed the labor bill on April 1. Meanwhile, Republicans and Democrats used delaying tactics to try to prevent passage of the budget bill. It eventually passed in May.[9]

Having secured a budget and a labor bill, Progressives focused on a long-standing demand of their rural constituents: public electrical power. Public power had long been an important issue for Progressives, and despite the defeat of the Wisconsin Finance Authority two years earlier, they now proposed the creation of a similar organization, the Wisconsin Development Authority, an independent corporation that would fund construction of power plants for both municipalities and rural areas and would direct federal Rural Electrification Administration funds to rural areas. Republicans and Democrats again fought the measure through a series of delaying tactics and by suggesting that the WDA was a step toward communism. Despite the specter of Communist electricians stalking the countryside, on June 16 the senate finally passed the bill, but only after opponents twice disappeared to prevent a quorum; Lieutenant Governor Henry Gunderson signed subpoenas compelling the absent senators to appear, and the sergeant at arms bolted the doors to the senate chamber to prevent further escapes. After the vote, opponents of the bill blasted Progressives and Phil for employing such dictatorial tactics.[10]

Rather than pursuing more Progressive legislation in such a hostile atmosphere, Phil supported a motion to adjourn *sine die* effective July 2. He was worried about how the Progressives would hold together and was growing irritated and frustrated with the "so-called leaders" who were eager to keep the session going: "Some—but not all—of these leaders," he wrote Robert, "were interested in keeping the session on—to keep open consideration of their 'pet' bills—some of which were 'shake downs.'" To further complicate matters, Progressive members all seemed to have separate agendas. There was much Phil wanted to accomplish, and rather than continuing to deal with bickering legislatures he planned to call a special session, which would allow the governor to specify what it could consider and prevent the introduction of unrelated bills. Not only was Phil tired of working with the fractious party, he was beginning to focus on other things. Prior to adjournment, Secretary Gordon Sinykin reported to Isabel that he and others in the governor's office, including Thomas Duncan and A. W. Zeratsky, thought Phil was neglecting his responsibility of dealing with the legislature and with party leaders and that they were overstepping their authority in making policy and strategy decisions. Duncan was in fact a familiar figure in the legislative chambers, acting as a party leader by directing legislators over matters of debate and parliamentary maneuvering.[11]

Phil also recognized that his goals—including labor and public power—could no longer be adequately addressed at the state level; any real change would have to come from Washington. Wisconsin simply did not have the resources to cope with the underlying economic problem, and dealing with the legislature was in many ways an exercise in futility. He had become preoccupied with national affairs during the session, especially about funding cuts for federal relief work. Shortly after his inauguration, he met with Roosevelt in the White House to inform him that the new Wisconsin legislature made it likely that his works bill could be enacted. Roosevelt, no longer concerned about wooing Progressives since his reelection, remained noncommittal. Recent WPA cuts, he said, made the federal funding impossible. Hoping to force Roosevelt's hand in spending, Phil and New York governor Herbert Lehman arranged a conference in New York on February 28 with other governors (George Earle of Pennsylvania, Henry Horner of Illinois, Elmer Benson of Minnesota, Robert Quinn of Rhode Island, and Charles Hurley of Massachusetts) to discuss relief issues. In early March, they met with the president to urge him to maintain funding for the WPA. Before the meeting, Phil outlined the group's goals to reporters, which included an ambitious proposal to maintain all "employables" on the WPA rolls until they could find private employment. The meeting was less than successful. The group demanded expanded federal relief work, but Roosevelt grew irritated by Lehman's blunt and aggressive manner; after the meeting, when Phil tried to appeal to Roosevelt personally, the president responded, "Phil, there have always been poor people—there always will be. Be practical!" A second meeting in April did not improve Phil's hope that the federal government would act or even make possible individual state action. After that meeting, Phil decided to be cool toward Roosevelt for the time being and make no new requests in the hopes that the administration would have a change of heart. He did eventually request cooperation in drafting a new works bill, but dropped the matter in favor of early adjournment of the legislature. Whatever influence Phil had thought he had with Roosevelt had clearly evaporated.[12]

Roosevelt's rebuff was particularly frustrating for Phil since he himself had gone out on a limb to support the president's ill-fated court-packing scheme in February. On February, 5, 1937, the president announced that he would be proposing legislation allowing him to appoint new justices to the U.S. Supreme Court. Phil and Robert were the only liberals of national standing to support the measure. Newspaper and magazine editors including Oswald Garrison Villard and William Allen White reacted in horror at the president's meddling with the court. Senators William Borah, Gerald Nye, Hiram Johnson, and Burton Wheeler opposed the plan, and George Norris supported it only half-heartedly. Phil, however, enthusiastically hailed the plan as the best means of making the court more responsive to the people's will. This was familiar territory for Progressives. In 1924, La Follette had made U.S. Supreme Court reform a major part of his presidential campaign and had urged a constitutional amendment that would allow Congress to override court decisions. The issue of a "judicial oligarchy" had become acute immediately following World War I, when the court struck down several progressive laws.[13] In February, Phil delivered a national radio broadcast in favor of the plan (a speech he "sweated over," according to Isabel). Rather than adopting the president's rather artless fiction that the court was overworked, Phil bluntly acknowledged that the move was to protect the New Deal policies but noted that the court stood in the way of democratic progress. "The spectacle," he said, "of five men blocking the progress of 130,000,000 people by twisting and distorting the plain terms of the Constitution to accord with outworn prejudices is a situation that needs correction." Phil even introduced a plan for the voluntary retirement and pension of Wisconsin justices and circuit court judges, causing a minor furor in the state capitol. His opponents charged that Phil was copying the president's move to dominate the U.S. Supreme Court.[14]

Supporting the president's controversial measure was one thing, but after Justice Willis Van Devanter announced his retirement in May,

Phil's support made him seem something of an opportunist. The *Capital Times* began hinting that Phil himself might be a judicial nominee; at a meeting in May at the White House, Phil (thinking perhaps that Roosevelt wanted to place him in a position where he would be unable to speak out against the president's policies) seemed to get that idea as well. Robert even sent a copy of a telegram from George Norris to the president endorsing Phil for the position. Phil insisted he did not want a seat on the court (and even tried to push the appointment of Robert) but the publicity made him appear to be currying favor with Roosevelt in hopes of a lifetime appointment.[15]

Frustrated with the federal government's unwillingness to maintain— let alone increase—relief spending and with the inadequacies of the state's own efforts, Phil increasingly began to promote national political realignment, a reshuffling of liberal Republicans, Democrats, and others into a single third party. In June he told students and alumni of the Harvard Business School that a national realignment was underway; its goal was to adapt government to changing conditions.[16] At Northwestern University he argued that the United States's future was not a choice between socialism and capitalism or between communism or fascism, as some popular intellectuals suggested. Instead he predicted a democratic cooperative state that would use government as an instrument to promote economic expansion and economic equality, rather than smaller measures that kept workers and farmers better paid but still captive to an economic system run for the profits of business owners. Opportunity alone was no longer enough: "Apply the doctrine of equality," he said, "but apply it not only in giving to every individual an equal chance to live, but to likewise develop at the same time a definite sense of equality of responsibility."[17] Ironically, Phil came to this conclusion just as some former third party enthusiasts, including Thomas Amlie and Alfred Bingham, had resigned themselves to the New Deal, concluding that liberal reform would have to come via a Roosevelt-led Democratic Party.[18]

In that same address, Phil noted the need for massive political organization, and he knew what hard work organizing a new party would be. In the summer and fall of 1937, he actively promoted the formation of new parties in Iowa and Nebraska. After meeting with Phil, a number of Iowa liberals, including a small farmer-labor party, agreed to unite behind the "Progressive Party" label. The move effectively created a nascent regional party in the upper Midwest incorporating Wisconsin, Minnesota, Iowa, and to a lesser extent the Dakotas and Nebraska.[19] But even modest talk of "realignment" or "national third party" carried the implication that Phil was a self-promoter. In February 1937, the *Capital Times* had reported that some Wisconsin congressmen wanted Phil to be a presidential candidate in 1940. Reports circulated that Phil had his eyes on F. Ryan Duffy's senate seat, which would be open in 1938, as a steppingstone to the White House. Visits with Roosevelt on the presidential yacht only seemed to confirm that one or the other La Follette was planning a presidential run.[20]

The break after the legislature adjourned allowed Phil to confer with Robert and other Progressives on national affairs and to prepare for the special session. After consulting with agricultural and labor interests, Republicans, Democrats, and all factions of the Progressive Party, Phil issued a call on September 11, 1937, for the legislature to convene on September 15. A strict routine was established to keep the session as short as possible. No resolutions or memorials to Congress could be introduced, nor could any new bills be introduced after September 22 unless approved by the Progressive-controlled Joint Finance Committee. Both houses were to meet five days a week. The main business would be a $3 million emergency relief bill and a tax bill, but Phil promised to retract his opposition to further bills if his initial proposals were dealt with speedily. Conservative Republicans and Democrats demanded the governor amend his call, balking at what they saw as unconstitutional demands for a short session.[21]

Phil's vision for a quick and efficient session evaporated after the legislature took over three weeks to pass the relief bill, and then only after he strong-armed the squabbling Progressives to support it. By early October, he was furious at the lack of progress and eager for a rest and a return to his third-party organizing. "It has been such a long grind for a year now," Phil wrote Isabel, "that I count the days, and yes hours until I can leave." On October 4, Phil sent another message to the legislature scolding its members for slow action and promising to send more bills (for agricultural support, establishing a department of commerce, old-age pensions, and a sweeping governmental reorganization) if legislators agreed to certain rules of order, suggested by Thomas Duncan and intended to make them complete their work quickly. Phil proposed that the legislature meet for six days a week for at least eight hours a day, a fixed adjournment on October 16, and restrictions on amendments from the floor, all designed to curtail the kinds of delaying tactics that the opposition had used in the regular session. Such rules, Phil wrote Isabel, made Democrats and Republicans "raving mad," but both houses accepted them a few days later.[22]

Under strict control of Progressive speaker Paul Alfonsi, and with Thomas Duncan in the chamber directing Progressive members, the assembly worked quickly. The senate, however, continued to infuriate the governor by remaining in session only a few hours a day; Phil threatened to revoke the call entirely. Over the determined opposition of minority members, Progressives in the senate forced through a farm bill, a commerce bill, and a mortgage moratorium bill. Phil met daily with them, persuading individual members to vote for the measures and urging them to stay united. By October 13, the controversial reorganization bill had been engrossed and seven others passed. Phil was exhausted but pleased when he wrote Isabel that day:

> The legislature has done more work in the past five days than [it] did in three months of regular session. . . . More than that this knoc[k]-down and drag out scrap has [k]nitted our forces together, created better feeling, and should send them home pepped-up and in good shape for next year. All the party wrangling (publicly) has disappeared, and even more than that there is a sense of unity we have lacked ever since the Farmer-Labor Fed. came on the scene.[23]

As a result, eleven administration bills were introduced and passed in seven days with restrictions on debate and without public hearing; the presiding officers in both houses repeatedly ruled normal parliamentary motions dilatory and therefore inherently out of order. When the legislature adjourned on October 16, the *Milwaukee Sentinel* summed up the results: the establishment of a Department of Commerce and the Wisconsin Agricultural Agency (modeled on the national AAA and with broad powers to regulate agriculture), liberalized pension laws, extension of a home and farm mortgage moratorium, a chain store tax, a trades practices code, a relief bill funded by taxes on incomes and inheritances, and a government reorganization bill. The last half-hour of the senate session was dedicated to confirmation of twenty-four new (or "loyal," as opponents called them) government officials in what the newspaper referred to as a purge, as old officials lost their jobs to reorganization and new officials were appointed. Democrats and Republicans marched out of their chambers shouting "Heil" with upraised arms in a mock Nazi salute. The *Sentinel* reported that the special session "in seven days saw more important and far reaching measures enacted into law than any legislature since the days of the late dictator Huey P.

Long." The *Janesville Gazette* decried the "Louisiana methods of legislation," and the *Chicago Tribune* noted that "Democracy in Wisconsin seems to have gone as far as anywhere in its surrender to a one man form of government."[24]

Phil and other Progressives responded that they were merely responding to the will of the electorate; they viewed their party platform as a contract between them and the voters, and they were merely carrying out that contract. But some longtime followers of La Follette were extremely troubled by the spectacle. William Evjue wrote in the *Capital Times*:

> During the last few days of the session, orderly parliamentary procedure was thrown out of the window. The presiding officers in both houses made rulings in defiance of all accepted rules and procedure and the speaker of the house, on one occasion, made a ruling, unheard of in Wisconsin, denying the right to appeal from a decision of the chair. The rights of the minority were swept aside. The last few days of the session were characterized by tactics of the Huey Long variety and legislation was railroaded through in shotgun style. Bills were put through the legislative hopper under gag rule that never had an adequate hearing. Members voted on bills they had never read. It was a week in which we had legislation by executive decree through pressure exerted from the governor's office. It was a week in which democratic processes were abandoned and an executive dictatorship was in the saddle.[25]

He further noted that the long delays in the regular session were partly the product of lack of Progressive leadership, and he pointed to the danger of a special session in which the legislature could only respond to the governor's instructions.

Phil had anticipated the charges that were leveled at him by members of all parties. Writing to Isabel early in October, he noted that some legislators called him " 'dictator' and etc." He had been preoccupied for months with the abstract problem of how to make the government more responsive to the changing needs of society—probably the central question behind the progressive movement. Even Roosevelt had wrestled with this problem when he complained of the Supreme Court rulings invalidating major portions of the New Deal. The regular session of the 1937 legislature also seemed to have demonstrated how unproductive party rule could be. Having been reelected, Phil believed he had a mandate from the people and that the bickersome legislature actually hindered democracy; the intellectual in him could rationalize such action. Although he may have been prepared for charges of dictatorship by the opposition, he was probably not aware of how quickly he would be compared to Long or Mussolini or how damaging those comparisons would be. His model of vigorous and determined executive leadership continued to be his father between 1901 and 1906; his opponents charged that it more closely resembled Adolf Hitler after 1933.[26]

The reorganization bill was the most controversial measure passed during the special session, and Phil vigorously defended it as an embodiment of the central tenets of the progressive movement. Several careful studies had examined the responsibilities of each department or bureau and how the personnel in each could function most efficiently, and boards of commissioners (a nineteenth-century innovation) were replaced by single executives. The act also vested the governor, with the approval of an interim committee, with sweeping powers to change the state bureaucracy, transferring functions from one agency to another. The reorganization bill did rationalize the functions of government, transferring, for example, the old-age pension program from the board of control and the beverage tax division from the treasurer's office to the tax commission, and was a step towards a cabinet-style administration. Phil reconciled the centralization of state authority to the governor with democratic ideals by noting that no one questioned the ability of a democratic government to use force on individuals or small groups who threatened to violate the interests of the whole society. In other words, Phil believed that he was empowered by the people to use the authority of the government to pursue the public welfare, even at the expense of some individuals. He reiterated Wisconsin's past innovations—from workman's compensation to unemployment insurance—to defend the Progressives' claim to being democracy's agent. The same day senators marched out of the chamber imitating the Nazi salute, Phil delivered a radio address entitled "Democracy Functions in Wisconsin," in which he praised the legislature for passing relief appropriation and modernizing government. "The test of democratic government," he stated, "is whether it can function to meet the needs of the people as these arise and change." He promised that his administration would continue to make democracy function.[27]

Amid renewed newspaper speculation of a Progressive presidential ticket in 1940, Phil and Isabel departed for Central America for a brief vacation. In Costa Rica, Phil developed a sore throat and began experiencing chills; he was taken to a U.S. military hospital with a fever of 103°. Newspaper reports stated only that he had suffered an attack of influenza, but his condition was actually much more serious. Doctors recently trained at the Mayo Clinic diagnosed a streptococcus infection of a particularly aggressive nature, usually fatal, and treated him with sulfa drugs, which were just coming into use. Only a few years earlier the infection probably would have killed him. While he recovered in Panama, Phil pondered his close call, his future, and the future of the progressive movement. Isabel noted the impact that the illness had on him: "while he was lying those weeks in the Panama hospital with the retrospect of having nearly snuffed out, he was making up his mind that life was indeed to be used for what seems right to the individual." He thought about the years of conferences and meetings of liberals, all the speeches and proposals, and decided that if anything was ever to be actually done, he would have to take action.[28]

He returned to Madison in late November in a weakened condition. At the urging of Robert and Wisconsin Chief Justice Marvin Rosenberry, he "behaved" himself and took his recovery unusually slowly; Isabel reported that he was shocked to learn how hard the infection had hit his heart and blood system, a fact that had been kept from him during his early recovery. His absence from public life, Robert also noted, would do no harm, perhaps letting charges of dictatorship fade. Phil went into the office for only a few hours in the mornings. Yet at the same time, his mind was racing over the need to get people back to work, and he even urged Robert to compose a major speech urging greater relief spending.[29]

In the early months of 1938, Phil continued to hint at the development of a national Progressive Party in meetings in and out of the state. In New York he criticized Democrats and Republicans for failing to end the unemployment problem and acknowledged that it was really a national problem that individual states could not cope with alone. Dismayed at the federal cuts to relief programs, he made the curious point that "Democracy is based on the ability of the [people] to cut through the complicated maze of personalities and ideas to a judgment drawn from their own experience. . . . A grave danger [to] democratic government is that it has got bogged down with a complexity of detail and red tape." In saying this, he wasn't dismissing democracy as irrelevant, but he pointed to the need for an educated public who understood the issues and for elected officials who functioned efficiently in carrying out the will of the people. His experience with the 1937 legislation had reinforced this perception, and he saw a parallel in the federal relief bureaucracy and a divided Congress hobbled by reactionary southern representatives. His experience with the Progressive Party also underscored the need for cooperative action rather than trying to broker between a multiplicity of competing interest groups; uniting such elements, of course, was the major challenge facing the executive branch. His language alarmed some, and his vague arguments about national realignment in 1940 shed no light on his own future plans.[30] The one thing newspapers across the country did pick up on was a decidedly cold wind blowing between Phil and the president. As political commentator Winter Everett noted, "Mr. Roosevelt has decided that he and the La Follettes will not sleep in the same political bed in the future."[31]

Privately, Phil was not sure where his future lay. He believed he had three possible courses. He could stand for reelection as governor and just be "an office holder," merely the administrative head of the state. He could run again and, as Isabel wrote, "really go ahead and do things . . . and let them call him Dictator if they want, on the theory that he is elected to accomplish certain specified results and it is up to him to make democracy function." His third option was to resign and dedicate himself to organizing a national Progressive Party. Having decided that he would not like serving in the U.S. Senate, Phil had already ruled out running for Ryan Duffy's seat in 1938. His four years in office had worn heavily on him, and Isabel thought he would not be able to endure being governor much longer. As he had for other major decisions, Phil discussed his dilemma with Robert at length. Although he expected Robert to be angry at the possibility of his leaving politics, Robert merely wondered about when the best time would be. Robert also noted that being an elected official gave Phil's public statements greater weight; Phil's absence from Wisconsin would also have forced Robert to spend more time campaigning and maintaining the Progressive Party organization. As Robert grew increasingly worried about Roosevelt's foreign policy and Phil grew weary of state affairs, Phil gradually became convinced that his own future was in pushing for long-term economic and political change. But how to best do that remained unclear.[32]

Phil began meeting with groups of Progressive leaders from around the state to discuss the future. He told the state Progressive Central Committee to think hard about the party's future. For three or four hours a day Progressive leaders discussed whether they should begin a national movement. If so, should it be through one of the old parties or through a new party? What should Phil's role be—candidate for governor or senator, or national organizer? At these meetings, Phil made a crucial link between economic prosperity and democracy. During his terms in office, he had spoken repeatedly about the need for economic expansion and had criticized the New Deal's emphasis on restricting production. Based on what he had seen on his travels in Europe, he believed that the fundamental cause of dictatorship was economic scarcity; democracy depended not only on an educated citizenry but also on a prosperous one. Economic well being, he told Progressives, depended on the federal government; without federal leadership people would become desperate enough to embrace any "crackpot" movement. Phil bore heavily the burden of Wisconsin's progressive accomplishments and was unwilling to let the Wisconsin Progressives abrogate national leadership at what he saw as the most critical time in the nation's history since the Civil War.[33]

Phil asked Progressives to write him with their views, and they did. Isabel estimated that these letters were 90 percent in favor of a national party, but most of the letter writers also wanted Phil to run for reelection. The immediate result of the Central Committee meetings was to unite Progressives as never before—even some of the most difficult farmer-labor types realized that they needed Phil's prominence and abilities as a campaigner. No one was willing to challenge Phil lest he abandon politics altogether; he had made up his mind, and no one told him anything differently. Ironically, the one member of the Progressive Party who was adamant about not going forward immediately with the third party was Robert. He had avoided coming to these conferences, despite Phil's repeated requests. Isabel thought that Robert was for the idea of a national Progressive Party but could not bear the difficulties of organizing the effort. Robert refused to leave Washington during hearings by his Civil Liberties Committee, but he wanted to talk to Phil before he made any firm decision, perhaps worried about how Phil's actions would affect his chances for reelection in 1940. After outlining all the risks, Robert eventually agreed to support a national effort, but it was clear that Phil would have to do most of the work.[34]

Having received no major resistance from Progressives, Phil moved forward with his plans to launch a national party. He began with a rally in Madison. To build interest, he planned a series of radio talks to be broadcast statewide on thirteen stations in the weeks leading up to the event, and he sent drafts to Robert in early April. The broadcasts began on April 19, and the first gave little hint of the things to come; Phil defended the reorganization act at length, giving several examples of how state agencies had been shuffled for the sake of efficiency. Only at the end was there any suggestion that the rally would cover more expansive subjects, as Phil asked his listeners, "[W]hat can we do to help in the great task of bringing order, peace, and security to our people, and to the world in which we live? These problems must be faced, and it is concerning them that I will talk with you tomorrow night." The next night his address was more confrontational; he again posed the question that had been on his mind for the past year: How can democracy function more efficiently? But after repeating the state's accomplishments, he blamed the continuing economic problems on the Roosevelt administration, which, he argued, had failed to pursue meaningful relief and recovery after 1936. His third speech continued this attack on Roosevelt, scorning the policy of paying "great numbers of able-bodied men and women to do nothing productive." Yet he offered no clear alternative, aside from a vague call for "organized action." In the last of these radio speeches, he again challenged the notion of mere redistribution of wealth and called for government-coordinated work programs: "It does not seem reasonable to speak of a third of our people 'ill-fed, ill-clothed, and ill-housed,'" he remarked, "and then conclude that we are in trouble because of over-production." He then announced a public meeting to be held at the university gymnasium on Thursday, April 28.[35]

The radio addresses did indeed fuel speculation about what Phil was planning and what announcement he might make, although most reporters recognized that the Madison rally was likely the first step toward a national party. The Associated Press dispatched a features photographer, who spent two hours with Phil and his family at the Executive Residence the week before the rally. Phil himself holed up, preparing what he knew would be the most important speech of his career. While he was preparing, other national liberal leaders debated whether or not to participate. New York mayor Fiorello La Guardia phoned Phil and sounded supportive but declined to attend. Wisconsin Representatives Harry Sauthoff, Merlin Hull, Bernhard Gehrmann, and George Schneider enthused over the meeting but wanted to stay in Washington. Norris was uninterested. Labor groups and farmers' organizations were noncommittal, and the Minnesota Farmer-Labor Party sent no delegate. Some unions bluntly refused to have anything to do with the rally. Roosevelt responded to a reporter's question only that the more liberal organizations there were in the country the better; Roosevelt advisor Adolph Berle, he later commented, planned to attend but in no way represented the administration.[36]

Speculation continued as Phil changed the rally site from the gymnasium to the university Livestock Pavilion, a much larger venue.

William Evjue, by now completely loyal to the president and the New Deal, criticized Phil's comments on Roosevelt and warned repeatedly of the dangers of divided liberal forces. Most irritating to Phil was Robert's continued vacillation. Even though Robert reluctantly supported the third party, he continued to raise questions, and Phil had to reassure him. Robert refused to come to Madison to discuss a national third party but then got angry at Phil for moving ahead without him. In her diary, Isabel summed up Robert's reluctance: "He is tired; he sees all the risks; he's discouraged." Whenever the brothers did meet, Phil would reassure Robert and leave believing they were of one mind. Back in Washington, Robert would begin to doubt Phil's plans and convince himself that a national party would alienate voters and end both their careers. The Sunday before the rally, Robert met with Phil and other Progressives and again questioned Phil's plans; no one else would talk back to Robert, so Phil had to respond to all of his fears. On his way back to Washington, Robert told reporters that he supported his brother completely, but his privately expressed worries and disinterest in political organizing left Phil feeling abandoned.[37]

The rally was organized by Adjutant General Ralph Immell, and as people began to arrive, they were more than a little disturbed by what they saw. The pavilion was decorated in red, white, and blue, and a military band played marches and other patriotic music. University football players lined the stage and served as ushers and, in the event of a disturbance, bouncers. Attendees were startled to see a large banner immediately behind the stage that featured a large circle-and-x design, conceived by Phil himself and sewn by Isabel. The meeting was chaired by Progressive Representative Alvin Reis. As Phil delivered the keynote address, standing alone on the stage and illuminated by spotlights, many in the audience saw the trappings of fascism. People shuffled nervously in their seats as they wondered what it all meant. Phil's seventy-five-minute address summed up his thinking of the past few years. He emphasized the need for a nation to produce wealth in order to ensure not only prosperity but also democracy. Neither fascism nor communism offered a way out of the problems of depression, he told the crowd; the Republicans were too reactionary, and the Democrats were hopelessly divided. He announced the formation of a new party—the National Progressives of America—that would be built from the bottom up in every state. This party's principles were public control of money and credit, the right of every citizen to work, modernized government, guaranteed income, and individual responsibility. It was not a radical speech but one aimed firmly at the middle class that depicted a kind of cooperative society. The cross-in-a-circle, he explained, was a symbol of both a voter's "x" on the ballot (democracy) and of multiplication of wealth (prosperity). Ushers immediately began handing out lapel buttons and membership cards.[38]

The response to the NPA rally was far less enthusiastic than Phil had hoped; national liberals wanted nothing to do with the organization. La Guardia and CIO leader John L. Lewis refused to associate themselves with the NPA, and liberal Democrats refused to abandon Roosevelt. George Norris and others worried that a third party would sap strength from Roosevelt, causing him to lose crucial battles in Congress and ultimately the White House, even if he ran for a third term or tried to name a successor. Walter Lippmann doubted that a national liberal coalition, especially one that needed to house both the AFL and CIO, would accept Phil's leadership, since he had clearly identified the NPA as *not* a farmer-labor party. David Lawrence called it "a crude interjection of a personal program."[39] Harold Ickes was particularly furious at Phil for trying to assume national leadership of liberals and potentially cracking the Roosevelt coalition. Although the cabinet saw little hope for a third party, Ickes was discouraged that "some prima donna like Phil La Follette should seize upon the occasion to try to occupy the center of the stage." He later told reporters that Roosevelt was the "true" leader of American liberals.[40] Roosevelt responded with humor, writing to one correspondent on May 18:

> Did you know that Phil La Follette started his Third Party with a huge meeting in Wisconsin, the chief feature of which was the dedication of a new emblem—a twenty foot wide banner with a red circle and a blue cross on it? While the crowd present was carried away with the enthusiasm of the movement, most of the country seem to think this was a feeble imitation of the swastika. All that remains is for some major party to adopt a new form of arm salute. I have suggested the raising of both arms above the head, followed by a bow from the waist. At least this will be good for people's figures![41]

Even Robert seemed reluctant to associate himself too closely with his brother's endeavor. He told reporters that he supported the NPA and distributed lapel buttons to his congressional colleagues, but he gave no major comment until a radio address on May 9 in which he spoke in favor of the

NPA. Both Phil and Isabel thought the speech weak; Isabel called it "a rehashing of Phil's talk." Fola was faint in her praise, but Phil decided she probably thought launching the NPA "precipitous."[42]

The notion of a third party that might divide liberal forces was frightening enough, but many journalists and politicians were not quite sure just what Phil's plans were. Hugh Johnson, Heywood Broun, Dorothy Thompson, and others dismissed Phil's address as too vague, with some salient criticism of the New Deal but no practical proposals. Newspapers generally doubted the NPA's importance. The *Boston Herald* called the rally a "Midwestern trucked up version of Huey Long," and the *Chicago Tribune* suggested that the NPA would create "a new popular front by joining Dr. Karl Marx to the Marx Brothers." The confusion was justified. In trying to create a party that would appeal to the middle class, Phil combined radical suggestions such as a call for redistribution of wealth with apparently heartless comments, as when he declared that the government had a duty only to provide opportunity to every American, "but after that he can sink or swim."[43]

Journalists saved their harshest criticism for the cross-in-circle emblem and the tone of the meeting. Shortly after the event, columnist Heywood Broun commented on the slogans and banners and the self-conscious effort for middle-class appeal, writing, "In my opinion the most formidable fascist movement which has yet arisen in America is being nurtured in Madison, Wisc., by Phil La Follette." The cross may have represented the voter's secret ballot, but the symbol lost much of its power if that fact had to continually be explained. Another columnist suggested that the "x" also stood for illiterate citizens who signed their names with an x. The symbol was quickly dubbed a "circumcised swastika," rendering its appearance less menacing and slightly salacious.[44]

Despite the negative press, Phil professed to be "elated" with the results of the rally. Aides told reporters that ten thousand letters had come to Madison in support of the effort and that the NPA had enrolled eight thousand members in its first week. The NPA hired clerical workers to distribute and collect membership applications, moved into offices in Madison, and began to pursue articles of incorporation in other states. Phil defended the NPA against charges that it offered no real program by stating that the NPA intended to build itself up slowly in other states and then hold a convention to draft a platform to ensure that the organization (not yet formally a party) represented the views of its members. Nonetheless, other liberal groups continued to be wary of the NPA, still inherently a one-man show.[45]

The day after the NPA rally, Phil traveled to Iowa to promote the organization. He broadcast a summary of his speech and then began meeting with leaders of the Iowa Farmer-Labor Party to suggest that they affiliate with the NPA. The Iowa FLP delayed action into the summer and never formally joined the NPA.[46] In California, the NPA backed Raymond Haight for governor, and Phil planned to tour the state in support of his candidacy; however, by summer Haight began distancing himself from Phil and the NPA and insisted he was running as an independent, not as a Progressive.[47] Similar efforts in New England proved equally fruitless. Phil spent two weeks meeting with liberal leaders in northeastern states but was unable to draw much support for affiliation with the NPA.[48] Throughout the summer of 1938, Phil continued to promote the NPA. His themes continued to be the need for economic expansion and restoring opportunities, but he toned down the attacks on Roosevelt. The organization rented office space across from the state capitol, financed through the sale of the lapel pins and membership dues; the offices were largely empty. Immel predicted branches would open soon in twenty other states, but none ever materialized.[49]

While Phil embarked on his national crusade, the Progressive Party in Wisconsin became more disarrayed. Prior to the NPA rally, a number of older Progressives, including some in the legislature, wrote Phil looking for leadership in purging "false" Progressives from the party. Many regarded Phil's right-hand man behind the NPA, Ralph Immell, as much too conservative. At the same time Farmer-Labor-Progressive Federation members were clearly not interested in Phil's attempt at a national organization. At its conference on May 21 and 22, one delegate introduced a motion to forego endorsements of candidates since endorsements had caused much hostility among Progressives in 1936; another delegate sharply reminded him that it was a Farmer-Labor convention, not a Progressive convention. Milwaukee mayor Daniel Hoan received much applause when he obliquely knocked the NPA, and Thomas Amlie omitted without explanation a portion of his speech calling for cooperation with the NPA. There was no open discussion of the NPA, but the convention endorsed Hoan for U.S. Senate and Theodore Dammann for governor. A few days later more direct criticism appeared in the form of a letter signed by eleven Progressives and labor leaders, including Assembly Speaker Paul Alfonsi, accusing Phil of launching the party without "consultation or agreement" and charging that the new party would splinter the national liberal bloc. Thomas Duncan was perhaps the one figure who could work behind the scenes to get farmer-labor support behind the NPA, but he was in a Madison hospital and facing manslaughter charges for a drunk driving accident in March; he was later convicted but received only a two-year sentence from a Progressive judge from Ashland County.[50]

Phil's indecision about his own future threatened to set off a mad scramble for offices that pit former allies against one another. He was certainly reluctant to seek a fourth term, knowing that he could not be both governor and chief organizer of the NPA. Yet the resignation of Lieutenant Governor Henry Gunderson in 1937 left him a dilemma: when he was out of the state (as he was for much of 1938), Secretary of State Theodore Dammann became acting governor. Dammann had opposed the creation of the Progressive Party and now, ironically, was the FLPF's choice for governor. If Phil declined to run, Dammann would be the logical candidate. For some time, Phil had worked to convince Herman Ekern to be appointed lieutenant governor, a role Phil envisioned to be a fairly substantial "assistant governor" who would work far more closely with the governor and carry more responsibilities than the position had heretofore done. Ekern agreed in early May. Ekern's appointment (the first time a governor filled a vacant lieutenant governor's seat in any state) was an obvious way to groom him as a successor and leave a loyal follower in place when Phil went on the road for the NPA. Phil appointed Adjutant General Ralph Immel head of the NPA. The appointments made it look as though Phil was trying to establish a dynasty in both state and party leadership, and both the media and elected officials quickly responded. Cartoonist Ross Lewis drew Ekern, Phil, and Immell (outfitted with a sash, sword, and rows of medals) with arms upraised over the caption, "All We Need Now Are the Shirts." Milwaukee attorney William Rubin filed suit to block Ekern's appointment, arguing that the governor had no constitutional authority to make it. The state supreme court eventually confirmed the appointment's legitimacy, but perceptions were firmly in place; as in the Glenn Frank case, Phil appeared to be using the governor's office to perpetuate his own influence.[51]

Phil, still angry at the behavior of the 1937 legislature and eager to continue working to promote the NPA, was reluctant to seek a fourth term as governor. Exhausted from his last term, he knew he could not be both governor and organizer; others, he reasoned, could govern, but he believed he had the necessary campaigning experience and organizing ability to build up the Progressives nationally. He also wondered if he could be effective as governor since his works plan depended on federal money that was no longer forthcoming. Robert insisted that Phil run, arguing that it was necessary that Progressives maintain a strong presence in one state and use his role as governor to maintain national attention. In addition, Phil was reluctant to see Dammann assume the governorship, and Ekern had proven to be a big disappointment (according to Isabel, he had "floundered" as lieutenant governor). With no one else willing to step forward, Phil decided he had to run again, and his secretary, A. W. Zeratsky, began circulating Phil's nomination papers. On June 22 the *Capital Times* announced that Phil would run for reelection and that Ekern would run for a seat in the U.S. Senate. Dammann quickly began circulating his nomination papers for secretary of state. Having worn himself out in his third term and eager to move on to new national issues, Phil suddenly found campaigning to be hard work. He complained about having to organize his own campaign in Wisconsin when he wanted to be in California and other places where he thought he could help the progressive cause nationally. He even briefly considered issuing a public statement to the effect that he would serve as governor only if the Progressive Party elected a majority in both houses of the 1939 legislature.[52]

The Progressive primary campaign brought old divisions out into the open once again. Although Levitan, Dammann, and Loomis ran unopposed in the Progressive primary, the senatorial primary brought to the surface long-simmering tensions. The contest pitted old La Follette warhorse Herman Ekern against the younger and more radical Tom Amlie and symbolized the rift in the party between those who had supported Old Bob and those who came out of the farmer-labor organizations. Both candidates praised Roosevelt and both claimed to be the rightful successor to Old Bob. Phil and Robert remained officially neutral, pledging to support whomever the voters selected; privately they preferred Ekern. Rather than promoting unity, their position antagonized both sides, and supporters of each demanded a formal endorsement from the La Follette brothers. Friends of Amlie even threatened to break away from the Progressive Party if Phil did not support him. Socialist leader and FLPF member Daniel Hoan widened the split by endorsing Amlie. Near primary day the fight grew more intense: Ekern denounced Amlie's proposal for a national Industrial Expansion Administration as "un-American" and compared it to Soviet-style dictatorship.[53]

The primary election results were grim. Ekern beat Amlie by a mere 9,000 votes but ran 30,000 behind incumbent Democrat F. Ryan Duffy; the six Republican candidates collected a total of 214,000 votes. In the governor's race, Phil received 136,291, his poorest showing since 1934, but Republican candidates together garnered 227,159. The other statewide office races yielded similar results.[54] Not only did it look like a Republican victory in the making, but Democrats and Republicans ran coalition candidates in the primaries. Walter Goodland and John M. Smith won both the Republican and Democratic nominations for lieutenant governor and treasurer. Robert K. Henry ran as both a Democrat and as a Republican for governor, then withdrew in favor of the Republican nominee, Milwaukee businessman Julius Heil.[55]

Progressives realized that the election would be close, and so Phil cut back on his NPA work and dedicated himself to the campaign. Robert finally returned to the state and began campaigning himself, and Isabel frequently delivered speeches. In many ways it was a very traditional campaign. Phil began with a speech in Baraboo, denouncing both the Democratic and Republican parties as reactionary and reminding voters of Progressive accomplishment. He also regularly mentioned the NPA and its goals and defended himself against the charges of dictatorship. He and other candidates stumped the state repeating what had become Progressive dogma on the Depression and promoting economic expansion as a means to restore prosperity and ensure democracy. He tailored his addresses somewhat, but the message to his audiences was fundamentally the same: to hold together and remain united.[56]

With a coalition of Republicans and Democrats threatening to oust Progressives from office, a panicked sort of harmony also prevailed at the Progressive platform convention at the capitol. Both Phil and Robert denounced the "sordid, bald-faced deal" in which Henry had backed the millionaire Heil; the delegates knew they faced a united opposition for the first time since 1932. The convention dedicated itself a united-front campaign based on the Progressive record. The FLPF delegates did not raise the "production-for-use" language that had split the convention in previous years and cheered loudly for Phil, whom they had originally not wanted to run. The platform was similar to that in 1936, with additional planks for farm and labor interests, but it also called for national realignment of liberals into a new third party and more efficient legislative sessions. Republicans were unusually well organized and depended heavily on volunteer labor. In the last few weeks before the election, Progressives became increasingly desperate in the face of hostile press and public opinion, and radio addresses by Phil did little to dispel the sense of doom.[57]

On Election Day, Progressives faced disaster. With low voter turnout, Phil lost to Heil by almost 200,000 votes; he carried only thirteen counties, only three in the southern two-thirds of the state, and he lost the critical industrial lakeshore counties by 35,000 votes. The rest of the Progressive ticket went down to defeat as well. Alexander Wiley easily beat Ekern for the U.S. Senate seat with Duffy running a close third. Republicans captured eight congressional seats, failing only to defeat the immensely popular Merlin Hull and Bernhard Gehrmann in the rural northwestern part of the state. Republicans also increased their control of the senate to sixteen seats, leaving Progressives eleven seats and Democrats six, and gained solid control of the assembly for the first time since 1931.[58]

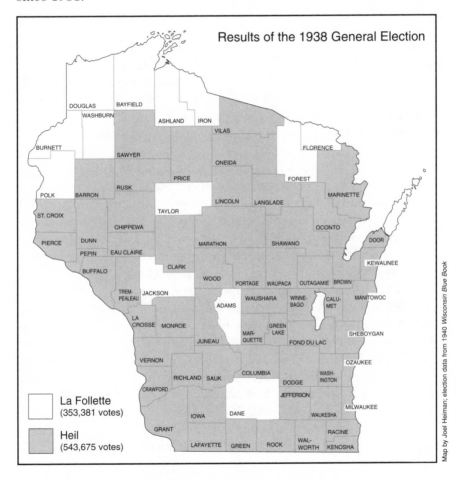

Results of the 1938 General Election

La Follette (353,381 votes)

Heil (543,675 votes)

Map by Joel Heiman; election data from 1940 *Wisconsin Blue Book*

The election was part of a national resurgence of Republicans and the result of anti–La Follette sentiment in the state. "Apparently people are dissatisfied all over the country," Mary wrote a few days later, "and the election was a means of registering their resentments." Robert agreed, as Fola wrote George in New York: "When you got out into the field you heard how bad the situation of people really was—that among the farmers as you campaigned up and down the state you couldn't help realizing how much genuine basis there was for disatisfaction." Writing for *The Nation* later that month, Phil also noted the sense of discouragement that resulted in low turnout. He was particularly bitter that the Progressives lost despite having campaigned on their record while the Republicans simply called for some kind of change. The intellectual in Phil was seriously annoyed at such a hollow issue. Phil's defeat also strained the relationship between the brothers, which had barely survived Phil's decision to launch the NPA. Robert rehashed questions about Phil's motives in establishing the NPA and claimed that his inability to fix Phil's mistakes had cost them the vote of organized labor. Phil was deeply hurt and decided to focus on the NPA and leave Robert's reelection bid in 1940 in his brother's hands.[59]

Historian John E. Miller suggested that Progressives were essentially victims of the continuing Depression, that voters were really no better off than they were when they voted out Republican Walter Kohler in 1930 and Albert Schmedeman in 1934.[60] In part this is true, since several other incumbents lost office was well. Yet Progressives—Phil especially—had been able to articulate an explanation for the economic dislocation and develop a platform to address those problems. What they could not do was carry it out; the vast appropriation that could have made the 1935 works bill a success was beyond the state's resources, and only the federal government could have adequately funded relief. Progressives had campaigned against the policies of the federal and state governments in the past, but now their own record was the issue. In 1938, voters did not see the state producing new employment or substantial reform; what they did see was the dismissal of Glenn Frank, the governor's secretary in jail, senators goosestepping from their chamber, and a national party that was neither national nor a party. Phil vastly overestimated the people's belief that Progressives could protect democracy from the vested interests and bring innovations to the machinery of government. In the end the people were no longer convinced.

CHAPTER EIGHT

Strange Bedfellows and Failed Crusades

When Philip La Follette left the governor's office in January 1939, four months shy of his forty-second birthday, he was the youngest former governor since Lucius Fairchild left office in 1866. Recent former governors either had moved on to higher office (as had James Blaine and Robert La Follette Sr.), retired to a lucrative private business (as had Walter Kohler and Emanuel Philipp), or received federal appointment (as had Albert Schmedeman). None of these was an option for Phil. He had run for governor five times since 1930 and was reluctant to pursue another state office. He had no interest in the House of Representatives or the U.S. Senate; he considered himself more of an administrator than a legislator and knew he would find the debate and parliamentary procedures tedious. Nor did he have a private business. His law practice had deteriorated during his terms in office, and he would have to virtually start it from scratch. A minor position in the federal bureaucracy, that haven for former elected officials, was unlikely because of his repeated criticism of Franklin Roosevelt and the New Deal. At forty-one, Phil essentially had his name and reputation but little money and no public position.

Even so, Phil did have a continued desire for public service. He was still haunted by his parents' expectations that he do great things, and he grew bored easily, needing something to engage his mind. His frustrating and bitter experiences during his last term ruled out a political comeback for the time being. He would direct his energies toward promoting the National Progressives of America (NPA), the would-be national party he had created a year before, but events abroad swept him into new pursuits, including involvement with the isolationist movement and a brief military career in the South Pacific. These endeavors appealed to Phil's intellectual side and allowed him to maintain some connection to his father. His absence left the Progressive Party of Wisconsin to gradually wither, as he neglected those fundamental political tasks of organizing and recruiting. The success of the party had depended on his willingness to travel around the state to meet with local leaders, to work with university experts to develop a legislative program, and to explain those proposals to the people. With no one to take his place, the party would ultimately disband, ending nearly fifty years of the Progressive movement in the state.

———•———

As they had in 1933, Phil and Isabel left for a vacation in Europe on inauguration day. It was to be a working vacation, since Phil wanted "to take a look-see" at the increasingly grim political and social conditions and prepare a series of magazine articles that would give him some financial security. Their itinerary included Great Britain, France, Italy, and Germany. Phil declined to make any comments or observations to the press before departing, explaining that he would be the guest of several countries and did not want to close off any potential source of information by making premature comments. "I always look first before I let my punches go," he joked to reporters. Nonetheless, he and members of the family were apprehensive about the trip, fearful that the Nazi government would use such a visit by a national figure to lend legitimacy to its regime. Both Phil and Isabel spent most of the crossing in bed, recovering from colds and their political upheavals.[1]

Once they arrived, however, Phil embarked on a busy schedule of meetings and speaking engagements. In London at the English-Speaking Union, he urged Great Britain to abandon appeals to the United States based on the countries' historic ties. Diplomatic relations, he told the luncheon guests, needed to be based on common interest, not a sentimental "hands-across-the-sea" appeal. As relations between Great Britain and Germany continued to deteriorate, it was apparent that Great Britain might need U.S. military and economic assistance. In Paris, Phil met with Premier Édouard Daladier, who had read Phil's speech launching the National Progressives of America at Madison and agreed with the basic premise that economic security was a prerequisite for a peaceful and democratic society. When Phil asked Daladier what France expected from the United States if war came, the premier responded quickly, "Money and men in great quantities and fast." It was perhaps the first direct example of the great tension that suffused the continent as it prepared for war. Phil believed that the French people were too divided by class and occupation to stand up to the German threat; although he perceived a general public sentiment for a strong stand against the fascist nations, he thought French leaders too unwilling to implement the military and domestic policies that would require sacrifice on the part of the French people in order for France to withstand a German attack.[2]

In Italy, Phil attended the last public audience of Pope Pius XI and had a long talk with the future Pope Paul VI, then Monsignor Montini. Phil was appalled at the economic situation in Italy (badly strained by Mussolini's military campaign in Ethiopia and his policy of exporting food in order to purchase war materiel) and the degree of government corruption and domestic espionage. As much as Sweden had impressed him as a progressive society, Fascist Italy seemed a nightmare: everything he believed most important—democracy and economic development—had been perverted by the aspirations of one man. Disgusted with the situation, he decided not to seek an appointment with Mussolini.[3] Germany was even more frightening. Phil was astonished at how much the country had changed under Nazi rule since his last visit in 1933. Fearful of espionage, he wrote only brief notes to his family until after he had crossed the border into Belgium, noting only that "I thought I knew something about this country from previous visits, and from following fairly closely what went on [through] the press. But one cannot understand it until one sees it, and gets into the atmosphere." In Copenhagen a few days after leaving Germany, Phil wrote that the majority of German people wanted peace but that Nazi censorship and propaganda prevented that sentiment from being recognized overseas. He further noted that the lack of an American ambassador in Germany increased this misunderstanding and served only to irritate the Nazi government. Phil was convinced that Hitler was still determined to destroy France and had in fact begun much larger schemes for Nazi domination of Eastern Europe. He predicted an invasion of Czechoslovakia just a month before German tanks rolled through Prague.[4]

Returning to the United States in late March, Phil immediately set to work on a series of magazine articles on the European situation, remaining in New York while Isabel returned to Madison. He had accumulated a great deal of information from his trip, and in addition to writing his articles, he also (rather brazenly) made public suggestions on

American policy toward Germany. On April 18, Phil delivered an address to the Economic Club of New York and outlined a program to "smash" European fascism, which he called the greatest menace facing the United States. His statements in no way suggested military intervention but urged measures for economic recovery at home, strengthening ties with Canada and Latin America, and aiding democratic forces in European countries. All of these actions, he believed, would address the root causes of the Depression and of fascism. On the last point, Phil criticized Great Britain and France, noting that conservative "cliques" in those countries had promoted the reckless and shortsighted policy of appeasement, greatly increasing the danger of the situation. In an even more inflammatory remark, he urged the immediate recall of American ambassador to Great Britain Joseph P. Kennedy: "Eloquent tributes to democracy here in America can be largely nullified if our representatives abroad by daily, public conduct support those forces in Europe least concerned about democracy. Speaking for myself alone, I do not hesitate to say that the President would perform a public service if he immediately recalled our Ambassador to Great Britain."[5]

His comments on Kennedy overshadowed his and Robert's White House visit with President Roosevelt two days later. Over the past few years, Robert had become particularly concerned with foreign affairs and had become one of the strongest advocates of congressional neutrality legislation. He had in fact introduced a Senate resolution that would require a congressional declaration of war to be ratified by a national referendum. Both Robert and Phil were convinced that war in Europe was imminent and worried that Great Britain and France would pressure the United States to become involved. After reporting on what he had seen in Europe, Phil was annoyed that the president seemed not to take him or his opinions seriously. When Phil predicted that France would collapse in six months if war came, Roosevelt patted Phil's knee and said, "Bob, Phil is a nice fellow, but he just doesn't know what he's talking about when he makes that kind of a prediction."[6] While in Washington, Phil also appeared before a joint congressional committee investigating legislation to permit United States entry of German refugee children. He described the terror of living under the Nazis and speculated that 75 percent of the German people would vote against the Nazi Party if free and secret elections were held. He urged the committee to amend the immigration quota laws to allow immigration of German children and described the "lasting shock" of the November 1938 anti-Jewish riots. By the end of April, Phil had become one of the best-known critics of the British and French appeasement policy toward Germany, and he argued that an American alliance with those governments would be a threat to democracy itself.[7]

Phil's distaste and fear of Germany made him sound like a proto-interventionist, and his stress on the need to "smash" Nazism sounded positively hawkish. In May, he told a Massachusetts gathering that the "Nazi way of life" could not coexist with democracies and proposed an American foreign policy based on protecting Latin America from Nazi overtures. Yet both he and Robert had been concerned with Roosevelt's foreign policy for some time, especially after the president proposed a massive naval expansion in early 1938. In January 1938, Robert had sent Phil a copy of a speech on foreign relations requesting that Phil read it carefully; Robert also remarked that he believed that Roosevelt would soon begin using a defense buildup as a means of economic recovery.[8]

Events in Europe also overshadowed state politics. "The Progressives are badly in the jitters," Isabel wrote Phil before he returned to Wisconsin. "[A]ll their attention is centered on international affairs." The conditions in Europe had captured people's attention, and Isabel urged Phil to keep his "eyes on the home base." Although Phil promised that he had not deserted the domestic situation (even if he was somewhat bitter at his being "kicked out of it"), he spent much of his time reporting on the European situation and did little to help organize state Progressives. Even before he had returned from Europe in 1939, political reporters wondered what he would do. Some speculated he would run for governor again in 1940, but after he returned to Madison he insisted that he planned only to build up his law practice and organize the NPA. He refused to comment on state politics and spoke only in national terms, insisting that a new party was "inevitable" if Republicans and Democrats failed to solve the fundamental problems in employment and agriculture. Yet he kept his comments abstract, and he insisted that the NPA was not in itself a party but rather an organization working with other liberal groups to form a third party. Spurning overtures from Roosevelt Democrats to take an administration post, Phil quietly resumed his law practice, wrote articles for *The Progressive*, and took speaking engagements. He was virtually retired from state affairs.[9]

Progressives still smarted from their defeat in 1938 and remained disorganized and discouraged, with no one willing to undertake a new organizing drive. Ralph Immell all but abandoned the NPA and focused on his National Guard duties, and former state officers retired from politics. No one was willing to try to get the Progressives back into shape. Still bitter about his loss to the popular but inept Julius Heil, Phil did not want to get involved with state politics, but he could not help but worry. Heil spent most of his time attending to his business in Milwaukee and generally neglected his job as governor, except for ceremonial duties. The 1939 legislature passed four different budgets, the last of which actually increased appropriations while cutting the budgets of state agencies, a situation that Phil believed would require the implementation of a sales tax, long anathema to Progressives. Heil and a coalition of Republicans and conservative Democrats enacted measures that restricted labor organizing, circumvented state civil service laws, and gutted most of the Progressive programs of the past four years. Progressives were unable to put up much of a fight and offered no substantive program of their own. Phil pressured Robert to offer some constructive leadership and return to Wisconsin during the summer of 1939. "The main reason," Phil wrote, "is our people FEEL the need for some leadership for them to rally around. Your presence will afford it." Phil believed that he himself had too little credibility to keep Progressives focused on developing a new program and so spent much of June and July traveling the country promoting liberal unity and speaking on the European situation.[10]

The outbreak of war in Europe, however, gave him a new debate in which to participate, mimicking the stand his father had taken prior to the last war; this was a chance to apply old progressive principles to a new situation. His immediate response was again critical of the British and French governments. In his New York Economic Club address earlier that spring, he had noted that those nations had done virtually nothing to stop Hitler and could not be depended on to do so in the future:

> I am convinced that we shall run the gravest risks if we attempt [to smash Nazi Germany] in alliance with the present ruling forces of Britain and France. Certainly the American people will never get into another European war consciously just to pull British and French chestnuts out of the fire. The only possible justification for such a course would be the argument that we were defending ourselves from Nazi-ism.[11]

Phil's articles on Europe had begun appearing in *The Commentator* in May and later in *The Progressive*, and they painted a bleak picture. He depicted France—weak and internally divided—as the key to European security, describing Hitler's determination to destroy it and how a French collapse would leave Great Britain and the Soviet Union too weak to resist Nazi aggression. He speculated that the French might accept an authoritarian regime out of fear of a German invasion; he also presciently noted that the Maginot line, France's fortified border with Germany, would do little to defend the country. Although he described the extreme power held by Mussolini and Hitler, Phil also suggested—overestimated, really—widespread discontent and latent opposition to the regimes. He was perhaps being naïve in thinking that Germans could not possibly go along with the Nazi regime for much longer. Even though he thoroughly described the terror of living in Germany, he had little sympathy for Great Britain, which he believed to be dominated by conservatives out to protect their commercial, financial, and industrial interests rather than defending the interests of the people.[12]

In this respect, Phil was echoing the arguments that his father and other Progressives had made prior to World War I, and his father's stand against war became a recurring theme in his public statements in 1939. "Twenty-two years ago," he said in an address over the Mutual Broadcasting network in October, just over a month after Germany invaded Poland, "a pitiless campaign of abuse raged around my father." The cause of the last war, Phil said, was the commercial and imperialistic competition among European countries; now the United States had to make certain it did not become entangled in the war as it had a generation earlier. The Neutrality Act of 1937, introduced by isolationist members of Congress and reluctantly signed by Roosevelt, prevented the United States from supplying belligerent nations. In September 1939, Roosevelt called Congress into special session to consider revision of the law, which did not allow the president to differentiate between aggressor and attacked nations. Phil argued against Roosevelt's proposed repeal of the arms embargo, declaring repeal a certain prelude to full participation. "The desire," he told his listeners,

> to see the tyranny of dictatorship ended . . . springs from America's deep-rooted love of liberty, and I yield to no man in my loathing of dictatorship as a denial of the free principles upon which America was founded. But we must not fool ourselves into thinking that we can help fight dictators in Europe and still stay out of war. We either go in or we stay out. Past experience and today's facts should have taught us that cash and carry before very long would become "charge it" and carry it too.

He further argued that modern war, with the requisite mobilization of the whole society, would inevitably lead to loss of liberty at home and produce only economic collapse. This was Old Bob's interpretation of the last war and the economic recession that followed, and Phil argued that the same thing would happen if the United States began supplying the Allies with armaments.[13]

The address, particularly the reference to his father, struck a responsive chord with others opposed to repeal of the arms embargo. Advertising executive Chester Bowles thought the speech "wonderful" and suggested Phil make a series of speeches aimed at specific groups to "take the shine off the armor" of Britain and France.[14] A week later, Phil debated the question of the embargo with Colonel Frank Knox on the radio program "Town Meeting of the Air" in New York. He again pointed to the financial commitments the United States had made to the Allies between 1914 and 1917 (a "tuition" of $42 billion and 350,000 casualties) that culminated in full participation in the war and three years of postwar depression. He also derided assertions that Great Britain and France fought for democracy, citing their harsh terms of the Versailles Treaty, their appeasement policy, and their machiavellian foreign policies in the 1920s and 1930s. Just as La Follette had derided British appeals to American democracy in 1917 in his speech against the war resolution, so, too, did Phil insist that the United States solve its own domestic problems first, before trying to rescue the British Empire. In both cases, the arguments had little effect; on November 4, Congress revised the Neutrality Act to allow nations at war to purchase armaments.[15]

The outbreak of war threatened to divert completely Phil's attention from politics, but the "phony war" that followed the collapse of Poland raised the enchanting prospect of a negotiated settlement and temporarily quieted the debate. For Progressives, it offered a chance to regroup. In October, Isabel took on a new project, editing and distributing *The Progressive Woman*, a small-format ("keep several copies in your purse," she urged readers) newsletter to be circulated among women sympathetic to the Progressive Party and to the movement to keep the United States out of war. The circular contained news on the efforts to maintain American neutrality, snide reports on the Heil administration, recipes, health tips, and book reviews. Phil continued to promote a national party, predicting a powerless Roosevelt unable to cope with a conservative Congress and unabated unemployment. He promised that "the Progressive movement is in the fight to stay until its principles prevail in all America." He predicted NPA candidates and NPA-affiliated independents in several states in 1940.[16]

In the early months of 1940, Phil continued his public speaking, stressing the need for economic expansion as a means of preserving democracy. In Cleveland, he compared the nation to a giant boiler loaded beyond capacity with production power and ready to explode unless means were found to tap that power; the explosion, he said, "would wreck the liberty and all that is good in the country."[17] At the urging of the state secretary of the Minnesota Farmer-Labor Association, Phil addressed its March convention to promote cooperation among farm bloc states.[18] Phil continued to promise ambitious plans to run Progressive candidates in congressional races, but he remained vague on the specifics.[19] Wisconsin politics, however, he continued to neglect. Robert was preoccupied with his duties in the Senate, and while a number of candidates sought nomination for offices, no other Progressive was willing to take up the vigorous organizing and campaigning that Phil had done. Henry Sauthoff and Harold Stafford planned gubernatorial bids but were unwilling to lead the party. Congressman Merlin Hull refused to run for governor because of his controversial dry record. Progressives' absence from the state scene irked some. "[W]hy can't liberals get together this year in Wisconsin?" one correspondent demanded. "I can't understand [what] you boys . . . seek to accomplish by starting a new national party and splitting up the liberal forces in the country just at a time when we are making some progress."[20] The death of Phil's secretary, A.W. Zeratsky, in February removed probably the only figure who could have substituted for Phil in behind-the-scenes organizing. Rumors began circulating that Robert, disappointed in the lackluster potential candidates to head the state ticket, was trying to convince Phil to run for governor again. Another rumor held that both Robert and Phil would run in both the Democratic and Progressive primaries. Thomas Amlie, one of the most vociferous activists for a third party in 1934, now wanted Robert to run as a Roosevelt Democrat. Phil agreed to weigh options very carefully, but he refused to respond to a draft movement.[21]

Phil was concerned not only with promoting a national Progressive organization, but also with generating an income. His speaking engagements brought him modest fees (usually $250 to $300), which he shared with the various speakers' bureaus he used. Such income, however, was far from steady, and he spent much of his time trying to rebuild his law practice, taking on both corporate clients and individuals. In March, Phil was elected to the board of directors of Fairbanks, Morse and Co. of Chicago, manufacturer of diesel engines and motors. Newspaper editors were quick to pick up on the irony of Phil joining the same corporate powers he had once denounced, but the position brought a number of contacts for legal business and future positions that would support his crusade as well as his family.[22]

The *blitzkrieg* of the spring and summer of 1940 turned national attention toward the European war, and especially after the collapse of France in June, Phil increased his antiwar activities. Urged on by Chester Bowles and others, Phil delivered a radio address in late June entitled "The Defense of America." Phil believed that the rapid German offense would produce either a quick Allied defeat or German collapse. The greatest danger to the United States came not from Europe but from Latin America, he argued, calling the United States susceptible to "boring from within," in which regimes sympathetic to the Nazis would threaten the United States economically and militarily. Domestic and foreign politics were still closely intertwined in Phil's mind as he described "the same dry rot that wreck Britain and France" affecting both the Democrats and Republicans. He urged the Democrats to adopt a "real program" for economic reform, rather than trying to prop up the Allies with war materials that would quickly be destroyed. He also called for a hemispheric defense system to keep the United States isolated from the war. As he had often done in the past, he infused the immediate crisis with historic importance and closed with a direct appeal: "If we can fulfill our own destiny we can save ourselves and by the example we set of what a free people can do, we can save the world. Will you help?"[23]

One correspondent understood Phil's general aims but challenged his immediate suggestions for national policy, which included nationalizing key industries, re-armament for defense, and some kind of protective supervision of Canada and Latin America, as "opposing totalitarianism with totalitarianism." Perhaps too enamored of national authority and clinging to a now old-fashioned progressive faith in government, Phil responded that he was not trying to pit class against class but wanted to "weed out" those individuals who put their own interests ahead of the general welfare. He also defended his own right to advocate increased governmental power without having to be tarred as a fascist: "[I]sn't the best test of what one is likely to do in the future, what one has done in the past: his record? That record will show, no doubt, many mistakes—but I don't think there is even a smudge of disloyalty to the fundamentals of American democracy."[24] Phil continued delivering radio addresses in the summer, all emphasizing his belief that the preservation of democracy required not intervention abroad but economic reform at home. "The money-changers," he remarked in July, "have not been driven from our temples."[25] By mid-July, the Democrats' decision to renominate Roosevelt effectively killed Phil's efforts toward a national Progressive organization, and he abandoned those efforts entirely in July.[26]

Phil's antiwar activities left him little time for Wisconsin politics. Even though he was frequently urged to head the ticket, he refused to be more than "a private in the ranks" and hoped that a crowded primary field would develop new leaders and build up their reputations in the state.[27] In May, Robert had finally quashed rumors that the Wisconsin Progressive Party would fold by announcing plans to run for reelection as a Progressive. As Phil had hoped, the primary field was indeed crowded. Five candidates competed for the Progressive nomination for governor, two each for secretary of state and state treasurer, and three for attorney general. Only the lieutenant governor's nomination was unopposed. Most county Progressive parties also ran full slates for local offices, although Progressives were much less organized in the southeastern counties and the Fox River Valley. By August, Phil was on the campaign trail for Robert and other Progressives, but he worried that political feeling might still be running against incumbents. Not all were pleased with the candidates, some of whom were virtual unknowns outside of Madison and others of whom were poor campaigners.[28]

Phil tried to remain optimistic that by going after Heil's record as governor, Progressives could come back from their defeat two years earlier, and he did indeed repeatedly mock the administration of "Julius the Just." After the primary in September, he began his familiar routine of four to five speeches a day around the state as well as radio addresses. The numerous billboards erected in support of Heil were easy targets, and Phil compared the Heil campaign with advertising for Camel cigarettes. He had been accused of raising taxes and spending too much as governor, so he made sure to mention that under the Republicans the state had the highest taxes and biggest budget in history. Yet because he spent much of his time campaigning for Robert, who remained in Washington, foreign affairs intruded into his message. During the primary, Phil told audiences that by their example the very act of voting in the primary was the first step in destroying dictatorship. Robert ran unopposed in the primary and gained only 144,692 votes; the Republicans (including the late Glenn Frank, who had died in a car accident two days before the primary) split nearly 350,000 votes. In the general election, Robert's Republican opponent was Fred Clausen, a lobbyist for the Manufacturers' Association who had battled Phil's measures for years. Phil discussed his record but also demanded to know how Clausen would vote on "steps leading to war." He praised his brother's leading role against American involvement in the war and urged voters to join him. By voting Progressive, he told one radio audience, "YOU are a soldier for peace and democracy."[29]

The results of the election were profoundly disappointing to Progressives. Republicans retained all constitutional offices and increased their majority in the senate from seventeen to twenty-five and in the assembly from fifty-three to sixty-one; Progressives lost five seats in the senate and eight seats in the assembly. Robert was reelected to the U.S. Senate, but only just. In a three-way race, he captured 45 percent of the vote, the first time he had not captured a majority; Clausen received 41 percent. But there was some hope for the future. The gubernatorial candidate, former attorney general Orland Loomis, received 40 percent of the vote, losing to Heil by just over twelve thousand votes and running far ahead of other Progressive nominees. Progressive energy had focused almost entirely on the Senate race, and Loomis and other state candidates were unable to drum up much enthusiasm for local issues.[30]

After the disappointment of the elections, Phil returned to his crusade against American intervention in Europe and got involved with the founding of the America First Committee. America First had formed late that summer in response to Roosevelt's exchange of destroyers for bases with Great Britain, and its prime mover, R. Douglas Stuart Jr., had requested Phil's aid in organizing it shortly after General Robert E. Wood of Sears, Roebuck and Co. accepted its chairmanship. After spending an afternoon with Phil in August, Stuart was convinced that the committee needed Phil's support:

> Your name will give confidence to the great middle groups—i.e. farm, labor and consumer groups. Your support can avert the danger of this Committee being smeared as a business men's organization and will make it a really American movement. If you believe at all in what many of us are dedicating our energies toward doing, I am sure we will have your help.

Phil responded with a list of potential members and by writing directly to a number of his associates encouraging them to contact Wood. He also arranged for several U.S. senators to make fifteen-minute recorded speeches for the committee; the senators included such unlikely bedfellows as Robert Wood, Robert A. Taft, Hiram Johnson, and Henry Cabot

Lodge. Phil did, however, rebuff suggestions that he join the board, and his name never appeared on the organization's stationery.[31]

Phil's support for America First raised eyebrows among his liberal-intellectual friends. Stuart Chase refused Phil's suggestion to join: "General Wood's outfit is undoubtedly splendid," he wrote Phil in late August, "but I just don't want to appear on the same letterhead with some of his buddies." Elmer Davis was more blunt: "The spectacle of the Chicago Tribune [*sic*] and the La Follettes on the same side moves me to a brief missionary sermon." Davis then went on to warn Phil about the dangers of teaming up with those who promoted freedom for business rather than freedom for the people. The war had become the big issue in American politics and overshadowed past differences with conservative members of the isolationist movement. Phil was willing to work with them because they all viewed the problem the same way and was willing—as his father had been—to risk taking an unpopular stand on his principles. The alliance also demonstrated an important lesson in practical politics, as Phil later remarked to his daughter: one must be careful in making comments to or about another person in a fight because they might be allies on the next issue.[32]

Throughout 1940 and 1941, Phil's rhetoric against American involvement in the war escalated as the Roosevelt administration's policy shifted from "cash-and-carry" to "lend-lease." In a Fireside Chat on December 29, 1940, Roosevelt announced that the United States had to become a "great arsenal for democracy" and that he would send legislation to Congress to allow Great Britain to borrow war materiel in exchange for long-term leases on military bases. Early in January 1941, in direct response to the president's proposal, Phil delivered a national radio address over NBC sponsored by the America First Committee in which he accused the president of "preaching the doctrine of fear" by suggesting the United States would be vulnerable to a German invasion unless it delivered arms to Great Britain.[33] Phil amplified these views in a debate over the Lend-Lease Bill with Secretary of the Interior Harold Ickes, also broadcast on NBC. Ickes referred to the bill as "probably our last effective chance" to stop Nazi aggression and reiterated the president's oft-repeated pledge to do everything short of war to aid Great Britain. In addition to criticizing the administration's escalating commitment to Great Britain as a direct prelude to war, Phil described the bill as "the most far-reaching grant of power ever seriously proposed for any one man in the history of the United States." The bill, he said, so broadly defined weapons of war that they could be almost anything designated as such by the president. Furthermore, the bill granted the president the authority to dispose of that property to any foreign government as he wished. In his message to Congress, Roosevelt had pledged to deliver weapons to Great Britain in sufficient quantity to ensure overwhelming victory; since the British government also had said that it could not win without a conquering army on the continent, Phil argued that Lend-Lease effectively gave the president the power to raise and equip another expeditionary force. His comments were tinged with anti-British sentiment as well; Phil suggested that once Great Britain was guaranteed American aid the country would not be above seeking a peace treaty, leaving the United States as sole combatant against Nazi Germany. When Ickes quoted the Nazi journal *Will and Power*, in which a government official praised Phil as a good Nazi, Phil responded—much to the audience's delight—by noting that the only attention he had ever gotten from the German government was to be trailed by the Gestapo in 1939.[34]

His increasing prominence in the public debate earned Phil an appearance before the Senate Foreign Relations Committee in February 1941. During the hearings on the Lend-Lease Bill he continued to mock the threat of a German invasion, noting that the Germans were hardly likely to cross the Atlantic Ocean when they had been incapable of crossing the English Channel. The main point of his statements, however, was that the bill would inevitably cost American liberty at home. He bluntly declared that the bill vested in one man the decision for peace or war, and that such a war would plunge the nation even further into economic stagnation. The effects of the Depression continued to haunt Phil, and he urged increased efforts toward domestic economic reform lest the conditions that spawned Hitler and Mussolini produce an American dictator. As he had said in his first message to the legislature in 1931, if the United States was capable of spending $7 billion for war, it could certainly afford a similar investment at home.[35]

After the Lend-Lease resolution was passed in March, Phil continued to speak on behalf of the America First Committee, in one instance pinch-hitting for Charles Lindbergh. Phil's reputation as a liberal reformer made him a particularly valuable ally after Roosevelt's proclamation of the Four Freedoms. The question of "aid short of war" was now moot, since there was virtually nothing else the United States could now do that was not war, and Phil began to propose what R. Douglas Stuart called "a philosophy of peace" as a way to promote economic and political freedom worldwide. During a public debate with Upton Sinclair, Phil told the audience that the best way for the United States to "strike a blow for freedom" was not only to protect the Western Hemisphere but also to demonstrate that people did not have to choose between a job with no freedom or freedom with no job. In short, the United States had to lead by example. In advocating this twentieth-century version of the city on the hill, Phil was convinced that the United States could promote democracy simply by demonstrating to oppressed people its dedication to democracy.[36] Dedicated to keeping the United States out of the war, Phil appeared often on the radio during the spring of 1941, making speeches or participating in discussions. He usually had his remarks transcribed and then edited them for articles in *The Progressive*. The America First Committee also engaged him for appearances in Florida, New York, North Carolina, Florida, Ohio, and Pennsylvania. By May, however, Phil began to sense that the United States could do little more to aid Great Britain and would have to decide either to declare war on Germany or acquiesce to the German conquest of Great Britain. He remarked to Fola that Churchill continued to push Roosevelt for more assistance and the president would have to either make a firmer commitment to British defense or rebuff Churchill's overtures once and for all. Throughout the battle, he clung to the stubborn conviction that he was right and that the majority of people agreed with him. He saw himself as a champion of the people: the fight "has registered in the minds of the common folks that there is leadership in this country . . . that is fighting for their side." In every address, Phil criticized the Roosevelt administration's scare tactics and urged further reform at home. The effort exhausted him. In October, Isabel wrote that she had never seen him so "depleted."[37]

Phil's absence from Wisconsin politics and his participation in the isolationist crusade seriously hurt the Progressive Party, not only because the party shuffled along without a leader but also because the war raised a bitterly divisive issue among former comrades-in-arms. Throughout 1941, Phil received letters from those who had supported his father or who had supported Phil in the past, complaining about his association with conservatives like Wood, Robert Taft, and Robert McCormick. *Capital Times* editor William Evjue was the most vocal former supporter who now argued that Phil had abandoned the liberal position of his father and urged Progressives to support the president.[38] Phil was well aware of the tension he was exacerbating in party ranks, and he tried to convince Progressives to put differences in foreign policy aside. At the opening of "Progressive House," the new national headquarters of the National Progressives of America on North Carroll Street, he stressed the need to focus on domestic issues and to not let the Progressive movement be torn apart over issues of intervention. "We Progressives," Phil solemnly told those in attendance, "who are isolationists and we Progressives who are interventionists have very special and grave responsibilities in this critical period. The Progressive movement and what it stands for believes in the American way of life."[39] An August special election to elect a successor to the late Stephen Bolles from the first congressional district, however, indicated how much foreign policy was dominating Phil's political outlook. In letters supporting Progressive candidate Kenneth Greenquist, Phil wrote supporters that the election was of vital importance since Greenquist was the only noninterventionist candidate. Although he ran unopposed, Greenquist received five hundred votes too few to qualify for the general ballot, and the choice came down to Thomas Amlie, who supported Roosevelt's domestic and foreign policy, and isolationist Republican Lawrence Smith. The La Follettes did nothing, and Smith defeated Amlie by a two-to-one margin. The emphasis of the brief campaign was not domestic issues but the president's foreign policy.[40]

A series of encounters between U.S. naval ships escorting merchant ships and German U-boats in the North Atlantic culminated in the sinking of the USS *Rueben James* on October 27. On November 1, Phil delivered his most controversial address on the war. It was also his angriest, since he believed that everything he had predicted in terms of escalating American involvement had happened due wholly to Roosevelt's determination that the United States assist Great Britain. Phil accused the president of following the same road as the European dictatorships in using a military buildup as a quick fix for the complicated problem of the Depression, rather than addressing its root causes. From start to finish, Phil depicted the foreign policy of the administration (which he referred to as "the War Party") as nothing more than a series of misguided steps that had brought the nation closer to war, defrauding the American people by the same methods as Hitler and Mussolini. In one particularly grim passage, he warned of a potential assault on American liberties and promised that if those in power made any attempt to "dynamite the American ballot-box" then "they will find that the fighting spirit and love of liberty which inspired our ancestors to rise up against George III is as fearless today as it was at Lexington and Concord."[41]

Unlike Phil's previous addresses, which received generally favorable response, the November 1 address generated a great deal of hostility. "You and the rest of your damned traitors start something," threatened one letter writer, "and we will have an organization that will take good care of you within 24 hours."[42]

Phil's fighting mood finally spurred him to formally assume a leadership role in the America First Committee, and he agreed to become its vice chairman in early November. Before he assumed the position, however, Japanese forces bombed Pearl Harbor, and at its December 11 board meeting, America First disbanded. His erstwhile colleagues were unrepentant and assured Phil of their admiration. "The leadership and statesmanship which you have shown," wrote one, "is a challenge to succeeding generations to show the same heroic determination to uphold the American way of live, to preserve American Democracy." R. Douglas Stuart told Phil that he had been an inspiration. It may or may not have been a comfort to Phil, but he at least could be satisfied that he had waged a battle as fervently—and as futilely—as his father had in 1917.[43]

In his last letter to Phil, Stuart told him that he had decided to enlist in the army. Phil did likewise on December 12, 1941. The news shocked his family, even though he had said as early as 1940 that he would enlist if the United States declared war. In his last column for *The Progressive*, he declared that "everything we are and hope to be is being hammered out on the bloody anvil of this war," and he had to be part of it. He encouraged his readers to resist blind patriotism and continue to fight for progressive reforms of the economic and political system. Progressives—and other critics of state or national policy—had often been accused of being unpatriotic, but Phil had learned from his father that the most patriotic thing one can do in a democracy is to criticize the government when it is wrong. Progressives defended democracy by trying to make the nation better. Phil was by no means abandoning his political beliefs and adopting the unquestioning "blind patriotism" he warned his readers about, but he believed the most valuable service he could render was to join the military fight. After passing a physical examination in early January, he received notice on March 15 to report for active duty. The forty-four-year-old former commander in chief of the Wisconsin National Guard was commissioned a captain in the military police and was sent to Fort Myer Military School in Virginia.[44]

Phil's enlistment was devastating to Isabel. She had belonged to the Women's International League for Peace and Freedom and had lobbied for peace proposals in the 1920s. She couldn't bear the sight of a uniform, and when Phil donned his for the first time, she remarked that he was now "dressed fit to kill" and could barely help him pin on his insignia. Phil also left her at a particular burdensome time, as they had just purchased two adjoining farms in the town of Roxbury in northwestern Dane County. The purchase fulfilled a longing of Phil's to get back to the land after having not really lived at Maple Bluff Farm since 1925. Phil had inherited from his parents a romantic vision of farm life, but Isen had to deal with the hard realities. With his departure, Isabel took on the onerous tasks of repairing the nineteenth-century sandstone house and farm buildings and the general running of both the farm and their residence in Madison, without the household help she was accustomed to. Her letters throughout 1942 suggest a profound loneliness masked by overwork. She did visit frequently with the wives of other servicemen and with her regular Friday lunch group. Every morning she sat at her typewriter and wrote a letter to Phil describing her activities on the farm as also she coped with raising their three children and taking a greater hand in the management of *The Progressive*. Family issues began to become more important than politics for both Phil and Isabel during the war as the children grew older. Robert III disappointed Phil by not taking an interest in the farm. (He did, however, make the Madison West High School football team, which won the state championship.) Robert III was drafted into the army following his graduation in 1944.[45]

Phil did not have an easy time of it, either. Although long accustomed to (and somewhat fond of) long work days, Phil in middle age could not stand the pace as well as he had when he was in his twenties, and the military routine at Fort Myer left him exhausted most days. Some subjects—military law and criminal investigation—were familiar and interesting, but others, especially map triangulation, confounded him. He resisted attempts to transfer him to the Judge Advocate General's School, preferring to remain near the troops and witness as much as he could, but the military bureaucracy frequently infuriated him.[46]

A chance encounter with a doctor from Wisconsin, Colonel Martin F. DuFrenne, ended Phil's career with the military police and sent him to the front. Further administrative work held little appeal, and the chance to see the war closer to the action appealed to Phil's curiosity. DuFrenne used his personal connections to arrange for Phil to go to the Pacific Theatre. As his family speculated about where he was (his location was classified), Phil flew from San Francisco to New Caledonia to New Zealand. Another old friend from Wisconsin arranged his transfer to the staff of General Douglas MacArthur in Port Moresby, New Guinea. Phil remained on MacArthur's staff as a public relations officer from October 1942 until June 1945, although in a spectacular example of bad timing he missed the Leyte landing in 1944. The general immediately impressed him with his bearing, a living example of the kind of leader that Phil had admired since childhood, and Phil compared him to Caesar, Washington, and Grant. Over the years of his service, Phil developed a profound respect for MacArthur as an intellectual, as one who had years earlier perceived the nature of the next war and prepared for it in great detail. MacArthur possessed another trait that Phil greatly admired: the ability to stand up to authority figures, particularly President Roosevelt.

In a sense, MacArthur was a new father figure. Phil wrote enthusiastically about the general in his letters home, and his family evidently kidded him on the subject. "I have not become a hero-worshipper of MacArthur," he wrote defensively, "but I do have immense respect for his military capacity." He defended MacArthur against charges of being too dramatic by pointing out that Roosevelt, Churchill, and Stalin were more so and speculated that he was the one man who could end the war quickly.[47] MacArthur was "very remindful of Dad," Phil wrote Robert in 1943. "The only sad note in it all is that a man with these gifts, and capacity for leadership should not have a wider field." For the rest of his life, Phil remained an ardent admirer of MacArthur, and he would take an active part in the general's presidential aspirations in 1948.[48]

Phil may have thanked fate for sending him to the South Pacific to meet MacArthur, but his absence from Wisconsin during the war effectively ended the Progressive Party. As the war dominated the newspapers and people coped with rationing and shortages, there seemed little room for traditional Progressive proposals, and even the most active supporters settled into a general sense of apathy. No one took up Phil's role of traveling the state and meeting with local leaders or even delivering the regular radio addresses that had been fixtures of his last term in office. Phil was aware of how his absence affected the party; he hoped others would pick up where he left off, and he badgered Robert to make sure the party remained active. In March 1942, Phil again urged Robert to return to Wisconsin: "I think it is critically important for you to get back here. You need to get around the state—stir our people up—meet with leaders and for your own thinking you should know what the people are thinking and feeling." Robert, however, remained mostly in Washington attending to Senate business; he delayed his return to the state until the three remaining Progressive congressmen could accompany him. Robert sensed a growing reaction against the administration and was unwilling to try to convert voters and politicians alike to Progressive ideals. At the same time, some Democrats urged Progressives to abandon their party and join them; a few Republicans, including former

Assembly Speaker Paul Alfonsi, suggested that Progressives return to the Republican Party. According to former Milwaukee mayor Frank Zeidler, Socialists had believed for some time that Progressives wanted them for their votes and not their principles. In 1942, Socialists reclaimed their ballot status, adopted a defiantly left-wing platform, and insisted that their party would be an appropriate home for Progressives.[49]

Phil finally convinced Robert to go to Wisconsin in April, and Robert was pleasantly surprised by the warm reception; he ended all speculation about what Progressives would do by convincing party leaders to stay united on their own ticket. Nonetheless, he dreaded the trips and avoided them when at all possible.[50] Phil remained annoyed at what he perceived was a dependence on him by other Progressive leaders. When Progressives were at a loss as to how to raise money, Phil wrote Isabel, "For Once I could keep quiet—though I wouldn't be surprised if they thought I ought to take a few days off and raise the money for them even now."[51]

In Phil's absence, Progressives had done virtually nothing to advance or even devise a program, instead relying on criticism of Governor Julius Heil, the incompetent incumbent whom even the Republican leadership did not like. Nor was there much interest among potential candidates: Orland Loomis ran unopposed for the nomination, and only the attorney general and state treasurer races were contested. As a result, the Progressive primary vote was very light; Robert had ensured that the party would continue to exist, but he did little to give it life or direction. Loomis received only about 14 percent of the total vote cast, although some Progressives voted for Heil, believing him to be the weakest of the three Republican candidates. Neither Isabel nor Robert was optimistic about the general election. Robert refused to return to Wisconsin until late October, and Isabel found the formerly well-organized Progressive campaign confused without either Phil's or Robert's firm leadership. Furthermore, Progressive candidates still smarted from their 1938 defeat and did not want the campaign to turn into a La Follette family affair, and they did not invite Isabel to take part. She in turn declined whatever speaking requests came her way, but she followed the campaigns closely so she could report to Phil. Loomis tried to distance himself from the La Follettes and did not ask Robert to campaign on his behalf until two weeks before the election.[52]

The general campaign did little to raise Progressive spirits. With gas rationing in place, mass political rallies were out of the question since farmers, who needed their gas to fuel tractors and other machinery, were reluctant to travel. Campaign finances were in worse than usual shape, so radio and newspaper advertising was curtailed. But as one correspondent noted, "[O]ur big hurdle is 'Old Man Apathy.' People are very busy and very much preoccupied with the war, rationing, home defense, bond & war chest drives, etc." With no aggressive organizing and no major proposals, Progressives were left mainly to campaign against Heil's record. The absence of both Robert and Phil at the platform convention, according to news reports, left it "spiritless." Loomis himself was not much of a campaigner, and after one meeting Isabel wrote that "Orlando [*sic*] dampened everyone's spirits with his frightful egotistical dullness." Glenn Roberts took control of the state central committee just after the gloomy primary election and gradually built up voter interest in the weeks leading up to the general election, but Progressives continued to hammer away at Heil's record, especially his lavish use of the state contingency fund. In that they were successful. Loomis defeated Heil by more than 100,000 votes. Yet the victory masked other, more worrisome contests. Republicans retained all other constitutional offices by wide margins and controlled the legislature with twenty-three of thirty-three seats in the senate and seventy-one of one hundred in the assembly.[53]

The Progressives' victory was remarkably short-lived. "Spike [Loomis] is going to be up against a very difficult situation next winter because both the senate and the assembly will be strongly Republican," Alf Rogers wrote Phil in November. "I am afraid he will be disposed to compromise, but we will wait and see." Loomis himself was worried. He wrote Phil to tell him he had evened the score with Heil, but he realized what a monumental job he had on his hands and planned to remain as nonpartisan as possible in dealing with the legislature. Isabel complained that he did nothing but attend banquets and listen to flattery and had done nothing to prepare for the budget hearings. Whatever cautious optimism Progressives possessed was abruptly quashed when Loomis died suddenly of a heart attack in early December. After a few weeks of doubt as to who should succeed the office, the Wisconsin supreme court ruled that Lieutenant Governor-elect Walter Goodland would take office as "acting governor." Progressives had not only lost their one statewide office, they had also lost their chief issue: Goodland was a popular and curmudgeonly Republican with a strong independent streak who regularly bucked the party leadership almost as much as Fighting Bob La Follette had. Without Heil, Progressives essentially had no issue. Some Progressives hoped that Republican factionalism might help them in the future, but most remained dispirited.[54]

Loomis's death was a killing blow to the Progressive Party. Glenn Roberts, now state party chairman, promised Phil that he would start organizing for 1944, but he himself refused to be a candidate; he eventually became too involved in a number of wartime projects, including a potato-dehydrating plant in Duluth, that took his attention away from politics. Robert became increasingly absorbed with national affairs and the war. Even as removed as Robert was from the state, Phil continued to urge his brother to return to Wisconsin and organize for his own Senate reelection in 1946 and to rally Progressives for the difficult future: "There is no substitute for personal contact . . . there is nothing more important for your personal and political point of view than your relations with your constituents."[55] Privately, Phil complained to Isabel about Robert's failure to provide political leadership. "Bob enjoys the luxury of being a statesman," he wrote. "I hope and trust he can as long as he likes—but it will take a lot of work on the part of others." Robert continued to demur, postponing trips to the state again and again.[56]

Isabel, too, was frustrated with Robert's behavior: "When I had that serious talk with him last summer he referred to your going off and leaving him 'holding the bag' politically. He never wants to make decisions or steps forward and he has been accustomed to the role of constantly holding you back or checking rather than initiating." She worried that since Phil had done all the legwork in organizing and talking to people and no one had taken over for him, the people were becoming more and more aware that they were being neglected. Glenn Roberts did some organizing, but he accomplished little in setting forth an agenda. Some party members and supporters even began suggesting folding the party.[57]

When Robert finally did travel to Wisconsin in late July, he was appalled at the deteriorated political conditions he found. He again promised to do more to pull Progressive forces together, and he convinced Progressive leaders to pull together a full slate of candidates. Just as he had two years earlier, Robert kept the party alive in name, but he did nothing to encourage a platform or any real direction. Phil suggested that if Roberts was serious about becoming a candidate that he begin a tour of the state and visit every county official and editor. "The election of 1930," Phil reminded Isabel, "was won in the 1925–26–27–28–29—those years of combing the cross-roads and by-ways. Glenn has a good personality, people like him, and he can be elected IF he will get out and HUMP NOW—Warn him (I'll write him too) not to do a Herman Ekern."[58]

Yet again, Robert became too enmeshed in his congressional duties, proposing a massive federal governmental reorganization plan that would occupy him through 1946, to return frequently enough to the state. An ongoing battle with depression and illness distracted him as well, and the pressures of work frequently left him tense, irritable, and depressed. His occasional forays in the state did little to cheer him, as he found little organizing being done and a popular Republican governor who would make a formidable candidate.[59]

Progressives seemed to regroup somewhat in the spring of 1944. A Progressive meeting in Milwaukee generated some enthusiasm and produced four candidates for governor.[60] But 1944 was a Republican year in Wisconsin. Presidential candidate (and New York governor) Thomas Dewey carried the state, and Progressives had a desperate time trying to overcome their differences on the presidential race and on foreign policy. Everywhere Progressives encountered an apathetic public and a chronic inability to raise funds. The primary was a disaster. Progressive candidates for governor received a total of just 6 percent of the vote. Other statewide Progressive candidates faired even worse, and for a while it was unclear if any of the candidates would even qualify for ballot status in the general election. Democrats, however, buoyed by Roosevelt's candidacy, did remarkably better than in the recent past, and Robert sensed an abrupt shift in the Progressives' traditional bases of support: "Labor seems to have gone into the Democratic Primary," he wrote Fola, "and the farmers into the Republican."[61] A month after the primary, Progressives were still unorganized and unable to raise funds, even with Robert and Phil (on a short leave) in the state. Everywhere, they encountered apathetic voters, more interested in the presidential contest than in state politics. Robert spent much of September and October trying to rally Progressive voters, but he met with little success. Gasoline rationing continued to prevent mass meetings around the state and much travel by the candidates. Radio advertising had grown even more expensive. Former U.S. Senator Gaylord Nelson recently noted that most Progressives considered themselves Democrats on the national level; he cited both the war and the fact that the Roosevelt administration had co-opted the Progressives' boldest policies as causes of the apathy now endemic among Progressives. Phil urged Robert to remain optimistic, at least in front of the crowds, in the hope that confidence would breed confidence. Not much could be expected, however, when the longtime Progressive newspaper the *Capital Times* endorsed Daniel Hoan for governor and 5th district Congressman Howard McMurray—both Democrats.[62]

A Progressive revival was not to be. Up against Milwaukee Mayor Daniel Hoan and Governor Walter Goodland, the Progressive candidate for governor, Alexander Benz, received less than 6 percent of the total vote. Harry Sauthoff, running for the U.S. Senate against Democrat Howard McMurray and incumbent Republican Alexander Wiley, also received less than 6 percent. Republicans claimed all state offices and seven congressional seats. They controlled the legislature with twenty-two of thirty-three seats in the senate and seventy-five of one hundred seats in the assembly. More telling, Democrats had clearly asserted themselves as the state's second party. Democrats controlled six senate seats and nineteen assembly seats as well as two congressional seats. Progressives were left with Robert's Senate seat, Merlin Hull's congressional seat, five seats in the senate, and six in the assembly, all from either Dane County or predominantly rural counties of the north and west. Robert's interpretation of the general election was precisely right: Republicans made great inroads in Progressive rural areas, and Democrats made great gains in industrial counties along the lakeshore and Fox River Valley. Without anyone to hold it together, the Progressive alliance between Socialists, farmers, and laborers came apart at the seams.[63]

By May 1945, Robert was ready to abandon politics altogether and let the Progressive Party disband. After the 1944 elections, Phil increased his demands on Robert that he focus on his own political future ("Use those two years—don't drift."), but Robert had grown tired and discouraged by the incessant demands of electoral politics. He was angry that Phil had abandoned leadership of the party to embark on his isolationist crusade and military service and that state leaders had floundered without clear instructions from him. Robert was resentful, too, about the burden of political leadership and about perceived slights by voters. Yet after Glenn Roberts informally canvassed members of both the Progressive and Republican Parties and assured Robert both of continued popular support and that Republicans would welcome him back into the fold, Young Bob reluctantly decided to seek another term in the Senate.[64] But on which ticket? Over the past three years, Progressive voters had gradually drifted back to the Republican column, and with the Republicans' control of state politics, it seemed safer for Robert to run as a Republican than as a Progressive. William Evjue and Thomas Amlie, the party's most vigorous supporters in 1934, had become loyal Roosevelt Democrats and wanted Progressives to join them.

In January 1946, a Progressive committee recommended a party convention whose sole duty would be to decide the future of the party.

Conventional wisdom was that Progressives would return to the Republican Party. The party convened in March in Portage, while Phil was on leave (he would be formally discharged that summer). Robert and other older Progressives wanted to return to the Republican Party and were well aware of Phil's oratorical ability to sway a crowd. They feared that if Phil addressed the meeting, he would persuade the delegates to keep the Progressive Party alive. As Phil and Isen were about to leave for the convention, their telephone rang; the caller was Phil's law partner, Gordon Sinykin, who conveyed Robert's insistence that Phil stay away from the convention. Devastated, Phil once again deferred to his brother's preference and stayed in Madison. Without Phil, however, the convention participants had trouble making a decision. More than forty delegates spoke, and opinion ranged from remaining independent, returning to the Republicans, or joining the Democrats. Tensions ran high as the Progressives remained true to form, divided and antagonistic. By early afternoon, Robert finally decided to take a firmer hand and delivered his address—originally scheduled for after the vote— and recommended that the Progressives return to the Republican Party. The convention obediently agreed, voting 284 to 131 to join the Republican Party.[65]

Phil knew very well that his absence from the convention meant the death of the party he had formed twelve years earlier, yet since Robert was the candidate, he deferred to his brother's wishes. Phil was sure that if he appeared and spoke his mind, the convention would not vote to disband, but Robert and others clearly were ready to disband the party. Phil later recalled:

> I was not invited to attend; and then, I guess, to safeguard against my causing any disruption to their plans for burying the party, I was formally advised that I could attend the convention if I desired, providing it was understood that I would not participate or speak. I did not know what to do. If I appeared and spoke my convictions, I was reasonably sure the convention would not vote for disbandment. Yet I had been away from Wisconsin for more than three years. I knew there was a good chance that this long absence had deprived me of the "feel of the situation" that is essential to sound judgement.[66]

Bowing to the habit of a lifetime, he deferred to Robert's wishes and Robert's career and remained in Madison, although he took some satisfaction in the fact that the decision to disband was not a foregone conclusion and that some in attendance tried to keep the party alive.[67]

Phil eventually resigned himself to his party's death and to supporting former Progressives in the Republican primary, although he took no active part in the campaign, worried that as a "controversial figure" he might jeopardize Robert's reelection. "He does not want my face or voice stirring up controversy—so I shall keep out of it," he wrote his son in July. Phil was initially optimistic about the former Progressives' chances: "Everything considered," he wrote Robert in May, "I think things are becoming okay—Ralph [Immell, running for governor] is off to a good start—and got unusually good press." But by late summer, interest in the campaigns had waned badly. At one campaign speech in Sparta, Immell had to play records over a loudspeaker to attract a handful of people to listen to what he had to say. Phil was particularly upset that Robert waited until ten days before the primary to even begin his own campaign. The lack of enthusiasm meant that no one had any sense how the Progressives would do in their first Republican contest since 1932.[68]

What's more, some Republican Party leaders did not want them back. The party chairman, conservative businessman Thomas Coleman, had developed a great antipathy toward the La Follettes and deliberately set out to end Robert's career by any means necessary. In 1945, Republicans introduced a bill in the legislature, aimed directly at Young Bob, that would have prevented anyone who had been a candidate or member of one party in 1944 from being the candidate of another party in 1946. Governor Walter Goodland vetoed the bill, but it was clear that conservative Republicans would not gladly welcome back the Progressives and risk turning over party leadership to the La Follettes. Robert remained in Washington and did not campaign at all until just over a week before the primary. His entire strategy was to stress his record as a good representative of the people and to refrain from taking any controversial stand. His opponent in the primary, the politically unknown Appleton judge Joseph McCarthy, however, ran a vigorous campaign that involved a great deal of the door-to-door politicking that had made Fighting Bob La Follette such a success in the 1890s. Coleman and the Republican organization vigorously supported McCarthy. Even more decisive, a disgruntled Governor Goodland decided late in the campaign to endorse McCarthy after Robert endorsed Goodland's opponent Immell—a mistake even more costly than the late start of the campaign, since it alienated the one Republican who had been receptive to Robert's candidacy and who could have aided his campaign.[69]

In the primary McCarthy defeated Robert by just over five thousand votes, a startling turn of events that seemed to take most people by surprise. The *Milwaukee Journal* called the defeat "one of the most startling stories in the political history of Wisconsin." Friends came to Isabel in tears, confessing they had voted in the Democratic primary on the assumption that Robert would easily defeat McCarthy. In returning to the Republican Party, Robert lost the industrial lakeshore labor vote to Milwaukee Democrat Howard McMurray, a decisive indication of the Progressive Party's difficulty in uniting the interests of rural and urban voters. Of all the former Progressive Party members, only congressman Merlin Hull won reelection as a Republican. In the 1947 legislature, only one Progressive remained: Madison senator Fred Risser hung on to the party identification until he ran for reelection in 1948 as a Republican. In that contest, he lost to another former Progressive, now running as a Democrat, an obscure young lawyer from Polk County named Gaylord Nelson.[70] Isabel proposed the idea of Robert running in the special election to fill a second district congressional seat after the death of Robert Henry, but Robert refused, unwilling to face another election.[71] The Progressive Era was over.

The Legacy of the Great Experiment

When writing to his brother, Robert, in November 1946 to commiserate over Robert's defeat in the Republican senatorial primary, the forty-nine-year-old former governor Philip La Follette noted his lack of involvement in the magazine the family had run since 1909, *The Progressive*: "I have had nothing to do with the paper since before the war—and have not wanted to get involved."[1] Indeed, Phil seemed to have nothing to do at all when he returned from the army to Madison in the summer of 1945. After a few months of "loafing" he rented out a small office and tried to rebuild his former law practice; a few old clients returned, but the business did not absorb his time or his energy. He filled his time by reading law reports and the newspaper and chatting with old friends; he also spoke to various civic groups about his experiences in the South Pacific and even addressed the state legislature on the subject. In February 1946, he appeared before the House Military Affairs Committee to give testimony against universal military service; there he readily shared his thoughts on American foreign policy. Phil was still something of a public figure, but the once tireless campaigner had become more of an after-dinner speaker.[2]

Without the pressures of a public career, Phil was able to become more involved with his children, and he tried to be more supportive than his own father had been. From 1944 to 1947, Phil's son Robert III served in the army and planned after his enlistment was over to enroll in the University of Wisconsin. When his son was in the process of being discharged and was unable to return to Madison to register for classes in the fall of 1947, Phil took his place in the registration line, creating the unusual sight of a middle-age former governor and professor lined up with eighteen-year-olds. Yet Phil's relationship with his own father continued to haunt him. As a young man, Phil would have done anything to get his father's approval and wanted more than anything to follow in his father's political footsteps. Years later, he could not understand his own son's independence from politics. Robert III had little interest in pursuing a political career, especially in light of the depression Phil withstood after his loss to Julius Heil and Robert felt after his loss to Joseph McCarthy. His son's indifference to politics disappointed Phil, especially since he had given him the magical name "Robert M. La Follette" at birth in anticipation that he would pursue politics. Phil told his son he could do whatever he wanted—he even helped him get into the University of Wisconsin Law School—but he expressed his disappointment to others. After earning a law degree, Robert III served as a judge in Alaska and later moved to Michigan and pursued a career in animal behavior.[3]

Phil and Isabel gave much more direction to their daughter Judy. Perhaps regretting his own decision not to pursue an academic career, Phil advised Judy to pursue higher education. Both parents could be critical and demanding, and the close direction coming after years of being rather distant frustrated Judy, who eventually quit college and went to work as a secretary for Sears in Minneapolis. In 1981 she earned a master's degree in English from Washington State University, having inherited her parents' strong affection for literature, and she taught there until 1994.

Phil's and Isabel's youngest daughter, Sherry, was ten when Phil returned from the Pacific, and she presented significant familial challenges. She was a high-energy child, as precocious and intense as Phil had been. She suffered from bouts of depression and mysterious pains in addition to symptoms of bipolar disorder, which went undiagnosed until she was an adult. Judy and Robert attended public schools in Madison, but Phil and Isabel sent Sherry to private schools because of her frequent illness. She followed her aunt Fola's footsteps and moved to New York to pursue an artistic life, appearing in several Broadway plays and writing several books with her husband George Zabriskie, including a biography of her grandmother, Belle Case La Follette. In an ironic way, Phil's family life had come full circle. Each of his children inherited a major aspect of his personality—Robert his legal abilities, Judy his academic bent, and Sherry his dramatic flair—but the demands of politics and for his children to live up to their grandfather's public service frustrated the La Follettes' home life.[4]

Family life supplemented by a stagnant law practice and occasional lectures were not enough, however, to keep Phil's active mind occupied, and the adjustment to civilian life was difficult. Quite simply, without politics, he was bored. "As we have agreed," Isabel wrote him in a letter, "you do not have enough to do[,] which drives you nuts." For a time he considered giving up his law practice completely and devoting all of his energies to the farm, despite the fact that the day-to-day requirements of farm life would have kept him away from Madison. Phil even considered running for office again, but the disappointment of the Progressive Party's disbanding was too painful, and it was an enduring disappointment that he was not courted by either the Democrats or the Republicans.[5]

In the end, although he was exiled from state politics, Phil did not step away from the political scene. He was eager to promote his old commander, Douglas MacArthur, for president in 1948. Phil had been attracted to powerful leaders since his youth, and all his life he devoured biographies of "great men" with whom he believed MacArthur shared important qualities. When serving under MacArthur in the Pacific, he had been deeply impressed by the man's leadership and intellect; MacArthur had been awarded the highest grades ever achieved at West Point and excelled in the sciences, which demanded precision and detail, both qualities Phil admired and qualities he found lacking in most politicians. He was especially impressed by how MacArthur handled the Japanese after the war, which he thought demonstrated great cultural insight. This admiration was tempered by what Phil recognized as serious flaws in MacArthur's personality. The general had no humility and never admitted mistakes, often resorting to petty attempts to cover them up.[6]

Phil believed that the same vigorous leadership and intellectual abilities were critical in the early years of the Cold War. He had witnessed firsthand the political repression in the Soviet Union, and he feared that Joseph Stalin might take advantage of the devastation in Europe to dominate the continent, jeopardizing American interests and eventually threatening American democracy. In November 1947, a Chicago meeting hosted by Robert Wood included Phil, who outlined the strategy for securing MacArthur's nomination at the Republican National Convention. Phil recognized that the powerful image of a former military leader reluctantly agreeing to serve the people as a political officeholder, as George Washington had, could boost MacArthur's popularity. Phil's role in this was particularly valuable because of a quirk in the Wisconsin election laws that allowed a candidate's name to be placed on the ballot without that candidate's support or even permission. This would allow MacArthur to be a candidate and still appear to be uninterested. In January 1948, Phil began actively campaigning on MacArthur's behalf, delivering a radio address in which he declared that the general would "do more than any one else to salvage the world's peace." In March, he delivered several radio addresses in support of MacArthur emphasizing his intellect and leadership. That spring, he also opened MacArthur's Madison campaign headquarters.[7]

Phil also took on a larger role: after initially refusing, he agreed to be a candidate for delegate-at-large pledged to MacArthur to the Republican National Convention. Until 1968, voters in the presidential primary voted for a slate of delegates who pledged to support a candidate at the convention, which would nominate the candidate with the majority of delegates. As one of several MacArthur delegates, Phil ran against other delegates who were pledged to other nominees, hoping to win enough votes to gain MacArthur's nomination. The results of the presidential preference primary, however, were disappointing. Overall, Harold Stassen defeated MacArthur with Thomas Dewey running third. Phil could take some satisfaction in the fact that he had won more votes than any other MacArthur delegate, even though the general lost the election. After the defeat, Phil remained philosophical, noting that he felt about the same as he did after his 1932 loss: "We fought for something, and everything we said before election was just as true afterwards—I was and am convinced that MacArthur is the one man most likely to keep us out of war, and if we are thrust into a third war, he would be by far the one most likely to win for those that are against dictatorship and police state." After Dewey secured the Republican nomination nationally, Phil endorsed him rather than the much more liberal incumbent president, Harry S Truman, the first time Phil had ever publicly supported a Republican presidential candidate. He lost Wisconsin but won enough other states to secure the national nomination. He later aided California Governor Earl Warren's efforts toward the presidential nomination in 1952 and proposed an unlikely slate of electors headed by himself, Walter Kohler Jr., Oscar Rennebohm, and Fred Zimmerman. It appeared that Phil had drifted far to the conservative side of politics, but he really made the same decision he had made in supporting the isolationist cause in 1940 and 1941: to work with those who shared his goals regardless of their stand on other issues or of past political conflicts.[8]

The spark of energy that the MacArthur crusade gave Phil quickly dissipated, and he again grew bored and irritable, unwilling to grow old.

He repeatedly dissuaded admirers who urged him to run for office, writing to William Ihrig in 1952:

> During the past twenty-five years I have put in over half of it working for the public (D.A., Governor, Army). It has been a rewarding experience—but not financially. It required throwing a law practice "out the window" three times. And I don't need to tell you it is not easy to build it back. And when I reached the point of fairly good earnings from my practice, it coincided with this period of high income taxes.[9]

It was not exactly that he had grown tired of public service, but he believed he had never been sufficiently recognized for the sacrifice of his career and private life. He was also worried about money. The La Follettes had never been rich, and financial worries had hounded Phil for most of his young adulthood. He wanted to use his talents in a way that would leave his children a financial legacy.[10]

One new opportunity was the governorship of occupied Bavaria. In 1948, he was summoned to Washington by Secretary of War Kenneth Royall, who informed him of the situation in occupied Germany. General Lucius Clay, military governor of the American Occupation Zone, wanted Americans with administrative experience to assist him. Phil flew to Germany and met with Clay, who urged Phil to accept the position of military governor of Bavaria, the largest state in the American Occupation Zone. The offer—and the administrative challenges it brought—sorely tempted Phil. Two considerations convinced him not to accept. The first was financial: the salary was only $10,000 a year, and the food and hospitality expenses that the job entailed—which Phil would have to bear —would be enormous. The second consideration was political. Would Phil's authority be supported by the U.S. government? After returning to the United States, Phil met with Secretary of State George C. Marshall, who also urged Phil to accept. Phil remained unconvinced and wanted a personal commitment from President Truman. When the president's secretary failed to make an appointment, Phil took it as a rebuff and refused the post, unwilling to risk his financial stability without the full support of the president.[11]

Bored by civilian life and frustrated with being cut out of politics, Phil turned to alcohol. Both he and Isabel drank heavily, and she self-consciously speculated that alcohol was becoming a "crutch" to get them through their painful lives in Madison, surrounded by former friends and bad memories. An enthusiastic radical in his youth, Phil in middle-age found himself out of step with liberalism and unwilling to connect himself with the younger politicians out to reform the state Democratic Party. He did not approve of editor Morris Rubin's *The Progressive*, especially after the magazine supported the Rosenbergs during their 1951 trial, and he grumbled that his father's name was still associated with it.[12]

Depression continued to stalk the La Follette family. Robert, still living in Washington, struggled to come to terms with his electoral failure of 1946. Convinced that he had betrayed the family honor by losing to McCarthy ("I was at the helm and the ship has foundered," he remarked to Phil), Robert committed suicide in 1953 at the age of fifty-eight. The event shocked the family and deepened Phil's own depression. Aware of her husband's state of mind, Isabel worried for his safety, listening at the bedroom door on the mornings that Phil overslept to make sure he was still alive.[13]

Eventually some of Phil's "eastern connections" provided an opportunity that would relieve Phil of both his boredom and his financial worries. Phil already sat on the boards of directors of several corporations and had been associate general-counsel for the Hazeltine Corporation, an electronics firm, since 1946. The business frequently took him to New York, and in 1955 Phil and Isabel moved to Long Island when Phil was elected president of Hazeltine's Electronics Division; in 1957, he was elected president of the corporation. The departure again fueled speculation that Phil had turned into a corporate conservative, but for Phil the electronics industry was a new and interesting challenge. In many ways it was an ideal position for him: the cutting-edge technology appealed to his intellectual curiosity, and managing a corporation fit his administrative skills. The job also provided a sizable income that would enable him to leave money for his children, which had become a preoccupation.[14]

Phil had never managed to leave Wisconsin entirely during his political career, and even in his new role, he could not stay away from Madison for very long. Isabel felt out of place in Long Island and missed her friends. There was unfinished business as well. Phil wanted to write his memoirs—to tell his side of the story—hoping to inspire young readers to enter politics. After he retired from Hazeltine in 1959, Phil and Isabel returned to Madison. Phil was now a gray old man, dapper in dress if stout in appearance. He and Isabel rented an apartment on North Pinckney Street, just a few blocks from the old Executive Residence, where he had lived for five years as a child and six as an adult. The couple spent weekends on the farm near Roxbury. Phil appeared at his law office every morning, read the newspaper, and went to lunch. He spent his afternoons at the State Historical Society, where he sifted though boxes of correspondence and began working on his memoirs. He enjoyed visiting with others at the Historical Society, both students and professors, puffing away on a small cigar as he discussed his views on politics. As old hurts faded, he eased more comfortably into the role of elder statesman.

By the 1950s, Wisconsin politics had changed a great deal. Republicans had dominated the state since after the war, but the Democrats underwent a rebirth. Led by admirers of the La Follettes like Gaylord Nelson and William Proxmire and supported by former Progressive voters, the Democrats had grown into a competitive liberal party. In 1957 voters elected Proxmire to a U.S. Senate seat, and in 1958 voters elected Nelson governor, the first Democrats to hold these offices since the New Deal era. In 1960, on the twenty-fifth anniversary of the Rural Electrification Act, Phil stood with Governor Nelson in his old office as Nelson signed a proclamation naming May "Rural Electrification Month." He happily posed for photographers in the executive office next to his successor and beneath portraits of himself and his father, hung side by side. Certainly he must have been very aware that the man standing next to him, viewed by many as his intellectual and political heir, was a Democrat.[15]

Yet without an active role in politics, Phil remained sad, and work on his memoirs could not measure up to the heady days of the Great Depression when he was a young man ready to rescue civilization. He had grown prematurely old, and like his father, he began to suffer health problems, particularly with his heart. In August 1965, Phil was hospitalized with chest pains. He died soon after, on August 18, from pneumonia. In his last days, visited by his wife and children, Phil's thoughts turned not to politics but to his contrasting impulse toward a peaceful rural life, asking his daughter about the crops on the Roxbury farm. He took comfort in the fact that he had managed his chief goal in retirement: he left a modest financial legacy for his children. His body lay in state at the capitol rotunda, the first governor to be so honored since Walter Goodland in 1947. Phil was buried next to Robert and his parents in Forest Hill cemetery on Madison's west side. Isabel soldiered on, still devoted to her husband and his cause, preparing his papers to be opened to the public and seeing that his memoirs were eventually published. Like his father's biography, finally published in 1953, Phil's story of an ambitious politician during the 1920s and 1930s was quaint to a generation raised in the 1960s. His childhood home, Maple Bluff Farm, had been placed on the National Register of Historic Places the year before his death. His obituaries depicted him as an ambitious politician and cited the Glenn Frank case and the National Progressives of America as the events that ended his political career.[16]

Yet the obituaries missed an important point. Yes, Phil was a radical in an era of radicals, and he was best known for launching the National Progressives of America in an era of would-be new parties. What set Phil apart from other liberal critics of the New Deal was his ability to articulate a rational explanation for the causes of the Great Depression and gather a group of intellectuals who could offer a coherent and workable program to address the problems of widespread unemployment and misdistribution of wealth. Until 1938, he was also remarkably successful in convincing voters to support his proposals. The Progressive works bill of 1935 was perhaps the most cogent potential challenge to the vagaries of New Deal relief. As long as the Progressive Party could develop those proposals and make its case persuasively it thrived, winning elections and implementing innovative programs. When Phil became discouraged and left politics after 1939 to pursue other crusades, however, the party lost the one figure who could hold it together and make it a legitimate political force.

After Phil's death, Isabel remained in Madison, finishing Phil's memoirs and working on her own autobiography, which remains unpublished. She continued to be something of a public figure, presiding over the opening of Phil's papers at the State Historical Society and at the dedication of La Follette High School in Madison. She continued her hobbies and sold her paintings at art fairs, knowing that people purchased them more for their celebrity provenance than for their artistic merit. She died in 1973.

Phil's and Isen's children never entered politics, but they did pursue careers that reflected their father's interests. Robert excelled in college, graduating Phi Beta Kappa from the University of Wisconsin and in the top fifth of his UW Law School class. After serving as a magistrate judge in Alaska he moved to Michigan and earned a master's degree in animal behavior—another subject Phil would have found fascinating. Judy earned a master's degree in English and married a geologist who taught at Washington State Univeristy in Pullman, Washington, settling into an academic household that Phil would have found comfortable. Sherry became an actress and author in New York, living a life filled with drama and literature that Phil would have enjoyed. Phil's nephew, Bronson La Follette, Young Bob's son, carried on the family business of politics, and Phil lived to see him elected Wisconsin attorney general in 1964.

Bronson lost a race for governor in 1968 to popular incumbent Republican Warren Knowles, but he served three more terms as attorney general from 1975 to 1987.[17]

Phil's significance as a historical figure is manifold. His difficult relationship with his father and his efforts to live up to Fighting Bob's reputation make an interesting episode in the study of political dynasties. Certainly he attained far more than the children of his contemporaries Franklin Roosevelt and Joseph Kennedy, and few American families rival the La Follettes' record of public service. More tangibly, Wisconsin under Phil's governorship again proved to be a leader in innovative public policy. Faced with the economic crisis of the Great Depression, Progressives inaugurated successful relief and employment programs that served as models for other states and in part as a model for the New Deal. Several important figures of the Roosevelt administration—including Edwin Witte and David Lilienthal—got their start in the La Follette administration.

The most striking thing about Philip La Follette was his profound grasp of the meaning of America. His parents instilled in him an almost religious faith in democracy, but it was not the mindless patriotism of Gilded Age robber barons, World War I super-patriots, or McCarthy-era anticommunists. The La Follettes saw the United States the same way that the founding generation did: as a great experiment, a new *kind* of nation. During Old Bob's 1924 presidential bid, those who attended his rallies were treated to a lantern slide show that flashed images of Washington, Jefferson, Lincoln, and other great American leaders. The common thread in those depicted was not that they had served their country but that they had served the *idea* of their country. Americans had to work at democracy and adapt the United States to changing circumstances. Lincoln told his audience at Gettysburg that it was up to them to give the nation "a new birth of freedom." Fighting Bob wanted to restore economic liberty to those losing out to unscrupulous corporations. Phil saw the Great Depression not just as an economic crisis but also as a political crisis that threatened to end American democracy. It was up to his generation to restore economic opportunities to the people and to maintain democracy when the rest of the world was falling to totalitarianism. Phil asserted such determination in his National Progressives of America speech in the Livestock Pavilion at the University of Wisconsin: "Men can have work AND be free."[18]

Phil never tired of campaigning because he never tired of that message. And he never gave up hope that every person could grasp that message and work to preserve American democracy, whether they were farmers, industrial workers, housewives, college students, or business-men. Forty years after Phil's death, the nation continues to face eco-nomic problems that divide the poor and the wealthy and deprive children of food, housing, and opportunity. For many people, the prom-ise of democracy remains unfulfilled. This does not represent a failure on the part of Progressives but rather—as Phil would have seen it—a challenge for the next generation of Americans who believe that politi-cal democracy and economic opportunity belong to all and are willing to commit to leaving the United States a better nation than they found it. The great experiment goes forward.

WHi Image ID 34109

Phil enjoyed campaigning even more than he did governing. Meeting and greeting often enthusiastic supporters renewed his energy and his confidence in progressive ideas. When heckled on the stump, he relished fighting back and gave as good as he got.

Notes

In citing correspondence, the following abbreviations have been used for names that appear frequently:

BCL   Belle Case La Follette
PFL   Philip Fox La Follette
RML Jr.   Robert Marion La Follette Jr.
RML Sr. Robert Marion La Follette Sr.
ML   Mary La Follette
IBL   Isabel Bacon La Follette
GM   George Middleton
FL   Fola La Follette
RS   Ralph Sucher

INTRODUCTION

1. Belle Case La Follette and Fola La Follette, *Robert M. La Follette: June 14, 1855–June 18, 1925* (New York: The MacMillan Company, 1953), 1170–73; Bernard A. Weisberger, *The La Follettes of Wisconsin: Love and Politics in Progressive America* (Madison: University of Wisconsin Press, 1994), 273–75; *Capital Times*, June 17, 1926, and June 14, 1927.

2. *New York Times*, June 19, 1925; *St. Paul Pioneer Press*, June 19, 1925; *Portland Oregonian*, June 19, 1925; *Chicago Tribune*, June 19, 1925; *Washington Post*, June 19, 1925. All newspapers commented on his national significance, some neglecting to even mention which state he represented in the Senate. "Obituary," *The Outlook* 140 (July 1, 1925): 323. *The Outlook* had a long history of denigrating La Follette. See also George E. Mowry, *The Era of Theodore Roosevelt and the Birth of Modern America* (New York, 1956), 291–95; Sinclair Lewis, "Be Brisk with Babbitt," *The Nation* 119 (October 15, 1924): 411. Babbitt provided readers with his profound insight on all three candidates; he supported Calvin Coolidge. *The Saturday Evening Post* repeatedly tried to link La Follette with communism. See Samuel Blythe, "Let X=La Follette," *Saturday Evening Post* 197 (October 18, 1924): 3–4+.

3. *The Nation* 115 (September 6, 1922): 224. The magazine often compared La Follette to Abraham Lincoln, a comparison La Follette used in his 1924 campaign. Weisberger, *La Follettes of Wisconsin*, 264–72. For an extended study of how La Follette himself cultivated his image as a quasi-religious crusader, see John Milton Cooper Jr., "Robert M. La Follette: Political Prophet," *Wisconsin Magazine of History* 69 (Winter 1985–86): 90–105. See also "Robert Marion La Follette: A Swashbuckling Dumas Hero Caught and Civilized," *Current Opinion* 77 (September 1924): 298–99.

4. John Dos Passos, "Fighting Bob" in *The 42nd Parallel* (Boston: Houghton Mifflin Company, 1930); Bruce Bliven, "Robert M. La Follette's Place in Our History," *Current History* 22 (August 1925): 716; *New York Times*, June 19, 1925.

5. "Address by Philip F. La Follette," in Congress, Senate, *Acceptance and Unveiling of the Statue of Robert Marion La Follette*, 71st Cong., 1st Sess., 1929, Senate Document No. 4, pp. 26–29. See also Philip F. La Follette, *Adventure in Politics: The Memoirs of Philip La Follette*, Donald Young, ed. (New York: Holt, Rinehart and Winston, 1970), 133–34; *Capital Times*, April 25 and 27, 1929.

6. In 1933, Phil delivered a memorial address to the Wisconsin Legislature on the death of Lieutenant Governor Henry Huber. He praised Huber's role in social legislation and for his stand defending La Follette against attacks of disloyalty "under the cloak of perverted patriotism." See *Henry A. Huber, Late Lieutenant Governor: Memorial Exercises, Wisconsin Legislature*, Supplement to Senate Journal, 61st Session, May 31, 1933.

7. For Wisconsin's unusual party system, see Leon D. Epstein, *Politics in Wisconsin* (Madison: University of Wisconsin Press, 1958), 33–56.

8. The earliest work on the Wisconsin Progressive Party is Donald McCoy, "The Formation of the Wisconsin Progressive Party in 1934," *The Historian* 14 (Autumn 1951: 70–90). Two dissertations also discuss the third party movement but were completed before the opening of the Philip La Follette Papers at the Wisconsin Historical Society and the La Follette Family Papers at the Library of Congress: Lester F. Schmidt, "The Farmer-Labor Progressive Federation: The Study of a 'United Front' Movement among Wisconsin Liberals, 1934–1941" (University of Wisconsin, 1955) and Charles H. Backstrom, "The Progressive Party of Wisconsin, 1934–1946" (University of Wisconsin, 1957). The most thorough discussion is John E. Miller, *Governor Philip F. La Follette, the Wisconsin Progressives, and the New Deal* (Columbia: University of Missouri Press, 1982), although Miller spends little time with the Wisconsin politics in the 1920s or on Phil's young adulthood, both of which were major factors in his public career and the movement behind the Progressive Party.

9. Transcript of interview, November 23, 1936, in folder 6, box 63, PFL Papers.

10. Book review of John Gunther, *The Riddle of MacArthur*, in *The Freeman*, May 7, 1951, copy in folder 4, box 120, ibid.

11. See Otis L. Graham, *An Encore for Reform: Old Progressives and the New Deal* (New York: Oxford University Press, 1967), especially chapter one. On the "moralism" of the Progressives, see Richard Hofstadter, *The Age of Reform: From Bryan to F.D.R.* (New York: Vintage Books, 1955), 174–214. For the different interpretations of the Great Depression by New Dealers and Progressives, see Hofstadter, *Age of Reform*, 302–16, and Gary Gerstle, "The Protean Character of American Liberalism," *American Historical Review* 99 (October 1994): 1068.

CHAPTER ONE

1. Bernard A. Weisberger, *The La Follettes of Wisconsin: Love and Politics in Progressive America* (Madison: University of Wisconsin Press, 1994), 14–27.

2. George Middleton, *These Things Are Mine: The Autobiography of a Journeyman Playwright* (New York: The Macmillan Company, 1947), 87; Patrick J. Maney, *"Young Bob": A Biography of Robert M. La Follette, Jr., 1895–1953* (Columbia: University of Missouri Press, 1978), 11–12; Belle Case La Follette and Fola La Follette, *Robert M. La Follette: June 14, 1855–June 18, 1925*, 2 vols. (New York: The Macmillan Company, 1953), 1:111–12; Weisberger, *La Follettes of Wisconsin*, 66–67; Philip F. La Follette, *Adventure in Politics: The Memoirs of Philip La Follette*, Donald Young, ed. (New York: Holt, Rinehart and Winston, 1970), 1, 21–22. The "when we were governor" remark is from Zona Gale, "Americans We Like," *The Nation* 126 (February 15, 1928): 180–82.

3. La Follette, *Adventure in Politics*, 6–7.

4. Ibid., 8–9.

5. Merle Curti and Vernon Carstenson, *The University of Wisconsin: A History, 1848–1925*, Volume II (Madison: University of Wisconsin Press, 1949), 11–13; La Follette, *Adventure in Politics*, 10–11. See also Horace Samuel Merrill, *William Freeman Vilas: Doctrinaire Democrat* (Madison: State Historical Society of Wisconsin, 1954), 253. Vilas objected to the university's increasingly close relationship to the state government, known generally as "The Wisconsin Idea."

6. La Follette and La Follette, *Robert M. La Follette*, 1:197.

7. Ibid.; Mary Ellen Chase, *A Goodly Fellowship* (New York: Macmillan, 1940), 87–121; La Follette, *Adventure in Politics*, 6.

8. PFL to BCL and RML Sr., January 9, February 2, March 28, and April 25, 1906, box A5, La Follette Family Papers, Manuscript Division, Library of Congress.

9. PFL to BCL, February 2 and 15, 1906, box A5, ibid.

10. The La Follette family, like all congressional families, maintained two homes, one in Madison and one in Washington. Where the children lived was determined by how long Congress was in session. If the session was only a few months, Belle preferred to keep them in their schools in Madison; if La Follette faced more than a few months in Washington, the family stayed there.

11. La Follette and La Follette, *Robert M. La Follette*, 1:226; Weisberger, *La Follettes of Wisconsin*, 66–69. See also RML Sr., correspondence to his family in box A5, La Follette Family Papers.

12. La Follette's response to the pony's blindness is mentioned in La Follette and La Follette, *Robert M. La Follette*, 1:225.

13. PFL to RML Sr., January 29, February 4 and 27, and October 10, 1907, all in box A6; and April 16 and May 14, 1907, box A6; all in La Follette Family Papers.

14. La Follette, *Adventure in Politics*, 17–18; BCL to RML Sr., October 23, 1909, box A7, La Follette Family Papers.

15. PFL to BCL, June 16 and 18, 1910, box A9, La Follette Family Papers.

16. PFL to BCL, June 23, 1910, box A9, ibid.

17. PFL to BCL, April 24, 1914, box A15, ibid; La Follette, *Adventure in Politics*, 28–29.

18. In the La Follette Family Papers see PFL to Louis Brandeis, August 6, 1910, box A9, and PFL to Lord Rosenberry, May 14, 1913, box A13. Photographic request

file, box F1. George V declined the request ("not his majesty's policy"), as did Haakon VII of Norway. There was occasional confusion on the part of foreign correspondents, who sometimes addressed replies to "Senator Philip La Follette."

19. Weisberger, *La Follettes of Wisconsin*, 215; Maney, *"Young Bob,"* 16 (quotation), 31; La Follette, *Adventure in Politics*, 38, 6; La Follette and La Follette, *Robert M. La Follette*, 1:281; "Recollections of Philip La Follette's Childhood by Mrs. Gilbert E. (Netha King) Roe," August 21, 1965, box F2; and BCL to RML Sr., April 16 and May 14, 1907, box A5, all in La Follette Family Papers.

20. Lucy Freeman, Sherry La Follette, and George A. Zabriskie, *Belle: The Biography of Belle Case La Follette* (New York: Beaufort Books, 1986), 47; BCL to PFL, July 29, August 7, October 21–25, November 10, 1913; the quotation is from BCL to PFL, August 17, 1913, all in box A12; and Philip La Follette journal, box F2, all in La Follette Family Papers.

21. Phil thought Robert needed to stay in school. PFL to BCL and RML Sr., no date [1911], box A11, La Follette Family Papers.

22. BCL to PFL, August 10, 1913, box A12; PFL to RML Sr., August 1913 [no day], box A13; and Journal of Philip La Follette, February 20, 1913, box F1, all in La Follette Family Papers.

23. La Follette, *Adventure in Politics*, 30–34; PFL to "Dear Ones," August 1, 1914, and PFL to RML Sr., August 3, 1914, both in box A15, La Follette Family Papers.

24. La Follette, *Adventure in Politics*, 33; PFL to "Dear Ones All," September 4 and 14, 1914, box A15, La Follette Family Papers.

25. La Follette, *Adventure in Politics*, 32–33; Weisberger, *La Follettes of Wisconsin*, 182–83.

26. PFL correspondence, fall 1915; BCL to PFL, September 28, October 10, November 2 and 3, December 10, 1915; and BCL to "Dear Ones," September 20, 1915, all in box A17, La Follette Family Papers.

27. La Follette, *Adventure in Politics*, 38–39; Weisberger, *La Follettes of Wisconsin*, 215; *Wisconsin State Journal*, February 24, 1916; RML to PFL, January 30, 1916, box A19, La Follette Family Papers. Judith Sorem and Robert La Follette III to the author, October 9, 2005.

28. La Follette, *Adventure in Politics*, 37–38; PFL to RML Jr., March 20, 1916; and PFL to RML Sr., March 20, 1916, both in box A19, La Follette Family Papers.

29. PFL to "Dear Ones," July 18 and 28, 1916; and PFL to RML Sr., December 8, 1916, all in box A19, La Follette Family Papers.

30. La Follette and La Follette, *Robert M. La Follette*, 1:618.

31. Ibid., 1:651, 666–68; *Congressional Record* (April 4, 1917), 65th Congress, 1st Sess., Vol. 55, part 1, p. 235.

32. PFL to RML Sr., March 10, 1917, box A20, La Follette Family Papers; La Follette, *Adventure in Politics*, 32–33; Weisberger, *La Follettes of Wisconsin*, 214–15.

33. RML Sr. to PFL, March 27, 1917, box A21, La Follette Family Papers.

34. PFL to RML Sr., February 6 and March 10, 1917; PFL correspondence, March through May, 1917; and BCL to "Loved Ones," July 19, 1917, all in box A20, ibid.

35. La Follette, *Adventure in Politics*, 48–49; La Follette and La Follette, *Robert M. La Follette*, 2:765–72; Richard Barry, "A Radical in Power: A Study of La Follette," *The Outlook* 132 (November 29, 1922): 566; *St. Paul Pioneer-Press*, October 6, 1917.

36. Irvin S. Cobb, "The Thunders of Silence," *Saturday Evening Post* 190 (February 9, 1918): 3–5, 38–42.

37. Curti and Carstensen, *University of Wisconsin*, 115; Wisconsin Legislative Journal, special session, 1918.

38. PFL to BCL, April 3, 1917; and BCL to PFL, April 16, 1917, both in box A20, La Follette Family Papers.

39. PFL to RML Sr., April 2, 1917; PFL to BCL, April 9, 1917; BCL to PFL, April 11, 1917; and PFL to "Dear Ones," April 16, 1917, all in box A20, ibid.

40. PFL to BCL, April 9 and 14, 1917, box A20, ibid. The quotation is from PFL to "Dear Ones All," April 28, 1918, box A23, ibid.

41. RML Sr. to "Dear Hearts," June 20, 1917, box 21; PFL to BCL, April 9 and 18, 1917; PFL to RML Sr., August 25, 1917; PFL to "Dear Ones," October 10, 15, 30, and November 5, 1917; and BCL to ML, December 14, 1917, all in box A20, ibid.

42. Undated correspondence (drafts of letter to unnamed friend), box F1, ibid.; La Follette, *Adventure in Politics*, 52–53; Weisberger, *La Follettes of Wisconsin*, 214–15; La Follette and La Follette, *Robert M. La Follette*, 643–44.

43. PFL to BCL, February 1, 1918, box A23, La Follette Family Papers; La Follette, *Adventure in Politics*, 52–53.

44. RML Sr. to PFL, April 3, 1918, box A23, La Follette Family Papers.

45. RML Sr. to PFL, January 19, March 6, and April 20, 1918; PFL to "Dear Ones," January 20 and February 18, 1918; PFL to RML Sr., March 8 and 25, 1918; and PFL to BCL, March 13 and 15, 1918, all ibid.

46. Undated poetry (1917?); and PFL to RML Sr., January 19, 1917, both in folder 1, box 131, Philip F. La Follette Papers, Archives Division, Wisconsin Historical Society.

47. Weisberger, *La Follettes of Wisconsin*, 216–21; La Follette, *Adventure in Politics*, 56.

48. PFL to "Dear Ones," June 6, 1918; RML Sr. to FL, October 10, 1918; PFL to FL, October 13, 1918; PFL to RML Sr., October 15 and 29 and November 9, 1918, all in box A23, La Follette Family Papers; the "accuracy" quotation is from RML Sr. to PFL, June 1918 (no exact date), box A23, ibid.

49. PFL to RML Sr., November 19 and December 3, 1918, box A23, ibid.; PFL to RML Sr., January 10 and 24, 1919, box A26, ibid. Phil blamed the problems at the University of Wisconsin on the lack of leadership of the recently deceased Van Hise, although he wrote a note of condolence (with some difficulty) to Van Hise's widow. See PFL to RML Sr., November 24, 1918, box A23, ibid.

50. PFL to "Dear Ones," March 1, 1919; PFL to BCL, March 15, 1919; and PFL to RML Sr., March 20, 1919, all in box A26, ibid.

51. PFL to RML Sr., February 26, 1919; and PFL to "Dear Ones," May 28 and June 14, 1919, all in box A26, ibid.

52. PFL to "Dear Ones," February 4 and 24, 1919; PFL to BCL, February 11, 1919; and PFL to RML Sr., February 7 and 8, 1919, all in box A26, ibid.

53. Max Otto to PFL, November 19, 1919; and Joe Farrington to PFL, November 6 and 19, 1919, all in folder 1, box 131, PFL Papers. Phil's pledge to his father appears in Weisberger, *La Follettes of Wisconsin*, 257.

54. PFL to BCL, May 29 and September 27, 1919, box A26; and BCL to "Loved Ones," February 19 and 28 and May 9, 1920, box A28, all in La Follette Family Papers.

55. BCL to PFL, January 6, 1921; and PFL to BCL, March 18 and May 15, 1921, all in box A29, ibid.; La Follette, *Adventure in Politics*, 63–64; Weisberger, *La Follettes of Wisconsin*, 258.

56. RML Jr. to PFL, June 24 and September 21, 1921; and IBL to BCL, September 19, 1921, all in box A29, La Follette Family Papers; La Follette, *Adventure in Politics*, 79–80; Isabel Bacon La Follette, "If You Can Take It," 61, unpublished manuscript in box 165, PFL Papers. See also Weisberger, *La Follettes of Wisconsin*, 260–62.

57. Nancy Unger, "The Two Worlds of Belle Case La Follette," *Wisconsin Magazine of History* 83 (Winter 1999–2000): 83–110; Weisberger, *La Follettes of Wisconsin*, 77–101.

58. BCL to PFL, [January 1921] and June 6, 1921, box A29; PFL to RML Sr., January 3, 1923; PFL to "Dear Ones," April 3 and 7, 1923; and PFL to "My dear hearts," April 13, 1923, box A30, all in La Follette Family Papers; La Follette, *Adventure in Politics*, 79–81; Weisberger, *La Follettes of Wisconsin*, 260–62.

59. IBL to RML Jr., January 26, 1925; and BCL to PFL and IBL, December 29, 1925, all in box A32; IBL correspondence, 1926–27, boxes 33 and 34; BCL to IBL, January 15 and April 16, 1926, box A33; PFL to "Dear Ones," January 14, 1926, box A34; and PFL to "Dear Ones," December 4, 1927, box A35, all in La Follette Family Papers; Weisberger, *La Follettes of Wisconsin*, 262.

60. RML Sr. to PFL, April 28, 1925; PFL to "Dear Ones," February 22, 1925; IBL to RML Jr., January 26, 1925; and IBL to BCL, January 24, 1925, all in box A32, La Follette Family Papers.

CHAPTER TWO

1. George Middleton, *These Things Are Mine: The Autobiography of a Journeyman Playwright* (New York: The Macmillan Company, 1947), 173; "Speech of Robert M. La Follette: Hearings Before a Subcommittee of the Committee of Privileges and Elections," U.S. Senate, 65th Congress, 1st Sess., 1917.

2. Philip F. La Follette, *Adventure in Politics: The Memoirs of Philip La Follette*, Donald Young, ed. (New York: Holt, Rinehart and Winston, 1970), 53–54, 48; PFL to BCL, RML Sr., and ML, July 3, 1919, box A26, La Follette Family Papers, Manuscripts Division, Library of Congress. Roe also represented La Follette before the Senate Committee investigating his alleged disloyal comments in his St. Paul speech and wrote a brilliant brief defending free speech during war—see "Speech of Robert M. La Follette." Phil mentioned John Bright in his speech accepting the statue of his father in 1929, and he mentioned the book often in letters. See George Macaulay Trevelyan, *Life of John Bright* (New York: Houghton Mifflin, 1913).

3. Belle Case La Follette and Fola La Follette, *Robert M. La Follette: June 14, 1855–June 18, 1925*, 2 vols. (New York: The Macmillan Company, 1953), 2:1015; La Follette, *Adventure in Politics*, 68; Bernard A. Weisberger, *The La Follettes of Wisconsin: Love and Politics in Progressive America* (Madison: University of Wisconsin Press, 1994), 259.

4. La Follette and La Follette, *Robert M. La Follette*, 2:1025.

5. Ibid., 1025–26; La Follette, *Adventure in Politics*, 69–70; Weisberger, *La Follettes of* Wisconsin, 242.

6. Phil graduated from the University of Wisconsin in 1920, attended one year of law school at George Washington University, and received a law degree from the University of Wisconsin law school in 1922.

7. PFL to IBL, February 21 and March 2, 1922, folder 4, box 131, Philip F. La Follette Papers, Archives Division, Wisconsin Historical Society. For details of Robert's and Phil's work in the early part of the campaign, see RML Jr. to "Dear Ones," April 30 and May 2, 3, 4, 6, and 7, 1922, box A29, La Follette Family Papers.

8. PFL to IBL, March 17 and 19, 1922, PFL Papers. In the March 19 letter, Phil first mentions that various people have been encouraging him to run for district attorney for Dane County, which he is reluctant to do because the large amount of work would detract from his home life. He does admit, however, that it would be excellent experience and advertising for his law practice. Phil wrote almost daily letters to his wife from wherever he was staying, describing the crowds he spoke to. See PFL to IBL, August 9, 11, 14, and 28, 1922, ibid. See also Isabel Bacon La Follette, "If You Can Take It," 57–58, unpublished manuscript, box 165, ibid.

9. BCL to IBL, September 10, 1922, folder 5, box 131, ibid; La Follette, *Adventure in Politics*, 70. See also Weisberger, *La Follettes of Wisconsin*, 259; Paul W. Glad, *History of Wisconsin: War, a New Era, and Depression, 1914–1940* (Madison: State Historical Society of Wisconsin, 1990), 315–17.

10. 1923 *Wisconsin Blue Book*, 500; La Follette, *Adventure in Politics*, 73; La Follette and La Follette, *Robert M. La Follette*, 2:1061.

11. La Follette and La Follette, *Robert M. La Follette*, 2:1062; *Capital Times*, November 1, 1922; La Follette, *Adventure in Politics*, 73–74. The State Board later explained that the Farmer-Labor Party refused to pay the one-thousand-dollar rental fee.

12. *St. Paul Pioneer-Press*, November 2, 1922.

13. *Milwaukee Journal*, November 2, 1922; *Milwaukee Sentinel*, November 2, 1922.

14. La Follette, *Adventure in Politics*, 75.

15. *Milwaukee Sentinel, Milwaukee Journal, Superior Telegram, St. Paul Pioneer-Press, Capital Times*, November 3, 1922.

16. La Follette and La Follette, *Robert M. La Follette*, 2:1062; *Capital Times*, November 4, 1922.

17. *Wisconsin State Journal*, November 4, 1922.

18. La Follette, *Adventure in Politics*, 76; La Follette and La Follette, *Robert M. La Follette*, 2:1063. Belle did indeed chide her husband for his remarks. See BCL to FL and GM, November 4, 1922, box A29, La Follette Family Papers.

19. La Follette, *Adventure in Politics*, 89; PFL to IBL, February 10, March 17, 21, 22, and 26, 1924, all in folder 4, box 132, PFL Papers.

20. John F. Sinclair to PFL, March 12, 1924; and RML Jr. to PFL, March 22, 24, and 25, 1924, all in folder 4, box 132, PFL Papers. Old Bob twice spurned nominations by left-wing parties, in part because he did not adhere to revolutionary Marxism and also because he feared having his own Progressive movement dismissed as red. See La Follette and La Follette, *Robert M. La Follette*, 2:996–1010; Kenneth Campbell MacKay, *The Progressive Movement of 1924* (New York: Columbia University Press, 1947), 85–91; Russel B. Nye, *Midwestern Progressive Politics: A Historical Study of Its Origins and Development, 1870–1950* (East Lansing: Michigan State Press, 1951), 327–31.

21. IBL to "Dearest Family," March 24, 1924, box A30; and PFL to "Dear Ones," March 23, 1924, box A31, both in La Follette Family Papers.

22. *Capital Times*, June 14, 1924.

23. *Freeport (IL) Journal-Standard*, April 3, 1924; La Follette, *Adventure in Politics*, 89.

24. La Follette, *Adventure in Politics*, 92–93; La Follette and La Follette, *Robert M. La Follette*, 2:1122–25; undated newspaper clippings, folder 5, box 132, PFL Papers; "La Follette, Dictator," *The Nation* 118 (April 2, 1924): 360; William Hard, "That Man La Follette," ibid., 119 (July 16, 1924), 65; MacKay, *Progressive Movement of 1924*, pp. 179–83.

25. *Cleveland Plain Dealer*, September 29, 1924; address at Rochester, New York, October 6, 1924, MS folder 5, box 132, PFL Papers.

26. *Chicago Herald-Examiner*, October 12, 1924, clipping in folder 5, box 132, PFL Papers. See also James A. Frear, *Forty Years of Progressive Public Service Reasonably Filled with Thorns and Flowers* (Washington, D.C.: Associated Writers, 1937), 166.

27. FL to IBL, October 22, 1924, folder 5, box 132, PFL Papers; La Follette and La Follette, *Robert M. La Follette*, 2:1145.

28. RML Sr. to PFL and IBL, May 7, 1924, box A31, La Follette Family Papers.

29. *New York Times*, October 7, 1924; *Chicago Tribune*, October 12, 1924; *St. Louis Globe-Democrat*, October 15, 1924; MacKay, *Progressive Movement of 1924*, pp. 187–95.

30. PFL to IBL, December 3, 1921, folder 3, box 131, PFL Papers.

31. *Capital Times*, October 15 and 16, 1924; and PFL to IBL, October 15, 1924, folder 5, box 132, PFL Papers.

32. La Follette, *Adventure in Politics*, 98–99; La Follette and La Follette, *Robert M. La Follette*, 2:1147; *Capital Times*, August 30 and November 5, 1924; *New York Times*, November 6, 1924; *Wisconsin State Journal*, November 3, 1924.

33. Robert M. La Follette, *La Follette's Autobiography: A Personal Narrative of Political Experiences* (Madison: The Robert M. La Follette Company, 1913), 6–14; La Follette and La Follette, *Robert M. La Follette*, 1:47; John Dos Passos, *U.S.A.* (New York: Houghton Mifflin Company, 1946), 324. See also Weisberger, *La Follettes of Wisconsin*, 18–19. This interpretation of La Follette's victory has been challenged by historian David P. Thelen, who argues that La Follette faced little opposition from

Republican leaders and ran a campaign totally in harmony with the rest of the ticket. See Thelen, *The Early Life of Robert M. La Follette, 1855–1884* (Chicago: Loyola University Press, 1966), 51–72. Nonetheless, by the 1920s this was the standard account and familiar to most people.

34. In his autobiography, La Follette, referring to his meetings with voters, wrote: "'Ain't you over-young?' was the objection chiefly raised." Phil faced similar questions about his age. After giving a talk at the Royal Institute of International Affairs in London in 1933, according to Phil's memoirs, one distinguished member of his audience rose to ask a question: "'Governor La Follette, there is one question on everyone's mind here tonight which has not been asked.' (Here it comes, thought I, bracing myself for some weighty problem to be posed.) 'What we really want to know is this: Actually, how old are you?'"

35. Thelen, *Early Life of Robert M. La Follette*, 53–54; La Follette, *Adventure in Politics*, 100–101; *Wisconsin State Journal*, October 7, 1880.

36. La Follette, *Adventure in Politics*, 101–2; *Capital Times*, January 7, 9, 1925.

37. In 1925 there were about five hundred first- and second-generation Italians living in Greenbush. Many of them had arrived in Madison to work on the marble carvings adorning the new capitol and the State Historical Society building.

38. Robert A. Goldberg, "The Ku Klux Klan in Madison, 1922–1927," *Wisconsin Magazine of History* 58 (Autumn 1974): 34–36; William T. Evjue, *A Fighting Editor* (Madison, WI: Wells Printing Company, Inc., 1968), 468–74; *Capital Times*, December 3, 30, 1924. There remains the question of bribery; although little evidence of police corruption exists, certainly some constables must have been at least approached with bribery.

39. *Capital Times*, February 3, 1925; *Wisconsin State Journal*, February 8, 9, 1925; *Capital Times*, February 9, 10, 1925; *Milwaukee Journal*, February 8, 1925; *Milwaukee Sentinel*, February 8, 9, 1925; La Follette, *Adventure in Politics*, 103–5.

40. *Capital Times*, March 6, 7, 20, 24 and April 3, 1925. The *Capital Times* reported raids regularly between April and December. The amount of liquor destroyed is astonishing—hundreds of gallons and at least one still every week.

41. BCL to PFL, March 9 and April 28, 1925; and RML Jr. to "Dear Ones," January 29, 1925, all in folder 1, box 133, PFL Papers.

42. *Capital Times*, February 21, 25, 28, March 13, and April 3, 4, 18, 1925.

43. *Capital Times*, August 30, 1924, March 5, 7, 1925. The Musso incident appears only in Phil's memoirs, and in his account, Phil reacted with the same grim (and articulate!) determination seen in his father's famous encounter with Philetus Sawyer in Milwaukee in 1891. La Follette, according to his autobiography, responded, "Senator Sawyer, you can't know what you are saying to me. If you struck me in the face you could not insult me as you insult me now." Phil likewise told Musso, "Musso, you have just committed the crime of attempted bribery, which is a state prison offense." Musso left the state that day. See La Follette, *La Follette's Autobiography*, 145, and La Follette, *Adventure in Politics*, 109.

44. *Wisconsin State Journal*, February 21, 22, 1925; *Capital Times*, February 21, 1925. Phil himself showed restraint: the maximum sentence was a total of 252 months

in jail and $32,000 in fines. PFL to "Dear Ones," February 22, 1925, box A32, La Follette Family Papers.

45. *Capital Times*, February 23, 27, and March 3, 1925.

46. Ibid., May 2, 5, 1925; *Wisconsin State Journal*, May 5, 1925; *Capital Times*, January 27, 31, June 30, 1927; La Follette, *Adventure in Politics*, 104, 109–10. Stolen later charged Phil with irregularities in his prosecution of slot machines in Dane County, but these charges were quickly dismissed.

47. William Evjue of the *Capital Times* called for an organized effort to combat slot machines (see May 12, 1925), and Phil found himself involved in a complicated legal argument over whether police could confiscate such machines before they were proven to be gambling devices. He demonstrated that they could be (see ibid., August 29, September 21, 1925). In an infamous case at the time, one driver was found not guilty after the defense claimed that he never realized he had hit someone. The alleged "vampire driver" was William Parr. See *Capital Times*, November 4, 5, 1925. Another boy was killed in May 1926, prompting another crackdown on bad drivers.

48. The *Capital Times* devoted almost daily coverage to the story. See La Follette, *Adventure in Politics*, 105–6, for Phil's version of events. IBL to RML Jr., March 22 and April 14, 1926, box A33; and PFL to "Dear Ones," January 14, 1926, box A34, all in La Follette Family Papers.

49. *Capital Times*, March 19, 1925. See also address to the Knights of Columbus, ibid., April 30, 1925.

50. Ibid., March 3, 1926.

51. Ibid., December 18, 22, 1925.

52. *Wisconsin State Journal*, June 25, 1926; *Chicago Tribune*, June 28, 1926; *Capital Times*, June 25, 28, 1925; "Enforcement of the Criminal Law: An Address by Philip F. La Follette," pamphlet from PFL Papers.

53. *Capital Times*, July 9, 1928, July 31, October 22, August 5–17, 1926.

54. La Follette's death and funeral are recounted most thoroughly in La Follette and La Follette, *Robert M. La Follette*, 2:1166–74.

55. BCL to PFL, December 18, 1926, folder 4, box 133; RML Jr. to PFL, February 12, 1927, folder 1, box 134; and RML Sr. to PFL, May 18, 1923, folder 3, box 132, all in PFL Papers.

56. Patrick J. Maney, *"Young Bob": A Biography of Robert M. La Follette, Jr., 1895–1953* (Columbia: University of Missouri Press, 1978), 26–35; Weisberger, *La Follettes of Wisconsin*, 176–78; Alfred R. Schumann, *No Peddlers Allowed* (Appleton, WI: C. C. Nelson Publishing Co., 1978), 177; G. M. Sheldon to La Follette, Rogers and La Follette, March 11, 1922, folder 1, box 132, PFL Papers. "The firm" refers to La Follette's law office, La Follette and Rogers, which Phil joined after law school.

57. La Follette, *Adventure in Politics*, 113; Lucy Freeman, Sherry La Follette, and George A. Zabriskie, *Belle: The Biography of Belle Case La Follette* (New York: Beaufort Books, 1986), 229–30. See also folder 4, box 49, in the John J. Blaine Papers, for the numerous recommendations for the Senate seat. Blaine had no authority to appoint a senator, but he was constitutionally responsible for calling a special election to fill the seat.

58. Freeman, La Follette, and Zabriskie, *Belle*, 230–31.

59. Ibid.; Oswald Garrison Villard to John J. Blaine, June 18, 1925, folder 6, box 48; W. R. McCabe to John J. Blaine, July 22, 1925, folder 4, box 49, both in the Blaine Papers, Archives Division, Wisconsin Historical Society; Roger T. Johnson, *Robert M. La Follette, Jr. and the Decline of the Progressive Party*, reprint edition (New York: Archon Books, 1970), 6; La Follette, *Adventure in Politics*, 111–15; Maney, *"Young Bob,"* 38–40; Judith Sorem and Robert La Follette III to the author, October 9, 2005.

60. Ralph Sucher to PFL, April 21, 1926, folder 3, box 133, PFL Papers; *Capital Times*, November 27, 1925, March 31, June 4, 18, 1926; *Fennimore Times*, March 4, 1926; *New York Times*, October 4, 1925.

61. PFL to Gilbert Roe, "Personal," October 18, 1925, folder 3, box 132; and Ralph Sucher to PFL, May 20, 1926, folder 3, box 133, all in the PFL Papers. The Dane County district attorneyship did in fact prove to be an excellent launching point for Wisconsin politicians. The next two district attorneys, Glenn Roberts and Fred Risser Sr., went on to careers in the Wisconsin senate.

62. La Follette, *Adventure in Politics*, 116–18; *Capital Times*, June 3, October 1, 7, 1926. One of Phil's students was Dorothy Lenroot Black, daughter of Senator Irvine Lenroot. PFL to "Dear Ones," May 12, 1926, box A34, and May 7, 1929, box A38, La Follette Family Papers; PFL to Louis Brandeis, "Confidential," March 14, 1928, folder 3, box 134, PFL Papers.

63. La Follette, *Adventure in Politics*, 118–19; Harry P. Harrison to PFL, August 1, 1927, folder 3, box 134; PFL to IBL, August 16, 1927, and A. M. Weiskopf to PFL, July 5, 1927, both in folder 1, box 134, all in PFL Papers; RML Sr. to PFL, July 30, 1923, box A30, La Follette Family Papers. La Follette recommended the Redpath and Midland companies and suggested a salary of $250 per week plus expenses for an eight-to-twelve-week commitment.

64. La Follette, *Adventure in Politics*, 81.

CHAPTER THREE

1. Herbert F. Margulies, *The Decline of the Progressive Movement in Wisconsin: 1890–1920* (Madison: State Historical Society of Wisconsin, 1968), 84–85; Bernard A. Weisberger, *The La Follettes of Wisconsin: Love and Politics in Progressive America* (Madison: University of Wisconsin Press, 1994), 43. La Follette's motives are unclear: not only did he indeed want to maintain Progressive unity in order to continue political reform in the state, he also wanted a national stage and probably had been looking toward a return to Congress since he lost his House seat in 1891. La Follette himself does not mention the conditions of his election in his autobiography, but for the "official" version, see Belle Case La Follette and Fola La Follette, *Robert M. La Follette: June 14, 1855–June 18, 1925*, 2 vols. (New York: The Macmillan Company, 1953), 1:188–89, and Albert O. Barton, *La Follette's Winning of Wisconsin* (Madison: Homestead Company, 1922), 332–33. The question of whether La Follette was a political boss

is also problematic. Certainly he saw himself as *the* Progressive leader, but he never controlled the faction on the state or national level that his detractors claimed. Moreover, La Follette supported his associates not through patronage or graft, but through electoral support. He articulated progressive ideas, and those who sought to ally themselves with the Progressive faction recognized the value in accepting La Follette's ideas and his support.

2. Margulies, *Decline of the Progressive Movement*, 86–99; La Follette and La Follette, *Robert M. La Follette*, 1:194–95 and 213–14; Philip F. La Follette, *Adventure in Politics: The Memoirs of Philip La Follette*, Donald Young, ed. (New York: Holt, Rinehart and Winston, 1970), 15–16. For La Follette as a "reform boss" see Robert S. Maxwell, *La Follette and the Rise of the Progressives in Wisconsin* (Madison: State Historical Society of Wisconsin, 1956), 56–73. Only recently had Republican leaders begun to recognize the usefulness in deliberately courting Scandinavian elements. Spooked by their defeats in 1890 and 1892, Republicans started nominating Norwegians to statewide office, usually as the state treasurer, beginning in 1894 with Sewell Peterson of Rice Lake, Wisconsin. By nominating Davidson for lieutenant governor, the Progressives effectively one-upped the Stalwarts.

3. Margulies, *Decline of the Progressive Movement*, 104–23; Maxwell, *La Follette and the Rise of the Progressives in Wisconsin*, 173–94; Weisberger, *La Follettes of Wisconsin*, 140–43; Nancy C. Unger, *Fighting Bob La Follette: The Righteous Reformer* (Chapel Hill: University of North Carolina Press, 2000), 215–20.

4. 1915 *Wisconsin Blue Book*, 236–37; Robert. S. Maxwell, *Emanuel Philipp: Wisconsin Stalwart* (Madison: State Historical Society of Wisconsin, 1959), 82–85. See also Margulies, *Decline of the Progressive Movement*, 123, for the influence of geography on political loyalty.

5. PFL to "Dear Ones," July 15, 1919, box A26, and BCL to "My Dear Ones," March 30, 1920, box A28, both in the La Follette Family Papers, Manuscripts Division, Library of Congress; La Follette, *Adventure in Politics*, 66–67. For Blaine, see Patrick G. O'Brien, "Senator John J. Blaine: An Independent Progressive during 'Normalcy,'" *Wisconsin Magazine of History* 60 (Autumn 1976): 25–41.

6. For roll call votes on the Matheson Bill (no. 16, A.) see *Wisconsin Assembly Journal*, 1921 session, 502, and *Wisconsin Senate Journal*, 1921 session, 774. See also Jeffrey Lucker, "The Politics of Prohibition," master's thesis, University of Wisconsin, 1968. The influence of Germans on Wisconsin politics has been hotly debated, but that ethnic group's influence may help explain some of the more unusual phenomena of Wisconsin politics. For example, the most Democratic areas of the state equate fairly closely with those areas most influenced by German settlement. Germans voted Democratic in the post–Civil War years out of a resentment of Republican flirtation with social regulation in the state. The Bennett Law is the best example. In 1889, Representative Michael John Bennett introduced a compulsory education for children and requiring that schools be taught in English. German and Norwegian Lutherans and German Catholics were furious at the state's intrusion to their ethnic parochial education. The controversy helped elect the only Democratic governor and legislature between 1873

and 1932. By the 1920s and 1930s, this resulted in a state Democratic Party that was conservative and opposed progressive government and therefore found itself at odds with both the Progressives and the New Deal.

7. Veto message for bill No. 16, A. in *Messages to the Legislature and Proclamations of John J. Blaine, Governor, 1921–1927* (Madison: Democrat Printing Company, 1926), 125–28; *Wisconsin State Journal*, June 7, 1923.

8. Veto message for bill No. 283, S., in *Messages to the Legislature and Proclamations of John J. Blaine*, 452–58; Paul F. Glad, *The History of Wisconsin, Volume V: War, a New Era, and Depression, 1914–1940* (Madison: State Historical Society of Wisconsin, 1990), 304. The attempt to override the vote in the senate failed, 17 to 16. See *Wisconsin Senate Journal*, 1923 session, 1406.

9. Harold M. Groves, "The Wisconsin State Income Tax," 1933 *Wisconsin Blue Book*, 51–53; Thomas E. Lyons, "The Wisconsin Tax System," 1923 ibid., 85–87; W. Elliot Brownlee Jr., "Income Taxation and the Political Economy of Wisconsin, 1890–1930," *Wisconsin Magazine of History* 59 (Summer 1976): 317–19.

10. Glad, *War, a New Era, and Depression*, 302; RML Jr. to BCL and RML Sr., June 5, 9, 10, 14, 20, 21, 22, 26, 27 and 28, 1923, box A30, La Follette Family Papers.

11. PFL to RML Jr., May 21, 1923, box A30; RML Jr. to RML Sr., May 20, 1924, box A31; PFL to RML Jr., April 28, 1924, box A31, all in La Follette Family Papers; Glad, *War, a New Era, and Depression*, 303; *Wisconsin State Journal*, July 2, 1923. The election returns are in the 1923 and 1925 *Wisconsin Blue Books*, 565 and 562–63, respectively.

12. PFL to RML Jr., December 6, 1923, box A30; BCL to "Dear Ones," February 22, 1924, box A31; and RML Jr. to "Dear Ones," March 1 and 4, 1924, box A31, La Follette Family Papers. La Follette's tirade is from RML Sr. to "Dear Kids," February 12, 1925, box A32, ibid.

13. PFL to RML Sr., May 21, 1923, and RML Jr. to RML Sr., May 29, 1923, both in folder 3, box 132, Philip La Follette Papers, Archives Division, Wisconsin Historical Society. PFL to RML Jr., January 21, 1925; and RML Jr. to RML Sr. and BCL, January 22, 1925, both in folder 1, box 133, ibid.

14. The John J. Blaine Papers at the Wisconsin Historical Society contain the governor's correspondence from this time, and he received copious advice. See box 48, folder 6, and box 49, folders 1 and 2.

15. Frank C. Morgenroth to John J. Blaine, June 30, 1925; Philip Lehner to Fred L. Holmes, July 13, 1925; John Reynolds to John Blaine, July 17, 1925; J. C. Kieffer to Blaine, July 21, 1925; Frank C. Morgenroth to Blaine, August 6, 1925; Philip Lehner to Blaine, July 22, 1925; and the quotation from Harold Shannon to Blaine, June 26, 1925, all in boxes 48 and 49, ibid.; Stanley Frost, "The Scramble for 'Fighting Bob's' Shoes," *Outlook* 140 (July 29, 1925): 460–62; "After La Follette—What?" *Literary Digest* 86 (July 4, 1925): 9–11.

16. "Young Bob," *The Nation* 121 (July 8, 1925): 59.

17. See Lavern Mertz to Blaine, June 24, 1925, H. H. Peavey to Blaine, no date, and S. J. Gwidt to Blaine, August 20, 1926, all in the Blaine Papers; *Capital Times*, September 3,

1925; Patrick J. Maney, *"Young Bob": A Biography of Robert M. La Follette, Jr., 1895–1953* (Columbia: University of Missouri Press, 1978), 59. Years later, Phil denied any deal between Blaine and Robert and insisted that Blaine had no choice but to support his brother for the Senate.

18. Maney, *"Young Bob,"* 38–40; *Capital Times*, August 29, September 1, 1925. Two Democrats and another Republican also ran but received only small numbers of votes. For attacks on the "Madison Ring," see *Capital Times*, August 28, September 4, 14, 1925.

19. *Portage Register-Democrat*, September 1, 1925; *Janesville Daily Gazette*, September 7, 1925. Phil also demonstrated his father's gift for the ad lib. When a few drops of rain fell from a thundering sky, Phil urged his listeners not to leave: "This storm is just like the Stalwarts—all wind but nothing behind it."

20. PFL to IBL, July 31, 1925; and PFL to IBL, August 9, 1925, both in box 133, PFL Papers.

21. Maney, *"Young Bob,"* 39–40; La Follette, *Adventure in Politics*, 115.

22. 1926 *Wisconsin Blue Book*, 500, 578.

23. Roger T. Johnson, *Robert M. La Follette, Jr., and the Decline of the Progressive Party in Wisconsin*, reprint edition (New York: Archon Books, 1970), 9; BCL to PFL, March 9, 1925, folder 1; and RML Jr. to PFL, November 9, 23, 1925, folder 2, all in box 133, PFL Papers; IBL to BCL, March 4, 1926, box A33, La Follette Family Papers. See also Herbert F. Margulies, *Senator Lenroot of Wisconsin: A Political Biography, 1900–1929* (Columbia: University of Missouri Press, 1977), 392–97.

24. La Follette, *Adventure in Politics*, 123–24; Maney, *"Young Bob,"* 46–47; BCL to "Dear Ones," March 13, 1926; and RML Jr. to PFL, March 16, April 9, June 3, 1926, all in folder 3, box 133, PFL Papers; BCL to "My Dear Ones," March 30, 1921, box A28, La Follette Family Papers; RML Jr. to PFL, March 16, 1926; PFL to RML Jr., May 3, 1926; and PFL to "Dear Ones," May 12, 1926, all in box A34, ibid.

25. G. M. Sheldon to Charles M. Dow, January 30, 1926; and RML Jr. to PFL, May 1, 1926, both in folder 3, box 133, PFL Papers.

26. IBL to BCL, May 26, 1926, box A33, La Follette Family Papers; La Follette, *Adventure in Politics*, 124; Alfred Schumann, *No Peddlers Allowed* (Appleton, WI: C. C. Nelson Publishing Co., 1948), 195–96; Maney, *"Young Bob,"* 46; *Wisconsin State Journal*, July 2, 6, 1926; *New York Times*, September 2, 1926.

27. See, for example, *Sheboygan Press*, August 9, 1924; *Manitowoc Pilot*, August 12, 1926. The quotation is from the *Manitowoc Herald-News*, August 6, 1926. For Phil's itinerary, see *Capital Times*, July 28, 31, 1926; PFL to RML Jr., September 16, 1926, box A33, La Follette Family Papers; PFL to IBL, September 19, 1926, folder 4, box 133, PFL Papers.

28. 1927 *Wisconsin Blue Book*, 494.

29. *New York Times*, September 5, 10, 1926; 1927 *Wisconsin Blue Book*, 494–99.

30. *Capital Times*, November 4, 1926, January 6, 7, 1927, May 20, July 3, 1928; Glenn Roberts to PFL, August 3, 1927, folder 2, box 134, PFL Papers; *Racine Times-Call*, May 11, 1928.

31. La Follette, *Adventure in Politics*, 123.

32. *Wisconsin State Journal*, July 12, 1927.

33. Ibid.; *Milwaukee Journal*, September 26, 1927; Schumann, *No Peddlers Allowed*, 211; PFL to IBL, August 11, 1928, folder 3, box 134, PFL Papers.

34. La Follette, *Adventure in Politics*, 126.

35. *Capital Times*, October 26, 28, 1927.

36. Ibid.; October 15 through November 8, 1927; *Wisconsin State Journal*, July 12, 1927; John Blaine to RML Jr., November 11, 1927, folder 2, box 134, PFL Papers; Isabel Bacon La Follette, "If You Can Take It," 57, unpublished manuscript, box 165, ibid.

37. *Capital Times*, November 14, 1927; *Wisconsin State Journal*, November 14, 1927; *Green Bay Press Gazette*, November 14, 1927; *Superior Evening Telegram*, November 14, 1927. Levitan's biographer, Alfred Schumann, depicts Levitan as a modest and disinterested figure awaiting the call of destiny. Although he did nothing to advance his own candidacy, it seems likely that he would have accepted quickly any support.

38. *Capital Times*, November 15, 1927; *Wisconsin State Journal*, November 15, 1927; *Milwaukee Journal*, November 15, 1927; *Milwaukee Sentinel*, November 15, 1927; *Superior Evening Telegram*, November 15, 1927; Schumann, *No Peddlers Allowed*, 220.

39. *Capital Times*, November 16, 1927; *Wisconsin State Journal*, November 16, 1927; *Milwaukee Journal*, November 16, 1927; *Milwaukee Sentinel*, November 16, 1927; *Superior Evening Telegram*, November 16, 1927; *Green Bay Press Gazette*, November 16, 1927.

40. *Antigo Journal*, November 20, 1927; *Wisconsin State Journal*, November 17, 21, 1927; *Milwaukee Journal*, November 18, 1927; *Milwaukee Sentinel*, November 24, 1927; Schumann, *No Peddlers Allowed*, 248; *Capital Times*, December 12, 1927. See also PFL to BCL, February 5, 1928; and PFL to BCL and RML Jr., February 12, 1928, both in box A38, La Follette Family Papers.

41. *Capital Times*, August 8, 13, 17, 20, 23, 1927.

42. The *Capital Times* kept its readers informed of various speakers' itineraries. In August and early September, Phil spoke at La Valle, Milwaukee, Roxbury, Sauk City, Hollandale, Lake Mills, Platteville, Reedsburg, Pardeeville, Wonewoc, Milladore, Auburndale, Arpin, Marshfield, Morris, Niagara, Marrinette, Oconto, Oshkosh, Manitowoc, Waupun, Watertown, and Kaukauna.

43. BCL to RML Jr., April 5, 1928, box A35, La Follette Family Papers; *Manitowoc Herald-News*, September 1, 1928; 1929 *Wisconsin Blue Book*, 736. A fourth Republican captured 3,448 votes.

44. 1929 *Wisconsin Blue Book*, 735 and 816; Maney, *"Young Bob,"* 60–61; Johnson, *Robert M. La Follette, Jr.*, 19. The quotation is from Henry F. Pringle, "Youth at the Top: United States Senator Robert M. La Follette, Jr.," *World's Work: A History of Our Time* 58 (May 1929): 85.

CHAPTER FOUR

1. Lincoln Steffens, "Enemies of the Republic, Wisconsin: A State Where the People Have Restored Representative Government—The Story of Governor La Follette," *McClure's Magazine* 23 (October 1904): 563–79; Lincoln Steffens to BCL, October 2, 1929, folder 1, box 135, Philip La Follette Papers, Archives Division, Wisconsin Historical Society.

2. *Capital Times*, November 27, 1925, and September 10, 1926; *New York Times*, October 4, 1925. For letters booming Phil for the Senate, see *Capital Times*, March 6 and 31, June 4 and 18, and August 18, 1925; editor William Evjue frequently reprinted these suggestions from other newspapers. The *Record Herald* editorial is from "The State Press" column of the *Capital Times*, May 2, 1929; "In La Follette-Land," *Time*, October 2, 1928, pp. 11–12; Henry F. Pringle, "Youth at the Top: United States Senator Robert M. La Follette, Jr., *World's Work: A History of Our Time* 58 (May 1929): 85.

3. Philip F. La Follette, *Adventure in Politics: The Memoirs of Philip La Follette*, Donald Young, ed. (New York: Holt, Rinehart and Winston, 1970), 135; Isabel Bacon La Follette, "If You Can Take It," unpublished manuscript, box 165, PFL Papers, 59; *Capital Times*, May 6, 1929; "In La Follette-Land," 11–12; Pringle, "Youth at the Top," 85.

4. PFL to RML Jr., May 13, 1929; and PFL to BCL, August 8 and November 17, 1929, all in box A38, La Follette Family Papers, Manuscripts Division, Library of Congress; *Capital Times*, November 12, 13, and 15, 1929.

5. The *Capital Times* printed daily updates on the case (all of which must be read with some caution) between early October 1928 and January 1929. See especially November 19 and December 13, 1928, and January 26, 1929. See also William T. Evjue, *A Fighting Editor* (Madison, WI: Wells Printing Co., 1968), 492–93, for a melodramatic discussion of Evjue's role, and La Follette, *Adventure in Politics*, 127–28, for a more objective narrative.

6. *Capital Times*, November 30, 1928, January 27 and 29, July 1, 2, 13, and 17, and September 1, 1929; Evjue, *A Fighting Editor*, 495; La Follette, *Adventure in Politics*, 127–28; PFL to RML Jr., June 27, 1929, box A38, La Follette Family Papers. There was a delay for several months when the original judge, Edward Voight, recused himself; Wickersham was brought in from Eau Claire County.

7. *Capital Times*, February 4, 9 (for the *Tribune* comment), and 18, 1930; PFL to IBL, February 9, 1930, folder 6, box 134, PFL Papers. For biography and politics of the justices, see the 1929 *Wisconsin Blue Book*, 479–80.

8. State papers carried daily accounts of the trial. The best coverage is in the *Milwaukee Journal*, the *Wisconsin State Journal*, and the *Capital Times*, all April 21 through May 16, 1930. With the exception of the *Capital Times*, newspapers were fairly sympathetic to the governor. See also Evjue, *A Fighting Editor*, 497–503, and La Follette, *Adventure in Politics*, 127–28.

9. James I. Clark, *Wisconsin Meets the Great Depression* (Madison: State Historical Society of Wisconsin, 1956), 4–6; H. W. Perrigo, *General Relief in Wisconsin:*

1848–1935 (Madison: Wisconsin Public Welfare Department, 1939), 14–16; Don D. Lescohier and Florence Peterson, *The Alleviation of Unemployment in Wisconsin* (Madison: Industrial Commission of Wisconsin, 1931), 9.

10. Lescohier and Peterson, *Alleviation of Unemployment*, 10–15. The quotation is from page 13.

11. Ibid., 17; James I. Clark, *Cutover Problems* (Madison: State Historical Society of Wisconsin, 1956), 12–16.

12. Lescohier and Peterson, *Alleviation of Unemployment*, 25–30; Edwin Witte, "Wisconsin in the 1930 Census," 1933 *Wisconsin Blue Book*, 103–32; Orrin A. Fried, "Wisconsin Manufacturing Since 1929," ibid., 141–42. See also *Bankshares Review*, January 20, 1931, in folder 6, box 4, PFL Papers.

13. Perrigo, *General Relief*, 34; Clark, *Great Depression*, 8–9; Lescohier and Peterson, *Alleviation of Unemployment*, 101.

14. Perrigo, *General Relief*, 40–41.

15. Ibid., 40; Lescohier and Peterson, *Alleviation of Unemployment*, 103–8.

16. Perrigo, *General Relief*, 27, 35–37; Lescohier and Peterson, *Alleviation of Unemployment*, 33, 52–53.

17. Perrigo, *General Relief*, 33–37; Lescohier and Peterson, *Alleviation of Unemployment*, 43, 47–53.

18. Perrigo, *General Relief*, 28–32; Lescohier and Peterson, *Alleviation of Unemployment*, 25–39.

19. Lescohier and Peterson, *Alleviation of Unemployment*, 38.

20. *Capital Times*, May 6, 1929; La Follette, "If You Can Take It," 59–60; La Follette, *Adventure in Politics*, 134–38; PFL to IBL, January 8, 1930, folder 6, box 134, PFL Papers.

21. RML Jr. to PFL, c. January 9, 1930, folder 6, box 134, PFL Papers. Solomon Levitan and Henry Huber were from Dane County, and Alvin C. Reis, Dane County representative and Progressive floor leader, planned to run for attorney general. It is unclear why Blaine assumed there would be a "dump Sol" movement, since Levitan was an extraordinarily popular candidate. For Perry, see PFL to BCL, November 17, 1929, box A38, La Follette Family Papers.

22. PFL to IBL, January 16, 1930, folder 6, box 134, PFL Papers. The comments from the *News-Herald* were reprinted in the *Capital Times*, November 12, 1929.

23. La Follette, *Adventure in Politics*, 137–38; *Capital Times*, May 2, 1929.

24. La Follette, *Adventure in Politics*, 137–38; the comment from Alf Rogers is on page 137. La Follette, "If You Can Take It," 64.

25. La Follette, *Adventure in Politics*, 138–41. Unfortunately there is little correspondence among the La Follettes since by now they had become dependent on the telephone for this kind of hurried, detailed discussion.

26. La Follette, *Adventure in Politics*, 140–41; La Follette, "If You Can Take It," 62. Frequent and extensive edits of the platform are in folder 4, box 1, PFL Papers.

27. *New York Times*, July 1, 1930; first scrapbook of the 1930 campaign, PFL Papers.

28. *The Progressive*, July 26, 1930; *Milwaukee Journal*, August 11, 1930; Alf Rogers to PFL, September 20, 1930, folder 6, box 1, PFL Papers.

29. La Follette, *Adventure in Politics*, 137.

30. *The Progressive*, July 19 and 26, 1930.

31. La Follette, "If You Can Take It," 65, 131–33; *Wisconsin News*, September 10, 1930; PFL to "Dear Ones," July 22, 1930, box A39, La Follette Family Papers.

32. *Capital Times*, August 29, 31, September 5, 1930; *Milwaukee Journal*, August 15, September 4, 9, 10, 16, 1930.

33. La Follette, "If You Can Take It," 69–77. Phil's quotation is from page 70.

34. *Milwaukee Journal*, August 20, 1930.

35. *The Progressive*, July 26, 1930.

36. *Capital Times*, August 20, 1930; *The Progressive*, August 23, 1930.

37. *Milwaukee Journal*, August 27, September 7, 1930; *Milwaukee Sentinel*, September 16, 1930. Kohler's name-calling is found in La Follette, *Adventure in Politics*, 143.

38. *New York Times*, July 1, 1930; *The Nation*, August 9, 1930; *Labor*, September 2, 1930. *The Nation* suggested something akin to heresy in the campaign by suggesting that the Depression "cannot be cured by the program and the philosophy of the elder La Follette."

39. Vote totals can be found in the *Wisconsin Blue Books*: 1931 (p. 464), 1929 (p. 736), and 1927 (p. 494). To some extent, however, old patterns held true. Phil did best in western and northern counties, where Progressives had traditionally been strongest, and significantly less well in southeastern counties. Two aberrations to this pattern are Vilas and Marinette Counties, both of which went for Kohler. Additionally, in those counties that he did win, Phil did somewhat less well in those that had a class-two city (with a population of more than thirty-nine thousand—Kenosha, Dane, Milwaukee, La Crosse, and Douglas), suggesting perhaps that his greatest strength lay with small town and rural areas dependent on agriculture.

40. The platform appeared in *The Progressive*, July 26, 1930, and was reprinted widely in state newspapers. See also 1931 *Wisconsin Blue Book*, 446–58.

41. La Follette, *Adventure in Politics*, 146–48. Numerous invitations and letters to officials and members of the legislature can be found in the PFL Papers, folders 3, 4, and 5, box 2. See especially PFL to John Anderson, December 1, 1930, PFL to Orland Loomis, December 19, 1930, PFL to Harold Groves, December 20, 1930.

42. La Follette, *Adventure in Politics*, 148–50; *Capital Times*, January 5 and 6, 1931; inaugural address manuscript in folder 1, box 117, PFL Papers and reprinted in an abridged form in the *Capital Times*, January 6, 1931.

43. *Capital Times*, January 7 and 15 (especially the column "The State Press"); "Message of Philip F. La Follette to the Wisconsin Legislature, Regular Session, 15 January 1931" in *Messages and Addresses to the Legislature, Philip F. La Follette* (Madison: Democrat Printing Co., 1933); Roy Wilcox to PFL, folder 3, box 4, PFL Papers.

44. "Message of Philip F. La Follette to the Wisconsin Legislature, Regular Session, 15 January 1931"; John E. Miller, *Philip F. La Follette, the Wisconsin Progressives, and the New Deal* (Columbia: University of Missouri Press, 1982), 14–15.

45. The use of the frontier thesis by 1930s intellectuals and politicians is well documented. See David M. Wrobel, *The End of American Exceptionalism: Frontier Anxiety from the Old West to the New Deal* (Lawrence: University of Kansas Press, 1993), especially pages 122–42; Curtis Nettels, "Frederick Jackson Turner and the New Deal," *Wisconsin Magazine of History* 17 (March 1934): 257–65; Theodore Rosenof, "'Young Bob' La Follette on American Capitalism," *Wisconsin Magazine of History* 55 (Winter 1971–72): 130–39; Steven Kesselman, "The Frontier Thesis and the Great Depression," *Journal of the History of Ideas* 29 (April 1968): 253–68; Theodore Rosenof, *Dogma, Depression, and the New Deal: The Debate of Political Leaders over Economic Recovery* (Port Washington, NY: Kennikat Press, 1975). An especially entertaining conversation among intellectuals is "Dark Days Ahead: A Dialogue on the Bankruptcy of Business Leadership," *The Forum* 84 (October 1930): 200–207.

46. " Message of Governor Philip La Follette to the Wisconsin Legislature, Regular Session, 15 January 1931"; *Capital Times*, January 15–17, 1931, which includes a sampling of comment from other newspapers; FL to PFL, January 20, 1931, folder 1, box 135, PFL Papers. See also Mauritz A. Hallgren, "Governor La Follette," *The Nation*, April 20, 1931, p. 473.

47. "The State Press" in the *Capital Times*, January 7 and 8, 1931.

48. Letters to university professors are in folder 7, box 4, and to Wisconsin manufacturers are in folder 1, box 4, all in the PFL Papers; *Capital Times*, January 7, 14, 17, and 20, 1931. The manufacturers included L. R. Clausen of the J. I. Case Company, Otto Falk of the Allis-Chalmers Company, and C. W. Nash of Nash Motors.

49. The daily routine of the governor's office is reported by Calmer Browy in the *Capital Times*, January 3, 1932; IBL to BCL, April 13, 1931; and PFL to BCL, May 10, 1931, both in box A41, La Follette Family Papers. The "Little Lord Fauntleroy" comment appeared in an undated *Capital Times* clipping, probably early January 1932, in volume 2 of the PFL Papers.

50. "Budget Message of Philip F. La Follette, Governor of Wisconsin, to the Wisconsin Legislature, Regular Session, 1931, Thursday, January 29, 1931," in *Messages and Addresses to the Legislature, Philip F. La Follette*; *Capital Times*, January 29, 1931, and (for University of Wisconsin pay cuts) March 3, 1932; A. O. Barton to PFL, January 29, 1931, folder 1, box 5, and undated *Capital Times* clipping ("Lops $1500 Off Own Salary") in volume 2, PFL Papers.

51. Max Otto to PFL, February 3, 1931, and E. E. Schwartztrauber to PFL, February 4, 1931, both in folder 4, box 5, PFL Papers.

52. See especially "The La Follette Myth," January 30, 1931, "Phil and the Rail Chiefs," January 29, 1931, and editorials for February 10, 1931, all in the *Capital Times*. Letters like these continued for several months.

53. H. William Ihrig to PFL, January 17, 1931; and A. W. Lueck to PFL, January 19, 1931, both in folder 5, box 4, PFL Papers. See also the comments of Oscar Hammersly and party chair Otto La Budde in the *Capital Times*, March 9, 1931.

54. BCL to PFL, February 12, 1931, folder 1, box 135; George Reid to PFL, January 28, 1931, with attached clipping from the *Elkhorn Independent*, folder 1, box 5; PFL

to Joseph Poss, March 30, 1931, folder 3, box 5, all in the PFL Papers; PFL to BCL, February 7, 1931, and PFL to RML Jr., February 10, 1931, both in box A41, La Follette Family Papers; *Capital Times*, January 27 and 31, 1931. Walter Kohler appointed Fowler to the supreme court in 1929 to fill an unexpired term, but voters had to ratify that appointment in the next spring election, April 1930. Fowler then ran again for his own full term in 1931.

55. La Follette, *Adventure in Politics*, 159–60; Miller, *Philip F. La Follette*, 18–20; *Capital Times*, March 18, 23, and 24, June 17, 19, 28, and 29, 1931; *New York Times*, March 23, 1931; BCL to PFL and IBL, May 15, 1931, folder 1, box 135, PFL Papers; Hallgren, "Governor La Follette," 474.

56. PFL, Message to the Legislature, June 4, 1931, manuscript in the PFL Papers, folder 3, box 117; Isabel La Follette, "To the Progressive Women of Wisconsin," box A41, La Follette Family Papers.

57. *Capital Times*, July 7, 8, and 17, 1931; PFL to BCL, May 10, 1931, box A41, La Follette Family Papers.

58. In folder 2, box 117, PFL Papers: "The Challenge," March 17, 1931, untitled manuscript, dated May 2, 1931, "Equality of Opportunity," undated; "Labor Day— Fond du Lac."

59. *Capital Times*, August 11, October 30, 1931; *Wisconsin State Journal*, October 30, 1931; *Milwaukee Journal*, October 30, 1931.

60. *Capital Times*, September 15, 16, and 17, and November 23, 1931.

61. RS to IBL, October 12, 1931; and RS to PFL, November 16, 1931, both in folder 2, box 135, PFL Papers; IBL to FL, December 4, 1931, box A41, La Follette Family Papers. On Belle's death, see the *Capital Times*, August 17, 18, and 19, 1931; Lucy Freeman, Sherry La Follette, and George Zabriskie, *Belle: The Biography of Belle Case La Follette* (New York: Beaufort Books, 1986), 237–38; Bernard A. Weisberger, *The La Follettes of Wisconsin: Love and Politics in Progressive America* (Madison: University of Wisconsin Press, 1994), 287–88.

62. RML Jr. to PFL, November 21, 1931, and RS to PFL, November 24, 1931, both in folder 2, box 135, PFL Papers; PFL to RML Jr., November 15 and 22, 1931, box A41, La Follette Family Papers.

63. "Message to Special Session, November 24, 1931," in *Messages and Addresses to the Legislature, Philip F. La Follette*; *Milwaukee Journal*, November 25, 1931; *Capital Times*, November 25, 1931; *Wisconsin State Journal*, November 25, 1931. The Associated Press picked up the message, which appeared in many large metropolitan newspapers.

64. "A Great Message," *The Nation*, December 9, 1931; RS to PFL, November 28, 1931, folder 2, box 135, PFL Papers; Charles A. Beard to Roy Nash, December 9, 1931 (misdated as 1935), in vol. 2, PFL Papers.

65. Frazier Hunt, "A Job for Every Man in This State," *Cosmopolitan*, January 1932, no page numbers, in vol. 2, PFL Papers, emphasis original.

66. *Capital Times*, November 24, 25, and 29, and December 4, 7, 8, 9, 10, 11, 19, 28, 29, and 30, 1931; PFL to RML Jr., December 11, 19, and 28, 1931, box A41, La Follette Family Papers.

67. *Wisconsin Senate Journal* for January 5, 1932, pp. 259–68. The quotation appears on page 265. *Capital Times*, January 5, 6, 7, 8, and 14 (Isabel's article), 1932; *Milwaukee Journal*, January 7, 1932; *Wisconsin News*, January 7, 1932; "Radio Speech, PFL, Jan. 1932 (Revised)," folder 1, box 117, PFL Papers; PFL to FL, January 27, 1932, box A42, La Follette Family Papers.

68. *New York Times*, February 7, 1932, and "Relief in Wisconsin" editorial, *New York Times*, February 7, 1932; PFL to RML Jr., January 31, 1932, box A42, La Follette Family Papers; La Follette, *Adventure in Politics*, 163–64: Miller, *Governor Philip F. La Follette*, 21–22.

69. Paul A. Raushenbush and Elizabeth Brandeis Raushenbush, *Our "U. C." Story: 1931–1967* (Madison: privately printed, 1979), 110–14.

70. La Follette, *Adventure in Politics*, 163–65; Harold M. Groves, "In and Out of the Ivory Tower," unpublished manuscript, 1969, Wisconsin Historical Society, 143–46; Daniel Nelson, "The Origins of Unemployment Insurance in Wisconsin," *Wisconsin Magazine of History* 50 (Winter 1967–68): 119–21. In the John R. Commons Papers in the Wisconsin Historical Society: "Broadcast from WISJ," March 29, 1931; "Memorandum on Groves and Nixon Bills," April 6, 1931; and "Brief Summary Comparison of the Groves Bill and the Nixon Bill," February 28, 1931, all in box 4, folder 5. See also Glad, *War, a New Era, and Depression*, 394–95. For Harold Groves's ideas on Progressive taxation, see John O. Stark, "Harold M. Groves and Wisconsin Taxes," *Wisconsin Magazine of History* 74 (Spring 1991): 196–214.

CHAPTER FIVE

1. *Capital Times*, February 12, 1932; Philip F. La Follette speech over NBC Radio, February 14, box 117, Philip F. La Follette Papers, Archives Division, Wisconsin Historical Society.

2. *"Progressive Government: Speeches of Hon. Philip La Follette, Governor of Wisconsin, and Hon. Robt. M. La Follette, U.S. Senator from Wisconsin,"* March 14, 1932, in box 117, folder 3, PFL Papers.

3. PFL to RML, February 23, 1932, box 42, La Follette Family Papers, Manuscript Division, Library of Congress; Progressive Republican Platform, March 17, 1932, box 117, folder 3; and RML to PFL, March 15, 1932, box 135, folder 3, both in the PFL Papers; *Capital Times*, March 15 and 19, 1932.

4. IBL to FL, February 17, 1932, box A42, La Follette Family Papers; RS to PFL, January 26, 1932, box 135, folder 3, PFL Papers; *Capital Times*, March 10 and 16, 1932; *New York Times*, March 24, 1932.

5. Philip F. La Follette, *Adventure in Politics: The Memoirs of Philip F. La Follette*, Donald Young, ed. (New York: Holt, Rinehart and Winston, 1970), 177–78. The first issue of the *Uncensored News* appears in volume 15 of the PFL Papers. PFL to RML Jr., April 23, 1932, box A42, La Follette Family Papers. For an example of the influence of the *Uncensored News* on the state press, see stories of Phil hobnobbing with Wall Street

bankers in the *Milwaukee Journal*, May 29, 1932.

6. Vote totals for the presidential primary elections are calculated by dividing the total number of votes cast for all district delegates by two, since each voter marked a ballot for two delegates. Because some voters may have voted for only one delegate, the numbers are approximate.

7. Vote totals are from the 1929, 1931, and 1933 *Wisconsin Blue Book*s.

8. *Capital Times*, May 13, 1932.

9. La Follette, *Adventure in Politics*, 180; PFL to RML Jr., April 23, 1932, box A42, La Follette Family Papers; PFL to RML Jr., May 15, 1932; and PFL to IBL, June 14, 1932, both in box 135, folder 3, PFL Papers.

10. *Capital Times*, June 17 and 18, 1932, especially the Evjue editorial on June 18.

11. *Progressive Campaign Textbook* in box 162, folder 2, PFL Papers. The platform is on pages 4 to 13. Isabel Bacon La Follette, "If You Can Take It," unpublished manuscript, box 135, PFL Papers; RS to IBL, August 13, 1932, ibid.

12. Alfred Schumann, *No Peddlers Allowed* (Appleton, WI: C. C. Nelson Publishing Co., 1940), 269–70; La Follette, "If You Can Take It," 144.

13. *Capital Times*, May 22, 23, 24, and 25, 1932. Phil's budget cut $1.5 million from state departments, $700,000 from the University of Wisconsin, $570,000 from the Board of Control, $150,000 from the nine Normal Schools, $32,000 from Stout Institute, and $2,300 from the Platteville mining school.

14. *Capital Times*, June 6, 7, 8, and 9, 1932.

15. Ibid., June 10 and 12, 1932. For a discussion of Democratic strategy, see ibid., July 27, 1932.

16. Ibid., June 5, 13, and 15, 1932. NEA correspondent Rodney Dutcher's report appeared in ibid., June 1932.

17. "Announcement of Philip F. La Follette," in box 117, folder 3, PFL Papers; *Capital Times*, July 6, 7, and 9, 1932.

18. Phil's itinerary and accounts of his speeches appear in the *Capital Times*, July 18 to 30, 1932. The Chapple incident occurred on July 28 and is also recounted in La Follette, *Adventure in Politics*, 181–82. For early comment on the contest, see the *New York Times*, July 17, 1932.

19. *Merrill Daily Herald*, August 23, 1932. The quotation is from the *Wausau Record-Herald*, August 28, 1932. See also *Milwaukee Sentinel*, August 26, 1932, and *Eau Claire Leader*, September 1, 1932, all in the PFL Papers, vol. 15. Isabel later recounted the campaign in "If You Can Take It," 141–48, in box 165, folder 3, ibid.

20. *Capital Times*, August 7, 9, 10, 11, and 30, 1932. The spending estimate is from ibid., September 13, 1932.

21. Ibid., September 15–17, 1932. Phil's speech appeared on the seventeenth.

22. For Schmedeman, see ibid., July 31 and August 13, 1932; for Rubin, August 11, 1932; for the rumor, see September 12, 1932.

23. Official vote totals are from the 1933 *Wisconsin Blue Book*, 514–19. The *Capital Times* printed editorials from the *Milwaukee Sentinel*, *Racine Journal-Times*, and *Marshfield News-Herald*, among others, in the week following the primary.

24. Official vote totals are from the 1933 *Wisconsin Blue Book*, 514, and the 1931 *Wisconsin Blue Book*, 462 and 467.

25. La Follette, *Adventure in Politics*, 182–83; ML to PFL, September 21 and 22, 1932, box 135, folder 3, and undated clippings, vol. 15, all in the PFL Papers; *Capital Times*, September 21 and 23, 1932; *The Progressive*, October 1 and 8, 1932. A letter to Phil from Ralph Sucher, dated October 4, 1932, suggests that Phil himself considered running as an independent candidate for the United States Senate.

26. *Capital Times*, November 9 and 10, 1932; *Wisconsin State Journal*, November 9 and 10, 1932; *Milwaukee Journal*, November 9 and 10, 1932.

27. La Follette, *Adventure in Politics*, 179–80; RS to PFL, November 17, 1932, box 135, folder 3, PFL Papers; PFL to RML Jr., December 9, 1932, box A42, La Follette Family Papers. See also William Leuchtenberg, *Franklin Delano Roosevelt and the New Deal, 1932–1940* (New York: Harper and Row, 1963), 12; James MacGregor Burns, *Roosevelt: The Lion and the Fox, 1882–1940* (New York: Harcourt Brace, 1956), 149; Russel B. Nye, *Midwestern Progressive Politics* (East Lansing: Michigan State College Press, 1951), 356; and Arthur Schlesinger, *The Crisis of the Old Order* (Boston: Houghton Mifflin, 1957), 469–72.

28. La Follette, *Adventure in Politics*, 183–84; La Follette, "If You Can Take It," 151; PFL to ML, January 2, 1933; and PFL to RML Jr., January 4, 1933, both in box A43, La Follette Family Papers.

29. PFL diary for January 3 and 4, 1932; and RML Jr., to PFL, January 6, 1933, both in box 135, folder 3, PFL Papers.

30. RML Jr. to PFL, January 9, 1933, box 135, folder 3, ibid.; La Follette, "If You Can Take It," 212.

31. La Follette, *Adventure in Politics*, 184–85; PFL diary, 2–6, box 134, folder 3; and *London Times*, *London Daily Telegraph*, and other unidentified clippings, especially "No Sentiment in America's Attitude to Europe," vol. 15, all in PFL Papers.

32. La Follette, *Adventure in Politics*, 190–93; PFL diary, 22–28, box 134, folder 3, and newspaper clippings, vol. 15, both in the PFL Papers; PFL to "Dear Ones," January 29 and February 5 and 18, 1933; and PFL to RML Jr., February 5, 1933, all in box A43, PFL Papers.

33. La Follette, *Adventure in Politics*, 193–99; PFL to "Dear Ones," February 19, 1933, box A43, La Follette Family Papers; *The Progressive* and *New York Evening Post* clippings, vol. 15, PFL Papers.

34. La Follette, *Adventure in Politics*, 200–203; FL to PFL and IBL, January 31, February 6, and March 6, 1933, box 135, folder 3; and La Follette, "If You Can Take It," 212, all in PFL Papers; PFL to RML Jr., February 5, 1933, box A43, La Follette Family Papers; *New York Times*, March 5, 1933.

35. La Follette, "If You Can Take It," 213–16; RML Jr. to FL and GM, February 24, 1933, box A43, La Follette Family Papers.

36. La Follette, *Adventure in Politics*, 179–80 and 204–6; La Follette, "If You Can Take It," 214–15. Phil's detailed description of his meeting with Roosevelt, written later that same day, is in box A43, La Follette Family Papers.

37. La Follette, "If You Can Take It," 216–17; *New York Sun*, March 20 and 24, *New York World-Telegram*, March 20, 1933, and *Washington Herald*, March 2, 1933, all in vol. 15, and PFL to IBL, March 21 and 27, 1933, box 135, folder 4, all in PFL Papers; *Capital Times*, March 22, 1933; *The Progressive*, March 25, 1933. Phil probably told Evjue his reasons off the record, and Evjue passed on the information to writers at the *Capital Times* and *The Progressive*, since the same story appears in both.

38. La Follette, *Adventure in Politics*, 206–9; PFL to IBL, April 20, 1933; and PFL to RS and ML, July 8, 1933, both in box 135, folder 3, and unlabeled clipping "Progressives Press for Big Job Program," vol. 15, all in PFL Papers.

39. *Chicago Tribune*, September 21, 1933; *Los Angeles Illustrated Daily News*; *Los Angeles Examiner*, undated clippings (October 1933) in vol. 15, PFL Papers.

40. In the PFL Papers: PFL to IBL, December 9, 1933, box 135, folder 3, and the following newspaper clippings in vol. 15: *Albuquerque (NM) Journal*, October 12, 1933; *Spokane (WA) Herald*, no date (October 1933); *Rochester (NY) Evening Journal and Post-Express*, December 28, 1933; and *Rochester (NY) Times-Union*, December 28, 1933. The most developed iteration of Phil's ideas occurs in "Wanted—A New Machine," a speech delivered to the Purchasing Agents' Association of Chicago in November 1933, in box 117, folder 5, PFL Papers.

41. PFL to RML Jr., January 2 and 5, 1934, box A43, La Follette Family Papers; PFL to IBL, January 18, 1934, box 135, folder 4, PFL Papers.

42. Wisconsin, Public Welfare Department, *General Relief in Wisconsin, 1848–1935* (Madison, 1939), 24–29, 63–68, 95–104; Wisconsin, Public Welfare Department, *Financial Conditions of Wisconsin Counties* (Madison, 1936), 54 and 76; PFL to RML Jr., February 24, 1934, box A43, La Follette Family Papers.

43. A. William Hoglund, "Wisconsin Dairy Farmers on Strike," *Agricultural History* 35 (January 1961): 27–29; Herbert Jacobs, "The Wisconsin Milk Strikes," *Wisconsin Magazine of History* 35 (Autumn 1951): 30–35. See also Paul W. Glad, *The History of Wisconsin, Volume V: War, a New Era, and Depression, 1914–1940* (Madison: State Historical Society of Wisconsin, 1990), 410–19.

44. Walter H. Uphoff, *Kohler on Strike: Thirty Years of Conflict* (Boston: Beacon Press, 1966), 19–78; *Sheboygan Times*, July 16–30, 1934. The media tended to portray the strikers sympathetically, especially after it became known that the Kohler Company kept a stockpile of guns, dynamite, and tear gas. For a painfully unsympathetic account, see Garet Garrett, "Section Seven-A at Sheboygan," *Saturday Evening Post*, October 27, 1934, pp. 5–7+. See also Glad, *War, a New Era, and Depression*, 426 and 428–35.

45. Stuart L. Weiss, "Thomas Amlie and the New Deal," *Mid-America* 59 (January 1977): 19–23; Theodore Rosenof, "The Political Education of an American Radical: Thomas Amlie in the 1930s," *Wisconsin Magazine of History* 58 (Autumn 1974): 21–24; John E. Miller, *Philip La Follette, the Wisconsin Progressives, and the New Deal* (Columbia: University of Missouri Press, 1982), 42–43. For Amlie on the possibilities of a third party, see Amlie to Agnes Jenks, February 16, 1934, box 11, folder 5, Thomas Amlie Papers, Archives Division, Wisconsin Historical Society. See also Lester F. Schmidt, "The Farmer-Labor Progressive Federation: The Study of a 'United Front' Movement

among Wisconsin Liberals, 1934–1941" (doctoral dissertation, University of Wisconsin, 1955).

46. There was an apparent assassination attempt on one or both of them on this night. Two masked men appeared at the Amlies' cabin door demanding to see them; Amlie's terrified wife and children were home at the time and told them to go away but were unable to call the police since the cabin had no telephone. Phil believed that the two men wanted to kill or beat them, since the La Follette family did not have enough money to make kidnapping a likely motive. See *Chicago Tribune*, October 1, 1933; *Milwaukee Journal*, October 1, 1933; and *Capital Times*, October 1, 1933. See also Amlie to Alfred Bingham, October 5, 1933, box 11, folder 1, Amlie Papers.

47. La Follette, *Adventure in Politics*, 208–9; PFL to RML, February 12, 1934, box A43, La Follette Family Papers; Miller, *Philip La Follette*, 42–43.

48. La Follette, *Adventure in Politics*, 208–9; Isabel B. La Follette, "Political Diary," 4–5, box 161, folder 6, PFL Papers; Miller, *Philip La Follette*, 46–49; PFL to RML Jr., February 12 and 21, 1934, box A43, La Follette Family Papers; Amlie to Seldon Rodman, March 5, 1934; Amlie to C. O. Wescott, March 12, 1934, both in box 12, folder 1, Amlie Papers. On those who opposed the new party, see Amlie to Alfred M. Bingham, October 19, 1933, folder 1; Amlie to J. G. Vennie, November 6, 1933, folder 2; and H. J. Kent to Amlie, February 23, 1934, folder 5, all in Amlie Papers, box 11. Patrick J. Maney describes Robert's alternating ambivalence and anger toward the third party in *"Young Bob": A Biography of Robert M. La Follette, Jr., 1895–1953* (Columbia: University of Missouri Press, 1978), 135–41.

49. La Follette, *Adventure in Politics*, 210–12; PFL to RML Jr., February 24, March 11 and 31, and April 10 and 16, 1934, all in box A43, La Follette Family Papers; *New York Times*, April 1, 1934. In May, Phil learned from Colonel House that James Farley had been trying to get an influential German-language newspaper publisher to oppose Robert; see PFL to RML Jr., May 14, 1934, box A43, La Follette Family Papers.

50. Unidentified clippings dated January 31, 1934 ("Phil La Follette in Plea for 'Politics'"), and *Chattanooga News*, April 24, 1934, both in vol. 17, PFL Papers.

51. La Follette, *Adventure in Politics*, 210; Miller, *Philip La Follette*, 50; PFL to RML Jr., April 10 and May 1, 1934, box A43, La Follette Family Papers; Amlie to Jack Kyle, March 10, 1934 (quotation); and Amlie to R. J. Forehand, March 22, 1934, both in box 12, folder 1, Amlie Papers; *Capital Times*, May 1, 1934; *Wisconsin Reports*, vol. 215, pp. 394–409.

52. La Follette, *Adventure in Politics*, 210–11; Miller, *Philip La Follette*, 51–52; La Follette, "Political Diary," 5; PFL to RML Jr., May 14, 1934, box A43, La Follette Family Papers; *New York Times*, May 19, 22, and 24, 1934; *Capital Times*, May 20, 1934; *Milwaukee Sentinel*, May 19, 1934; *Wisconsin State Journal*, May 22, 1934. The Milwaukee Progressive organization continued to cause problems for the state organization; see John Sprengeler to PFL, December [no day] 1934, folder 2, box 31, and Frank C. Durham to Thomas Davlin, December 5, 1934, copy enclosed in Durham to Gordon Sinykin, December 5, 1934, folder 1, box 31, both in PFL Papers. See also Donald McCoy, "The Formation of the Wisconsin Progressive Party in 1934," *The Historian* 14 (Autumn 1951): 70–90.

53. Miller, *Philip La Follette*, 52–55; La Follette, "Political Diary," 5–6; PFL to RML Jr., May 27, 1934, box A43, La Follette Family Papers; "The Birth of a New Party," address by Philip La Follette, box 117, folder 6, PFL Papers. In a letter to Louis Adamic, Duncan refuted charges that Phil did not want a separate party and that the Farmer-Labor group forced his hand; he compared the problem faced by the La Follette brothers as "that of the mythical western character who conducted a swarm of bees across the Rocky Mountains without losing a bee." See Duncan to Adamic, February 25, 1935, folder 6, box 33, PFL Papers. Adamic seems to have written in response to the assertions of Alfred Bingham, editor of *Common Sense*, that the La Follettes did not want a new party. See Freda Kuchurz [?] to Adamic, February 15, 1935, copy in folder 5, box 33, PFL Papers.

54. PFL to RML Jr., June 5 and 13, 1934, box A43, La Follette Family Papers; *Capital Times*, June 18, 1934; "Certificate of the Progressive Party," June 8, 1934, box 135, folder 4, PFL Papers.

55. PFL to RML Jr., June 13, 1934, box A43, La Follette Family Papers; "The Birth of a New Party," June 30, 1934, box 117, folder 6, PFL Papers.

56. "The Birth of a New Party," June 30, 1934, box 117, folder 6; and PFL to IBL, June 30, 1930, box 135, folder 4, both in the PFL Papers; Miller, *Philip La Follette*, 53–55; *Capital Times*, June 30, 1934.

57. PFL to IBL, July 2, 1934; and FL to IBL, July 1, 1934, both in box 135, folder 4, PFL Papers; La Follette, "Political Diary," 8–9. See also Weiss, "Thomas Amlie and the New Deal," 24–25.

58. La Follette, "Political Diary," 6–7; *Milwaukee Journal*, May 22, 1934.

59. La Follette, *Adventure in Politics*, 212–13; Amlie to Hans Amlie; July 13, 1934; Amlie to Horace Fries, July 2 and 28, 1934, both in box 12, folder 5, Amlie Papers; PFL to IBL, July 5, 10, 11, 13, and 16, 1934, box 135, folder 4, PFL Papers; La Follette, "Political Diary," 8–9; *Milwaukee Sentinel*, July 15 and 17, 1934; *Chicago Tribune*, July 22, 1934.

60. *New York Times*, August 2, 1934; *Chicago Tribune*, August 8, 1934; *Capital Times*, August 8, 9, and 10, 1934; *Milwaukee Sentinel*, August 12 and 15, 1934; La Follette, "Political Diary" for September 2, 1934, unpaged. For Roosevelt's visit, see Jonathan Kasparek, "FDR's 'Old Friends' in Wisconsin: Presidential Finesse in the Land of La Follette," *Wisconsin Magazine of History* 84 (Summer 2001): 16–25.

61. La Follette, "Political Diary" for September 2, 1934, unpaged. See newspaper clippings in vol. 16 of the PFL papers, especially *Chicago Tribune*, August 15 and September 6 and 13, 1934; *Augusta Union*, August 23, 1934; *Mondovi Herald*, August 24, 1934; *Wisconsin State Journal*, September 5 and 7, 1934; *Capital Times*, September 9 and 13, 1934; *Milwaukee Sentinel*, September 11, 1934; and *Milwaukee Journal*, September 12, 1934.

62. *Capital Times*, *Milwaukee Journal*, and *Wisconsin State Journal*, September 15, 1934. This document was also adopted as the Progressive State Platform and was printed in full in the 1935 *Wisconsin Blue Book*, 476–82; clippings in vol. 16, PFL Papers.

63. *New York Times, Capital Times, Milwaukee Journal, Milwaukee Sentinel,* and *Wisconsin State Journal,* September 20, 1934; IBL to FL and GM, September 17, 1934, box A43, La Follette Family Papers; 1935 *Wisconsin Blue Book,* 495–564. On Meisel, see the *Capital Times,* September 13, 1934.

64. *Chicago Tribune,* September 25, 1934; *Wisconsin State Journal,* September 20, 1934; "Extemporaneous speech of P. F. La Follette after delivery of platform at convention," box 117, folder 6; and untitled address (Madison, Wisconsin, September 1, 1934) in box 117, folder 6, PFL Papers.

65. La Follette, "Political Diary" for October 10, unpaged; *Milwaukee Journal,* November 2, 1934; IBL to FL, October 9, 1934, box A43, La Follette Family Papers; Radio speeches in box 117, folder 6, PFL Papers.

66. La Follette, *Adventure in Politics,* 215–16. Election data appear in the 1935 *Wisconsin Blue Book.*

CHAPTER SIX

1. For Coughlin, see Arthur M. Schlesinger Jr., *The Age of Roosevelt,* vol. III: *The Politics of Upheaval* (Boston: Houghton Mifflin, 1960), 18–27; Alan Brinkley, *Voices of Protest: Huey Long, Father Coughlin and the Great Depression* (New York: Vintage Books, 1983), 107–42 and 255–62; and William E. Leuchtenburg, *Franklin D. Roosevelt and the New Deal, 1932–1940* (New York: Harper Perennial, 1963), 100–103 and 181–83.

2. Schlesinger, *Politics of Upheaval,* 29–41; Leuchtenburg, *Franklin D. Roosevelt,* 103–106. The McGroarty bill died an ignoble death during a roll call vote in which half the representatives absented themselves out of the fear of antagonizing his supporters. Townsend's organization fell apart after charges of financial misconduct and the decision to endorse Union Party candidate William Lemke.

3. Leuchtenburg, *Franklin D. Roosevelt,* 96–100; Schlesinger, *Politics of Upheaval,* 42–68; Brinkley, *Voices of Protest,* 242–51.

4. John E. Miller, *Governor Philip F. La Follette, the Wisconsin Progressives, and the New Deal* (Columbia: University of Missouri Press, 1982), 78–79; Brinkley, *Voices of Protest,* 232. On Long, see *The Progressive,* December 27, 1934, and February 23, March 16, and May 4, 1935. On Coughlin, see ibid., November 10 and December 8, 1934, and February 2 and March 2, 9, and 16, 1935. On Townsend, see ibid., February 23, 1935. George P. Newbury to Philip La Follette, May 6, 1935, folder 1, box 36, Philip F. La Follette Papers, Archives Division, Wisconsin Historical Society.

5. *Kansas City (MO) Times,* June 21, 1935, clipping in folder 4, box 37, PFL Papers; *The Progressive,* March 2, 1935.

6. Philip F. La Follette, *Adventure in Politics: The Memoirs of Philip La Follette,* Donald Young, ed. (New York: Holt, Rinehart and Winston, 1970), 216; *Milwaukee Sentinel,* November 9, 1934. The quotation is from the *Pittsburgh Press,* November 23, 1934; PFL to RML Jr., December 27, 1934, box A43, La Follette Family Papers, Manuscripts Division, Library of Congress.

7. Miller, *Governor Philip F. La Follette*, 61–63. The quotation is from Lorena Hickok to Harry Hopkins, November 10, 1933, box 89, Hopkins Papers, Franklin Delano Roosevelt Library, Hyde Park, New York, quoted in James T. Patterson, *The New Deal and the States: Federalism in Transition* (Princeton: Princeton University Press, 1969), 177–78. For the relief appropriation, see Harry Hopkins to Albert Schmedeman, February 27, 1934, copy (dated January 3, 1935) in folder 2, box 31; Hopkins to PFL, January 14, 1935, folder 5, box 32; and "Memorandum of [*sic*] Relief Bill," no date, folder 1, box 33, all in PFL Papers.

8. Miller, *Governor Philip F. La Follette*, 63; PFL to IBL, December 7 and 8, 1934, folder 4, box 135, PFL Papers. The quotation is from the December 8 letter, emphasis original.

9. Miller, *Governor Philip F. La Follette*, 63; La Follette, *Adventure in Politics*, 220; PFL to RML Jr., December 27, 1934, box A43, La Follette Family Papers.

10. "Inaugural Address by Philip F. La Follette," January 7, 1935, folder 1, box 118, PFL Papers; *Capital Times*, January 7, 1935; *Wisconsin State Journal*, January 7, 1935. Two articles by Louis Adamic in *The Nation* particularly capture the theme of practical action: "La Follette Progressives Face the Future," January 20, 1935, pp. 213–16, and "A Talk with Phil La Follette," January 27, 1935, pp. 242–45.

11. "Executive Budget Message," January 9, 1935, folder 1, box 118, PFL Papers. For the radio address and message, see *Chicago Tribune*, January 22, 1935; *Capital Times*, January 22, 1935. Hopkins estimated that the state needed to allocate $11 million in relief funds in order to qualify for matching federal money; $6 million was to come from local governments and $5 million from the state. In 1934, $37 million had been spent on relief in Wisconsin, only $200,000 of which had come from the state. See *Capital Times*, January 18, 1935, and Harry Hopkins to PFL, January 14, 1935, folder 5, box 32, PFL Papers.

12. *Capital Times*, January 10, 21, 22, 23, and 24, 1935.

13. "Radio Address of Gov. La Follette," January 23, 1935, folder 1, box 118, PFL Papers; *Capital Times*, January 24 and February 1, 1935; *Chicago Tribune*, January 23, 1935. The Executive Chamber did in fact have a working fireplace. Miller, *Governor Philip F. La Follette*, 63; *Capital Times*, February 12–15, and March 1, 1935; "Radio Address," February 13, 1935, folder 1, box 118, PFL Papers.

14. "Work or Doles—Wisconsin's Answer," March 8, 1935, folder 1, box 118, PFL Papers; *Oshkosh Northwestern*, March 9, 1935. For comment from the *Wausau Record-Herald* and *Milwaukee Sentinel*, see "The State Press" column in the *Capital Times*, March 12, 1935. See also PFL to RML Jr., February 8, 1935, folder 3, box 33, PFL Papers.

15. See John E. Miller, "Governor Philip F. La Follette's Shifting Priorities from Redistribution to Expansion," *Mid-America* 58 (April–July 1976): 119–26.

16. Howard O. Hunter to PFL, February 16, 1935; and PFL to Hunter, February 18, 1935, both in folder 5, box 33, PFL Papers.

17. *Capital Times*, March 18, 26–30, and April 7, 1935.

18. *Capital Times*, April 2, 3, 7, and 19, 1935. See also clippings in vol. 17, PFL Papers.

19. Miller, *Governor Philip F. La Follette*, 64–65; RML to PFL, April 22, 1935; and IBL to PFL, May 6, 1935, both in folder 5, box 135, PFL Papers; *Capital Times*, May 3, 4, and 7, 1935, and other newspaper clippings in vol. 17, PFL Papers; Harold Ickes, *The Secret Diary of Harold Ickes: The First Thousand Days, 1933–1936* (New York: Simon and Schuster, 1954), 355; Roosevelt Press Conference No. 201 (May 3, 1935) in *The Complete Presidential Press Conferences of Franklin D. Roosevelt*, vol. 5 (New York: Da Capo Press, 1972), 269.

20. La Follette, *Adventure in Politics*, 222–23; PFL to Marguerite Le Hand, May 15, 1935, folder 4, box 36, PFL Papers; "Progressives Must Take Helm of Leadership in New Age, Phil Declares," from *The Progressive*, May 25, 1935, folder 1, box 118, ibid.; *Capital Times*, May 18–22, 1935; *Milwaukee Journal*, May 17, 1935; *Oshkosh Northwestern*, May 17, 1935.

21. Miller, *Governor Philip F. La Follette*, 66–67; La Follette, *Adventure in Politics*, 221–23. The study, *A Study of Wisconsin: Its Resources, Its Physical, Social and Economic Background*, ran nearly five hundred pages and included statistics, graphs, and charts providing a picture of the health, education, and economic conditions of the state; and "Radio Address, May 21, 1935," in *Addresses and Messages of Governor Philip La Follette*, both in Wisconsin Historical Society Library; "Data on the Wisconsin Plan," folder 4, box 36; "Questions and Answers" on works bill, June 1, 1935, folder 1, box 37; Ralph M. Hoyt to PFL, May 14, 1935, folder 3, box 36; Claire B. Bird to La Follette, Rogers, and Roberts, June 10, 1935, folder 2, box 37; and articles of incorporation for the Wisconsin Finance Authority, May 22, 1935, folder 5, box 36, all in PFL Papers.

22. *Capital Times*, May 25–26, 1935; the Steinle quotation is from May 25. *New York Times*, May 25, 1935; *Milwaukee Journal*, May 26, 1935; "Radio Address, May 24," folder 1, box 118, PFL Papers.

23. *Capital Times*, May 28–31, 1935; the quotation is from May 28; "Radio Address, May 31, 1935," folder 1, box 118, PFL Papers. For Isen, see *La Crosse Tribune*, May 25, 1935, clipping in vol. 17, ibid.

24. *Capital Times*, May 31– June 8, 1935; *Milwaukee Journal*, June 4 and 5, 1935; *Wisconsin State Journal*, June 11, 1935.

25. Miller, *Governor Philip F. La Follette*, 66–68; *New York Times*, June 2, 1935; *Wisconsin State Journal*, June 8, 1935; *Capital Times*, June 13, 1935; "Radio Address, June 7, 1935," folder 1, box 118; and Thomas M. Duncan, statement at hearing, May 29, 1935, folder 6, box 36, all in PFL Papers.

26. Daniel Hoan to PFL, May 31, 1935 (two letters), folder 6, box 36; PFL to Hoan, June 1, 1935, folder 3, box 37, all in PFL Papers.

27. "Radio Address, June 14, 1935," *Messages and Addresses of Governor Philip La Follette; Capital Times*, June 14–16, 1935. The disappointment was shared by other members of the family. Fola wrote that it was a bitter disappointment that "hit me hard." See FL to PFL and IBL, June 14, 1935, folder 5, box 135, PFL Papers.

28. Miller, *Governor Philip F. La Follette*, 68–70; *Capital Times*, June 18–22 and 28–29, 1935; *Wisconsin State Journal*, June 18, 1935; *Milwaukee Journal*, June 18,

1935; *Kenosha News*, June 19, 1935; *Oshkosh Northwestern*, June 21, 1935; Radio Address, June 28, folder 1, box 118, PFL Papers.

29. PFL to IBL, July 1, 1935, folder 5, box 135, PFL Papers; *Milwaukee Journal*, June 29, 1930; *Wisconsin State Journal*, July 1, 1930; Roosevelt Press Conference No. 217 (July 3, 1935) in *The Complete Presidential Press Conferences of Franklin D. Roosevelt*, vol. 6 (New York: Da Capo Press, 1972), 13.

30. Philip F. La Follette radio addresses for July 12 and 19, 1935 (box 118, folder 2, PFL Papers) and for September 2, 10, 20, 24, and 27, 1935, in *Messages and Addresses of Governor Philip F. La Follette*, Wisconsin Historical Society; *Capital Times*, July 28, 1935.

31. "Radio Address, October 1, 1935," folder 3, box 118, PFL Papers. On the Bermuda vacation, see clippings in vol. 17, especially *New York Herald-Tribune*, October 13, 1935, and *Rhinelander News*, October 14, 1935; and PFL to IBL, October 14, 15, 16, 18, and 21, 1935, folder 5, box 135. For New York speaking tour, see PFL to IBL, October 26, 28, and 30, 1935, folder 5, box 135, and clippings in vol. 17, especially *New York Times*, November 2, 1935, and *Rochester Journal*, November 1, 1935. For state speeches, see clippings in vol. 17, all in PFL Papers.

32. Bernard A. Weisberger, *The La Follettes of Wisconsin: Love and Politics in Progressive America* (Madison: University of Wisconsin Press, 1993), 306–8; FL to PFL and IBL, February 3 and June 14, 1935; GM to IBL, March 6, 1935; FL to IBL, May 26, 1935; RML Jr. to PFL, April 22, 1935; FL to PFL, May 1, 1935; and ML to PFL, May 19, 1935, all in folder 5, box 135, PFL Papers; PFL correspondence for March and April, A44, La Follette Family Papers.

33. The quotation is from GM to IBL, March 6, 1935, folder 5, box 135; see also FL to IBL, May 26, 1935, ibid.; FL to PFL, January 29, 1936; and FL to IBL, February 3, 1936, in folder 6, box 135, all in PFL Papers.

34. For the Department of Public Welfare, see 1937 *Wisconsin Blue Book*, 621. For Immell's appointment, see correspondence in folder 2, box 39, PFL Papers.

35. PFL to Harry Hopkins and Howard O. Hunter, both December 2, 1935, folder 4, box 39; and Hunter to PFL, August 26, 1935, folder 4, box 39, all in PFL Papers. The quotation is from PFL to Don Teach, November 19, 1935, folder 1, box 42, ibid.

36. FDR to Edward House, February 16, 1935, in Elliott Roosevelt, *FDR: His Personal Letters, 1928–1945* (New York: 1950), 452. For third party rumors, see articles by Louis Adamic in *The Nation*, February 20, 1935; R. L. Duffin, "Two States Test Third-Party Theories," *New York Times Magazine*, May 1935; *New York Times*, July 28, 1935, all in vol. 17, PFL Papers. Phil's remark on ending relief is from *The Secret Diary of Harold Ickes*, vol. 1, p. 487. Roosevelt Press Conferences No. 201 (May 3, 1935), vol. 5, p. 269; No. 217 (July 3, 1935), vol. 6, p. 13; and No. 236 (September 6, 1935), vol. 6, p. 41, all in *The Complete Presidential Press Conferences of Franklin D. Roosevelt*. For the Wisconsin Democrats' annoyance, see Miller, *Philip F. La Follette*, 64–65.

37. Executive committee memorandum, November 25, 1935, folder 2, box 42; Principles and Platform of Farmer Labor Progressive Federation, folder 3, box 42; and Thomas Duncan to B. C. Vladeck, December 4, 1935, folder 4, box 42, all in PFL

Papers; *Milwaukee Journal*, December 3, 1935; *Milwaukee Leader*, December 3, 1935. The Progressive Party executive committee included Phil, Robert, Harold Groves, and longtime La Follette supporters Charles Crownhart, Lawrence Brown, and E. Myrwyn Rowlands.

38. For the formation of the FLPF, see Miller, *Governor Philip F. La Follette*, 84–87; Glad, *War, a New Era, and Depression*, 475–77, especially the helpful footnote (No. 55) by John O. Holzhueter; and Donald L. Miller, *The New American Radicalism: Alfred M. Bingham and Non-Marxian Insurgency in the New Deal Era* (Port Washington, NY: Kennikat Press, 1979), 116–23; and clippings in vol. 17, PFL Papers. In the 1937 legislature, twenty-four of forty-eight Progressive assemblymen were FLPF members, as were eight of sixteen senators; see minutes of the FLPF executive board for November 9, 1936, copy in folder 3, box 63, PFL Papers.

39. Miller, *Governor Philip F. La Follette*, 79–82; *The Progressive*, December 1 and 8, 1934 , and May 11 and 25, 1935; Alfred Bingham to PFL, December 29, 1934, folder 2, box 31, and February 1, 1935, folder 2, box 33; and PFL to Bingham, February 22, 1935, folder 6, box 33, all in PFL Papers.

40. For Phil's public statements on a national third party, see *New York Times*, July 28, 1935; *Milwaukee Journal*, October 26, 1935; *Wisconsin State Journal*, October 29, 1935; and *Chicago Tribune*, December 21, 1935.

41. PFL to Seldon Rodman, July 25, 1935; and PFL to Don Fina, July 29, 1935, both in folder 6, box 38, PFL Papers.

42. "Can We Pay As We Go?" address, folder 4, box 118; and PFL to IBL, January 11 and 13, 1936, folder 6, box 135, all in PFL Papers.

43. Miller, *Governor Philip F. La Follette*, 87–88; IBL to FL, March 25, 1936, box A44, La Follette Family Papers; *Capital Times*, March 10–22, 1936.

44. La Follette, *Adventure in Politics*, 226–28; Miller, *Governor Philip F. La Follette*, 81–82; *Franklin D. Roosevelt*, 124–25 and 130–32.

45. Leuchtenburg, *Franklin D. Roosevelt*, 145–61, 170, and 183–84; Schlesinger, *Politics of Upheaval*, 271–87 and 291–342.

46. Miller, *Governor Philip F. La Follette*, 90–93; *Capital Times*, September 11 and 12, 1936. For the Progressive National Committee, see Schlesinger, *Politics of Upheaval*, 595–97; Maney, *"Young Bob" La Follette*, 190; and Donald R. McCoy, "The Progressive National Committee of 1936," *Western Political Quarterly* 9 (June 1956): 454–69. The quotation from Phil is from the *Houston Texan*, March 2, 1936, in vol. 18, PFL Papers.

47. Primary election results are from the 1937 *Wisconsin Blue Book*, 347–65; *Capital Times*, September 25, 1936; *New York Times*, September 16, 1936; "Radio Address—Green Bay," September 6, 1936, and "Radio Address—WIBA," September 14, 1936, both in folder 5, box 118, PFL Papers. On the FLPF, see Miller, *Governor Philip F. La Follette*, 85–86, and letter to the editor from Andrew Biemiller, *The New Republic* (July 15, 1936): 298.

48. The Democratic platform is in the 1937 *Wisconsin Blue Book*, 257–67; *Capital Times*, September 30, October 16 and 31, 1936.

49. *Capital Times*, October 15, 24, and 25, 1936. For *Wisconsin Facts*, see ibid., October 29, 1936. *La Follette Road to Communism* featured lurid photographs depicting the university as a hotbed of atheism and communism and documenting the evils of "LaFolletteism."

50. Gordon Sinykin to John Zahnd, July 23, 1936, folder 3, box 56, PFL Papers. For Phil on Roosevelt, see the *Capital Times*, September 19 (quotation), 20, 21, and 24, 1936. The formal endorsement came on September 23, 1936. For comments on Landon, see ibid., September 23, 1936. Not since 1904 did the leader of the Wisconsin Progressives support a president for reelection.

51. The *Capital Times* offered an almost day-by-day summary of Phil's speeches from September 25 to November 3, 1936. See especially October 2, 10, 18, 20, 21, 30, and 31, 1936. In the PFL Papers, see radio speeches for October 18 and November 1, notes for speech at Portage on October 15, and "Morning radio talk for women on education" from October 7, all in folder 5, box 118.

52. *Capital Times*, September 30, 1936.

53. Election statistics are from the 1937 *Wisconsin Blue Book*, 418–34. The Socialists had agreed to run no state candidates but did offer a slate of presidential electors.

54. RML Jr. and PFL to Franklin D. Roosevelt, day letter, November 2, 1936, folder 1, box 63; Roosevelt to PFL, November 21, 1936, folder 6, box 63, both in PFL Papers. See also La Follette, "If You Can Take It," 316, in ibid.

55. La Follette, *Adventure in Politics*, 228–29; PFL to IBL, November 19, 1936, folder 6, box 135; and Netha Roe to RML Jr. and PFL, November [?] 6, 1936, both in PFL Papers. The quotation is from the *Neillsville (WI) Journal*, December 10, 1936, clipping in vol. 18, ibid.

CHAPTER SEVEN

1. *Capital Times*, June 20, 1938.

2. For the 1904 gymnasium convention, see Robert M. La Follette, *La Follette's Autobiography: A Personal Narrative of Political Experiences* (Madison, WI: The Robert M. La Follette Co., 1911), 325; Albert O. Barton, *La Follette's Winning of Wisconsin* (Madison, WI: The Homestead Co., 1922), 348–50; and Belle Case La Follette and Fola La Follette, *Robert M. La Follette: June 14, 1855–June 20, 1925*, vol. 1 (New York: The Macmillan Company, 1953), 175–76. For Nils Haugen, see Barton, *La Follette's Winning of Wisconsin*, 53–68; and La Follette and La Follette, *Robert M. La Follette*, 106–9. For the Armed Ship Bill filibuster, see ibid., 603–35; and Bernard A. Weisberger, *The La Follettes of Wisconsin: Love and Politics in Progressive America* (Madison: University of Wisconsin Press, 1994), 198–202. These incidents did not escape contemporary comment, and La Follette's detractors often depicted him as a machine politician who used populist rhetoric to win election and keep his faction in power.

3. Philip F. La Follette, *Adventure in Politics: The Memoirs of Philip La Follette*, Donald Young, ed. (New York: Holt Rinehart and Winston, 1970), 233–35; E. David

Cronon and John W. Jenkins, *The University of Wisconsin: A History, Volume III: Politics, Depression, and War, 1925–1945* (Madison: University of Wisconsin Press, 1994), 215–30.

4. La Follette, *Adventure in Politics*, 237–38. Isabel noted in her "Political Diary" that the Franks kept trying to "butter them up." Cronon and Jenkins, *University of Wisconsin*, 297–99; Steven D. Zink, "Glenn Frank of the University of Wisconsin: A Reinterpretation," *Wisconsin Magazine of History* 62 (Winter 1978–79): 107–11. Through a combination of resignations and other circumstances, Phil had appointed five new regents in 1936; he was afraid of charges that Progressives were out to control the university and "get" Frank. See Walter Corrigan to PFL, January 28, 1935, and Wade Boardman to PFL, January 28, 1938, both in folder 1, box 33, Philip F. La Follette Papers, Archives Division, Wisconsin Historical Society.

5. La Follette, *Adventure in Politics*, 239–40; Isabel B. La Follette, "Political Diary" entry for February 19, 1937, folder 6, box 161, PFL Papers; Zink, "Glenn Frank," 118.

6. "Glenn Frank," 120–22; La Follette, *Adventure in Politics*, 240; La Follette, "Political Diary" for February 19, 1937, folder 6, box 161, PFL Papers. See also PFL incoming correspondence in boxes 64 and 65, ibid.

7. La Follette, *Adventure in Politics*, 240–41; La Follette, "Political Diary" for February 19, 1937, folder 6, box 161; "Statement of Governor Philip F. La Follette on the Presidency of the University of Wisconsin," folder 1, box 119; FL to PFL and IBL, December 17, 1936, folder 6, box 135; and RML Jr. to PFL and IBL, December 18, 1936, folder 6, box 135, all in PFL Papers; IBL to FL, January 20, 1937, box A44, La Follette Family Papers, Manuscript Division, Library of Congress. For the January meeting, see Zink, "Glenn Frank," 123–26. See also Lawrence H. Larsen, *The President Wore Spats: A Biography of Glenn Frank* (Madison: State Historical Society of Wisconsin, 1965), 139–51.

8. John E. Miller, *Governor Philip F. La Follette, the Wisconsin Progressives, and the New Deal* (Columbia: University of Missouri Press, 1982), 108–9; "Executive Budget Message," January 1937, folder 1, box 119; the budget received wide press: see clippings in vol. 18, especially *Chicago Tribune*, January 17, 1937; *Milwaukee Journal*, January 15, 1937; and *Wisconsin State Journal*, January 27, 1937, all in PFL Papers.

9. Miller, *Governor Philip F. La Follette*, 109–10; Radio Address, June 1, 1937, folder 1, box 119, PFL Papers; *Capital Times*, February 10, 1937. Labor continued to be a problem throughout 1937. The secession of the CIO locals from the AFL generated much conflict between the CIO and AFL, especially after the CIO locals were unwilling to abide by the labor board's decision. Phil wanted the board to be completely neutral and make decisions that would promote industrial peace and not simply serve to promote union organizing. In doing so, he alienated a number of labor leaders, including members of the Farmer-Labor-Progressive Federation. See Paul Glad, *History of Wisconsin: War, a New Era, and Depression, 1914–1940* (Madison: State Historical Society of Wisconsin, 1990), 533–34, for the AFL-CIO conflict, and see Isabel La Follette's "Political Diary" for May 8 through 15, 1937, 39–40, in box 161, PFL Papers.

10. Miller, *Governor Philip F. La Follette*, 110–11; *Capital Times*, June 17, 1937. For the WDA, see Samuel Mermin, *Jurisprudence and Statecraft: The Wisconsin Development Authority and Its Implications* (Madison: University of Wisconsin Press, 1963). A court challenge prevented the WDA from beginning operations until late June 1938 (see the *Capital Times* and *Wisconsin State Journal* for June 24, 1938), and the Republican-controlled 1939 legislature virtually defunded the agency.

11. PFL to RML Jr., June 25, 1937, box A45, La Follette Family Papers; La Follette, "Political Diary" for May 25, 1937, folder 6, box 161, PFL Papers.

12. Miller, *Governor Philip F. La Follette*, 105–6. The quotation is from La Follette, *Adventure in Politics*, 246–47; clippings dated January 9–12 in vol. 18 and La Follette, "Political Diary," 37, both in PFL Papers; *Capital Times*, March 9, 1937; *New York Times*, March 9, 1937; PFL to FDR, June 3, 1937, enclosed in PFL to RML Jr., July 4, 15, and 20, 1937; and RML Jr. to PFL, July 16, 1937, box A45, La Follette Family Papers.

13. For the court-packing scheme, see William Leuchtenburg, *Franklin D. Roosevelt and the New Deal, 1932–1940* (New York: Harper & Row, 1963), 232–38; Miller, *Governor Philip F. La Follette*, 106–7. For Robert La Follette Sr. on the court, see La Follette and La Follette, *Robert M. La Follette*, vol. 2, pp. 1128 and 1055–57; La Follette, "Political Diary," 35, folder 6, box 161, PFL Papers.

14. *New York Times*, February 26, 1937; *Wisconsin State Journal*, February 27, 1937; clippings in vol. 18, La Follette, "Political Diary," 34, folder 6, box 161; and "N.B.C Radio Address on President Roosevelt's Judicial Reorganization Plan," folder 1, box 119, all in PFL Papers. For the Wisconsin court plan, see *Milwaukee Sentinel*, February 17, 1937; *Capital Times*, February 17, 1937; and *New York Times*, February 17, 1937.

15. Miller, *Governor Philip F. La Follette*, 106; La Follette, "Political Diary," 44–45, folder 6, box 161; RML Jr. to PFL, August 3, 1937, folder 7, box 135; and clippings in vol. 18, PFL Papers.

16. For Harvard speech, see *Chicago Tribune*, June 19, 1937; and *New York Herald-Tribune*, June 19, 1937, both in vol. 18, PFL Papers.

17. "Political Democracy in America," July 22, 1937, folder 1, box 119, PFL Papers; the quotation is on p. 4.

18. On the FLPF's cold feet, see Donald L. Miller, *The New American Radicalism: Alfred Bingham and Non-Marxian Insurgency in the New Deal Era* (Port Washington, NY: Kennikat Press, 1979), 141–46; Stuart Weiss, "Thomas Amlie and the New Deal," *Mid-America* 59 (January 1977): 31; Bingham to PFL, July 28, 1938, folder 6, box 105; and PFL to Bingham, August 7, 1938, folder 4, box 106, both in PFL Papers.

19. Press release, July 31, 1937; and speech at Riverview Park, Des Moines, July 31, 1937, both in folder 1, box 119, PFL Papers; *Capital Times*, August 1, 1937; *New York Times*, September 6, 1937.

20. *Capital Times*, February 26 and April 22, 1937. See also clippings in vol. 18, PFL Papers.

21. Miller, *Governor Philip F. La Follette*, 115; La Follette, *Adventure in Politics*, 248. Proclamation for special session, folder 2, box 119, PFL Papers.

22. Miller, *Governor Philip F. La Follette*, 115; "Message to special session," October 4, 1937, folder 2, box 119; and PFL to IBL, October 6, 1937, folder 7, box 135, both in PFL Papers.

23. Miller, *Governor Philip F. La Follette*, 116; PFL to IBL, October 7, 10, and 13, 1937, folder 7, box 135, PFL Papers.

24. *Milwaukee Sentinel*, October 17, 1937; *Janesville Gazette*, October 17, 1937; *Chicago Tribune*, October 17, 1937. Phil himself went to the State Law Library (two floors above his office) and looked up a precedent by the Speaker of the House of Representatives for the controversial ruling ending debate.

25. *Capital Times*, October 19, 1937.

26. La Follette, *Adventure in Politics*, 249; PFL to IBL, October 6, 1937, folder 7, box 135, PFL Papers.

27. "Reorganization of the State Government"; "Progress and Democracy," *The Beacon*, October 1937; and "Democracy Functions in Wisconsin: The Record of Achievement of the 1937 Legislature," all in folder 2, box 119, and clippings in vol. 18, all in PFL Papers.

28. La Follette, *Adventure in Politics*, 250–51; newspaper clippings for November 1 to 3, vol. 18, PFL Papers. The quotation is from Isabel Bacon La Follette, "If You Can Take It," unpublished manuscript, box 165, ibid., 326.

29. RML to PFL, November 10, 1937; and Marvin Rosenberry to PFL, undated (November 1937), both in folder 7, box 135, PFL Papers; PFL to RML Jr., November 27 and December 20, 1937, box A45; and IBL to FL, December 4, 1937, box A44, all in La Follette Family Papers.

30. The quotation is from "Speech at Town Hall and Economic Club Dinner," February 28, 1938; and Radio Speech, WNYC, February 28, 1938, both in folder 2, box 119; clippings in vol. 18, especially *New York Times*, March 3, 1938, and *Wisconsin State Journal*, March 4, 1938, all in PFL Papers.

31. *Wisconsin State Journal*, March 11, 1938, also in *La Crosse Tribune and Leader Press*, March 11, 1938, all in vol. 18, PFL Papers.

32. La Follette, "Political Diary," 47–49, folder 6, box 161, ibid.

33. PFL to RML Jr., March 17, 1938, box A46, La Follette Family Papers; La Follette, "Political Diary," 50, folder 6, box 161, PFL Papers.

34. The letters are in boxes 94–97, PLF Papers; La Follette, "Political Diary," 50–55, and PFL to RML Jr., March [?] 22, 1938, and RML Jr. to PFL, both attached to p. 52. See also Maney, *"Young Bob,"* 204–5.

35. PFL to RML Jr., April 8, 1938, box A46, La Follette Family Papers. The speeches are in folder 3, box 119, PFL Papers. See also clippings in vol. 18, ibid.

36. La Follette, "Political Diary," 56–58, folder 6, box 161, PFL Papers; *Wisconsin State Journal*, April 24, 1938; *Capital Times*, April 24, 1938; FDR press conference no. 454, April 26, 1938, in *Complete Presidential Press Conferences of Franklin D. Roosevelt* (New York: Da Capo Press, 1972), 389–90. See also clippings in vol. 18, PFL Papers.

37. La Follette, "Political Diary," 55–58, folder 6, box 161, PFL Papers.

38. "A New Movement, the National Progressives of America Is Under Way," folder 3, box 119, PFL Papers. The rally was thoroughly covered by the press; see clippings

in vol. 18, ibid. See also "April Hopes in Madison," *The New Republic*, May 11, 1938, pp. 13+; *Life* (May 9, 1938); and *Time* (May 9, 1938).

39. "La Follette Thunder," *The Nation*, April 30, 1938, pp. 492–93; *New York Times*, May 5, 1938; *Capital Times*, May 5, 1938. The quotation from David Lawrence is from the *Washington Star*, May 4, 1938. See also clippings from vol. 25, PFL Papers, especially columns by Raymond Clapper, Hugh Johnson, and Walter Lippmann.

40. Harold Ickes, *The Secret Diary of Harold Ickes, Volume Two: The Inside Struggle, 1936–1939* (New York: Simon and Schuster, 1954), 378–80; *New York Times*, May 5, 1938.

41. FDR to William Phillips, May 18, 1938, in Elliott Roosevelt, ed., *FDR: His Personal Letters, 1928–1945* (New York: 1950), 785.

42. La Follette, "Political Diary," 58–59, folder 6, box 161; "Radio Speech Delivered by Senator Robert M. La Follette Jr.," May 9, 1938, folder 4, box 119; and FL to PFL, May 8, 1938, folder 8, box 135, all in PFL Papers.

43. See clippings in vol. 25, PFL Papers, especially *Washington Daily News*, May 2, 1938; *New York Tribune*, May 2, 1938; and *Chicago Tribune*, May 7, 1938.

44. For comments on the symbol and other Fascist trappings, see clippings in vol. 25, ibid., especially *New York World Telegram*, May 3, 1938, and undated columns by Paul Y. Anderson and Heywood Broun.

45. PFL to RML Jr., May 5, 1938, and PFL to GM, May 7, 1938, box A46, La Follette Family Papers; *Capital Times*, May 8 and June 3, 1938; *Wisconsin State Journal*, May 8, 1938. An editorial in *Common Sense* ("Progressives, What Now?," June 1938) warned its readers of the dangers of a one-man party. James McMullin, writing in *The Commentator* ("Progressive—1938 Model," July 1938), was more optimistic about the organizing efforts.

46. *New York Times*, April 29 and May 1, 1938; *Capital Times*, May 1, 1938; *Wisconsin State Journal*, April 30 and May 1, 1938. For the outcome of the Iowa situation, see clippings in vol. 26, PFL Papers; and Miller, *Governor Philip F. La Follette*, 145–46.

47. For California, see *Capital Times*, May 6, 1938; *Milwaukee Journal*, May 8, 1938; and other clippings in vol. 26, PFL Papers. See also Miller, *Governor Philip F. La Follette*, 148–49.

48. For New England, see *Capital Times*, May 29, 1938; *Chicago Tribune*, May 29, 1938; and other clippings in vol. 26, PFL Papers. See also Miller, *Governor Philip F. La Follette*, 14–47.

49. *Capital Times*, May 26, 1938; La Follette, "Political Diary," 65–66, folder 6, box 161, PFL Papers.

50. *Chicago Tribune*, May 22, 1938; *Capital Times*, May 22 and 25, 1938; *Wisconsin State Journal*, May 22, 1938; *Milwaukee Sentinel*, May 23, 1938. Dammann later said he would withdraw from the race if Phil decided to seek another term. For letters critical of Phil's NPA efforts, see folders 1 and 2, box 94, and folder 5, box 95, PFL Papers.

51. La Follette, "Political Diary," 56–57, folder 6, box 161, PFL Papers; *Capital Times*, May 7, 16, 17, and 18, 1938. The Lewis cartoon appeared on the front page of the *Milwaukee Journal*, May 22, 1938.

52. La Follette, "Political Diary," 68–69, folder 6, box 161, PFL Papers; PFL to RML Jr., July 12, 1938, box A46, La Follette Family Papers; *Capital Times*, June 22, 1938; *Wisconsin State Journal*, June 23, 1938.

53. Miller, *Governor Philip F. La Follette*, 152–53; *Milwaukee Journal*, July 24, 1938; *Milwaukee Leader*, August 4, 1938; *Chicago Tribune*, September 7 and 11, 1938.

54. 1940 *Wisconsin Blue Book*, 536–41.

55. Miller, *Governor Philip F. La Follette*, 154–55; *Chicago Tribune*, August 14 and September 7, 1938.

56. *Capital Times*, September 23, 27, and 29, and October 6, 7, 8, and 9, 1938; *New York Times*, September 23, 1938.

57. *Capital Times*, October 5, 1938; radio addresses, October 23 and November 6, 1938, folder 4, box 119, PFL Papers. The Progressive platform appears in the 1940 *Wisconsin Blue Book*, 470–82.

58. 1940 *Wisconsin Blue Book*, 606–21.

59. ML to IBL and PFL, November 11, 1938, folder 8, box 135; La Follette, "Political Diary," 73, folder 6, box 161; and "The Wisconsin Election," folder 4, box 119, all in PFL Papers; FL to GM, November 11, 1938, box 46, La Follette Family Papers.

60. Miller, *Governor Philip F. La Follette*, 160–61.

CHAPTER EIGHT

1. *New York Sun*, January 3, 1939 (quotations), and *Newsweek*, January 16, 1939, both clippings in vol. 28, and GM to PFL and IBL, December 12, 1938, folder 8, box 135, both in the Philip La Follette Papers, Archives Division, State Historical Society of Wisconsin; PFL to "Dear Ones," January 16, 1939, box A47, La Follette Family Papers, Manuscripts Division, Library of Congress. Prior to writing to Phil, Middleton discussed the trip with "the Justice," who thought it a "great mistake" to visit Germany. This was probably Louis Brandies, who had been a close friend of Robert M. La Follette Sr. and who had given Phil political and professional advice in the past.

2. Philip F. La Follette, *Adventure in Politics: The Memoirs of Philip La Follette*, Donald Young, ed. (New York: Holt Rinehart and Winston, 1970), 257–58; *Chicago Tribune*, January 18, 1939, clipping in vol. 28; PFL to "Dear Ones," January 25, 1939, folder 8; and notes on French visit dated January 28, 1939, folder 8, all in box 135, PFL Papers; IBL to "Dearest Family," January 22, 1939, box A47, La Follette Family Papers.

3. La Follette, *Adventure in Politics*, 258, 261; PFL to "Dear Ones," February 4, 1939, box A47, La Follette Family Papers. Notes on Italy visit dated February 4, 1939, folder 8, box 135, PFL Papers.

4. La Follette, *Adventure in Politics*, 258; PFL to "Dear Ones," February 11 and 23 and March 3, 1939; and IBL to FL and GM, February 17, 1939, both in box A47, La Follette Family Papers.

5. In the PFL Papers: PFL to IBL, April 3 and 4, 1939, folder 8, box 135; "The Outlook for Democracy: Address Delivered before the Economic Club of New York," April 18, 1939, folder 6, box 119. Phil's address, particularly his comments on Kennedy, were widely reported in the press; see clippings in vol. 28, ibid., especially *New York Times*, April 19, 1939.

6. La Follette, *Adventure in Politics*, 262–63; Associated Press clipping ("Bob, Phil Talk with FR; Latter Denies Asking Kennedy Recall") vol. 28, PFL Papers.

7. *New York Times*, April 22, 1939; *New York Journal-American*, April 21, 1939; *New York Herald-Tribune*, April 22, 1939; Robert Dell, "Phil La Follette Is Right," *The Nation* (April 29, 1939): 487–88. For Robert's foreign policy concerns, see Patrick J. Maney, *"Young Bob": A Biography of Robert M. La Follette, Jr., 1895–1953* (Columbia: University of Missouri Press, 1978), 201–3.

8. *New York Times*, May 7, 1939; *New York Herald-Tribune*, May 7, 1939; RML Jr. to PFL, January 6, 1938, folder 8, box 135, PFL Papers.

9. IBL to PFL, April 6, 1939; and PFL to IBL, April 7, 1939, both in folder 8, box 135, PFL Papers; clippings in vol. 28, ibid., from March to April 1939, especially *Capital Times*, April 23, 1939, and *New York Times*, April 23, 1939.

10. PFL to RML Jr., April 26 (quotation) and May 12, 1939, both in box A47, La Follette Family Papers; Stanley Price Devens, "Wisconsin After LaFollette," *The Christian Century*, June 21, 1939, p. 793; *Milwaukee Journal*, July 30, 1939.

11. "The Outlook for Democracy," folder 6, box 119, PFL Papers, 8.

12. Copies of *The Commentator* and *The Progressive* are in folder 6, box 119, ibid. See also "What's Going On in Europe?" June 2, 1939, ibid.

13. Radio speech by Philip F. La Follette, October 3, 1939, folder 1, box 120, ibid.; the quotation is from page 4. On neutrality laws and their revision, see David M. Kennedy, *Freedom from Fear: The American People in Depression and War, 1929–1945* (New York: Oxford University Press, 1999), 432.

14. Chester Bowles to PFL, October 4, 1941, folder 8, box 135, PFL Papers.

15. *Capital Times*, October 13, 1941; "Should the Arms Embargo Be Lifted?" *Town Meeting: Bulletin of America's Town Meeting of the Air* 5 (October 16, 1939): 11–17.

16. See issues of *The Progressive Woman* and IBL to "Dear Friend," October 14, 1939, both in box A47, La Follette Family Papers; "Where Do We Go from Here?," PFL speech, November 1939, folder 1, box 120 (quotation); "Hon. Philip F. La Follette Saturday Forum Speaker," *The City* 25 (January 17, 1940): 1–4, folder 1, box 136; and Lillian McCarthy telegram to G. C. Gallati, January 13, 1940, folder 1, box 136, all in PFL Papers.

17. *Cleveland Plain Dealer*, January 21, 1940; *Cleveland Press*, January 20, 1940.

18. Harold Peterson to PFL, February 13, 1940, folder 1, box 136, PFL Papers; *Capital Times*, March 8, 1940.

19. *New York Times*, January 13, 1940; *Capital Times*, February 20, 1940.

20. RML Jr. to PFL, February 19, 1940, box A47, La Follette Family Papers; Alfred Van De Zande to PFL, May 24, 1940, folder 3, box 136, PFL Papers. The quotation is from Edmund D. Walsh to PFL, January 31, 1940, folder 1, box 136, ibid.; *Milwaukee*

Journal, March 10, 1940. By March, likely gubernatorial candidates included former tax director John Theil, former tax commissioner Henry Gunderson, former Assembly Speaker Paul Alfonsi, Stafford, former Attorney General Orland Loomis, and state senator Philip Nelson. None were particularly promising to the La Follette brothers.

21. Roger T. Johnson, *Robert M. La Follette and the Decline of the Progressive Party in Wisconsin*, reprint ed. (New York: Archon Books, 1970), 54–55; *Racine Journal-Times*, March 5, 1940, clipping in vol. 28; Evan A. Evans to PFL, March 7, 1940, folder 2, box 136; and PFL to Evans, March 11, 1940, folder 2, box 136, all in PFL Papers.

22. For Fairbanks, Morse and Co., see clippings in vol. 28, PFL Papers.

23. Chester Bowles to PFL, May 16 and 29, 1940; and PFL to Chester Bowles, May 18, 1940, all in folder 3, box 136, PFL Papers; "The Defense of America," national radio address, June 20, 1940, folder 2, box 120, ibid.

24. Boyd [?] to PFL, June 27, 1940; and PFL to Boyd [?], June 28, 1940, both in folder 3, box 136, PFL Papers.

25. The money-changers quotation is from an untitled speech dated July 6, 1940 ("For years we have lived in a fool's paradise.") in folder 2, box 120, ibid. See also "The Defense of America," dated July 10, 1940, and another untitled speech dated July 13, 1940 ("Let us have a heart-to-heart talk tonight."), both ibid.

26. *Milwaukee Journal*, July 7, 1940. See also "Phil and NPA Ahead of Crowd Future Will Tell," State Politics column by Aldric Revel, from the *Capital Times*, no date (early Fall 1940), vol. 28, PFL Papers.

27. PFL to Clough Gates, July 22, 1940, folder 4, box 136, PFL Papers.

28. Johnson, *Robert M. La Follette*, 56; PFL to RML Jr., August 5, 1940; and IBL to RML Jr., August 13, 1940, both in box A47, La Follette Family Papers; Adam J. Gates to PFL, September 4, 1940, folder 5, box 136, PFL Papers. For county organization, see six-page summary in folder 4, box 136, ibid.

29. Johnson, *Robert M. La Follette*, 56–58. In the PFL Papers: PFL to Adam J. Gates, September 6, 1940; Lillian McCarthy to Victor G. Gilbertson, September 10, 1940; PFL itineraries for September and October, all in folder 5, box 136; "Address by Philip F. La Follette," September 15, 1940, folder 2, box 120. The quotation is from "Radio Talk by Philip F. La Follette," October 27, 1940, folder 1, box 120, ibid.

30. Election figures are from the 1940 and 1942 *Wisconsin Blue Book*s. See also Maney, *"Young Bob,"* 238–44.

31. R. Douglas Stuart to PFL, July 30 and August 5 (quotation), 1940; PFL to John T. Flynn, et al., August 16, 1940; PFL to Chester Bowles, August 24, 1940; and PFL to R. Douglas Stuart Jr., August 27, 1940, all in folder 4, box 136, PFL Papers.

32. Stuart Chase to PFL, August 29, 1940, folder 4, box 136; and Elmer Davis to PFL, January 6, 1941, folder 1, box 138, both in PFL Papers; Judith Sorem and Robert La Follette III to the author, October 9, 2005.

33. "Radio Comment on President Roosevelt's Message to Congress," January 6, 1941, folder 1, box 138, PFL Papers. The address was reprinted in *The Progressive*, January 11, 1941, and *Vital Speeches of the Day*, February 15, 1941; *Capital Times*, January 7, 1941.

34. "Second Session on the President's Lend-Lease Plan," *Town Meeting* 6 (February 3, 1941): 4–21; *Wisconsin State Journal*, January 31, 1941; *Capital Times*, January 31, 1941. August Derleth called Phil's debate "one of the most masterful addresses you ever made"; see Derleth to PFL, February 11, 1941, folder 2, box 138, PFL Papers. For Lend-Lease, see Kennedy, *Freedom from Fear*, 465–70.

35. Congress, Senate, Committee on Foreign Relations, *To Promote the Defense of the United States: Hearings before the Committee on Foreign Relations*, 77th Congress, 1st Sess., February 3, 1941, pp. 262–87; *New York Times*, February 4, 1941; *Capital Times*, February 3, 1941; *Wisconsin State Journal*, February 3, 1941; Kennedy, *Freedom from Fear*, 470–75.

36. R. Douglas Stuart to PFL, February 18, 1941, and proposed itinerary for California cities in late February, both in folder 2, box 138; R. Douglas Stuart telegram to PFL, March 29, 1941; and Ivan H. Light to PFL, March 31, 1941, both in folder 3, box 138; and "Peace or War in America: A Debate Between Upton Sinclair and the Hon. Philip F. La Follette," March 13, 1941, folder 3, box 120, all in PFL Papers.

37. R. Douglas Stuart to PFL, May 9, 1941, and Lillian McCarthy to James H. Meuler, May 10, 1941, both in folder 4, box 138; Robert Bliss to PFL, August 14, 1941, folder 6, box 138, PFL Papers. See also clippings from May and June in vol. 28, ibid.; PFL to FL, May 11, 1941 (quotation), and IBL to FL, October 20, 1941, both in A48, La Follette Family Papers.

38. See, for example, G. Erle Ingram to PFL, January 3, 1941, folder 1; PFL to G. Erle Ingram, March 3, 1941, folder 3; and T. E. McGillian to PFL, May 15, 1941, folder 4, all in box 138; Robert A. Scott to PFL, November 8, 1941, folder 2, box 139; and clippings from February and March, vol. 28, all in PFL Papers; *Wisconsin State Journal*, June 20, 1941.

39. *Capital Times*, March 6, 1941.

40. Johnson, *Robert M. La Follette, Jr.*, 79–81; PFL to John Burnham, et al., August 4, 1941; and John T. Flynn to PFL, August 6, 1941, both in folder 6, box 138, PFL Papers.

41. "What Next for America?" November 1, 1941, folder 3, box 120, PFL Papers; the quotation is from p. 20. A slightly different version of the address was printed on the front page of *The Progressive*, November 15, 1941. For North Atlantic escorts, see Kennedy, *Freedom from Fear*, 498–500.

42. For correspondence in reaction to the address, see folder 2, box 139, PFL Papers. The quotation is from George H. Corey to PFL, November 17, 1941.

43. Evelyn Palmer to PFL, November 17, 1941; and William S. Foulis to PFL, December 20, 1941, both in folder 2, box 139; and R. Douglas Stuart to PFL, January 3, 1942, folder 4, box 139, all in PFL Papers.

44. Philip F. La Follette, "With MacArthur in the Pacific: A Memoir by Philip F. La Follette," *Wisconsin Magazine of History* 64 (Winter 1980–81): 85; Lois [?] to IBL, January 14, 1942; and ML to IBL and PFL, March 22, 1942, both in folder 4, box 139, PFL Papers; IBL to FL, March 16, 1942, box A48, La Follette Family Papers; "Until

We Meet Again," *The Progressive*, March 21, 1942; Judith Sorem and Robert La Follette III to the author, October 9, 2005.

45. La Follette, *Adventure in Politics*, 267–68. For the farm, see IBL to FL, November 13, 1941; and PFL to FL, November 20, 1941, both in box A48, La Follette Family Papers. Judith Sorem and Robert La Follette III to the author, October 9, 2005.

46. See PFL correspondence for April and May 1942, folders 4 and 5, box 139, PFL Papers.

47. PFL to RML III, November 17, 1942; PFL to IBL, December 7, 1942; and Robert E. Wood to PFL, December 10, 1942, all in folder 1, box 140; and PFL to IBL, March 18, 1943, folder 3, box 142, all in PFL Papers. The quotation is included in IBL to RML Jr., January 12, 1943, box A49, La Follette Family Papers. For a detailed account of Phil's experiences with MacArthur in the South Pacific, see La Follette, "With MacArthur in the Pacific," 86–106.

48. PFL to RML Jr., March 18, 1943, box A49, La Follette Family Papers.

49. PFL to RML Jr., March 5, 1942, box A49, ibid.; RML Jr. to PFL, March 9, 1942, folder 4, box 139, PFL Papers; Johnson, *Robert M. La Follette*, 83–87; Frank P. Zeidler to the author, March 11, 2003. Zeidler was the Socialist nominee for governor in 1942.

50. Johnson, *Robert M. La Follette*, 87; PFL to IBL, April 4, 1942; and Morris Rubin to PFL, c. April 18, 1942, both in folder 4, box 139, PFL Papers.

51. PFL to IBL, May 15, 1942, folder 5, box 139, PFL Papers.

52. Primary election figures are from the 1944 *Wisconsin Blue Book*, 504–8; RML Jr. to PFL, September 17, 1942; IBL to PFL, September 16, 21, 22, and 24, 1942; and Alf Rogers to PFL, September 25, 1942, all in folder 6; and RML Jr. to PFL, November 2, 1942, folder 7, all in box 139, PFL Papers; IBL to RML Jr., October 1, 1942, box A48, La Follette Family Papers.

53. Herb Zander to PFL, no date (late September 1942); IBL to PFL, November 3, 1942; and RML Jr. to PFL, November 10, 1942, all in folder 7, box 139; and Thomas Haydon to PFL, January 5, 1943, folder 2, box 140, all in PFL Papers. Election results are from 1944 *Wisconsin Blue Book*, 572–85. *Chicago Tribune*, October 3, 1942, enclosed in IBL to RML Jr., October 6, 1942, box A48, La Follette Family Papers; *Wisconsin State Journal*, November 4, 1942. See also Johnson, *Robert M. La Follette*, 93–94.

54. Alf Rogers to PFL, November 18, 1942; Orland Loomis to PFL, November 24, 1942; and IBL to PFL, November 27, 1942, all in folder 7, box 139; Glenn Roberts to PFL, December 10, 1942, folder 1, box 140; and RML Jr. to PFL, January 5, 1943, folder 3, box 140, all in PFL Papers.

55. Glenn Roberts to PFL, January 2 and 28, 1943; and Alf Rogers to PFL, February 2, 1943, all in folder 2, box 140, PFL Papers; PFL to RML Jr., February 12, 1943, box A49, La Follette Family Papers.

56. PFL to IBL, February 20, 1943; and RML Jr. to PFL, February 24, 1943, both in folder 2, box 140; IBL to PFL, March 7, 1943, folder 3, box 140; and IBL to PFL May 10, 1943, folder 4, box 140, all in PFL Papers; RML Jr. to PFL, June 24, 1943, box A49, La Follette Family Papers.

57. The quotation is from IBL to PFL, May 12, 1943. See also IBL to PFL, May 20 and 27, 1943, both in folder 4, box 140; Gordon Sinykin to PFL, June 3, 1943; and Alf Rogers to PFL, June 4, 1943, all in folder 5, box 140, PFL Papers.

58. RML Jr. to PFL, July 24, 1943, box A49, La Follette Family Papers; PFL to IBL, June 30, 1943, folder 5, box 140, PFL Papers.

59. IBL to PFL, July 4, 1943, and PFL to IBL, July 14, 1943, both in folder 5, box 140; PFL to RML Jr., and August 6, 1943; and RML Jr. to PFL, September 1, 1943, both in box A49, La Follette Family Papers. See also Maney, *"Young Bob,"* 259–64.

60. PFL to RML Jr., May 11 and 24, 1944; IBL to RML Jr., May 13, 1944; and RML Jr. to PFL, May 19, 1944, all in box A49, La Follette Family Papers.

61. Primary election results are from the 1946 *Wisconsin Blue Book*, 590–607; RML Jr., to FL, August 9, 1944, box A49, La Follette Family Papers; Johnson, *Robert M. La Follette*, 98.

62. RML Jr., to "Dear Ones," September 18 and 20, 1944; RML Jr. to FL, September 28, 1944; and PFL to RML Jr., October 22, 1944, all in box A49, La Follette Family Papers.; *Capital Times*, November 2, 1944; Gaylord Nelson, telephone conversation with the author, February 25, 2003.

63. Election statistics are from the 1946 *Wisconsin Blue Book*, 664–78.

64. PFL to RML Jr., November 21, 1944; and Glenn Roberts to RML Jr., May 12 and 24, 1945, all in box A49, La Follette Family Papers.

65. Johnson, *Robert M. La Follette*, 104–5; Judith Sorem and Robert La Follette III to the author, October 9, 2005.

66. La Follette, *Adventure in Politics*, 275.

67. Ibid., 275–76.

68. Ibid., 225–26; PFL to RML Jr., May 13, 1946, box A50, La Follette Family Papers; PFL to RML III, July 28 and 31, 1946, folder 5, box 143, PFL Papers. The quotation is from the July 31 letter.

69. William T. Rawleigh to PFL, August 15, 1946. Wisconsin senator Fred Risser explained that the conservatives had so consolidated their grip on the party machinery during the Progressives' absence that they stood no chance of doing well in the primary campaigns.

70. Election results are from the 1948 *Wisconsin Blue Book*, 604. Robert's defeat received extensive notice in the state and national press. See *Wisconsin State Journal*, August 14, 1946; *Milwaukee Sentinel*, August 14, 1946; *Milwaukee Journal*, August 14, 1946; *Capital Times*, August 14, 1946; *New York Times*, August 15, 1946; "La Follette's Defeat," *Life*, August 26, 1946, pp. 26–27; "La Follette's Folly," *The Nation*, August 24, 1946, pp. 200–201; "La Follette Nadir," *Newsweek*, August 26, 1946, pp. 16–17. Nelson was aided by a last-minute endorsement by the *Capital Times* despite the fact that Risser had a 100 percent Progressive voting record. Judith Sorem and Robert La Follette III to the author, October 9, 2005.

71. IBL to RML Jr., November 21, 1946, folder 5, box 143, PFL Papers. The best account of Robert's primary defeat is in Maney, *"Young Bob,"* 287–304. There is some disagreement as to where Progressives went after 1946. Fred Risser suggested that

many did try to follow the La Follettes back to the Republicans, but Gaylord Nelson recalled that most supporters looked to the Democratic Party, especially in Dane County and the northern counties. For the "progressivization" of the Democrats, see Richard C. Haney, "The Rise of Wisconsin's New Democrats: A Political Realignment in the Mid-Twentieth Century," *Wisconsin Magazine of History* 58 (Winter 1974–75): 91–106.

EPILOGUE

1. PFL to RML Jr., November 7, 1946, box A50, La Follette Family Papers, Manuscripts Division, Library of Congress. In 1940 the La Follettes had hired Morris H. Rubin as editor. Over the next six years, Rubin ran the magazine with little supervision from Phil, who was in the army, or Robert, who was preoccupied with his duties in the United States Senate.

2. Philip F. La Follette, *Adventure in Politics: The Memoirs of Philip La Follette*, Donald Young, ed. (New York: Holt Rinehart and Winston, 1970), 271–72; PFL to RML III, June 13 and August 24, 1945, folder 4, box 143; statement on universal military service and "A Sound American Policy," both in folder 4, box 120, all in Philip F. La Follette Papers, Archives Division, Wisconsin Historical Society; *Milwaukee Journal*, September 27, 1945.

3. Judith Sorem and Robert La Follette III to the author, October 5, 2005.

4. Lucy Freeman, Sherry La Follette, and George A. Zabriskie, *Belle: The Biography of Belle Case La Follette* (New York: Beaufort Books, 1986), 241; Judith Sorem and Robert La Follette III to the author, October 9, 2005.

5. IBL to PFL, February 20, 1947, folder 2, box 146, PFL Papers.

6. Edward M. Coffman and Paul H. Hass, eds., "With MacArthur in the Pacific: A Memoir by Philip F. La Follette," *Wisconsin Magazine of History* 64 (Winter 1980–81): 94–95.

7. Robert E. Wood to PFL, December 4, 1947, and enclosures, folder 3, box 144; PFL to Frank B. Keefe, January 24, 1946, folder 1, box 144; and radio address for Douglas MacArthur for President, folder 5, box 145, all in PFL Papers; *Chicago Tribune*, January 26, 1948.

8. Election results are from the 1948 *Wisconsin Blue Book*, 700–703. PFL to GM, April 15, 1948, box A50, La Follette Family Papers; press release, October 18, 1948, folder 3, box 146; and PFL to Earl Warren, January 10, 1952, folder 4, box 147, both in PFL Papers.

9. PFL to H. William Ihrig, January 30, 1952, folder 4, box 147, PFL Papers. See also PFL to Edward M. Blumenfeld, April 21, 1952, folder 5, box 147, ibid., for similar sentiments.

10. Judith Sorem and Robert La Follette III to the author, October 5, 2005.

11. La Follette, *Adventure in Politics*, 279–80.

12. IBL to PFL, November 29, 1948, folder 5, box 146, PFL Papers; Bernard Weisberger, *The La Follettes of Wisconsin: Love and Politics in Progressive America* (Madison: University of Wisconsin Press, 1994), 315–16.

13. Judith Sorem and Robert La Follette III to the author, October 9, 2005.

14. Ibid. For Phil's involvement with the corporation, see Edward Litchfield to PFL, September 13, 1947, folder 2, box 146; PFL to Kenneth Royall, September 20, 1947, folder 2, box 146; PFL to Hugo H. Hauser, October 14, 1947, folder 2, box 146; IBL to PFL, November 29 and December 2, 1948, folder 5, box 146; PFL to FL, November 4, 1953, folder 2, box 148; and Gordan Sinykin to PFL, April 22, 1957, folder 3, box 148, all in PFL Papers.

15. *Capital Times*, December 7, 1959; *Wisconsin State Journal*, April 27, 1960.

16. *Capital Times*, August 19, 1965; *New York Times*, August 19, 1965; Weisberger, *La Follettes of Wisconsin*, 316; Judith Sorem and Robert La Follette III to the author, October 9, 2005.

17. Weisberger, *The La Follettes of Wisconsin*, 315–17; Judith Sorem and Robert La Follette III to the author, October 9, 2005.

18. "A New Movement, the National Progressives of America, Is Under Way," folder 3, box 119, PFL Papers.

Bibliography

MANUSCRIPT COLLECTIONS

Thomas Amlie Papers. Archives Division. Wisconsin Historical Society.
John J. Blaine Papers. Archives Division. Wisconsin Historical Society.
John R. Commons Papers. Archives Division. Wisconsin Historical Society.
La Follette Family Papers. Manuscripts Division. Library of Congress.
Philip F. La Follette Papers. Archives Division. Wisconsin Historical Society.
Albert Schmedeman Papers. Archives Division. Wisconsin Historical Society.

INTERVIEWS AND CORRESPONDENCE WITH THE AUTHOR

La Follette, Bronson. Telephone conversation. January 2, 2003.
Nelson, Gaylord. Telephone conversation. February 25, 2003.
Risser, Fred A. Interview. November 13, 2002.
Sorem, Judith, and Robert La Follette III. Letter to the author. October 9, 2005.
Zeidler, Frank P. Letter to the author. March 11, 2003.

PRIMARY ARTICLES

Adamic, Louis. "La Follette Progressives Face the Future." *The Nation* 140 (February 20, 1935): 213–15.

_____. "A Talk with Phil La Follette." *The Nation* 140 (February 27, 1935): 242–45.

"After La Follette—What?" *Literary Digest* 86 (July 4, 1925): 9–11.

"Another La Follette in the Senate?" *Literary Digest* 86 (September 26, 1925): 10–11.

Barry, Richard. "A Radical in Power: A Study of La Follette." *Outlook* 132 (November 29, 1922): 566–67.

Bliven, Bruce. "Robert M. La Follette's Place in Our History." *Current History* 22 (August 1925): 716.

Blythe, Samuel G. "Let X=La Follette." *Saturday Evening Post* 197 (October 18, 1924): 1–4+.

Cobb, Irvin S. "The Thunders of Silence." *Saturday Evening Post* 190 (February 9, 1918): 3–5 and 38–42.

Conway, W. J. "Taxation in Wisconsin." *Wisconsin Blue Book* (1927): 115–38.

"Dark Days Ahead: A Dialogue on the Bankruptcy of Business Leadership." *Forum* 84 (October 1930): 200–207.

Davenport, Walter. "Fighting Blood." *Collier's* 89 (April 23, 1932): 10–11+.

_____. "An Uncertain Party." *Collier's* 97 (May 23, 1936): 14–15+.

Dell, Robert. "Phil La Follette Is Right." *The Nation* 148 (April 29, 1939): 487–88.

Devens, Stanley Price. "Wisconsin after La Follette." *Christian Century* (June 21, 1939): 793.

Fried, Orrin A. "Wisconsin Manufacturing Since 1929." *Wisconsin Blue Book* (1933): 141–42.

Frost, Stanley. "The Scramble for 'Fighting Bob's' Shoes." *Outlook* 140 (July 29, 1925): 460–62.

Gale, Zona. "Americans We Like." *The Nation* 126 (February 15, 1928): 180–82.

Garrett, Garet. "Section Seven-A at Sheboygan." *Saturday Evening Post* (October 27, 1934): 5–7+.

"A Great Message." *The Nation* 133 (December 9, 1931): 403.

Groves, Harold. "The Wisconsin State Income Tax." *Wisconsin Blue Book* (1933): 51–67.

Hallgren, Mauritz A. "Governor La Follette." *The Nation* 82 (April 29, 1931): 473–75.

Hard, William. "That Man La Follette." *The Nation* 119 (July 16, 1924): 65.

"In La Follette-Land." *Time* (October 22, 1928): 11–12.

Kent, Frank R. "Little Bob Wins." *The Nation* 121 (December 30, 1925): 758.

"La Follette as a Boss Ventriloquist." *Current Opinion* 77 (August 1924): 143–44.

"La Follette, Dictator." *The Nation* 118 (April 2, 1924): 360.

La Follette, Philip F. Review of John Gunther, *The Riddle of MacArthur.* *Freeman*, May 7, 1951, n.p.

"La Follette Nadir." *Newsweek* (August 26, 1946): 16–17.

"La Follette Thunder." *The Nation* 146 (April 30, 1938): 492–93.

"La Follette's Defeat." *Life* (August 26, 1946): 26–27.

"La Follette's Folly." *The Nation* 163 (August 24, 1946): 200–201.

Lewis, Sinclair. "Be Brisk with Babbitt." *The Nation* 119 (October 15, 1924): 411.

Lovett, Robert M. "April Hopes in Madison." *New Republic* 95 (May 11, 1935): 13–14.

Lyon, Thomas E. "The Wisconsin Tax System." *Wisconsin Blue Book* (1925): 111–33.

McMullin, James. "Progressive—1938 Model." *Commentator* (July 1938).

"Obituary." *Outlook* 140 (July 1, 1925): 323.

"A Political Realignment in Wisconsin." *New Republic* 92 (September 1, 1937): 89.

Pringle, Henry F. "Youth at the Top: United States Senator Robert M. La Follette, Jr." *World's Work: A History of Our Time* 58 (May 1929): 85+.

"Progressives at Madison." *Time* (May 9, 1938): 3–4.

"Recessional." *Saturday Evening Post* 209 (August 1, 1936): 22.

"Robert Marion La Follette: A Swashbuckling Dumas Hero Caught and Civilized." *Current Opinion* 77 (September 1924): 298–99.

"Second Session on the President's Lend-Lease Plan." *Town Meeting* 6 (February 3, 1941): 4–21.

"Should the Arms Embargo Be Lifted?" *Town Meeting* 5 (October 14, 1939): 1–32.

Steffens, Lincoln. "Wisconsin: A State Where the People Have Restored Representative Government—The Story of Governor La Follette." *McClure's* 23 (October 1904): 563–79.

"Success to Robert La Follette." *The Nation* 115 (August 16, 1922): 160.

Turner, Frederick Jackson. "Contributions of the West to American Democracy." *The Frontier in American History*. New York: Henry Holt and Company, 1920: 243–68.

———. "The Middle West." *The Frontier in American History*. New York: Henry Holt and Company, 1920: 126–56.

"Young Bob." *The Nation* 121 (July 8, 1925): 59.

Witte, Edwin. "Wisconsin in the 1930 Census." *Wisconsin Blue Book* (1933): 103–32.

PRIMARY BOOKS

Barton, Albert O. *La Follette's Winning of Wisconsin*. Madison, WI: Homestead Printing Company, 1922.

Chapple, John B. *La Follette Road to Communism—Must We Go Further Along That Road?* Ashland: privately printed, 1936.

Complete Presidential Press Conferences of Franklin D. Roosevelt. New York: Da Capo Press, 1972.

Dos Passos, John. *The 42nd Parallel*. Boston: Houghton Mifflin Company, 1930.

Roosevelt, Elliott, ed. *FDR: His Personal Letters, 1928–1945*. New York: 1950.

Roosevelt, Franklin D. *Looking Forward*. New York: John Day Company, 1933.

Trevelyan, George Macaulay. *Life of John Bright*. New York: Houghton Mifflin, 1913.

Wallace, Henry A. *New Frontiers*. New York: Reynal and Hitchcock, 1934.

MEMOIRS AND AUTOBIOGRAPHY

Chase, Mary Ellen. *A Goodly Fellowship*. New York: The MacMillan Company, 1940.

Evjue, William T. *A Fighting Editor*. Madison, WI: Wells Printing Company, Inc., 1968.

Frear, James A. *Forty Years of Progressive Public Service Reasonably Filled with Thorns and Flowers*. Washington, D.C.: Associated Writers, 1937.

Groves, Harold. "In and Out of the Ivory Tower." Unpublished manuscript, 1969, Wisconsin Historical Society.

Ickes, Harold. *The Secret Diary of Harold Ickes*. Two vols. New York: Simon and Schuster, 1954.

Jorgenson, Arthur W., Sr. "Getting By: A Schoolteacher's Recollection of the Depression Years." *Wisconsin Magazine of History* 68 (Summer 1985): 266–83.

La Follette, Isabel Bacon. "If You Can Take It." Unpublished manuscript, box 165, Philip F. La Follette Papers.

La Follette, Philip F. *Adventure in Politics: The Memoirs of Philip La Follette.* Donald Young, ed. New York: Holt, Rinehart and Winston, 1970.

———. "With MacArthur in the Pacific: A Memoir by Philip F. La Follette." *Wisconsin Magazine of History* 64 (Winter 1980–81): 83–106.

La Follette, Robert M., Sr. *La Follette's Autobiography: A Personal Narrative of Political Experiences.* Madison, WI: The Robert M. La Follette Company, 1913.

Middleton, George. *These Things Are Mine: The Autobiography of a Journeyman Playwright.* New York: The MacMillan Company, 1947.

Raushenbush, Paul A. and Elizabeth Brandeis Raushenbush. *Our "U. C." Story: 1930–1967.* Madison, WI: privately printed, 1979.

NEWSPAPERS AND MAGAZINES

Albuquerque (NM) Journal
Antigo Journal
Augusta Union
Chicago Herald-Examiner
Chicago Tribune
Cleveland Plain Dealer
Eau Claire Leader
Fennimore Times
Freeport (IL) Journal-Standard
Green Bay Press Gazette
Janesville Gazette
Kansas City (MO) Times
Kenosha News
La Crosse Tribune
London Daily Telegraph
London Times
Los Angeles Examiner
Los Angeles Illustrated Daily News
Madison Capital Times
Marshfield News-Herald
Milwaukee Journal

Milwaukee Journal-Sentinel
Milwaukee Sentinel
Mondovi Herald
The Nation
New York Evening Post
New York Herald Tribune
New York Times
New York World-Telegram
Oshkosh Northwestern
Pittsburgh Press
Portage Register-Democrat
Portland Oregonian
The Progressive (Founded as *La Follette's Weekly Magazine*)
Richland Center Republican and Observer
Racine Journal-Times
Racine Times-Call
Rhinelander News
Rochester (NY) Evening Journal and Post-Express
Rochester (NY) Journal
Rochester (NY) Times-Union
Sheboygan Press
Sheboygan Times
St. Louis Globe-Democrat
St. Louis Post-Dispatch
St. Paul Pioneer Press
Superior Evening Telegram
Superior Telegram
Washington Herald
Washington Post
Washington Star
Wausau Record-Herald
Wisconsin State Journal

GOVERNMENT PUBLICATIONS

Lescohier, Don D. and Florence Peterson. *The Alleviation of Unemployment in Wisconsin*. Madison: Industrial Commission of Wisconsin, 1931.

Perrigo, H. W. *General Relief in Wisconsin: 1848–1935*. Madison: Wisconsin Public Welfare Department, 1939.

U.S. Congress. Senate. *Acceptance and Unveiling of the Statue of Robert Marion La Follette*. 71st Cong., 1st Sess., 1929. Senate Document 4.

U.S. Congress. Senate. Committee on Foreign Relations. *To Promote the Defense of the United States: Hearings before the Committee on Foreign Relations*. 77th Cong., 1st Sess., February 3, 1941.

U.S. Congress. Senate. Debate over declaration of war with Germany. 65th Cong., 1st Sess. *Congressional Record* (April 4, 1917), vol. 55, part 1.

U.S. Congress. Senate. "Speech of Robert M. La Follette: Hearings Before a Subcommittee of the Committee of Privileges and Elections." 65th Cong., 1st Sess., 1917.

Wisconsin Blue Book.

Wisconsin. Industrial Commission. *Unemployment Relief in Wisconsin, 1932–1933*. Madison: 1933.

Wisconsin. Legislature. *Henry A. Huber, Late Lieutenant Governor: Memorial Exercises*. 61st Session, 1933.

Wisconsin. Legislature. *Report of the Wisconsin Legislative Interim Committee on Unemployment, Submitted to the Governor and the 1931 Special Session of the Wisconsin Legislature*. Madison: 1931.

Wisconsin. Legislature. *Senate Journal*. Special Session, 1918.

Wisconsin. *Messages and Addresses to the Legislature: Philip F. La Follette*. Madison: 1933.

Wisconsin. *Messages and Addresses of Governor Philip F. La Follette*. Madison: 1939.

Wisconsin. *Messages to the Legislature and Proclamations of John J. Blaine, Governor, 1921–1927*. Madison: 1927.

Wisconsin. Public Welfare Department. *Financial Conditions of Wisconsin Counties*. Madison, 1936.

THESES AND DISSERTATIONS

Backstrom, Charles H. "The Progressive Party of Wisconsin, 1934–1946." Doctoral dissertation, University of Wisconsin, 1957.

Lucker, Jeffrey. "The Politics of Prohibition." MA thesis, University of Wisconsin, 1968.

Schmidt, Lester F. "The Farmer-Labor Progressive Federation: The Study of a 'United Front' Movement among Wisconsin Liberals, 1934–1941." Doctoral dissertation, University of Wisconsin, 1955.

SECONDARY ARTICLES

Altmeyer, Arthur J. "The Wisconsin Idea and Social Security." *Wisconsin Magazine of History* 42 (Autumn 1958): 19–25.

Brownlee, W. Elliot, Jr. "Income Taxation and the Political Economy of Wisconsin." *Wisconsin Magazine of History* 59 (Summer 1976): 311–30.

Cooper, John Milton, Jr. "Robert M. La Follette: Political Prophet." *Wisconsin Magazine of History* 69 (Winter 1985–86): 90–105.

Gerstle, Gary. "The Protean Character of American Liberalism." *American Historical Review* 100 (October 1994): 1043–73.

Goldberg, Robert A. "The Ku Klux Klan in Madison, 1922–1927." *Wisconsin Magazine of History* 58 (Autumn 1974): 31–44.

Haney, Richard C. "The Rise of Wisconsin's New Democrats: A Political Realignment in the Mid-Twentieth Century." *Wisconsin Magazine of History* 58 (Winter 1974–75): 91–106.

Hoglund, A. William. "Wisconsin Dairy Farmers on Strike." *Agricultural History* 35 (January 1961): 25–42.

Jacobs, Herbert. "The Wisconsin Milk Strikes." *Wisconsin Magazine of History* 35 (Autumn 1951): 30–35.

Kasparek, Jonathan. "FDR's 'Old Friends' in Wisconsin: Presidential Finesse in the Land of La Follette." *Wisconsin Magazine of History* 84 (Summer 2001): 16–25.

Kesselman, Steven. "The Frontier Thesis and the Great Depression." *Journal of the History of Ideas* 29 (April 1968): 253–68.

Link, Arthur. "What Happened to the Progressive Movement in the 1920s?" *American Historical Review* 64 (July 1959): 833–51.

McCoy, Donald R. "The Formation of the Wisconsin Progressive Party in 1934." *The Historian* 14 (Autumn 1951): 70–90.

———. "The Progressive National Committee of 1936." *Western Political Quarterly* 9 (June 1956): 454–69.

Miller, John E. "Governor Philip F. La Follette's Shifting Priorities from Redistribution to Expansion." *Mid-America* 58 (April–July 1976): 119–26.

Nelson, Daniel. "The Origins of Unemployment Insurance in Wisconsin." *Wisconsin Magazine of History* 51 (Winter 1967–68): 109–21.

Nettels, Curtis. "Frederick Jackson Turner and the New Deal." *Wisconsin Magazine of History* 17 (March 1934): 257–65.

O'Brien, Patrick G. "Senator John J. Blaine: An Independent Progressive During 'Normalcy.'" *Wisconsin Magazine of History* 60 (Autumn 1976): 25–41.

Rosenof, Theodore. "The Political Education of an American Radical: Thomas Amlie in the 1930s." *Wisconsin Magazine of History* 58 (Autumn 1974): 21–34.

_____. "'Young Bob' La Follette on American Capitalism." *Wisconsin Magazine of History* 55 (Winter 1971–72): 130–39.

Stark, John O. "Harold M. Groves and Wisconsin Taxes." *Wisconsin Magazine of History* 74 (Spring 1991): 196–214.

Unger, Nancy. "The Two Worlds of Belle Case La Follette." *Wisconsin Magazine of History* 83 (Winter 1999–2000), 83–110.

Weiss, Stuart L. "Thomas Amlie and the New Deal." *Mid-America* 59 (January 1977), 19–23.

Zink, Steven D. "Glenn Frank of the University of Wisconsin: A Reinterpretation." *Wisconsin Magazine of History* 62 (Winter 1978–79): 91–127.

SECONDARY BOOKS

Brinkley, Alan. *Voices of Protest: Huey Long, Father Coughlin and the Great Depression.* New York: Vintage Books, 1983.

Burns, James MacGregor. *Roosevelt: The Lion and the Fox, 1882–1940.* New York: Harcourt Brace, 1956.

Clark, James I. *Cutover Problems: Colonization, Depression, Reforestation.* Madison: State Historical Society of Wisconsin, 1956.

_____. *Wisconsin Meets the Great Depression.* Madison: State Historical Society of Wisconsin, 1956.

Cronon, E. David and John W. Jenkins. *The University of Wisconsin: Politics, Depression, and War.* Madison: University of Wisconsin Press, 1994.

Curti, Merle and Vernon Carstenson. *The University of Wisconsin: A History, 1848–1925.* Two vols. Madison: University of Wisconsin Press, 1949.

Epstein, Leon D. *Politics in Wisconsin.* Madison: University of Wisconsin Press, 1958.

Freeman, Lucy, Sherry La Follette, and George A. Zabriskie. *Belle: The Biography of Belle Case La Follette.* New York: Beaufort Books, 1986.

Glad, Paul. *History of Wisconsin: War, a New Era, and Depression, 1914–1940.* Madison: State Historical Society of Wisconsin, 1990.

Graham, Otis L. *An Encore for Reform: Old Progressives and the New Deal.* New York: Oxford University Press, 1967.

Hofstadter, Richard. *The Age of Reform: From Bryan to F.D.R.* New York: Vintage Press, 1955.

Johnson, Roger T. *Robert M. La Follette, Jr., and the Decline of the Progressive Party.* Reprint edition. New York: Archon Books, 1970.

Kennedy, David M. *Freedom from Fear: The American People in Depression and War, 1929–1945.* New York: Oxford University Press, 1999.

Larsen, Lawrence H. *The President Wore Spats: A Biography of Glenn Frank.* Madison: State Historical Society of Wisconsin, 1965.

La Follette, Belle Case and Fola La Follette. *Robert M. La Follette: June 14, 1855–June 18, 1925.* New York: The MacMillan Company, 1953.

Leuchtenberg, William. *Franklin Delano Roosevelt and the New Deal, 1932–1940.* New York: Harper and Row, 1963.

MacKay, Kenneth Campbell. *The Progressive Movement of 1924.* New York: Columbia University Press, 1947.

Maney, Patrick J. *"Young Bob" La Follette: A Biography of Robert M. La Follette, Jr., 1895–1953.* Columbia: University of Missouri Press, 1978.

Margulies, Herbert F. *The Decline of the Progressive Movement in Wisconsin: 1890–1920.* Madison: State Historical Society of Wisconsin, 1968.

_____. *Senator Lenroot of Wisconsin: A Political Biography, 1900–1929.* Columbia: University of Missouri Press, 1977.

Maxwell, *Robert S. La Follette and the Rise of the Progressives in Wisconsin.* Madison: State Historical Society of Wisconsin, 1956.

_____. *Emanuel Philipp: Wisconsin Stalwart.* Madison: State Historical Society of Wisconsin, 1959.

Mermin, Samuel. *Jurisprudence and Statecraft: The Wisconsin Development Authority and Its Implications.* Madison: 1963.

Merrill, Horace Samuel. *William Freeman Vilas: Doctrinaire Democrat.* Madison: State Historical Society of Wisconsin, 1954.

Miller, Donald L. *The New American Radicalism: Alfred M. Bingham and Non-Marxian Insurgency in the New Deal Era.* Port Washington, NY: Kennikat Press, 1979.

Miller, John E. *Governor Philip F. La Follette, the Wisconsin Progressives, and the New Deal.* Columbia: University of Missouri Press, 1982.

Mowry, George E. *The Era of Theodore Roosevelt and the Birth of Modern America.* New York: Harper and Row, 1953.

Nye, Russel B. *Midwestern Progressive Politics: A Historical Study of Its Origins and Development, 1870–1950.* East Lansing: Michigan State University Press, 1951.

Patterson, James T. *The New Deal and the States: Federalism in Transition*. Princeton: Princeton University Press, 1969.

Rosenof, Theodore. *Dogma, Depression, and the New Deal: The Debate of Political Leaders over Economic Recovery*. Port Washington, NY: Kennikat Press, 1975.

Schlesinger, Arthur. *The Crisis of the Old Order*. Boston: Houghton Mifflin, 1957.

———. *The Politics of Upheaval*. Boston: Houghton Mifflin, 1960.

Schumann, Alfred R. *No Peddlers Allowed*. Appleton, WI: C. C. Nelson Publishing Company, 1948.

Thelen, David P. *The Early Life of Robert M. La Follette, 1855–1884*. Chicago: Loyola University Press, 1966.

Unger, Nancy C. *Fighting Bob La Follette: The Righteous Reformer*. Chapel Hill: University of North Carolina Press, 2000.

Uphoff, Walter H. *Kohler on Strike: Thirty Years of Conflict*. Boston: Beacon Press, 1966.

Weisberger, Bernard A. *The La Follettes of Wisconsin: Love and Politics in Progressive America*. Madison: University of Wisconsin Press, 1994.

Wrobel, David M. *The End of American Exceptionalism: Frontier Anxiety from the Old West to the New Deal*. Lawrence: University Press of Kansas, 1993.

Index

Adams, Wisc., 132

Adams County, 29

Addams, Jane, xii

Agricultural Adjustment Act, 144, 145, 156, 191, 207

Agricultural Adjustment Administration, 144, 173, 183

Alfonsi, Paul, 207, 217, 242

Allegheny County (Pennsylvania) League of Women Voters, 176

American Association of University Women, 106

American Federation of Labor, xii, 202, 215; Federal Labor Union No. 18545, p. 148

American Federation of Teachers, 114

America First Committee, 234, 235, 236, 237, 239

American Occupation Zone, 255

Ames, Iowa, 34

Amlie, Thomas, 148, 149, 150, 151, 152, 153, 156, 157, 205, 217, 219, 231, 238, 239

Ancient Order of Hibernians, 27

Antigo Journal, 85

Anti-Saloon League, 68

Appleton, Wisc., 68, 94, 153, 185

Arbeiter Partei, 140

Armed Ship Bill, 11, 12

Ashland, Wisc., 94, 158, 193

Ashland County, 218

Ashland Press, 133

Associated Academic Conference, 145

Associated Charities, 99

Associated Press, 13, 102, 119, 213

Auburndale, Wisc., 132

Augusta, Wisc., 157

Babbitt, George F. (fictional character), quoted, xii

Bacon, Isabel (Isen). See La Follette, Isabel (Isen) Bacon

Bading, Gerhard, 107

Bancroft, Levi, 131

Baraboo, Wisc., 3, 6, 8, 220

Barron County, 70

Barry, Harry, 42

Barton, Albert O., 114

Bascom, John, 71

Battle Creek Sanatorium, 70–71

"Battle of Durham Hill," 147

Bayonne, N.J., 23

Beard, Charles A., 112, 119

Beaver Dam, Wisc., 86, 133, 192

Beck, Joseph, 7, 67, 82–83, 84, 87, 92, 102, 106, 115, 129

Beloit, Wisc., 94, 99

Bennet, J. Henry, 14

Benson, Elmer, 203

Benz, Alexander, 246

Berger, Victor, 73

Berle, Adolph, 213

Berlin, Germany, 140, 142

Beta Theta Pi fraternity, 15, 57

Biloxi, Miss., 91, 101

Bingham, Alfred, 189, 205

Blaine, Anna, 35; (illus.), 60

Blaine, Governor John, 27, 29, 32, 35, 42, 67, 68, 69, 70, 71, 72, 73, 74, 75, 77, 78, 79, 80, 81, 813, 84, 86, 89,

90, 91, 93, 101, 105, 106, 108, 126, 131, 133, 134, 149, 150, 155, 223; calls special Senate election, 74; runs for Senate, 75, 80; supports Robert Jr., 76; (illus.), 60
Blanchard, George, 148
Boer War, 26
Boileau, Gerald, 197
Bolens, Harry, 183
Bolles, Stephen, 238
Bootlegging, 38–39, 41, 42
Borah, William E., xiii, 2, 189, 204
Boston Evening Transcript, 12
Boston Herald, 216
Bowles, Chester, 230, 232
Brandeis, Alice, 2
Brandeis, Elizabeth, xvi, 122
Brandeis, Louis, 2, 7, 119
Brandt, Karl, 140
Bright, John, 26
Broun, Heywood, 216
Bryan, William Jennings, 12, 13
Bullitt, William, 139
Bureau of Unemployment Research, 97
Burke, Edmund, 26

Callahan, John, 72, 200
Capital City Bank, 128
Capital Times, 35, 38, 39, 40, 42, 80, 83, 86, 89–90, 91, 104, 114, 127, 134, 143, 205, 206, 208, 219, 237, 245
Carter, Hodding, 175
Case, Belle. *See* La Follette, Belle Case
Cassoday, John, 3
Causey, James, 138
Centuria, Wisc., 107
Chain banking, 90, 104
Chapple, John, 133, 134, 193
Chase, Stuart, 112, 235
Chenequa, Wisc., 134
Chicago, Ill., 33
Chicago Bar Association, 151
Chicago Tribune, 93, 208, 216, 235

China, 144
Chippewa County, 95, 99
Chippewa Falls, Wisc., 94, 98, 192
Churchill, Winston, 7, 237, 241
Congress of Industrial Organizations (CIO), 202, 215
Citizens' Committee on Employment, 97
Civil Liberties Committee, 212
Civil Works Administration, 145, 146
Clark County, 68, 95
Clausen, Fred, 117, 184, 233, 234
Clay, General Lucius, 255
Clay, Henry, 26
Clements, Robert, 174
Cleveland Plain Dealer, 33
Cobb, Irvin S., 14
Cold War, 253
Coleman, Thomas, 248
Columbia County, 132
Columbia University, 20
Comings, George F., 71
Common Sense, 189
Commons, John R., xvi, 16
The Commentator, 228
Communism, 119, 122, 158, 160, 179, 192, 193, 202, 214
Conant, James B., 201
Connor, William D., 64, 65, 66
Coolidge, Calvin, 33, 76, 80, 82, 87
Cooper, Henry Allen, 71, 73
Corrigan, Walter, 92
Coughlin, Charles, xvi, 173, 174, 175
Crimean War, 26
Croly, Herbert, xii
Crowley, Leo T., 184
Crownhart, Charles, 93
Curtiss, E. R., 52
Cutting, Bronson, 137, 138, 141, 143, 145, 146

Daggett, Harry B., state senator, 121
Dahl, Andrew, 67
Dahl, Harry, 131

Dahl, John, 70, 71
Dahl/Severson Bill, 70
Daily Cardinal, 11
Daladier, Édouard, 224–25
Dammann, Theodore, 85, 91, 132, 149, 150, 151, 152, 154, 155, 192, 217, 218, 219
Dane County, xiv, 35, 37, 41, 76, 81, 101, 240
Daniels, Josephus, 7
Darrow, Clarence, 73
Davidson, James O., 65, 66
Davis, Elmer, 235
Dawes, Charles, 125
Dawson, William, 127
Democratic Party, xv, 114, 127, 128, 130, 131, 134, 135, 137, 148, 151, 158, 160, 188, 192, 194, 206, 228, 233, 241, 245, 246, 257
Dewey, John, 201
Dewey, Thomas, 245, 254
Dithmar, Edward, 67
Dole system, 100, 122, 140
Dos Passos, John, xiii, 36
Douglas County, 68, 99
Duffy, F. Ryan, 157, 183, 206, 211, 219, 221
DuFrenne, Martin F., 240
Duncan, Thomas, 115, 121, 142, 177, 179,, 184, 188, 203, 206, 207, 217–18
Dunn, Nellie. *See* McKenzie, Nellie Dunn

Earle, George, 203
Eau Claire, Wisc., 14, 75, 90, 94, 98, 101
Eau Claire County, 95
Economic Club of New York, 226
Edison, Thomas, 7
Eighteenth Amendment, 68
Ekern, Herman, 7, 32, 65, 67, 70, 72, 75, 77–78, 79, 80, 81, 84, 85, 86,

102, 106, 115, 127, 218, 219, 221, 244
Emergency Highway Relief Bill, 115
Emergency Relief Appropriation Act, 191
Emergency Relief Board, 115
Emerson, Ralph Waldo, 8, 19
England, 9
English-Speaking Union, 140, 224
Esch, John, 82
Esch-Cummins law, 32
Essen, Germany, 140
Ethiopia, 225
Evans, Elizabeth Glendower, 7
Everett, Winter, 211
Evjue, William, 38, 39, 40, 42, 80, 86, 90, 91, 92, 104, 127, 129, 135, 149, 152, 153, 175, 208, 214, 237, 246
Executive Budget Act, 109
Executive Council, 112, 115

Fairbanks, Morse and Company (Chicago), 231
Fairchild, Lucius, 223
Farm Holiday Association, 147
Farmer-Labor-Progressive Federation, 184, 192, 217, 218, 219, 220
Farmer-Labor Party, 29, 71, 153
Farmer-Labor Political Federation, 189
Farmer-Labor-Progressive League, 148, 153, 154, 155
Farmers' Holiday Association, 150
Farrington, Joseph 19, 20; (illus.), 57
Fascism, 214, 225, 226
Federal Deposit Insurance Corporation, 184
Federal Emergency Relief Act, 144
Federal Emergency Relief Administration, 146, 176, 177, 178, 180
Federal Trade Commission, 142, 143
Federation of Labor, 150
Fireside Chat, 235

First Baptist Church (Madison), 100
First Congregational Church (Madison), 40
First Wisconsin National Bank, 104
Fish, Carl Russell, 15
Fond du Lac, Wisc., 68, 117, 152
Fons, Leonard C., 132
Foreign Policy Association of New York, 143
Forest Hill Cemetery (Madison), 118, 197, 257
Fort Myer Military School (Virginia), 239
Fort Sheridan, Ill., 18
Four Freedoms, 236
Fowler, Chester, 93, 115
Fox Point, Wisc., 134
Fox River Valley, 68, 147, 161, 190, 233, 246
France, 9, 224, 229, 230
Frank, Glenn, 90, 114, 198, 199, 200, 218, 222, 233, 258; dismissed as university president, 201
Frankfurter, Felix, xii, 113
Frazier, Senator Lynn (North Dakota), 11
Freeport (Illinois) Journal-Standard, 32
Fritz, Oscar, 93
Furuseth, Andrew, 7

Gale, Zona, 73, 84, 107, 200
Ganfield, William, 29
Garfield, James, 37
Garrison, Lloyd, 181
Gates, Clough, 200
Gehrmann, Bernhard, 213, 221
Gehrtz, Gustave, judge, 93
George Washington University, 20
George, David Lloyd, 7, 26
Georgetown University, 20
Germany, 9, 33, 68, 140, 141, 224, 225, 227, 228, 229
Gettelman, Ben, 121, 131
Goodland, Walter, 80–81, 115, 121, 220, 243, 245, 248, 257

Grady, Daniel, 103, 200
Graham, Otis L., xvii
Great Britain, 140, 141, 224, 226, 229, 230, 236
Great Depression, xv, xvii, 94, 95, 97, 103, 105, 110, 111, 112, 117, 126, 129, 131, 134, 140, 141, 142, 144, 146, 151, 158, 160, 161, 165, 178, 180, 190, 192, 220, 222, 226, 236, 258
Green Bay, 68, 98
Green Bay Press-Gazette, 84
Greenbush ("the Bush," "Little Italy"), 37, 38, 39, 40, 41, 42; (illus.), 58
Greene, Howard, 130, 131, 158, 159
Greenquist, Kenneth, 238
Groves, Harold, xvi, 110, 122, 129, 156, 157
Gunderson, Henry, 202, 218

Haight, Raymond, 217
Hammersly, Oscar, 108
Handley, J. J., 153
Hanson Bill, 70
Hanson, Senator Charles, 70
Hansson, Per, 194
Harvard Business School, 205
Harvard University, 20
Hatton, William, 67
Haugen, Nils P., 198
Haydon, Eustace, 23
Hazeltine Corporation, 256
Head, Betty, 21, 22
Hearst Press, 143
Heil, Julius, 220, 227, 228, 230, 233, 234, 252
Henry, Robert K., 220, 249
Hickok, Lorena, 177
Hill, Robert Tudor, 111
Hillside Home School (Spring Green), 4
Hitler, Adolf, xvi, 140, 209, 225, 228, 229, 236
Hoan, Daniel, 120, 184, 217, 219, 245

Hoard's Dairyman, 19
Holmes, Fred, 24, 200
Hoover, Herbert, 80, 98, 105, 119, 126, 129, 135, 137, 182
Hopkins, Harry, 177, 178, 180, 181
Hoppmann, August C., 41, 42
Horicon, Wisc., 117
Horner, Henry, 203
House, Edward, 139, 188
House Military Affairs Committee, 251
Hoyt, Ralph, 182
Huber, Henry, 67, 71, 80, 81–82, 85, 87, 91, 92, 122, 132, 133
Huhn, Oscar, 107
Hull, Merlin, 213, 221, 231, 246, 249
Hunt, Frazier, 119
Hunt, Senator Walter, 121
Hunter, Howard, 180
Hurley, Charles, 203

Ickes, Harold, 112, 137, 181, 183, 215, 235, 236
Ihrig, William, 255
Immell, Ralph, 147, 155, 187, 190, 214, 217, 218, 227, 248
Industrial Expansion Administration, 219
Institute for Agricultural Co-operatives, 140–41
Internal Revenue Service, 116
Invictus, 135
Iowa Agricultural College, 34
Iowa Farmer-Labor Party, 217
Ireland, 27
Italy, 142, 225, 226

James, O. B., 73
James, William, 8
Janesville, Wisc., 28, 94
Janesville Daily Gazette, 76, 112, 208
Jefferson, Thomas, xii, 31, 33
Jefferson Club of Milwaukee, 114
Jefferson County, 27
Jenkins, Newton, 32

Jessner, Rudolf, 42–43
Johnson, Charles, 4
Johnson, Hiram, 137, 204, 234
Johnson, Hugh, 112, 175, 176
Jones, Ellen, 4
Jones, Jane Lloyd, 4
Juneau County, 29, 68, 132

Kaiser Wilhelm II, 7
Kellogg, Senator Frank B., 29, 30, 31
Kennedy, Joseph P., 226
Kenosha, Wisc., 68, 98, 185
Kenosha County, 135, 137
Kewaunee County, 135
Keyes, Elisha, 36
Kirby, Roland, 12
Kittleson, Milo, 38
Knowles, Warren, 259
Knox, Frank, 230
Kohler, Wisc., 86, 148
Kohler Plumbing Company, 147–48
Kohler, Walter J., 86, 87, 91, 92, 93, 96, 97, 101, 102, 103, 104, 105, 106, 107, 108, 126, 128, 129, 130, 131, 133, 134, 135, 148, 151, 160, 164, 222, 223, 254
Kronshage, Theodore, 84, 114, 199
Ku Klux Klan, 38, 43, 80, 84

La Crosse, Wisc., 68, 131
La Crosse County, 68
La Fayette (ship), 139
La Follette, Belle Case, 6, 9, 10, 14, 15, 19, 21, 22, 23, 24, 29, 30, 31, 40, 43, 72, 77, 78, 83, 87, 89, 102, 103, 104, 106, 113; engaged, 1; graduates from the University of Wisconsin Law School, 2; teaches school, 2; moves to Washington, D.C., 2; cares for ill husband, 3; writes to her husband, 5; father suffers stroke, 6; death, 7, 118; biography of, 252; (illus.), 53, 54, 55, 56, 61

La Follette, Bronson, 258, 259

La Follette, Flora (Fola). See Middleton, Flora (Fola) La Follette

La Follette, Isabel (Isen) Bacon, 21, 22, 24, 29, 32, 34, 43, 79, 82, 91, 93, 102, 103, 106, 107, 113, 116, 121, 127, 128, 129, 133, 146, 150, 153, 155, 160, 177, 181, 183, 187, 200, 203, 211, 212, 214, 216, 220, 224, 227, 237, 239, 240, 242, 243, 244, 249; engagement and marriage to Phil, 22, 23; social work, 23; works at *La Follette's Magazine*, 23; travels, 101, 138–39, 140, 141, 176, 194, 209; edits *The Progressive Woman*, 230; drinks heavily, 255; death, 258 (illus.), 58, 60, 168, 171, 172

La Follette, Josephine. See Siebacker, Josephine La Follette

La Follette, Judith (daughter of Phil), 101, 252, 258; (illus.), 168, 169, 172

La Follette, Mary. See Sucher, Mary La Follette

La Follette, Philip F., 67, 70, 71, 85, 86, 89, 127; leader of Progressive faction of Republican Party, xiv; Dane County district attorney, xiv, 35; governor, xv, 93–94, 102, 103, 104, 108, 132, 157, 159, 161, 219; speaks at unveiling of his father's statue, xi; lectures at University of Wisconsin Law School, xvi; opposes Roosevelt administration and programs, xvi, xvii, 144, 145; and National Progressives of America Party, xvi, 214, 217; birth, 1; lives with his grandmother Case, 3; attends Hillside Home School, 4; homesick, 4, 6; accompanies family to Washington, D.C., 5; difficulty with school, 6; travels, 8–9, 19, 101, 117, 138–39, 140, 141, 142, 176, 194, 209, 224; enters University of Wisconsin, 9, 10; argues with father, 10–11; urges father to campaign in Wisconsin, 11; joins Union board, YMCA committee, and Joint Debate Board, 13; considers enlisting, 14, 15; enlists in army, 17, 18; commissioned second lieutenant, 18; discharged from army, 19; enters George Washington University Law School, 20; engaged, 21, 22; delivers speeches, 28, 29, 32, 90, 101, 145; marriage, 23; denounces Esch-Cummins law, 32; denounces Senator McCormick, 32; campaigns for father for president, 33; compared with father, 33; works to keep Wisconsin Progressives united, 64; University of Wisconsin president, 72; campaigns for Robert Jr., 75–76; opposes U.S. entry into World Court, 79; endorses Joseph Beck, 83, 85; denounces Smoot-Hawley Tariff Act, 105; reduces his salary, 114; ill, 118, 210, 224; loses gubernatorial primary and election, 134, 220; meets with Roosevelt, 137, 142, 177, 181, 203, 226; declines position in Roosevelt administration, 143; writes articles, 143, 225–26; addresses Associated Academic Conference, 145; works on bills to present to Congress, 146; favors third party, 149, 150; attacks Albert Schmedeman, 151; criticizes New Deal, 151, 186, 190, 212, 213, 238; chairs Progressive Central Committee, 153; criticizes Agricultural Administration Act and Administration, 156, 183; delivers radio addresses, 160, 180; angry over defeat of Wisconsin Works Plan, 184, 185, 186; speaks at Milwaukee South Side armory, 185; and Roosevelt, 187–88, 191, 193, 211; describes Alfred Landon, 193; launches national Progressive Party, 198; wants to fire

Glenn Frank, 199; reputation tarnished, 200; delivers budget message, 202; supports motion to adjourn legislature, 202; promotes a national third party, 205, 212–13; calls for special legislative session, 206; charged with dictatorship, 210; hints at national Progressive Party, 210; urges Congress to allow immigration of German children, 226; urges recall of ambassador to Great Britain, Joseph Kennedy, 226; criticizes Great Britain and France, 226, 228; dislikes and fears Germany, 227; against American involvement in World War II, 229, 232, 234, 235; elected to board of Fairbanks, Morse and Company, 231; and America First Committee, 234, 239; enlists in army, 239; purchases farms in Wisconsin, 240; appears before House Military Affairs Committee, 251; promotes Douglas MacArthur for president, 253, 254; aids Earl Warren in bid for presidential nomination, 254; endorses Thomas Dewey, 254; drinks heavily, 255; declines governorship of Bavaria, 255; and Hazeltine Corporation, 256; moves to Long Island, 256; death, 257; (illus.), 52, 54, 55, 56, 57, 60, 61, 163, 164, 165, 166, 167, 169, 170, 171, 172, 261

La Follette, Rachel, 118

La Follette, Robert M., Sr. ("Fighting Bob," father of Phil), xii, 53, 64, 67, 73, 86, 89, 107, 154, 198, 223, 229, 230; statue unveiled, xi; runs for U.S. Senate, xi, 25, 28, 65; votes against war with Germany, xiv, 9, 10, 12; engaged, 1; enrolls in law school, 2; elected Dane County district attorney, 2, 35–36; elected U.S. congressman, 2; elected Wisconsin governor, 3; ill, 3, 31; resigns as governor to become U.S. senator, 4; writes to children, 5; starts *La Follette's Magazine*, 8; proud of son Phil, 10; argues with Phil, 10–11; filibusters Armed Ship Bill, 11; delivers speeches, 13, 27, 28, 30, 31, 33; compared to Judas and Benedict Arnold, 14; burned in effigy, 16; candidate for president, 25; files libel charges, 26; endorses John Blaine for governor, 27; wins Republican primary, 29; compared with son, 33; controls Progressive faction in Wisconsin, 63; death, 63; at Battle Creek Sanatorium, 70–71; memorial for, 197; (illus.), 52, 55, 56, 59, 60; memorial for, 197

La Follette, Robert M., Jr. (brother of Phil), 5, 11, 21, 22, 23, 24, 31, 32, 39, 40, 67, 70, 71, 72, 75, 76, 84, 89, 101, 102, 105, 107, 139, 142, 143, 146, 149, 155, 156, 157, 181, 191, 204, 205, 210, 211, 214, 220, 221, 222, 227, 231, 241, 244; birth, 1; homesick, 4; closer to father than his brother, 7; poor performance at University of Wisconsin, 7; ill, 17, 18, 19, 245; elected and reelected to Senate, 63, 77, 87, 91, 161, 234, 246; delivers first campaign speech, 76; supports Joseph Beck, 83; denounces Fred Zimmerman, 84; loses baby, 118; opposes third party, 150; declares he will run on Progressive Party ticket, 153; meets with Roosevelt, 177, 226; agrees to support third party, 212; recommends Progressives return to Republican Party, 247; defeated in primary, 249; commits suicide, 256; (illus.), 54, 55, 56, 60, 163, 166

La Follette, Robert M., III (son of Phil), 240, 251, 252, 258; (illus.), 61, 168, 169, 172

La Follette, Sherry. See Zabriskie, Sherry La Follette

La Follette High School (Madison), 258

La Follette Road to Communism: Must We Go Further Along That Road?, 193

La Follette's Magazine, 8, 10, 13, 19, 22, 23. *See also The Progressive*

La Guardia, Fiorello, 213, 215

La Jolla, Calif., 18, 19

Labor, 108

Labor Code, 115, 117

Lake Mendota, 3

Lake Winnebago, 99

Landis, James, 113

Landon, Alfred, 193

Lane, Harry, 11

Latin America, 227, 232

Lawrence, David, 215

League for Independent Political Action, 148, 189

League of Women Voters, 106

Legislative Reference Library, 175

Lehman, Herbert, 203

Lehner, Philip, 74

Lemke, William, 174

Lend-Lease Bill, 235, 236

Lenroot, Irvine, 19, 27, 65, 66, 74, 75, 76, 77, 79

Lescohier, Don D., 96, 97, 100

Levitan, Solomon, 7, 80, 82, 83, 84, 85, 86, 87, 91, 132, 133, 219

Lewis, John L., 215

Lewis, Ross, 167, 170, 183, 218

Lewis, Sinclair, xii

Lewis, Theodore G., 37, 38

Lilienthal, David, 113, 114, 177, 259

Lincoln, Abraham, xii, 26, 31, 33, 178

Lindbergh, Charles, xviii, 236

Lindley, Ernest K., 137

Lippmann, Walter, 215

Lodge, Henry Cabot, 234–35

London School of Economics, 140

Long, Huey P., xvi, 173, 174–75, 183, 201, 207–8, 209, 216

Loomis, Orland, 110, 219, 234

Loomis Bill, 115

Lorraine Hotel (Madison), 129

Los Angeles Illustrated Daily News, 144

Louisiana Railroad Commission, 174

Louisiana State University, 201

Loverud, Alvin M., 35

Lovett, Robert Morss, 72

Lueck, Arthur W., 192, 194

MacArthur, Douglas, xvi, xviii, 240, 241

MacDonald, Ramsay, 7, 9

Madison Club, 13, 26

Madison Democrat, 26

Madison Gas and Electric, 129

Madison Ring, 75, 78, 79, 81, 83, 102

Madison West High School, 240

Maginot line, 229

Mallard, Jason (fictional character), 14

Manitowoc, Wisc., 79, 87, 116

Mankato, Minn., 30

Manufacturers' Association, 233

Maple Bluff Farm, 5, 6, 23, 83, 84, 85, 103, 118, 149, 155, 156, 199, 240, 257

Marathon County, 68, 95

Marshall, George C., 255

Marshfield News-Herald, 101

Matheson Bill, 68

Matheson, Alexander, 68

Mayo Clinic, 210

McCarthy, Joseph, 248, 249, 252

McClure's Magazine, 89

McCormick, Medill, 32

McCormick, Robert, 237

McGoarty, John S., 174

McGovern, Francis, 66, 75, 76, 106

McKenzie, Fred, 10

McKenzie, Nellie Dunn, 6, 9, 10, 187

McMurray, Howard, 245, 246, 249

Meikeljohn, Alexander, 72

Meisel, Henry, 157, 159
Mellon, Andrew, 76
Mexican War, 26, 33
Middleton, Flora (Fola) La Follette (sister
    of Phil), 1, 9, 33, 89, 109, 128, 141,
    155, 187, 201, 216, 221; (illus.), 163
Middleton, George, 109, 155, 221
Miller, Anton, 153
Miller, John E., 180, 222
Milwaukee Association of Commerce,
    120
Milwaukee, Wisc., 66, 68, 73, 76, 84, 90,
    94
Milwaukee County, 99, 128, 135, 152,
    159, 183
Milwaukee Journal, 82, 104, 106, 121,
    129, 160, 167, 183, 249
Milwaukee Sentinel, 89, 112, 134, 180,
    207
Milwaukee South Side armory, 185
Mineral Point, Wisc., 90
Minneapolis, Minn., 30
Minneapolis University of Wisconsin
    Alumni Club, 13
Minnesota, 173, 188
Minnesota Farmer-Labor Association,
    231
Minnesota Farmer-Labor Party, 213
Minnesota National Guard, 30
Minnesota Public Safety Commission, 13
Mitchell, Billy, 73
Mondovi, Wisc., 157
Monroe County, 90, 132, 159
Montini, Monsignor, 225
Morgan, J. P., 76
Morgenbladet, xv
Morgenroth, Frank, 74
Morgenthau, Henry, Sr., 139, 145
Morris, Oscar H., 120, 121
Muscle Shoals, Ala., 140
Musso, Tony, 41
Mussolini, Benito, xvi, 209, 225, 229,
    236

Mutual Broadcasting System, 229
Myrdal, Gunnar, 194

The Nation, xii, 19, 108, 119, 175, 222
National Association for the
    Advancement of Colored People, xii
National Association of Retail Grocers,
    117
National Industrial Recovery Act, 147
National Labor Relations Act, 202
National Progressives of America Party,
    xv, 170, 191, 214, 215, 216, 217, 218,
    220, 222, 223, 224, 227, 230, 237,
    258
National Recovery Administration, 144,
    145, 173
National Register of Historic Places, 257
National Union for Social Justice, 173
Nazis, 140, 224, 225, 226, 227, 228,
    229, 232, 236
NBC radio, 126, 235
Neenah Paper Company, 129
Neilsville, Wisc., 133
Nelson, Gaylord, 245, 249, 257
Nelson, John, 71
Nelson, Philip, 120
Neutrality Act (1937), 229, 230
New Deal, xvii, 144, 145, 146, 149, 151,
    158, 159, 173, 175, 177, 179–80,
    192, 204, 208, 212
New Era, xiii
New Nationalism, xvii
The New Republic, xii
New York Economic Club, 228
New York Herald-Tribune, 137
New York Times, xi–xii, 35, 89, 108
Niemann, Lucius, 129
Nonpartisan League, 13
Normal Schools, 113
Norman, Okla., 18, 57
Norris, George, 2, 84, 126, 136, 137,
    138, 189, 204, 205, 213, 215
North Dakota, 11

Northwestern, 180
Northwestern University, 205
Norway, 194
Norwegians, 65, 68
Nova Scotia, 117
Nye, Gerald, 204

O'Connor, T. P., 9
Oconto, Wisc., 90
Ohl, Henry, 193
Ojibwe tribe, 107
Oshkosh, Wisc., 28, 68, 94, 99, 185
Otto, Max, xvi, 19, 105, 114
Our Savior's Lutheran Church (Madison), 40
Outagamie County, 135
Outlook, xii
Owen, Walter, 93

Padway, Joseph T., 184
Palmer, A. Mitchell, 20
Paoli, Wisc., 37
Park Hotel (Madison), 149
Pederson, Eli, 36
People's Reconstruction League, 27
Perry, Charles, 91, 101, 121, 130
Peterson, Florence, 96
Philipp, Emanuel, 10, 27, 67, 223
Pitt, William, 26
Platteville, Wisc., 181
Polakowski, Walter, 121
Polk County, 249
Pope Paul VI, p. 225
Pope Pius XI, pp. 142, 225
Portage, Wisc., 73, 76, 247
Portage County, 70, 95, 135
Portland Oregonian, xii
Pound, Roscoe, 72
Power Commission, 142, 143
Primrose, Wisc., 36
The Progressive, 175, 189, 227, 228, 237, 239, 240, 251, 256. *See also La Follette's Magazine.*

Progressive Campaign Textbook, 129
Progressive Central Committee, 153, 154
The Progressive Woman, 230
Progressive Party, xiv, xvii, xviii, 63, 78–79, 81, 82, 83, 84, 86, 91, 93, 110, 111, 112, 113, 120, 125, 128, 129–30, 134, 135, 136, 137, 139, 152, 154, 155, 158, 159, 160, 161, 175, 182, 188, 189, 190, 192, 194, 217, 219, 224, 233, 234, 237–38, 239, 241, 246
Prohibition, 41, 68, 84, 85, 104
Proxmire, William, 257
The Public Domain and Democracy, 111
Public Service Commission, 115, 129, 177

Quarles, Senator Joseph, 64
Quinn, Robert, 203

Racine, Wisc., 115, 185
Racine County, 135, 137
Railroads, 111, 113
Railway Brotherhoods, 32
Raushenbush, Paul, xvi, 122
Reconstruction Finance Corporation, 125, 182
Reis, Alvin C., 92, 115, 214
Relief efforts, 98, 99, 100, 119, 120, 121, 122, 146, 180
Rennebohm, Oscar, 254
Republican National Convention, 1, 83, 84, 87, 253, 254
Republican Party, xiv, xv, 63, 75, 82, 85, 87, 126, 127, 128, 129, 135, 137, 148, 152, 154, 158, 160, 188, 192, 194, 206, 221, 228, 233, 234, 242, 245, 246, 247, 248
Reynolds, James, 37
Reynolds, John, 80, 85, 91, 92, 115
Rhinelander, Wisc., 133
Rice Lake, Wisc., 90, 101
Richland Center Republican and Observer, 73

Ridgway, Eldo, 71
Risser, Fred, 249
River Hills, 134
Road construction, 69
Roberts, Glenn, 39, 43, 92, 243, 244, 246
Rochester, Minn., 33
Rock County, 28, 68
Rockford, Ill., 138
Rodman, Seldon, 189
Roe, Gilbert, 26, 39, 194; (illus.), 55
Roe, Netha, 194; (illus.), 55
Rogers, Alf, 65, 77, 101, 102, 104, 141, 243
Rome, Wisc., 27
Roosevelt, Franklin D., xv, xvi, xvii, 112, 126, 127, 128, 135, 136, 137, 139, 142, 144, 146, 148, 149, 150, 151, 157, 158, 160, 161, 167, 173, 177, 181, 186, 190, 205, 215, 229, 233, 235, 238, 241; approves Wisconsin Works Plan, 181; and Phil, 187–88, 211; signs Social Security Act, 191; wins 1936 election, 194; meets with Phil and Robert Jr., 203, 226; rebuffs Phil, 204
Roosevelt, Theodore, xii, xiii, xvii, 9, 13, 66, 145
Rosenberry, Marvin, 20, 93, 210
Roxbury, Wisc., 240, 256
Royal Institute of International Affairs, 140
Royall, Kenneth, 255
Rubin, Morris, 256
Rubin, William, 134, 156, 157, 159, 218
Rural Electrification Act, 257
Rural Electrification Administration, 202
Russia, 9

Samp, Elmer, 131
Saturday Evening Post, xii, 14
Sauk City, Wisc., 104, 105, 132
Sauk County, 132

Sauthoff, Harry, 81, 156, 213, 231, 246
Scandinavians, 65, 68
Schafer, John, 71
Scheller, Frank, 130
Schmedeman, Albert, 92, 131, 134, 137, 139, 147, 148, 154, 157, 158, 159, 161, 177, 178, 180, 181, 186, 188, 222, 223
Schneider, George, 153, 213
Scripps-Howard, 119
Seamen's Union, 7
Sears, Roebuck and Company, 234
Sellery, George, 201
Seltzer, Louis, 33
Senate Committee of Elections and Privileges, 26
Senate Foreign Relations Committee, 236
Serbia, 9
Severson, Herman, 69, 70, 113, 120
Severson Act, 69
Shannon, Harold, 74
Share Our Wealth organization, 175
Sheboygan, Wisc., 86, 99, 107, 183
Sheboygan County, 92, 108, 148
Sheldon, G. M., 78
Shipstead, Henrik, 29, 30, 31
Siebecker, Josephine La Follette, 80
Siebecker, Robert, 11, 80
Sigman, Sam, 153
Sinclair, Upton, 173, 236
Singler, Walter M., 147
Sinykin, Gordon, 203, 247
Smith, Al, 127
Smith, Gerald L. K., 175
Smith, John M., 220
Smith, Lawrence, 238
Smith, Peter J., 112
Smoot-Hawley Tariff Act, 105
Social Security Act, 174, 191
Socialist Party, xii, 69, 75, 117, 120, 137, 148, 155, 160, 188, 189, 242, 246
Soviet Union, 141, 142–43, 144, 228, 253

Sparta, Wisc., 248
Spohn, William, 151
Spring Green, Wisc., 2
St. Paul, Minn., 30
St. Paul Pioneer Press, xii
Stafford, Harold, 231
Stalin, Joseph, 241, 253
Stalwarts, xiv, 64, 72, 75, 79, 80, 81, 84,
    87, 103, 105, 112, 115, 116, 119,
    120, 121, 125, 127, 128, 129, 130,
    131, 133, 134, 135, 148, 151, 154
Stassen, Harold, 254
State Historical Society of Wisconsin,
    118, 257, 258
State of Wisc., ex rel. La Follette v.
    Kohler, 92
Staudenmayer, George, 70
Steffens, Lincoln, 2, 89, 144, 145
Steinle, Roland J., 183
Stephenson, Isaac, 64, 65, 66
Stevens, E. Ray, 93
Stevens Point, Wisc., 101
Stolen, Ole, 42, 80
Stone, James A., 65
Stoughton, Wisc., 35, 41, 76
Strikes, 147–48
Student Army Training Corps Unit
    (University of Oklahoma), 18, 19, 57
Stuart, R. Douglas, Jr., 234, 236, 239
Sucher, Mary La Follette (sister of Phil),
    1, 4, 5, 10, 16, 19, 57, 102, 135, 139,
    187, 221; (illus.), 55, 56, 163
Sucher, Ralph, 82, 102, 103, 118, 127,
    155, 163, 187; (illus.), 57
Sunday, Billy, 30
Superior, Wisc., 65, 68, 80, 93, 94, 99, 100
Sweden, 194
Swedes, 65

Taft, William Howard, 66
Taft, Robert A., 234, 237
Taxes, 69–70, 96, 98, 103, 110, 116,
    119, 121, 130, 131–32, 182, 186

Taylor County, 68, 96
Thompson, Dorothy, 216
Thompson, James, 27
Time, 90
Tittenmore, James, 130
Titus, William, 71
Tomahawk, 74
Townsend, Charles, 173, 175
Townsend, Doctor Francis, 174
Trevelyan, George Macaulay, 26
Truman, Harry S, 254, 255
Tuberculosis, 101
Tucker, Herman, 69
"Tucker Bill," 69
Tugwell, Rexford, 181
Turner, Frederick Jackson, 111
Two Rivers, Wisc., 99

Uncensored News, 127, 133
Unemployment Compensation Act, 125
Unemployment Compensation program,
    xviii
Unemployment Reserves and
    Compensation Act, 122
Unemployment, 94–95, 96, 97, 98, 104,
    117, 144, 146, 176
Union Party, 174
United States Supreme Court, 191, 204,
    208
University of Chattanooga, 151
University of Chicago Divinity School, 23
University of Wisconsin, 1, 11, 15, 34,
    53
University of Wisconsin Board of
    Regents, 3, 71, 72, 103, 114, 199, 201
University of Wisconsin Department of
    Economics, 96
University of Wisconsin Extension, 95
University of Wisconsin Law School, xvi,
    20, 21, 181, 252
University of Wisconsin Livestock
    Pavilion, 213
USS *Rueben James*, 238

Van Brunt Manufacturing Company, 117
Van Devanter, Willis, 204
Van Hise, Charles, 3, 14, 15
Vernon County, 132
Versailles Treaty, 230
Vilas, William F., 3
Villard, Oswald Garrison, 204
Voight, Edward, 83
Von Hindenburg, Paul, 140

Wagner, Robert, 98, 146
Wagner labor bill, 191
Wall Street, 76; crash, 94
Wallace, Henry A., 112, 137, 181
Walrus Club, 21
Walsh, Thomas, 141
Warren, Earl, 254
Washington Star, 126
Washington State University, 252
Waukesha County, 147
Waupaca County, 70, 95
Wausau Record-Herald, 90, 180
Wauwatosa, Wisc., 101
Wayland Club of the First Baptist Church
    (Madison), 100
Webster, Daniel, 26
Westby, Wisc., 90
Wheeler, Burton K., 35, 189, 204
White, William Allen, 204
WIBA, radio station, 40
Wickersham, James, 92
Wilcox, Roy P., 14, 27, 75, 76, 77
Wiley, Alexander, 192, 194, 220, 246
Wilkie, Harold, 92, 200
Will and Power, 236
Williams, John Sharp, 12
Wilson, Woodrow, xii, xiii, 9, 11, 15,
    139, 188
Wisconsin Agriculture Commission, 115
Wisconsin Agricultural Agency, 207
Wisconsin Bankers' Association, 184
Wisconsin Board of Control, 179
The Wisconsin Citizen, 86

Wisconsin Conference of Social Workers,
    96
Wisconsin Co-operative Milk Pool, 147,
    150
Wisconsin Department of Commerce, 207
Wisconsin Department of Public Welfare,
    187
Wisconsin Development Authority, 202
Wisconsin Emergency Relief
    Administration, 146, 187
Wisconsin Facts, 193
Wisconsin Federation of Labor, 153, 184
Wisconsin Finance Authority, 182, 184,
    202
Wisconsin Industrial Commission, 82,
    96, 97, 187
Wisconsin Insurance Commission, 78
Wisconsin Joint Finance Committee, 206
Wisconsin Manufacturers Association,
    117, 120, 184
Wisconsin National Guard, 147, 148,
    227, 239
Wisconsin Progressive Central
    Committee, 211, 212
Wisconsin Public Welfare Department,
    146
Wisconsin Railroad Commission, 114,
    115
Wisconsin Rapids, Wisc., 193
Wisconsin Regional Planning Committee,
    177
Wisconsin Socialist Party, 117
Wisconsin State Board of Agriculture, 95
Wisconsin State Journal, 15, 26, 82, 83
Wisconsin State Planning Board, 177
Wisconsin State Regional Planning
    Committee, 182
Wisconsin Supreme Court, 91, 152
Wisconsin Works Plan, 176, 179, 182,
    184, 185
WISN, radio station, 121
Witte, Edwin, xvi, 96, 175, 259
Women's Christian Temperance Union, 40

Women's International League for Peace
and Freedom, 239
Wood, Robert E., 234, 235, 237, 253
Work, John M., 75
Works Progress Administration, 176,
185, 186, 190, 191, 203
World War I, xiv, 95, 97, 117
World's Work, 90
Wright, Frank Lloyd, 4
Waupaca, Wisc., 69
Wylie, Fred, 92, 152, 155

Zabriskie, George, 252
Zabriskie, Sherry La Follette, 252, 258
Zeidler, Frank, 242
Zeratsky, A. W., 191, 203, 219, 231
Zimmerman, Fred, 71, 78–79, 80, 81,
82, 84, 86, 87, 1012, 159, 254
Zimny, Arthur, 185